This book combines original theoretical analysis with real life case studies to examine the nature of the standoff. Starting with the standoffs of Wounded Knee, MOVE, Ruby Ridge, Waco, the Freemen of Montana, Tupac Amaru, and the Republic of Texas, the author explores the archetypal patterns of human action and cognition that move us into and out of these highly charged situations and seeks to theorize the contingency of all such moments. As an emergency situation where interaction is both frozen and continuing, the standoff evokes original ideas about time, space, and appropriate or anticipated action, and individuals and organizations often find their standard operating procedures and categories deflected and transformed. By tracking and analyzing such impositions and deflections, this book aims to develop a theory of the fundamental existential indeterminacy of social life and the possible role that improvisation can play in navigating this indeterminacy and preventing a violent and destructive conclusion.

ROBIN WAGNER-PACIFICI is a Professor of Sociology in the Department of Sociology and Anthropology, Swarthmore College, Pennsylvania. She has taught and researched in the USA and Italy and her previous publications include *The Moro Morality Play: Terrorism as Social Drama* (1986) and *Discourse and Destruction: The City of Philadelphia vs MOVE* (1994).

Theorizing the Standoff
Contingency in Action

Cambridge Cultural Social Studies

Series editors:
JEFFREY C. ALEXANDER, *Department of Sociology, University of California, Los Angeles, and* STEVEN SEIDMAN, *Department of Sociology, University at Albany, State University of New York.*

Titles in the series
ILANA FRIEDRICH SILBER, *Virtuosity, Charisma, and Social Order*
0 521 41397 4 HARDBACK
LINDA NICHOLSON AND STEVEN SEIDMAN (eds.), *Social Postmodernism*
0 521 47516 3 HARDBACK   0 521 47571 6 PAPERBACK
WILLIAM BOGARD, *The Simulation of Surveillance*
0 521 55081 5 HARDBACK   0 521 55561 2 PAPERBACK
SUZANNE R. KIRSCHNER, *The Religious and Romantic Origins of Psychoanalysis*
0 521 44401 2 HARDBACK   0 521 55560 4 PAPERBACK
PAUL LICHTERMAN, *The Search for Political Community*
0 521 48286 0 HARDBACK   0 521 48343 3 PAPERBACK
ROGER FRIEDLAND AND RICHARD HECHT, *To Rule Jerusalem*
0 521 44046 7 HARDBACK
KENNETH H. TUCKER, *French Revolutionary Syndicalism and the Public Sphere*
0 521 56359 3 HARDBACK
ERIK RINGMAR, *Identity, Interest and Action*
0 521 56314 3 HARDBACK
ALBERTO MELUCCI, *The Playing Self*
0 521 56401 8 HARDBACK   0 521 56482 4 PAPERBACK
ALBERTO MELUCCI, *Challenging Codes*
0 521 57051 4 HARDBACK   0 521 57843 4 PAPERBACK
SARAH M. CORSE, *Nationalism and Literature*
0 521 57002 6 HARDBACK   0 521 57912 0 PAPERBACK
DARNELL M. HUNT, *Screening the Los Angeles 'Riots'*
0 521 57087 5 HARDBACK   0 521 57814 0 PAPERBACK
LYNETTE P. SPILLMAN, *Nation and Commemoration*
0 521 57404 8 HARDBACK   0 521 57683 0 PAPERBACK
MICHAEL MULKAY, *The Embryo Research Debate*
0 521 57180 4 HARDBACK   0 521 57683 0 PAPERBACK

Series list continues at end of book

Theorizing the Standoff

Contingency in Action

Robin Wagner-Pacifici

Swarthmore College

HM
1121
,W34
2000

PUBLISHED BY THE PRESS SYNDICATE OF THE UNIVERSITY OF CAMBRIDGE
The Pitt Building, Trumpington Street, Cambridge, United Kingdom

CAMBRIDGE UNIVERSITY PRESS
The Edinburgh Building, Cambridge, CB2 2RU, UK   http://www.cup.cam.ac.uk
40 West 20th Street, New York, NY 10011–4211, USA   http://www.cup.org
10 Stamford Road, Oakleigh, Melbourne 3166, Australia

First published 2000

Printed in the United Kingdom at the University Press, Cambridge

Typeset in Times NR (MT) 10/12½pt, QuarkXPress™   [SE]

A catalogue record for this book is available from the British Library

Library of Congress cataloguing in publication data
Wagner-Pacifici, Robin Erica.
Theorizing the Standoff: Contingency in Action / Robin Wagner-
Pacifici.
    p.   cm.
Includes bibliographical references and index.
ISBN 0 521 65244 8 (hardback)
1. Social conflict.   2. Social conflict – United States Case
studies.   3. Conflict management.   I. Title.
HM1121.W34   1999
303.6 – dc21   99–29695   CIP

ISBN 0 521 65244 8 hardback
ISBN 0 521 65479 3 paperback

to Adriano, Laura and Stefano
with all my heart

Contents

Preface

This book has had a double aim from the outset: to theorize contingency in social life and to analyze and extract the essence of real-life standoffs. By proposing the standoff as a privileged archetypal situation, the project has read contingency through the standoff and the standoff through its own contingency. Of course I am concerned with moments of danger and imminent violence for the damage they can do to lives and social systems. But I am also, and equally, concerned with ferreting out the "standoffish" aspects of everyday interactions and charting the various thresholds we all work hard to elude, thresholds that will take a conversation into the realm of the confrontation.

One of the striking aspects of researching responses to real-life standoffs is the discovery of the habitual connections made between situations and standardized categories. The book attempts to locate and theoretically press the idea of standard operating procedures as agents of the law and adversaries alike summon up their warrants, ultimatums, deadlines, electrical generators, fire engines, and so forth when an "emergency" has been declared. One category of standard agent, the "Hostage Rescue Team," has particular theoretical resonance. As a specific group within the Federal Bureau of Investigation, this team is obviously trained to rescue hostages in situations of danger and potential violence. As will be explored, sometimes this team is sent into situations where there is no clear hostage (this was particularly true in the case of the Ruby Ridge, Idaho standoff of the Randall Weaver family). At such a moment, a kind of aporia opens up, a conceptual and strategic gap between the reality of the situation and the means determined to deal with it. Much of the book's investigation will peer into that gap to try and understand it. But in a larger sense, if the claim here is that all social situations are working overtime to avoid becoming standoffs, then perhaps we do indeed need a kind of metaphorical Hostage

Rescue Team to periodically rescue us hostages of social life from ourselves and each other. Ultimately, this study aims to suggest some strategies of rescue, though perhaps not of final reconciliation.

My analysis of the standoff aims to develop a systematic and three-dimensional understanding of the indeterminacy that is the existential stuff of such situations. I want both to begin and end with an image of the standoff as a moment of pure contingency and with an analytical stance that seeks to foreground action in the subjunctive mood.

It should be the goal of all analysis to make the phenomenon under observation simultaneously familiar and strange. We all have an instinct that we know what a standoff is and how it acts in the world. The goal here is to clarify and expose the lineaments of that instinct. In this regard, I'll end the Preface and begin the book with a quotation from Walter Benjamin who, in contemplating the exposed "standstill" of dramatis personae and plot, gives expression to my own analytical animus:

Again and again, in Shakespeare, in Calderon, battles fill the last act, and kings, princes, attendants and followers, "enter, fleeing." The moment in which they become visible to spectators brings them to a standstill. The flight of the dramatis personae is arrested by the stage. Their entry into the visual field of non-participating and truly impartial persons allows the harassed to draw breath, bathes them in new air. The appearance on stage of those who enter "fleeing" takes from this its hidden meaning. Our reading of this formula is imbued with the expectation of a place, a light, a footlight glare, in which our flight through life may be likewise sheltered in the presence of onlooking strangers.[1]

Acknowledgments

As is always the case, this book was imagined into life with the participation of many people and by way of many different institutions. Of course, I wrote it and must take responsibility for it as it makes its way in the world. But I'd like to express my gratitude to those who have talked with me about the project and who have allowed me to experiment with ideas in their presence. Jeffrey Alexander has long known about my interest in contingency and my continuing preoccupation with social narrative, language and violence. He encouraged this project in many ways with his intellectual insight and editorial support. I thank him for his friendship and his confidence. Various friends and colleagues have demonstrated interest and have contributed much to my thinking. Such colloquy is perhaps the greatest gift we can give each other and stands as a testament to the existence of a counter universe to that of social life framed as a series of standoffs and near standoffs. Thus I thank Courtney Bender, Harold Bershady, Roger Friedland, Pier Paolo Giglioli, Jeff Goldfarb, John Hall, Nancy Hirschman, Ron Jacobs, Alberto Melucci, Magali Sarfatti-Larson, Rich Schuldenfrei, Barry Schwartz, Phil Weinstein, Barbie Zelizer, and Eviatar Zerubavel. My friend and colleague Bruce Grant deserves special thanks here for his energetic support, his wide-ranging associational mind, and his critical reading.

I'd also like to thank scholars Jayne Docherty and Catherine Wessinger, who generously sent me their own manuscripts on related topics to read. Two Swarthmore College students, Mark Hansen and Jim Harker, did a great deal of investigative work on several of the empirical cases examined here. They both became so much more than research assistants and I thank them for all their efforts. Rose Maio struggled mightily to convert my old word processing program into one that is currently legible by computer-based printing technology. Her great skill and good humor have helped me every step of the way.

Various institutions have provided me with forums for delivering talks based on this project. Thus, I would like to thank scholars at Indiana University, The University of Pennsylvania, Rutgers University, The New School for Social Research, Princeton University, the University of Bologna, The University of California-Santa Barbara, the University of Milan, and Swarthmore College for their engagement with my ideas.

Finally, and once again, I want to thank my husband, Maurizio, for all of his support and love. Our minds and hearts are joined in all sorts of ways – both directly and, through our children, indirectly. And to those children, with all my love, I dedicate this book.

1

Theorizing contingency

In every case the storyteller is a man who has counsel for his readers . . .
After all, counsel is less an answer to a question than a proposal concerning the continuation of a story which is just unfolding. To seek this
counsel one would first have to be able to tell the story.
(Walter Benjamin, "The Storyteller," *Illuminations*, p. 86)

God Himself probably preferred to speak of His world in the subjunctive
of possibility . . . for God creates the world and thinks while He is at it
that it could just as well be done differently.
(Robert Musil, *The Man Without Qualities*, p. 14)

The grammarian's activity could not in itself be considered autonomous
but must be seen as an aspect of an investigation conducted on two fronts,
one of enunciation and one of observation. Grammar then presents itself
as a theory of the event in its evolution.
(Ferdinand Gonseth, *Time and Method*, p. 106)

Imagine that your life is like being on a train and looking out the window.
Things fly past – houses, back yards, factories, forests, train stations, people
on platforms, people in cars on the highway. Sometimes, though rarely, you
catch the eye of a child playing in a yard or a motorist in a car. And then
you are gone. What can you say about all of this stuff which is, for you,
doubly in movement? Everything moves in its own right (motility, gesture,
bodily functions, growth, reproduction, death), and everything moves
before your eyes as the train of your life, flinging up one snapshot of reality
after another, hurtles on to its destination. Might not one say that the whole
project of sociology is to account theoretically for the contingent patterns
and shapes of this mutable and mutating social stuff of life – life as a speed-
ing train with windows, Leibniz's monads on parallel tracks? Certainly the

sociological preoccupation with cause and effect, where sequenced and predictable effects are tracked from their causes, seems to point in that direction. And yet, causality seems to imply a process that moves toward a stationary end point, that which is, or will be, given. Further, much of sociology, at least, has set a goal of identifying more overarching general patterns and hypothesizing laws – at both the macro and the micro levels.

So what does it mean to genuinely theorize contingency, to even want to theorize about what happens when things could literally go one way or another, when the station platform moves away as you approach it? In some sense, this is the opposite of what both the comparative-historical sociologists and the ethnomethodologists have, at their chosen levels of analysis, set out to do, that being to theorize the emergence of order, or regularity, and shared meaning. It also differs from these other approaches in aiming its illuminating light at what I call the "midro" life of the analytic object, that level where macro structure and micro interaction are *both* "in the picture." One might think here about a multiconstituency "event" as the characteristic object of analysis.[1] As well, such a project differs from the current preoccupations with trying to decipher patterns in apparent chaos, as theorists of chaos in physics, biology, and psychology, among other disciplines, are doing, though it shares with them the desire to keep up with that which is emerging out of the past into the present. Finally, and perhaps unusually, the emphasis is *not* on predicting the outcomes of contingent action (though outcomes are not irrelevant). The *focus* is rather on charting or describing the coming together of diverse elements, individuals, institutions, and languages, in a moment of action and interaction. It is the charting of a process in the present.

My goal is to theorize these moments – the moments just before and as a social interaction takes its definitive form. This is very difficult. How do you look head-on at something that is process, movement, fluid provisionality? To theorize contingency means to highlight rather than bracket the insight that reality is a moving target and that theory has to keep moving to try and keep up with it.

Probability theory may hold a clue here, but not in the way that it is normally invoked. Charles Sanders Peirce's insight that probability really applies to series of events, rather than to individual events provides an image of probability calculus chasing after a phantom, for example, chasing that which "could" but never actually does happen. For once happening, an event is no longer probable or, in the term significant here, contingent. It is momentarily in the shining light of the seemingly inevitable present tense, before slipping away into the past. So in a way, probability statements are masquerading as statements in and for the (near) future tense but are really assertions of a subjunctive or conditional mood. Probability statements in themselves refer to that which could happen (thus the conditional). If one adds a notion of contingent causality to such statements, the grammatical frame is the subjunctive (if x were to occur, then y would happen). Probability statements thus hover above reality, creating their own reality which is simultaneously both correct and in error. Probability statements never make contact with reality or – what may be the same thing – only in the long run, when, applied as it is to a series, the discrete event has long since come and gone. Contingency then, understood in this subjunctive, probabilistic way, traffics in hypothetical, merely imaginary worlds. That is its beauty and what makes it so elusive.

Indeed, perhaps there is a clue to be found in these heuristic characterizations of the grammatical tense or mood of the event. There may simply be no point to thinking about the contingent present – better to think about these moments as operating in and with the subjunctive mood. In this way, uncertainty, provisionality, a tentative quality is smuggled into our understanding of social interaction. Some languages, Italian is one, have baroquely well-developed subjunctive tenses, some, such as English, merely have a subjunctive mood – so maybe that is what I am aiming for – a theory of contingency as *action in the subjunctive mood.*

How is *action in the subjunctive mood* to be approached? The subjunctive is a subjective world in which strong emotions (statements of superlatives), uncertainty, and ambiguity are foregrounded. In his book, *Shakespearean Pragmatism*, Lars Engle writes that *"plays and poems* may be more suitable in some ways for the central pragmatic and economic enterprise of delivering finely tuned pictures of social operation and social change than is theoretical debate . . . in which there are always winners and losers."[2] As well, Michael André Bernstein's book, *Foregone Conclusions: Against Apocalyptic History*, elaborates its theory of sideshadowing techniques in fictional works such as novels, where the reader is moved to contemplate hypothetical, if generally unrealized, counterlives for the resident characters. Thus, we can profitably turn to the general frame of narrative in our project to understand social contingency, where the theorists of narrativity, authors of fiction, and directors of film have variably circled around this contingency problematic. The manners in which film directors, for example, have grounded the contingency issue in the plots of their films have inspired me to situate my own preoccupation more precisely. Thus, it is important to show how alternative dramaturgic approaches to contingency focus on diverse aspects of actors, events, and their causal ramifications.

One approach is best exemplified by the famous Kurosawa film *Rashomon*. This is the *retrospective interpretation* approach, looking at what Umberto Eco would call the diagnostic signs (signs moving from effects to causes). A violent event has occurred at a previous point in time. A man, his wife, a bandit, a murder. Various narrators, dead and alive, all invested in the event, present variable interpretations that reveal different realities, different stories of the *same* event. Characters and actions are moved about, positioned, and repositioned to highlight blame and guilt. While it's not true to say that in these retrospective theoretical dilemmas there is nothing at stake (certainly different interpretations will lead to different individual fates), it is also true that there is a finished quality to the event itself. It remains in the past and the focus has shifted to how it will reverberate into the future.

Alternatively, Krzysztof Kieslowski (the Polish film director famous for his *Red*, *White*, and *Blue* trilogy), has taken a *prospective*, or prognostic approach (moving with the cause to the possible effects) to what I'm calling the subjunctive problematic in his 1982 film, *Blind Chance*. Here, a young man is revealed to have three different alternate fates depending on whether or not he happens to catch a specific train. Will he become a Polish Communist Party hack, an activist in the underground Flying University publishing industry, or a play-it-safe doctor at a respectable medical academy? His various stories are like alternative narrative threads that are drawn out and examined. Time is an important dimension here, the protagonist catching or not catching the train with its inexorable schedule, the resultant narrative threads unwinding over a period of years. But I don't think time is the central philosophical preoccupation. Action is rather the hinge, the point at which past, present, and future align and realign in a variety of ways. Yet while Kieslowski's film gets us closer to that moment of contingency, with the pressure that it puts on the act of catching the train, it doesn't linger there. The man either catches the train or he doesn't. In one of the three possible lives, the hero responds to another character's assertion that life "isn't wholly a matter of chance," with the statement, "Sometimes I think it is."[3]

Sociologists haven't wanted to deal with chance or luck, according to Marc Granovetter, in his book *Getting a Job*. And indeed, it is hard to know what to do with chance theoretically other than to relegate it to some statistical purgatory. But contingency seems to me to be fairly close to chance, and a bit more amenable to theoretical analysis. So the question becomes, how is it possible to linger on the contingent quality of moments of action? Kurosawa and Kieslowski delicately examine the hinge quality of contingency by drawing out its repercussions. But I would like to approach contingency without either placing that moment (somewhat) safely in the past or barreling through that moment as you speed into the future to see how it plays out. The question becomes: is it possible to theorize what exactly happens during those moments when "fate hangs in the balance?" People move and gesture, and words are said so quickly. And there we are already in the future as the present falls over itself to get there over and over again. We simply do not usually have the liberty of slowing things down or freezing the frame to examine each transient moment and to link these moments theoretically to those that have come before or those that will come after. And besides, we never have the liberty, or luxury, of reliving a conversation or interaction, of seeing how it might have turned out differently . . . if only . . .

Reality, unlike films and novels, only provides us with gross approximations of those idealized visions of Kurosawa and Kieslowski, where alternative trajectories can be either retrospectively or prospectively lingered over. Bernstein's "sideshadowing" approach, specifically as he develops it within the context of literature about the Holocaust, aims to stick it out in the ongoingness of events. It's a bold and difficult task: simultaneously to acknowledge a (tragic) reality and to imagine its alternative. As he writes: "Rather than casting doubt on the event-ness of history, sideshadowing helps us to reckon the human cost of an occurrence by reminding us of all that its coming-into-existence made impossible. The nonlives of the sideshadowed events that never happened are a part of the emotional/intellectual legacy and aura of each actually occurring event . . ."[4]

Yet still, the events configured by the novelists analyzed reside resolutely in the past. The question is whether there is both an event that is self-conscious enough about its own contingent quality (leaning, as it were, on its contingency) and an analytical strategy for gainsaying such an event whereby the area illumined is precisely that space between the probability and the reality? In the aim of meeting this challenge, my approach to theorizing contingency has led me to focus on a very particular and decidedly contingent event, the standoff.

The standoff as an exemplar of contingency

At some level, it is ironic to indicate the standoff as the situation best suited to analyzing contingency. The standoff may be viewed as a frozen moment, where the mechanisms and processes of social interaction have ceased to function in their usual predictable and elastic way. They are neither the normal "structure" nor the periodic, but necessary "antistructure" in Victor Turner's terms. They are a heightened form of structure, frozen in the way that histological sections placed on a slide are, and, simultaneously, in the manner of live cell samples, engaging in their own forms of movement, threatening to slide off the social microscope. Participants in standoffs usually spend a good deal of time just waiting, waiting to see what the "enemy" will do. The basic social parameters of time, day and night, weekday and weekend (systematically analyzed by Eviatar Zerubavel in his works on the social construction of temporal boundaries), diminish their hold on the situation. Thus while we normally associate contingency with fluidity, I need to conjure up a different image of it, an image more bumpy and prone to stops and starts, both frozen and leaking at the same time.

But is a standoff – cops behind the rock , robbers in the hideout is a stereotypical image – just too eccentric a social situation to focus on for studying social processes that are relentlessly and continuously at work in all interactions? Standoffs, with their attendant expectations and dramatic denouements are interesting enough in their own right. But I would submit a larger claim – one that draws standoffs squarely into the ambit of social life more generally. In other words, I'd like to make that claim that most of social life can be understood as avoidance of standoffs and that there's something of the standoff lurking, contingently, behind every social situation. I'm trying to capture those things that contingently turn exchanges into standoffs.

Surely, we all have an image of what a standoff is, who the characters are, and even what is supposed to happen (someone is supposed to win and someone lose). Of course, history is replete with standoffs, the legendary case of Masada is a well-known example and in more recent historical time, that between US Federal Troops and John Brown and his fellows at the Harpers Ferry Federal Arsenal, is similarly famous. Certainly, we, in the United States, have been beset by such standoffs in the recent past. The following have figured prominently and will form the empirical basis for the analysis of this book. They are: Wounded Knee in 1973, MOVE in Philadelphia in 1985, the Randall Weaver family in Ruby Ridge, Idaho in 1992, the Branch Davidians in Waco, Texas in 1993, the Freemen of Montana in 1996, and the Republic of Texas in 1997. The details of these cases will be presented at the end of this chapter.

Other countries also experience their own standoffs: the recent occupation of the Japanese Ambassador's house in Lima, Peru by the indigenous group Tupac Amaru is a case in point. This standoff will also be examined in detail as it provides an interesting exogenous case with some similarities and some differences from those occurring in the United States. Despite their cultural and political differences, for all of these it is clear that the image of antagonists frozen in their opposition to each other is a first approximation of an adequate description of the situation. But can we conjure a different understanding of standoffs,[5] one that may provide the analytical leverage to concentrate on the contingent and provisional interactions that take place during its occurrence rather than on who wins and who loses? Can we assay a standoff in terms of its own subjunctivity?

The standoff as a conflict of meaning

Senator Kohl: And [Randall Weaver] is right in terms of fact. He is not a major firearms dealer. You are suggesting that he could have become but he was not. And you were in control of that whole operation to have made it, in fact, the case . . .

Mr. Byerly: There were only two firearms which were received by ATF, that is correct.

Sen. Kohl: I mean the rest is possibility, maybe, could have, did not happen, dispute over the price, but it did not happen. (The Federal Raid on Ruby Ridge, Hearings – Committee on the Judiciary, United States Senate, questioning by Senator Kohl of ATF Special Agent Herb Byerly regarding whether Randy Weaver was a big-time gun dealer, p. 110.)

Our sense of the completeness of a form, in other words, often depends upon a class of forms with which we identify it. We will know that a sonnet is complete as such only if we know what sonnets are. (Barbara Herrnstein-Smith, *Poetic Closure*, pp. 26–27.)

Let me begin by provisionally defining what I mean by a standoff. Stand-offs are situations of mutual and symmetrical threat, wherein the central parties face each other, literally and figuratively, across some key divide. Stand-offs engage committed adversaries in a frozen and exposed moment of interaction. Everything is placed in high relief – actions and reactions, language, gestures, behaviors. The moment is framed, often literally, in that a space of the standoff is, if possible, located and cordoned off. As well, temporal parameters are anticipated, cordoning off the period of the standoff in time, as X number of days are designated for waiting or nego-tiating or whatever.

A standoff may be viewed as the "eye of the storm" of a conflict in two ways. First, this image suggests the idea of calm before, during, or after a storm. This calm exists as a stalled moment of violence – a waiting, a holding until something happens. Alternatively it can come after an initial act of violence and places the reaction to that act in abeyance – it holds off the reaction. The second way in which the standoff is the "*eye* of the storm" is in the sense of vision, of revelation, of shedding some light on a situa-tion that has temporarily been frozen fast.

A paradox of the standoff is that while all participants have committed themselves to the situation (with highly variable degrees of freedom), they have, in a profound sense, committed themselves to *different* situations. They have taken their "stands," that is positioned themselves around some set of issues. And their definitions of the situation are usually diametrically opposed. Institutions of law and politics and organizations of law enforcement attempt to appropriate the standoff with preferred categories of assessment and control. The antagonist is alternately terrorist, cultist, fanatic, fundamentalist, or (as in the case of the long-running metaphorical standoff with the Unabomber) just plain old serial killer. Antistate groups, as well, have their own rigid and reified categories of identity and reality with which they operate. Thus the standoff is often as much about clashes of categorical imperatives as they are clashes of individuals and groups.

This conflict of meanings, at the levels of both cognition and experience of the participants, is what freezes the action. What needs to happen, at its most basic, is a restructuring of the situation so that there is some, however small, place of overlap between the definitions of the situation on the parts of the adversaries – to get a wedge into the frozen moment. (This is my own strong sense of what needs to happen; obviously others will define their goals differently – for example, the Bureau of Alcohol, Tobacco, and Firearms might say, at least before the Congressional hearings on the Waco disaster, that their goal was to arrest David Koresh.) I believe that my articulation of a goal is in accord with George Herbert Mead's notion of the relation of truth and the world: "Truth emerges in the process of experimental activity within a common world when problematic situations are resolved by *restructuring* a part of the world that is there in ways that work, which allow ongoing conduct that had been stopped by a conflict of meanings, to continue." [6]

Narrative as a bridge of meaning

What is the best way of analytically approaching this conflict of meaning and the contingent search for resolution in paralyzed situations? I believe that one needs two distinct, but contingently connected, analytical tools; a *theory* of situations (viz Pragmatism) and a *typology* of situations (viz Structuralism). And narrative is the connecting bridge between the two. Narratives tell stories about unique situations in ways that appeal both to recognizable archetypes and to contingent relations among the designated characters, events, and locales. All narratives are about the relationship between certainty and uncertainty. Past actions and past generic conventions of narrative forms provide a sense of predictability from beginning, through middles, to the end. And yet each narrative must inexorably ply its way through sequential time and social space (locales) – with characters, scenes, and plots acting and interacting and where, really, anything might happen.[7] Narratives thus provide both movement through time and space (sequence and action) and stopping points where socially meaningful transformative events (marriages, births, deaths, ruptures) are foregrounded and their consequences revealed. If the stopping-point of a standoff seems, at one level, literally to stop the action of ongoing narratives (or "conduct" in Mead's terms) in ways that typically emphasize binary opposition (us against them), an analysis that can handle this binarism is required. If, on another level, the standoff is viewed as having its own narrative life history of sequenced interaction, an analysis that can handle the processual syntax of the standoff is necessary.

As suggested above, I believe that such a combined project requires both the insights and tools of a general Structuralist approach and the insights and tools of Pragmatism. Such a combining is similar, in intent and theoretical patronage, to that described by anthropologist William Hanks in his analysis of discourse genres. For such analysis, he turns to the work of literary theorist, Mikhail Bakhtin and anthropologist Pierre Bourdieu. Hanks writes that:

. . . for the analysis of discourse, both "sociological poetics" [Bakhtin] and "practice" [Bourdieu] theory are insufficient when taken individually, but make up a coherent and revealing approach when combined. The former gives an inadequate account of the diachronic processes of discourse production, of the action-centric perspective of language users, and of the partial, open-ended realization of discourse forms in communicative practice. Bourdieu has written insightfully on each of these issues. On the other hand, Bakhtin's careful studies of formalist poetics, linguistics, and literary genres provide a nonreductive approach to verbal form, which will be necessary if practice theory is to come to terms with the linguistic processes embodied in action.[8]

Poetics and practice reflect, respectively, the Structuralist and Pragmatist approaches to social life. My own previous work has relied upon a methodological preference for a form of discourse analysis based primarily upon a Structuralist reading of discursive frameworks. At its most basic level, this Structuralist-oriented discourse analysis assumes an important relationship between systems of symbolic representation (most notably speech) and the organizations and institutions of the social world through which such symbol systems flow. It assumes, as Barry Schwartz and I have written elsewhere, that:

specific world views inhere in the specialized discourses of social organizations . . . These world views involve ideas of what it is to be a human being in society and how human beings ought to be represented. Discourse analysis moves back and forth between organizations and the contours of their world views by attending to the specific words and acts of organizational incumbents.[9]

Thus context is not sacrificed for formal assessment of the internal features of discursive formations, and internal features are not sacrificed for a context-derived covering explanation.

The substance of discourse analysis has been variously configured by different scholars and pitched at many different levels of social life. Michel Foucault identifies discourses with the "disciplines" of modern life, including such professions and attendant worldviews as medicine, psychiatry, and criminology. The notion of the human agent varies across these disciplines according to their paradigmatic worldviews. In the discipline of psychiatry, for example, the central norm is that of sanity, from which flows specific modes of assessing, naming, and treating human beings as either sane or sick. All discourses thus entail vocabularies of motives – the most essential engaging the question of what it means to be a human being. Working out of his own dramaturgical system, Kenneth Burke calls such centering and motivating images "God-terms" – the terms that literally stand in for God (or the first mover, or the final arbiter) in all human-made systems of knowledge, action, and truth. However, it has also been generally recognized, at least since the onset of modernity, that all discourses are partial – they can articulate some areas of human experience and literally *have no words* for others. These other areas of human experience then become unsayable.

But of course discourse, broadly interpreted, must include symbolic systems and acts beyond that of language *per se*. Analyses of three-dimensional social situations thus require a systematic assessment of more than just the linguistic features of the interactions. Algirdas Greimas, in his program to develop a semiotics of the natural world, speaks of the need to "consider the extralinguistic world as no longer being the absolute referent, but as the place where what is manifested through the senses can become the manifestation of human meaning, that is to say, of signification."[10] Put succinctly, bodies in time and in space move and gesture, build and demolish, come forward and go back in ways that are systematically signifying of the situation's narrative-in-the-making. As such, the features of this "extralinguistic" world need to be drawn into the analysis as well.

The orientation of Structuralism and the introduction of Pragmatism

As I noted above, my own engagement with discourse analysis has been heavily inflected with such Structuralist imperatives as seeking out oppositional pairs (of social genres or discursive formations), looking for formal patterns of organization, and charting their structured transformation.

While the social crises I have studied (the kidnapping of Italian political leader Aldo Moro in 1978 by the Italian terrorist group, the Red Brigades, and the confrontation between Philadelphia city police and the antisystem group MOVE[11] in 1985) have certainly called forth a sensitivity to the ongoingness of process, my chosen analytical strategies focused more on combinations and recombinations of the discrete symbolic items of these events viewed as systems. As T.S. Eliot wrote in "East Coker":

> For the pattern is new in every moment
> And every moment is a new and shocking
> Valuation of all we have been.

Eliot, in poetic shorthand, draws structure, pattern, and transformation together in precisely the way I understand Structuralism to do. Structuralism, founded as it is on the premise that the individual items of symbolic systems (from language, to totems, to kinship, to food) derive their meaning from their contrastive and correlative relations to other items in the system, rests on the claim that the items have no intrinsic meaning and must be assessed in terms of their systemic lives. So meaning is found in the mediating and enabling spaces between the items, in their relationships to each other. And, at the existential level, all such symbolic systems refer, according to such Structuralists as Claude Lévi-Strauss, to a defining general problematic; "how to make opposition, instead of being an obstacle to integration, serve rather to produce it."[12]

In terms of my own approach, I have tended, until quite recently, to resonate fairly exclusively with this Structuralist, neo-Kantian, Durkheimian, Lévi-Straussian vision of society as being comprised of categorical, collective representations – whether one assumes their source is in the mind, with Kant, or in society itself, with Durkheim. A more recent engagement with the process-oriented analytical framework of Pragmatism has pushed me to think beyond the Structuralist paradigm.

It was the work on the MOVE confrontation that ultimately drew my attention to Pragmatist models of interpretation. A series of overarching questions has motivated almost all of my research and was particularly true for that on MOVE. These questions include: How might we understand the actual trajectory taken in such cases, cases where a broad array of institutions and individuals confront each other in high stakes situations, where institutions (sometimes the very state itself) and organizations are either salvaged or broken, where lives are saved or lost, where power is ratified, accrued, or sacrificed? What are the roles of language in these cases (language here understood to be both cognitive and conceptual *and* normative and political)? Is language use and deployment during such emergencies different than it is during "normal time?" Should it be? How do we know when we are in an emergency? And finally, how might these crises have been resolved differently?

I concluded the book I wrote about MOVE (*Discourse and Destruction: The City of Philadelphia vs MOVE*) by theorizing a difference in the modes of discursive interaction I found operating in the case, that is, in the ways that the different discourses of action made contact with each other (or didn't).[13] The basic discovery was that there were two modes of interdiscursive interaction, *contamination* and *hybridization*. Both modes, despite their critical differences, provided the Burkean friction among the terms of order and motivation to move the narrative action of stories forward.

Narrative friction

Contamination refers to the process by which apparently insular, self-sufficient discourses experience discursive eruptions that reveal their dependency on other discursive formations. For example, the rules-bound, hierarchical, universalistic, disinterested discourse of Bureaucracy proved to be dependent upon the private and interested discourse of Sentimentality when bureaucracy had to articulate (justify) its actions to the outside world. Asked about his general expectations for MOVE members' actions at a moment of great tension during the day of confrontation, the singularly bureaucratic-minded managing director responded that: "Then I probably – I had an emotion that [the members of MOVE] might come out or that those who wanted to come out might come out." What was emotion doing in this sentence? What was it doing in Managing Director Brooks as he calculated the odds of a particular event? Certainly it appeared as a foreign body in both the discourse and the persona of Brooks as city bureaucrat. But its appearance was meaningful.

Similarly, the discourse of War demonstrated its dependence on images from a domestic discursive economy – literally from the kitchen. Tear gas was described as "like" powdered milk or talcum powder, shaped explosive charges were likened to different sizes of sausages. For all its striking strangeness, such dependency was revealed only in so-called marginal moments, in socially unconscious leaks in texts and speeches, and was thus unacknowledged as critical, essential. It happened, as it were, behind the backs of the very speakers.

Hybridization, on the other hand, means a *practical* acknowledgment of the incompleteness, the partiality of a given discursive formation. This involves discursive self-critique and an openness to other discourses. The constant aim of hybridization is the deinstitutionalization of discourse.

Those speakers engaged in discursive hybridization are structurally similar to those social agents about whom Foucault wrote, such as the professional, yet subordinate, caregiver nurse, who are in contradictory locations in disciplinary power formations. These agents have the metaphorical taste of two discursive worlds in their mouths, and their knowledge is "local," not completely caught up in the institutional relations of power, not completely constructed either as "in charge" or as "incarcerated." In this light it is interesting to note the voiced frustrations of the former hostages in the recent Tupac Amaru standoff in Lima, Peru who, rather than being actively solicited for help and advice as the standoff continued, were alternately ignored and placed under surveillance themselves by the Peruvian authorities. While former hostages are often given a kind of muted authority (the most positive role suggested by the government in the Peruvian case, for a former hostage, Canadian Ambassador Anthony Vincent, was that of "observer"), it is their discursive silencing that is striking.

An alternative conceptualization of the transdiscursive speakers I analytically identify as "organic mediators" might be Georg Simmel's idea of individuals located at the intersection of multiple "social circles," enacting, in the demanding and contradictory ways of modernity, multiple social roles and plural value systems. Sometimes, times such as those I am analyzing, such locations can be used to the advantage of the situation. In the MOVE conflict, there were such individuals. Shifting back and forth across discursive domains: doing elaborate forms of deference, invoking religious precepts, asserting their form of authority based on their civil rights activism (listing places and times where they had demonstrated against racism, poverty, disenfranchisement, etc.), these individuals cobbled speech acts together on the day of the confrontation through borrowings and reframings. Simply, they gave themselves the license to be creative and to act in the situation. That they were unsuccessful in catching and holding the attention of the authorities and in gaining an authoritative portfolio for action during the standoff, indicates, as we shall see in Chapter 4, the zealous reliance on legitimate experts in such cases.

Analytically, it is important to stress the relentlessly deinstitutionalized discourse (both during the crisis and in later testimony at the Hearings) of the "organic mediators" who were trying anything to preempt tragedy. By contrast, those participants bound up in institutional discourses were continually preoccupied with categories: who is in charge, who is a criminal, what kind of criminal, what category of crime, and – the biggest question of all – what is MOVE? Thus the irony – even those most attuned to strategy and tactics (the police, in an essential state of war) were *categorically* unable to focus on the situation. Thus I ended the MOVE book with the clear sense and suggestion that there was something important about the fluidity and flexibility of extrainstitutional discourses in social and political crises.

After finishing the book, and reading other case studies, it occurred to me that what I might be talking about when I was talking about hybridized discourses was perhaps akin to Pragmatism. Most importantly, the cases I was studying and reading about were inspiring me to think about the relationship between categories and institutions (law enforcement, medicine, bureacracy, etc.) and the social consequences of alternately clinging to or disengaging such worldviews and the categories they generate in moments of conflict and crisis. Perhaps the key lies in what kinds of questions are asked in such moments. If the question is, "how do we all get out of this intact?" rather than, for example, "what does the license and inspection code say about boarded-up houses?" then the repertoire of possible responses might be reconfigured. This is not a simplistic maxim to abandon the experts. Rather, in this formulation, the analytical issue becomes less that of "uncovering" a false distinction between experts and lay participants (i.e. problematizing expertise itself), than of problematizing what it is that the "experts" ought to be expert in. For example, as will be shown, academic and FBI (Behavioral Science Division) scholars of religion were not systematically consulted during the standoff between the Branch Davidians at Waco and the FBI. They were, in fact, ignored because the Branch Davidians had been labelled a "cult." As two such experts write, "This suggests that 'cult' stories are not perceived to be 'religion' stories."[14] Thus cult and religion, the illegitimate and legitimate categories of faith, have split themselves in two in the institutional mind, and reified in this way, become unavailable to each other.

Beyond such discursive splitting and segregation, I would like to consider what it would mean to invoke an apparently irrelevant type of expert in a standoff, experts in improvisation? But I'm getting ahead of myself. For now, what is key is that the qualitative difference between these kinds of questions (institutional versus situational questions), matters *analytically*, because the question about getting through a situation intact anticipates a theory of Pragmatism more than a theory of Structuralism. As Eugene Rochberg-Halton has written, in an article titled, "Situation, Structure, and the Context of Meaning," "[Charles] Peirce argued that a sign only has meaning in the context of a continuing process of interpretation. Because each sign is part of a continuous temporal process of interpretation, his theory is intrinsically processual and thus incompatible with Saussure's dyadic and intrinsically static theory . . . The continuity of the temporal interpretive process assures freedom in the pragmatic tradition. . ."[15] This is the key, the continuing process of interpretation in ongoing situations.

But, given my abiding interest in Structuralism, the route I have taken from Structuralism to Pragmatism has incorporated and sustained my preoccupation with form, and thus with the *specific forms of language* in crisis situations. The goal, then, is a large one – to be able to make theoretical sense of the formal discursive elements of the processual interaction. In order to do this an appropriate analytical language must be developed that can account for such a combination of the formally structured and the interactively procedural. In other words, as David Harvey poses Alfred North Whitehead's own project: "how to devise an adequate language with which to capture process, motion, flux and flow without abandoning the obvious commonsense idea that we are surrounded with things possessing relative stability and definable properties."[16] Or, to put this in symmetrical reverse, the aim is to develop a formalist analysis of language and the narratives of action from within the stance of Pragmatism.[17]

The Pragmatic stance

What then does "within the stance of Pragmatism" mean? Let me begin to explore this by way of a discussion of Jeffrey Alexander's essay, "Action and its Environments." In the context of his broader discussion of the relations of the macro to the micro, Alexander focuses on the crucial concept of effort. He writes: "Effort is the contingent element of action . . . the motor, the microprocess, that drives the combination of the other elements."[18] Ever since the days of the debate between Lévi-Strauss and Vladimir Propp about the respective analytical priority of the synchronic (axis of simultaneity where oppositional pairs are located) and the diachronic (axis of history where linear sequence is highlighted) in Structuralist analysis, precisely this contingent element of effort has been insufficiently addressed in discussions of the ongoing narrative composings of society. It is, I believe the crucial relationship between this contingent effort and the emergent symbolic combinings, viewed from both the synchronic and the diachronic perspective, that deserves our analytical attention. Alexander's essay points out some of the terms by which this relationship may be deciphered.

At the outset of the essay, Alexander asserts that the *macro* parameters of action have a determining role in interaction. Such a claim makes theoretical contact with my analysis of the institutional prerogatives of "official" participants and discourses in social conflicts. The impulse to locate the macro in the micro, through the crucial auspices of effort, leads, in an analysis of standoffs, to an articulation of the processes of interaction from several points of view; the various institutional representatives' points of view, the anti-institutional institutions' (MOVE, Branch Davidian, etc.) point of view, and the extrainstitutional individual's point of view. Given the inevitable presence of authoritative institutions and discourses in such situations, rather than ask the question – should we or should we not depend upon the presence of institutionalized authorities or experts in crises – we might more fruitfully look at the self-understandings of these institutions and the public's relation to them. How do we use institutions, or (with Foucault) how do they use us?

In his book, *The Imaginary Institution of Society*, Cornelius Castoriadis dwells on the nature of the relationship of society to its institutions: "Alienation occurs when the imaginary moment in the institution becomes autonomous and predominates, which leads to the institution's becoming autonomous and predominating with respect to society . . . in other words [society] does not recognize in the imaginary of institutions something that is its own product."[19] What is this "imaginary moment?" And, perhaps *counter* to the relentless disciplinizing process Foucault sees, how might we resurrect this imaginary moment, a moment of pure effort to intervene into the status quo, when we most need it?

To get at this, let me return to the central concept of action. "Every action," writes Alexander, "is both interpretation and strategization; each process ensues at every moment in time. Interpretation itself consists of two different processes: typification and invention."[20] One thing we know for sure about institutions is that they are fundamentally in the business of typification or, to put it another way, categorization. So the interpretive strategy of institutions when confronted with a new situation is inevitably to categorize or typify the situation with the particular classificatory schema at its disposal. On the face of it, such a process appears to be essentially simplifying – the institution takes a real-life, complex situation and calls it an X (religious cult, serial killer, terrorist, etc.). And then, once having made such a classificatory determination, the institution is clear on how to act with *that* kind of antagonist.

However, such a reading doesn't do full justice to the discovery of the "inventive moments of typification" as Alexander puts it. Even the process of typification requires the effort of making a connection, a connection between that which is known and that which is unknown. And any such effort must engage the processes of interpretation and fitting, both of which rely on the language of metaphor, which, as Eco reminds us, simultaneously illuminates the similarities and the differences between the two terms. Thus, a space opens up where the public, if able to recall the "imaginary moment" in institutions, can glimpse the process by which the institution makes the claim that X is a Y. I don't want to downplay the importance of this art of categorizing (even as I critique it for its inability to persevere with contingency over the long run). Categorizing does have going for it the benefit of recognition, knowing when you are encountering a species of experience you have encountered before. And even though institutional categories seem to catch people in their figurative net of definitions, to varying degrees, the categories must fit themselves to the specific individuals encountered. That process of fitting announces an existential contingency, or provisionality, at the core of the act of classification. In another context, that of employers seeking the right job candidate for the right job, Mark Granovetter has written, "The abstract categories of social theory discourage us from noticing that in many important situations, one has to obtain information about rather unstandardized alternatives."[21]

The notion of unstandardized alternatives appearing in a world that seems interested only in standards is especially important to the project of theorizing contingency because it invokes the issue of incommensurability. And here, where incommensurability announces its importance in a system of symbolic exchange, is where, I think, Pragmatism and Structuralism must work together.

I'd like to return to Durkheim and his *Elementary Forms of Religious Life*, by way of Lévi-Strauss in his *Totemism*, to capture something of the feeling I'm trying to conjure in this rapprochement of Pragmatism and Structuralism. Lévi-Strauss quotes Durkheim, who is himself quoting from a Native American Dakota wise man:

Everything as it moves, now and then, here and there, makes stops. The bird as it flies stops in one place to make its nest, and in another to rest in its flight. A man when he goes forth stops when he wills. So the god has stopped. The sun, which is so bright and beautiful, is one place where he has stopped. The moon, the stars, the winds, he has been with. The trees, the animals, are all where he has stopped, and the Indian thinks of these places and sends his prayers there to reach the place where the god has stopped and win help and a blessing.[22]

Lévi-Strauss goes on to write that there is a relationship here between this Native-American passage in Durkheim and Henri Bergson's philosophical metaphysics: "It seems that the relationship results from one and the same desire to apprehend in a total fashion the two aspects of reality which the philosopher terms continuous and discontinuous; from the same refusal to choose between the two; and from the same effort to see them as complementary perspectives giving on the same truth."[23]

Pragmatism would have us focus on the ongoing situation, on the changing meaning of the sign over the course of the continual process of interpretation. Structuralism would have us focus on the meaning-bearing relations of symbolic opposition and correlation within and between symbolic systems. There is both movement through time and stopping points, where meaning temporarily congeals as the result of recombinations of the symbolic items of the set.[24] Pragmatism's claim on temporality, or historicity and Structuralism's claim on social systems has led anthropologist Marshall Sahlins to invoke them both in his idea of the "structure of the conjuncture." Specifically, in his analysis of Captain Cook's visit to the Hawaiian Sandwich Islands, he reveals the way that Cook's reading of the Hawaiian categories of ritual and social status and the Hawaiian attempts to incorporate the European relations of trade into their ritual universe together work to demonstrate how the reproduction of structure becomes its transformation, for all parties involved, I might add. Thus, here is a case where classification reveals its existential contingency. As Sahlins writes: "Signs thus take on functional and implicational values in a *project of action, not merely the mutual determinations of a synchronic state.* They are subjected to analysis and recombination, from which arise unprecedented forms and meanings (metaphors for example)."[25]

Standoffs as interpretive moments

Senator Craig: My question – there was an official declaration of emergency by the Governor of Idaho?
Mr. Johnson (Former US Marshall, District of Idaho): Yes there was.
Sen. Craig: Did that allow the deployment of the National Guard?
Mr. Johnson: Yes it did Senator.
(The Federal Raid on Ruby Ridge, Hearings Committee on the Judiciary, United States Senate, p. 311.)

Let me now try and draw all of this together to talk about the ongoing process of institutional and extrainstitutional interpretation that occurs during standoffs. At this point, having made the point, convincingly I hope, that there is invention even in the archetypically conventional act of institutional classification, I'd like to refocus on those moments in standoffs when *predictable* classification makes restructuring less probable and where continuing paralysis is usually only broken by the emergence of violence.

One alternative to this standard operating procedure might be called a pragmatic stance: that is an approach that insists on directing the attention of consciousness to the continuous interpretive work in such situations. Interpretation as an ongoing process is the willed action of Alexander's schema as I understand it. Truth is discovered through this interpretive action in situ. This fits nicely with *The Oxford English Dictionary of Philosophy*'s statement that: "The driving motivation of Pragmatism is the idea that belief in the truth on the one hand must have a close connection with success in action on the other."[26]

The action driving the parties of a standoff to the standoff state and out through the other side of it is primarily a project of interpretation. Standoffs must be set off categorically from other situations. Participants must find themselves or declare themselves to be in an emergency. Such an existentially diacritical moment foregrounds the difference between *normal* time and space and *emergency* time and space.

There are several ways of understanding this difference between situations that are identified as normal and those that are identified as emergencies. Part of the larger task of this book is to try and elaborate a model of just such a difference by way of working through several empirical cases in which normal social life and emergencies are played off against each other. Here, at the outset, it might be useful simply to speculate on the analytical differences. For example, might one say that the normal is that which is structured in known and predictable ways and that emergencies are declared when such structure is either altogether absent or is dramatically increased, decreased, or distorted? Alternatively, one might claim that normal time is that time during which structure is merely implicit or latent (unmarked) and that emergencies are those situations in which structure becomes explicit (exposed). Thus, as a subset of emergencies, the standoff can be viewed as situations of either distorted, absent, predominant, or explicit social structure. Here, paralysis is a form of structural distortion.

Emergencies put stress on whatever organizations must deal with them, even those organizations like law enforcement, firefighters, the military, and hospital emergency rooms that are established precisely in order to meet emergency situations. Certainly, such organizations must prepare themselves for the emergencies within their purview – medical instruments, bandages, fire-fighting equipment, weapons, and so forth, must be stocked and ready to be used. But the exact nature, extent, time and shape of the contingent emergencies that do occur cannot be fully anticipated. "Normal accidents,"[27] a phrase that neatly captures the ironic acknowledgement of the cohabitation of the normal and the emergency, result from cascade effects of interdependent events. In his striking analysis of the famous Mann Gulch fire, in which many of the firefighters died trying to flee an unexpectedly escalating forest fire, Karl Weick charts what we might call an epistemological chronology of the fire and the interpretive paradoxes it throws up in the path of the fire-fighting team:

1. The crew expects a 10:00 fire [a fire that can be surrounded and isolated by 10:00 the next morning] but grows uneasy when **this fire does not act like one**. 2. Crewmembers wonder how this fire can be all that serious if Dodge and Harrison

eat supper while they hike toward the river. 3. People are often unclear who is in charge of the crew. 4. The flames on the south side of the gulch look intense, yet one of the smokejumpers, David Navon is **taking pictures,** so people conclude the fire can't be that serious, even though **their senses tell them otherwise** . . . 6. As the fire gains on them, Dodge says, "**Drop your tools,**" but if the people in the crew do that, then who are they? Firefighters? With no tools?[28]

The "who are we?" question is a key one for understanding the behavior of participants in a standoff, and will be dealt with at length in Chapter 4. In the case of standoffs between social groups, organizational self-understanding and situational sensitivity clearly hold the key. But for immediate purposes, it is useful to look more closely at Weick's chronology of the fire and the firefighters' reactions to it to try and identify the key parameters of the ongoing interpretations. Identity is clearly one of of them, but it is the variable relations of time, space, and action that most adamantly move the story forward towards its disjointed and tragic finale. Some things are going too slowly; others too quickly. Eating supper and taking pictures are activities that inhabit a leisurely world in which time exerts a minimal pressure. Such a temporal reading contradicts other sensory experiences that emphasize speed. The mixed-up times seem to cancel each other out. Such temporal and spatial dislocations create strange environments for situational action. Time and space coordinates normally provide anchors for individuals moving through social life. All presuppositions about what is appropriate (from eating breakfast, to sleeping, to stopping and going at a traffic light) rely on naturalized cues about where and when such things can and should occur. Not only is this so, but temporal and spatial ordering systems are *interdependent* in establishing such coordinates. As Carol Greenhouse writes: "Official time systems originating in the West, for example, claim to separate time and space as different dimensions of reality; however, their underlying unity can be recovered in the notion of 'events,' which situate temporal moments in social space, or [in the notion of] 'regime,' which does the inverse . . ."[29]

Contexts: time and space

Space and time are thus obviously key to the project of theorizing contingency in social crises, when these normally taken-for-granted coordinates go radically off course. Rhetoricians divide the world of rhetorical modes into the spatial (descriptive and classificatory) and the temporal (narrative and processual). But perhaps a better way to think about this is that in all social narratives, time and space coordinates are variably stressed. Recall the narrative and stylistic differences between the *Iliad*, with its long lists of boats and soldiers, and its staging of war as an endless repetition of battles that, in some sense, can be understood as occupying a single narrative time, and the *Odyssey*, with its singular protagonist and his long, progressive journey home (with stops along the way). Space and Time; War and Journey; List and Sequence. In the terms I'm developing here, the space of the Structuralists, the time of the Pragmatists. Imagine what it would take and what it would mean aesthetically and morally to intercalibrate the *Iliad* and the *Odyssey*, to combine them into one great work. The continuous and the discontinuous apprehended in, as Lévi-Strauss would say, a "total fashion."

Standoffs must be viewed, then, as situations in which the normal expectations about time and space are dramatically altered. In fact, new expectations explicitly emerge and are, precisely, fought over. Accordingly, I will now briefly introduce the conceptual apparatus of time and space coordinates in terms of their relevance to this project. Chapter 2 will deal explicitly with the temporal parameters of standoffs. Chapter 3 will address their spatial parameters.

Time

How is *time* experienced and conceptualized in standoffs? And, in complementary fashion, how are standoffs constructed in time? Obviously, a standoff is immediately determined to have "stopped time," stopped the normal flow of daily life, both mediated (as the mass-media often replace "normal" programming for coverage of the standoff) and face-to-face. Daniel Dayan and Elihu Katz, scholars of communication, have studied media events, such as the coronation of Queen Elizabeth, or the historic visit to Israel by Anwar Sadat. And they have termed these ritualized and media choreographed events, "Time-Out." Standoffs can be said to constitute their own Time-Out – at least for a while. Theoretically, time continues to have possible movement for those within the frame of the standoff (though obviously differently than before), but time seems to stop for those outside of the frame who can only wait. And after a while, something strange begins to happen – people (adversaries and public) get bored, or get fed up, or get too anxious and they want something to happen. This might sound obvious, but it still strikes me as strange that even in a crisis, we have certain expectations about how long "these things" should last. This isn't just my impression. Waco FBI Commander Jeff Jamar has claimed that "There's the 10-day rule. Usually these things are over in 10 days, okay, if you think about it. You think about all these crises, not many last past 10 days."[30] Jamar's almost casual, surely unreflective, invocation of "these things" might already alert us that we are in the presence of official category-making. How does he, and we, know when some situation is one of "these things"? But beyond that, a simple empirical check of the "ten-day rule" shows it to be a bureaucratic fantasy of the tallest order. None of the standoffs under analysis here actually lasted ten days. The standoff at Wounded Knee lasted seventy-one days; the 1985 MOVE confrontation lasted one day; that at Ruby Ridge, Idaho lasted eleven days; the standoff at Waco lasted fifty-one days; the Freemen of Montana standoff lasted eighty-one days, that of the Tupac Amaru, 127 days, and the Republic of Texas standoff lasted seven days. But where Jamar is accurate is in the fact that expectations invariably lead to actions – on the tenth day of the Waco standoff, the FBI turned off the electricity inside the Branch Davidian compound.

We may also want to rethink our common sense understanding of the concept of the "deadline" in crisis situations; deadlines deployed by those both inside and outside of the standoff spaces. Viewed from the Pragmatist perspective of the continuity of the interpretive process over time, *deadlines* can cut off not only electricity, but also the emergent interpretations that might serve to reconfigure the situation.

Thus, I want specifically to raise questions about temporal expectations in crises such as these. What does it mean to import into these situations our workaday notions of efficient use of time, delay, deadlines, patience, impatience, procrastination and the like? What about our importing, as well, our aesthetic sense of proper narrative time, with clear beginnings, middles and ends? Nonconceptual time keeps on going but, as Herrnstein-Smith writes: "The passage of time is . . . continuous; and although temporal sequence provides the poet with an excellent principle of generation, it does not provide him with a termination point."[31] Sometimes, only the contingencies of the situation can provide that. At any rate, the very act of waiting requires effort and faith – faith not in some inevitable clearing of the way but rather faith that time itself provides the unfolding of the real. As Mead, the Pragmatist wrote: "The real is qualitative and you cannot get quality at an instant. It occurs over a period, whether it be color, melody, or the ionization of an atom."[32]

The nerve strains of waiting also point to the emotional registers of individuals in stances of expectation. Here, the type of formal semiotic analysis performed by A.J. Greimas provides another vocabulary of interpretation for the temporal dynamics of patience and impatience, anticipation and anger. Working from what he calls the Narrative Program of the subject, we can track the unfolding of anger over time. As Greimas writes:

Yet, for all that the question of the patience of the patient is posed: At what moment can we say that the patient "becomes impatient," that he "runs out of patience," that he is "at the end of his patience? This problem is that of the introduction of discontinuity into the midst of duration, of segmentation into slices of passional life that appears to us in its ordinariness to be an alternation of tensions and relaxations . . .[33]

This book will examine all of the contingent expectations and actions relevant to temporal parameters in the case of standoffs. Deadlines, historical genealogies, waiting, patience, organizational calendars – all of these will figure in tracking time through the standoff.

Space

. . . There's a gas station
on a little square in Jericho,
and wet paint   Perhaps all fields are battlefields,
on park benches in Bila Hora.   all grounds are battlegrounds,
Letters fly back and forth   those we remember
between Pearl Harbor and Hastings,   and those that are forgotten:
a moving van passes   the birch, cedar, and fir forests,
beneath the eye of the lion at Chaeronea,   the white snows,
and the blooming orchards near Verdun the yellow sands, gray gravel,
cannot escape   the iridescent swamps,
the approaching atmospheric front . . .   the canyons of black defeat,
                                       where, in times of crisis,
                                       you can cower under a
                                                bush . . .[34]

Space is most clearly the domain of the Structuralists, even those Structuralists like Vladimir Propp who are sensitive to the sequential linearity of the narratives under analysis. Systemic boundaries are set – there are insides and outsides and spatial dislocations, and the symbolic elements of the spatial frame combine and recombine as so many variations on the themes of opposition and correlation. Thinking about the spaces of standoffs, one has an image of the relevant homes, compounds, and bunkers, where a morally inflected landscape is overlaid on the physical landscape of mountains, flatlands, or urban rowhomes. Thus spatial referents are usually reconfigured and renamed as a strict grid of inside and outside the perimeter; safe zones, demilitarized zones, and zones of danger replace the normal contours of street names, business districts, residential areas, farms, and wilderness. In the standoff of the Branch Davidians and the FBI/ATF, one could sense the palpable overlay of the topography of the cinematic Westerns, with their own inevitable scenes of shootouts. From the point of view of the authorities, inside the space of standoffs are the incorrigibles and their "hostages." (Like all standoff participants, hostages are dramatis personae with many and complex relations to the other characters in the story – often they are the children of the standoff protagonists. "Hostages" will be explored at length in Chapter 4 – The action of standoffs.) Thus there is more than a little moral and cognitive dissonance to the revelation that the Tupac Amaru members holding the hostages in the Japanese Ambassador's house allowed for the division of internal space into smoking and nonsmoking "sections." Outside the space, or rather, often creating the space by their very presence, are the normals, the law enforcers. A Structuralist sensitivity to the way meaning is created and engaged through symbolic oppositions and combinations can view the various readings of adult–child and male–female relations inside the various standoff compounds by those on the outside as attempts to "fit" the classification of the antagonists to the authorities' desired standoff tactics. Bad parents or bad husbands are clearly recognizable archetypes of the Structuralist analytic of over and undervaluing of existential relations as Lévi-Strauss' famous study of the Oedipus myth lays out the fatal social consequences of such excess.

The Pragmatist focus on the ongoing process of situational unfolding will further direct our attention to the question of the permeability of the spaces of a standoff. Points of ingress and egress are obviously highlighted by those with a strategic, military notion of space here – where houses become bunkers as windows are boarded up. But the analytic frame being developed here encourages a more narrative consciousness of messengers and messages coming and going into and out of the space of the standoff. In Peru, the representative of the Red Cross and the priest, in their respective uniforms of neutrality and transcendence, made the literal and symbolic journey daily. How do they, with their own symbolic and material loadings, restructure the processual narrative of interaction among standoff spaces? God and food and water sustain a partial overlap of meaning for the antagonists.

But I don't want to be too literal about what I mean by space here. The space of a standoff can be as big as a whole country (the United States as the staging ground for the Unabomber) or as small as a memo that lays out a tactical plan. What is interesting to me here is the way that any space, large or small, literal or figural, becomes morally charged. Some theorists of public education, such as the Australian Ian Hunter, have written of the metaphorical standoff that occurred in around the 1830s in England as the development of administrative strategies of population control converged with the moralizing ethics of Sunday School proponents to focus on the space of the school playground (which is suddenly viewed as being in a relation of symbolic opposition to the "streets"). According to Hunter, playgrounds became considered to be an essential part of school discipline, the morally charged space of "play."

Other standoff spaces need not be quite so literal. A collaborative academic article can show residual signs of a standoff between its two writers in the harmonic variations on a theme that appear in the main text and in the footnotes. Ethnomethodologist Howard Garfinkle, in his famous article on sexual identity, "Passing and the Managed Achievement of Sex Status in an Intersexed Person," co-authored with Robert J. Stoller, M.D. exposes the inner workings of a standoff between epistemological paradigms. The article begins by discussing the case of a young man who comes to Dr. Stoller in order to have a sex change operation. It's a complicated story but the bottom line is that this person, ultimately designated as Agnes in the article, believes himself to be truly a woman and wants to become so fully with all of a woman's genitalia. Medical and ethnomethodological perspectives work in tandem to move the story along, explaining Agnes' social and biological transformations and vicissitudes. At a certain key point the perspectives, and the narrative, split provocatively in two. This internal doubling occurs approximately one-third of the way through the article. At that point, a long footnote, authored by Stoller alone, advances an exclusively endocrinological explanation of the subject's postsurgery depression, while the main text continues to sustain the combination of sociological and medical explanatory frames. The beginning lines of the footnote are identical to the main body of the text on that page, and they parallel each other for a while. Then footnote and text diverge, with the footnote taking its own path. In that space that opens up between the text and the footnote, the reader (and, one might extrapolate, the subject of the study and of the medical treatment) stares into a kind of narrative abyss. It is both perplexing and liberating, as alternative explanations for the subject's experience cohabit in the same diagnosis/article without acknowledging each other. Thus the competition among discourses of knowledge, even the friendly sort, can interrupt the smooth work of professional authorities and announce an epistemological standoff. The residue of the standoff leaves its mysterious comet trail in the footnote. And all of this occurs within the privileged and charged space of a published academic article.

Thus, time and space will be foregrounded as the action of standoffs is tracked along its contingent path. Most often the times and spaces assessed will be literal (though always symbolically construed as well); sometimes, as in the Garfinkle and Stoller article, they will be largely metaphorical. The "stuff" of standoffs – identities, gestures, intermediaries, negotiations, rules, procedures, guiding and emergent texts, and so forth – will be analyzed at length in Chapter 4. In the concluding chapter, the developing theory of improvisation will be centrally related to the theoretical concern with contingency in social life. There, the focus will be on the way that standoffs end, and will reflect on the general project of theorizing contingency through exploring the standoff.

I will now briefly list and describe the rudimentary features of each of the seven standoffs referenced in this study. It is important to state that this is not a formal, comparative analysis of these particular standoffs. The aim instead is to play these standoffs off each other and off the analytical schema developed here. Thus, the hope is to extract the essence of "the standoff" from this interplay, and to engage this essence in the project of theorizing contingency more generally. Finally, the groups involved in these standoffs have different, though sometimes intersecting and cross-referencing, agendas and ideologies. These ideological differences (spanning the spectrum from ultraleft to ultraright), as well as the diverse demographic make-up of the respective groups and the way these demographic details feed into the issues put forward by them, make these selected standoffs a good set with which to forge a theory of the standoff. Some of the standoffs themselves were quite brief (MOVE's lasted one day). Some were quite long (the Tupac Amaru standoff lasted 127 days). But duration and complexity do not always coincide. All of the groups are self-identified as taking an antisystem stance, that system being variously configured as the extant government, modernity, neoliberalism, godlessness, and so forth. Some are explicitly religious, some are what might be termed political extremist. The reader may have sympathy for the stated goals of some of these groups while detesting those of others. For the purposes of this book, the analysis will aim to be steadfastly agnostic on such issues.

Presentation of selected empirical cases (in chronological order)

Wounded Knee, 1973

This standoff between members of the Independent Oglala Nation and the American Indian Movement (AIM) on one side, and the Bureau of Indian Affairs, the US Marshals, and the Federal Bureau of Investigation on the other, officially began on February 27, 1973. It took place in the village of Wounded Knee on the Pine Ridge reservation in South Dakota. The standoff lasted seventy-one days with three of the Sioux occupiers killed and one FBI agent shot and paralyzed. While criminal charges were brought against some of the occupiers, all of these charges were eventually dropped.

Some might say that this standoff actually began (had its roots) in the Fort Laramie Treaty of 1868 which set up the Great Sioux Reservation, 2.5 million acres of land occupying half of South Dakota, half of Nebraska and parts of North Dakota, Montana, and Wyoming, and provided the resident Native Americans the right to self-government. In fact, in Chapter 2, I will have reason to analyze this representation of the 1973 standoff as having precisely such a beginning-point. For now, suffice it to say that this treaty was broken and ignored in the intervening century, with such things as the Indian Reorganization Act of 1934, which removed the chiefs and headmen from their positions of formal authority over the tribes.

The more proximal and obvious background to the 1973 standoff involved the attempt, beginning in 1972, to impeach a Tribal Chairman, Richard Wilson, by the Oglala Sioux Tribal Council. Wilson had been accused of various acts of corruption, including hoarding monies distributed by the Bureau of Indian Affairs. At around the same time, the American Indian Movement, under the leadership of Russell Means, an Oglala Sioux, began its "Trail of Broken Treaties" tour, stopping at 300 reservation sites around the country in order to organize a caravan to Washington, DC to protest infringements of American Indian rights. While in Washington, frustrated by their inability to make contact with federal officials to air their grievances, AIM occupied the Bureau of Indian Affairs for three days. Following this, AIM began its return journey to report back to those reservations visited the lack of success in Washington.

Back at Pine Ridge, Richard Wilson denounced AIM's takeover of the Bureau of Indian Affairs and received $62,000 from the BIA ostensibly to guard the BIA building on the Pine Ridge Reservation. On February 11, 1973, as AIM neared Pine Ridge, eighty-four US Marshals were brought in to the Reservation. AIM was ordered not to enter and Wilson banished Russell Means from the Reservation forever. On February 12, there was a protest of some forty-five people against Wilson and, with an impeachment petition in hand, they demanded an impeachment trial. From February 21–23, fifty-five people attended the impeachment hearing, but the charges were dropped by a 14–0 council vote.

On the night of February 23, 800 people signed up to join the newly created Oglala Sioux Civil Rights Organization (OSCRO – approximately equal to half the registered voting population) and, after two days of deliberation, they decided to ask for AIM's help in removing Wilson from office. On February 27, the OSCRO met with AIM to develop a strategy. But Calico Hall, the site of several meetings, was too small. The groups decided to caravan to Porcupine, which had larger facilities. To do so, they had to travel through Pine Ridge and Wounded Knee. But when they got to Wounded Knee, they stopped to pray at the cemetery established there after the 1890 massacre, and decided that this was the place to make their stand. Thus, February 27 marked the beginning of the occupation of Wounded Knee.

The first actual building occupied was the Sacred Heart Catholic Church adjacent to the grave that contained 153 bodies of those killed in 1890. Next, the occupiers spread out to create roadblocks at each of the four roads leading in and out of Wounded Knee, but at this point there was still essentially free ingress and egress. Soon after, stores and white-owned trading posts were also occupied and food supplies and weapons were seized and distributed to the occupiers and the forty or so Sioux families living in Wounded Knee. The first shots were fired soon thereafter with an exchange of gunfire with BIA police, separated by two miles, a few hours after the occupation.

By morning on the 28th, the occupying chiefs issued a statement including three specific demands. First, Richard Wilson was to be removed from office. Second, the two ranking BIA officials on the Pine Ridge reservation were to be dismissed and a US Senate-led investigation was to be established to explore the alleged corruption in the national operation of the BIA. Finally, the Senate Foreign Relations Committee was to hold hearings on 371 treaties negotiated between the US and various Indian nations. During this time, the US Marshals moved in closer and arrested seventeen Indians who were leaving the area as they ran into new federal roadblocks just outside the Indian roadblocks. Each was charged with burglary, larceny, and conspiracy.

The two South Dakota Senators, George McGovern and James Abourezk, flew in specifically to secure the release of eleven white residents of Wounded Knee. However, these residents reported to the Senators that they did not want to leave. Ralph Erickson, special assistant to US Attorney General Richard Kleindienst, also flew to Wounded Knee to take charge of all federal forces and to initiate negotiations. Wilson threatened to invade Wounded Knee and the Justice Department, after a brief attempt at negotiation, issued a two-day ultimatum to the occupiers (which was quickly rescinded/denied by same). From March 9–15, over 300 Marshals and 100 FBI agents were assigned to control the roadblocks with a wide range of weapons (including M-16 automatic rifles, M-79 grenade launchers, and nighttime sensing devices). Negotiations broke down as the newly formed Independent Oglala Nation rejected the government's proposals, which called for a meeting with the Interior Department and the arrest of the occupying leaders.

After a twelve-day lull, negotiations restarted in the buffer zone between the two rings of roadblocks. On April 3, negotiations moved into Wounded Knee and a disarmament agreement was signed at an outdoor table in front of a sacred tipi. Several leaders of the occupation signed the agreement and Russell Means submitted to arrest (on April 5 Means and others flew to Washington to meet with White House officials, but the meeting was serially postponed. He eventually was allowed to address a meeting of the Indian Affairs Subcommittee in the House.) The standoff continued, however, and nearly 2,000 pounds of food was parachuted to Wounded Knee from six independent airplanes. An FBI helicopter shot at a group of occupiers attempting to collect the food and a firefight ensued that lasted for two hours and left one Indian, Frank Clearwater, fatally wounded. During the 24-hour period of April 26–27, a fierce firefight occurred during which another occupier, Lawrence "Buddy" Lamont, died as a result of a bullet wound. Negotiations resumed on April 28. (A historical footnote is important here. On April 30, President Nixon announced that administration officials Haldeman, Ehrlichman, Kleindienst, and Dean had been removed from their offices.)

Toward what would be the end of the standoff, the Council of Elders of the Teton Sioux Nation gathered to discuss the Wounded Knee situation and, in the name of the occupiers, sent a proposal to the government that called for a Presidential Treaty Commission, the firing of corrupt BIA officials and the opportunity for the people of Pine Ridge to vote Wilson out of office. The government responded by saying that five White House representatives would come to the home of Frank Fools Crow, 20 miles from Wounded Knee to discuss treaty issues and that Wounded Knee be evacuated by May 11 with all those with outstanding warrants submitting to arrest prior to that date. This proposal was accepted by the chiefs. Many, but not all, of the occupation leaders signed this agreement, and, on May 8, 1973, the seventy-first day of the standoff, disarmament and evacuation began. Scheduled meetings on May 17 and 18 at the house of Frank Fools Crow began the same day that televised coverage of the Watergate scandal began – subsequent meetings between White House officals and Sioux representatives were cancelled by the White House.

MOVE, 1985[35]

This standoff/confrontation between members of the group named MOVE and the Philadelphia Police Department occurred on May 13, 1985 and lasted just that one day. Certainly, as in all of the standoffs under analysis here, the situation between MOVE, MOVE's neighbors, and the City of

Philadelphia had been one of increasing tension since MOVE's inception in the early 1970s.

MOVE was founded by an African-American sometime handyman named Vincent Leapheart. Together with a graduate student in social work from the University of Pennsylvania, Leaphart (now calling himself John Africa) wrote a tract that laid out his developing system of beliefs, called *The Guidelines*. The largely African-American group MOVE grew up around John Africa and his *Guidelines*. From their house/headquarters in the Powelton Village section of West Philadelphia, an urban area of heterogeneous population, MOVE members walked dogs, washed cars, and did other odd jobs for money. They viewed themselves as a religious and a political organization and their beliefs included animal rights, antitechnology, Black Power, and vegetarianism. They demonstrated at pet stores, zoos, and local political rallies in the neighborhood. During these demonstrations, they were often arrested for, among other things, disturbing the peace.

MOVE members also confronted society in the ways in which they presented themselves personally. They wore their hair in the Rastafarian style of dreadlocks and their children did not wear diapers but defecated in the yard along with the many animals that MOVE kept. They all took the last name of Africa and considered themselves an extended family in which biological ties of parent to child were not salient. Diet was also important and MOVE members ate mainly raw fruits and vegetables, rejecting foods that were cooked. As well, MOVE deployed language in a most particular and provocative way. According to MOVE members themselves, they "strategized profanity to expose the profane circumstances of the system's injustice."[36] The combined effects of MOVE's issue-oriented demonstrations, irregular hygiene, and profane language antagonized some neighbors in the areas of the MOVE houses (Powelton Village in the mid to late 1970s; Osage Avenue in the early to mid 1980s) as well as the city police and politicians. MOVE claimed that the notoriously brutal police force of Frank Rizzo was specifically targeting MOVE for harassment and arrest.

In May 1977, with several MOVE members arrested and convicted of crimes and serving significant jail sentences, other MOVE members staged a demonstration with firearms on the front porch of their house in Powelton Village. Police surveillance intensified at this point and culminated in a blockade of the house that lasted for months. Negotiation attempts failed, including a plan to relocate MOVE to a farm. A shoot-out in August 1978 at the blockaded house left one policeman dead, one MOVE member badly beaten by police, and the house bulldozed to the ground. Nine adult members of MOVE were taken into custody and all were charged with and convicted of the policeman's death.

By the early 1980s MOVE members not currently serving prison sentences set up house in another section of West Philadelphia. The street, Osage Avenue, was in a predominantly African-American section of the city, and consisted of row homes largely owned by the inhabitants. People lived in close quarters, and much of the life of the block took place on the front porches that characterized the homes there.

During the early 1980s MOVE members lived in relative harmony with their neighbors. The house in which they lived had been owned for many years by an older woman who was a former MOVE member. MOVE members had themselves grown up in the neighborhood and were not unfamiliar to the other residents on the street. During this time, MOVE members repeatedly petitioned the newly elected African-American mayor, Wilson Goode, to reopen the trial of those convicted in 1978. Goode was willing to meet with them and listen but ultimately claimed not to have the authority to act on the matter. After this, MOVE took its campaign to the streets, literally. They mounted a loudspeaker on the outside of their house and, in language that was harsh, accusatory, threatening, and profane, lambasted a wide range of politicians and even, on occasion, their own neighbors. Many of MOVE's neighbors on Osage Avenue began their own campaign to rid their block of the "MOVE problem." They wrote letters to politicians at both local and state levels, with little in the way of consequent concrete action.

After an aborted police action on the sixth anniversary of the 1978 MOVE–city Powelton Village confrontation, MOVE members began to fortify their house on the inside and the outside with wood, steel, and railroad ties. The house took on the visage of a fortress. Faced with these transformations, and faced with the neighbors beginning to threaten to take things into their own hands, Mayor Goode handed the task of dealing with MOVE over to his managing director, the retired African-American army general Leo Brooks, and to the white police commissioner, Gregor Sambor.

On May 13, 1985, after evacuating the neighborhood and surrounding the MOVE house with five hundred police armed with military and commercial explosives [C-4 and Tovex], automatic and semiautomatic weapons, sharpshooter rifles, two M-60 machine guns, UZIs, a silenced .22-caliber rifle, and a Lahti antitank weapon, the police commissioner made the following announcement, via a bullhorn from the end of the block: "Attention MOVE, this is America. You have to abide by the laws of the United States." He also announced that he had warrants for the arrests of Frank James Africa, Ramona Johnson Africa, Theresa Brooks Africa, and Conrad Hampton Africa for various violations of the criminal statutes of

Pennsylvania. Further, all members and their children were to vacate the house within fifteen minutes. This ultimatum was immediately rejected by MOVE. At this point, the Philadelphia Fire Department's powerful squirt guns were trained on the house. Police fired tear gas and smoke projectiles at the house to provide cover for police insertion teams. An exchange of bullets ensued that lasted, intermittently throughout the day, until 5:27 p.m. At that point, a police helicopter dropped a satchel of explosives onto the roof of the MOVE house. Minutes later, the pilot reported seeing flames on the roof. After forty minutes, the "squirts" of the fire department were turned on for the first time that evening. By then the fire was out of control and, by morning, had destroyed the MOVE house and two city blocks of homes. Eleven MOVE adults and children died in the fire. One adult, Ramona Africa, and one child, Birdy Africa, escaped.

On May 22, 1985, Wilson Goode issued an Executive Order to create the Philadelphia Special Investigation Commission, composed of eleven private citizens, to "conduct a thorough, independent and impartial examination of the events leading up to and including the incident of May 13, 1985, in the neighborhood of 6221 Osage Avenue in Philadelphia, Pennsylvania."

Ruby Ridge 1992

This standoff in Ruby Ridge, Idaho, between the former Green Beret, right-wing exponent of white separatism and *The Protocols of the Learned Elders of Zion*, Randall Weaver and his family and the combined forces of the ATF, the FBI, and the US Marshals took place during the month of August, 1992, and lasted for eleven days. During the several gun fights that broke out over the course of those days, a US Marshal, William Degan, was shot and killed, Weaver's fourteen-year-old son, Sammy, was shot and killed (along with the Weaver dog), Weaver's wife, Vicky, was shot and killed, and both Weaver and his friend Kevin Harris were shot and wounded.

The story leading up to the standoff began as early as the late 1980s when Randall Weaver started to attend meetings of the ultra-right group, the Aryan Nations. The FBI, monitoring those attending such meetings, noted Weaver's presence. Meanwhile, in 1988, Weaver decided to run for county sheriff, with a slogan of "Get out of jail – free," and persisted in his decision not to pay taxes. At one of the Aryan Nations meetings he attended in October of 1989, Weaver met "Gus Magisano," who was actually Kenneth Fadeley, an undercover ATF agent. Fadeley became friendly with Weaver and managed to get Weaver to agree to sell him two sawed-off (thus illegal) shotguns. In June of 1990, Weaver was approached by two ATF agents concerning a weapons charge, and in December he was indicted on federal weapons charges connected to these shotguns. During the early stages of this encounter with Fadeley, the Weaver family moved from a rented house in Naples, Idaho to a cabin near Ruby Ridge, Idaho up in the Selkirk mountains. Neighbors were few and far between. Some of these neighbors would ultimately testify in Weaver's favor (claiming that he was a decent, family man), others would testify against him (referring to him as a right-wing, neo-Nazi).

After learning of the charges against him, Weaver claimed that he felt these charges were a scam and that he had been entrapped. The actual serving of the arrest warrant involved a fairly elaborate ruse on a road near Ruby Ridge. Weaver and his wife Vicky were driving home one day in January of 1991 and noticed a car pulled over on the side of the road. The driver seemed to be having engine problems and Weaver stopped to help. The driver and occupants of the car turned out to be ATF agents and they forcibly arrested Weaver, while holding down his wife. Soon after, Weaver was released on his own recognizance and given a date for appearance before an Idaho Federal Court. While there was some confusion about the court date (a letter sent to Randy Weaver indicated the wrong date), it is also true that Weaver secluded himself in his cabin with his family and his friend Kevin Harris. The cabin was equipped with a generator, but had no telephone or electricity lines. Local residents delivered mail and groceries. Weaver's status now became one of fugitive.

At this point, the US Marshals Service became involved and began an eighteen month period of low-visibility surveillance of the cabin. Finally, in August of 1992, six marshals, including William Degan, traveled to Ruby Ridge to conduct a more proximal surveillance of the Weaver residence in preparation for an undercover operation to arrest Weaver without harming his children. And, on August 21, they began to approach the house, attempting to stay hidden by the surrounding trees and rocks. During this approach, the Weaver's dog began barking and Weaver, his son Sammy, and his friend Kevin Harris left the cabin to investigate whatever it was that had made the dog bark. Realizing that they had been discovered, the US Marshals, dressed in camouflage uniforms, shot the dog and, they later state, sought to retreat. However, gunfire broke out at this point as Sammy Weaver, Randy Weaver, and Kevin Harris entered the scene at an out-cropped area called the "Y." In this firefight, Sammy Weaver was shot in the back and killed and US Marshal Degan was killed. It should be noted that the chronology of who shot first and who was advancing and who was retreating is contested by the surviving participants. Weaver retreated to the cabin with Kevin Harris.

On August 22, the next day, FBI sniper/observers from the "Hostage Rescue Team" were deployed to Idaho to deal with the crisis. They brought with them the specifically formulated "Rules of Engagement," that provides for their being allowed to shoot any armed adult male appearing outside the cabin, even prior to a surrender announcement. (I shall be discussing the controversy around the meaning of these "Rules" at length later in the book). Operating under these rules, FBI sharpshooter, Lon Horiuchi, fired and hit Randy Weaver as Weaver stood outside the building near the cabin called "the birthing shed" (where Weaver's wife and older daughter stayed during their monthly menses). A second shot was fired at Kevin Harris as he was retreating into the Weaver cabin. It seriously wounded him and killed Vicky Weaver who was standing inside, behind the cabin door, holding a baby in her arms.

During the next eight days, the FBI attempted, via a robot armed with a gun and a telephone and recorded messages from family members, to convince Weaver and Harris to surrender to federal authorities. They had little success in doing so. It was not until Bo Gritz, the well-known former Green Beret (who organized commando-type forays into Vietnam to rescue MIAs), right-wing Populist Party presidential candidate in 1992 ("God, guns, and Gritz" was his slogan) entered the scene and commenced negotiations with Weaver, that progress was made. Weaver knew Gritz from their days in the Army Special Forces and trusted him to orchestrate their surrender. On August 30, Kevin Harris surrendered and on August 31, Randall Weaver did as well. Kevin Harris was charged and acquitted of the federal murder charge regarding William Degan's death. Randy Weaver was aquitted of all charges, including the original one of selling illegal weapons to a federal agent, except that of failing to appear at his original firearms offense hearing. Harris sued two US Marshals in civil court and won as the judge found the Rules of Engagement to be unconstitutional. Congressional Hearings resulted from the FBI internal investigation of Ruby Ridge. Several FBI officials were demoted and/or suspended for their involvement in suspected perjury and/or destruction of documents pertaining to the case. Lon Horiuchi was indicted for involuntary manslaughter of Vicky Weaver and was eventually acquitted.

Waco, 1993

This standoff took place during the early months of 1993 outside of Waco, Texas and pitted the forces of the ATF and the FBI against a religious group, called the Branch Davidians, and, specifically, its leader, known as David Koresh. The standoff, which ended in a consuming fire, lasted fifty-one days.

At the time of the standoff, there were approximately 130 people living at Mount Carmel (the home/compound of the Branch Davidians), with roughly equal numbers of men, women, and children. By the end of the confrontation, four ATF agents had been killed and twenty wounded. Eighty-three Branch Davidians (including twenty-three children) had died.

Much has been written about the Branch Davidians and their charismatic and controversial leader, David Koresh. Most of the Branch Davidians, a group termed "catastrophic millennialist" by religion scholar Catherine Wessinger,[37] were former Seventh-Day Adventists. The group had a multiethnic composition; over half were persons of color, and they lived under one large roof at Mount Carmel. Koresh, born Vernon Howell, had many passions; cars, rock music, and the Bible figured prominently among them. He originally moved into Mount Carmel in 1981 when he was twenty-two years old. At this time, Mount Carmel was under the prophetic leadership of Lois Roden who identified Howell as the next prophet. Following this, Howell and his wife traveled to Israel where he claimed to have had a religious revelation and he would later (1990) take the name of David Koresh (after the biblical king of the Persians, Cyrus). Temporarily exiled from Mount Carmel by Roden's son, George, Howell/Koresh moved to nearby Palestine, Texas. During this time, along with his first, legal, wife Rachel Jones, Koresh "married" several other young girls (age twelve to twenty). In 1987, Howell/Koresh and George Roden engaged in a shootout essentially over their competing claims to be the prophet of Mount Carmel and Howell/Koresh was charged with attempted murder. He was released after a deadlocked jury could not reach a verdict. George Roden went on to murder another man in 1989 and was committed to a mental hospital.

Meanwhile, after paying the back taxes, Howell/Koresh moved back into Mount Carmel with his followers. In 1989, believing that he was a messiah, he declared that all the women in the community were his "wives" and that all the other men should be henceforth celibate. Koresh claimed this right after developing his own interpretations of various biblical texts. Koresh became renowned for his ability to "read" the Bible for the Davidians in the context of ongoing history and he recruited more members by traveling throughout the United States and the world. As an apocalyptical group, the Branch Davidians began to suspect that Armageddon might begin at Mount Carmel.

In the early 1990s, disgruntled former members of the Branch Davidians and proponents of the anticult movement had begun to levy charges against Koresh that he had physically abused the children living at Mount Carmel. Investigations were commenced by the Texas Department of

Human Services and the Texas Child Protective Services but the cases were closed for lack of evidence.

The investigation that did lead to federal agents taking action against the Branch Davidians was that of the ATF in June 1992. A United Parcel Service driver had reported delivering a parcel to Mount Carmel that contained hand grenade casings. ATF agent Davy Aguilera was given the assignment of investigating the Branch Davidian purchase of guns (specifically gun parts which, while legally purchased, could be illegal if modified and assembled in certain ways). This investigation included planting an undercover agent, disguised as a student who wanted to study the Bible with David Koresh and another undercover agent pretending to be a UPS driving trainee. Koresh began to understand that he was being surveilled by federal agents and he complained about this to the local sheriff's office.

In late January, 1993, the ATF decided to develop a plan of "dynamic entry" into Mount Carmel to deliver an arrest warrant to David Koresh (the warrant alleged that the Davidians were indeed converting semiautomatic weapons into automatic weapons without filling out the proper forms and paying the necessary fees). This operation, termed "Operation Trojan Horse" by the ATF, was actually discovered by the Branch Davidians when a news reporter tipped off a mail carrier who lived at Mount Carmel. Even though the undercover "Bible student" inside of Mount Carmel reported back to the ATF that the element of surprise had been compromised, the ATF went forward with the raid. Thus, on February 28, 1993, seventy-six ATF agents were deployed in order to deliver a search warrant. An eighty car, mile-long caravan of cattle cars contained agents and officers from a variety of federal agencies (including the ATF and the INS [Immigration and Naturalization Service]). The caravan left Fort Hood to arrive at the staging area at the Bellmead Civic Center and from there traveled to Mount Carmel. Two teams were to enter from the roof, with the support of helicopters overhead. The majority of ATF agents were on the ground, in the vicinity of the front door, announcing, within the noise, "Police, Search warrant, Lay down." As the shooting commenced, Branch Davidian member Wayne Martin actually called 911 to report the assault to the local sheriff's department. During the raid and resultant firefight, which lasted for much of that day, four ATF agents were killed and twenty were wounded; five Branch Davidians were killed and four were wounded. Later that day, another Davidian was killed as he tried to re-enter the compound. (The issue of who fired first is complex and important, both materially and theoretically. It will be addressed at length later in the book.)

With so many dead and wounded on both sides, the FBI was called in to take over on March 1. Jeffrey Jamar was the FBI Special Agent in Charge and the FBI Hostage Rescue Team arrived along with FBI negotiators trained in the behavioral sciences. During the standoff, a total of 668 FBI agents were deployed plus: "6 people from US Customs, 15 from US Army, 13 from Texas National Guard, 31 Texas Rangers, 131 from Texas Dept. of Public Safety, 17 from McLennan County Sheriff's Office and 18 Waco police."[38]

Over the course of the subsequent fifty-one days, negotiators attempted to convince David Koresh to send his fellow Branch Davidians out and to surrender himself. At various points, many children and some adults did exit the compound (thirty-five in total). Negotiations followed a tortuous path, with Koresh requesting the broadcast of his sermons on the Christian Broadcasting Network and engaging in biblical hermeneutics with the negotiators, including his ongoing interpretation of the Seven Seals of Revelation. Religious scholars attempted to offer assistance to the FBI negotiators at various points but were not engaged.

Meanwhile, the FBI tactical team was following its own course. As early as March 13, they cut off electricity to the Branch Davidians. This was followed by a series of tactics designed to put psychological pressure on those inside Mount Carmel to exit: shining bright lights, playing high decibel sounds of sirens, bagpipes, seagulls, Tibetan Buddhist chanting, and Nancy Sinatra's classic, "These Boots Were Made for Walking," among others. As well, the FBI employed tanks to destroy various Branch Davidian vehicles parked around Mount Carmel. On April 17, newly confirmed Attorney General Janet Reno approved a plan to insert tear gas into Mount Carmel. This plan called for the gradual insertion of C S gas by grenade launchers mounted on tanks (the same controversial tear gas as that used in the MOVE confrontation) and the dismantlement by tanks of the building if the Davidians did not exit. The assault was launched on April 19 and, as contingently programmed, the tanks did begin to demolish the building. A loudspeaker announcement by FBI agent Byron Sage contained the following message: "David, you have had your fifteen minutes of fame . . . Vernon is no longer the Messiah. Leave the building now."

A small flame appeared in a second-floor room around midday and larger fires were spotted soon thereafter in the dining room and the gymnasium. At 12:13 the fire department was called and at 12:41, fire fighters were allowed to begin putting out the fire. Fire continued, though, to consume the wood and plasterboard building. Seventy-four Davidians died in the fire on April 19, including David Koresh; twenty-three of these were children. Nine Branch Davidians escaped the fire and were subsequently arrested.

In 1994, a jury in San Antonio acquitted the surviving Branch Davidians of all murder and conspiracy charges while convicting them of lesser charges largely related to illegal weapons possession. A judge in the case, however, overturned much of the lenient verdict of the jury and sentenced the Davidians to lengthy jail terms.

Freemen of Montana 1996

The "standoff" (this confrontation was never officially declared to be a standoff by the authorities, a point I will deal with in Chapter 4) between the militant right-wing group, the Freemen on the one side, and the FBI, the Garfield Sheriff's Department, and the Montana Highway Patrol on the other, took place on and around a 960 acre wheat farm in Garfield County, Montana (near the high plains town of Jordan, Montana). At the outset of the confrontation, there were approximately thirteen men and several women and children inside the confines of the farm. It lasted from March 25 to June 13, 1996, a total of eighty-one days. The confrontation ended with the surrender of the sixteen remaining Freemen to FBI agents and without violence (certain violent incidents occurred during the six-month prelude to the "standoff," including the Freemen's seizure of equipment from an ABC television crew and the firing of a warning shot at a Polish reporter).

The Freemen of Montana are a group with an explicit ultra-right political and religious orientation. They have been described as "Christian Patriots" and many of them are partisans of "Christian Identity." (This movement is committed to white supremacy and claim that people of color are subhuman and that members of the Jewish religion are offspring of Satan and control the international banking system. There has been, apparently, some debate within the Freemen group as to the validity of these most extreme positions).[39] Freemen refer to such foundational documents as the Magna Carta, the Old Testament, the Declaration of Independence, the pre-Civil War Constitution, and prestatehood Montana county codes. They also rely on their own interpretation of the Common Law to generate their own legal documents. Freemen believe in a god named "Yahweh," and claim that their goal is to establish a "united States of America," as an association of sovereign state republics. The federal government of the United States of America is considered to be Babylon and the Freemen consider themselves in a holy war against this Babylon.

It was in 1992 that the Freemen, under the leadership of Rodney Skurdal, began to develop their campaign of what became known as "paper terrorism" by law enforcement agencies. This campaign consisted of printing and circulating a wide range of legalistic Common Law documents, including a

"Citizens Declaration of War." They brought a series of court cases in Musselshell county, Montana that pushed on the rules and regulations of the legitimate civil and penal codes. The Freemen refused to pay taxes, and refused to obtain the necessary licenses to drive automobiles. They also offered classes in the Common Law and taught Christian Patriots from around the country how to protest and withhold the payment of taxes. Eventually, in 1993, Skurdal's property in Musselshell was legally seized due to his refusal to pay taxes on it, and it was put up for sale (though he was not evicted). In 1994, the Montana Supreme Court fined Skurdal $1000 for filing "meritless, frivolous, vexatious" documents.[40]

Meanwhile, in Garfield County, some 150 miles from Musselshell County, other members of the Freemen group were flooding the Garfield County Courthouse with affidavits that were purported to be liens – for $1 million each – against the county attorney, the district justice, and the sheriff. When county clerk Jo Ann Stanton (whose husband was actually related to one of the Freemen) refused to file these affidavits, the Freemen threatened to kill her, the sheriff, and the county attorney.

Over these several years, law enforcement agents had arrested several members of the Freemen group for such things as impersonating public officials and committing criminal syndicalism. As well, Freemen sympathizers, the Clark family, had their farm/ranch in Jordan (in Garfield County) foreclosed on because they had stopped all payment on federal loans (they owed almost $2 million dollars by 1995). In early 1995, one Freeman, William Stanton, was convicted of criminal syndicalism and the FBI began to keep the group under surveillance.

In September of 1995, Freemen leaders Rodney Skurdal, LeRoy Schweitzer and others transferred via convoy to the Clark family farm, now renamed "Justus Township," and claimed by the Freemen to be its own sovereign state. Many like-minded advocates of the Christian Identity movement traveled to "Justus Township" to attend Freemen seminars, and some even to settle in Jordan. Neighbors, including many who were related to various Freemen members, felt increasingly under siege as the Freemen dug in and stockpiled food, water, fuel for backup generators and arms and ammunition (one reporter wrote that he had seen rifles stacked near every doorway and window next to piles of 30-round magazines of ammunition).[41]

The FBI took action on March 25, 1996 when they arrested Schweitzer and fellow Freeman Daniel Peterson while they were inspecting an antenna on the outskirts of the farm. The arrest warrants included the charges of threatening to kill a federal judge and issuing false financial documents. This action marked the beginning of the "standoff."

While the FBI did set up posts around the Clark farm, Attorney General Janet Reno made it very clear that this did not constitute an "armed perimeter" and that the situation was not to be designated as a "standoff." Thus a low-key, low-pressure orientation was chosen by the FBI from the outset.

The Freemen refused to negotiate with the FBI. Instead, relatives, Montana congresspersons, representatives of the right-wing CAUSE Foundation, the Christian Patriot leader and Colorado state Senator Charles Duke, several Religious Studies scholars, and the ubiquitous Bo Gritz all made attempts at formulating and/or participating in negotiations. A new and crucial FBI unit involved in this ongoing situation, created after the confrontation in Waco, was the Critical Incident Response Group. This unit coordinated the two sides of the FBI contingent, the tactical team and the negotiation/behavior science team.

During this period, LeRoy Schweitzer, in jail in Billings, Montana, began a hunger strike. Schweitzer, despite his physical absence, remained a powerful presence for those Freemen in "Justus Township." His participation would prove to be crucial to the resolution of the crisis.

Several individuals did leave the compound of their own free will during the months of April and June and the adults among them were arrested. It wasn't until May 16 that the FBI managed to meet face to face near the gate of the farm, with four of the key Freemen leaders. Two days later, with the mediation of Charles Duke, the FBI actually set up a table and folding chairs at the site in order to seriously engage the process of negotiation. This phase of negotiations failed and, on May 22, the Freemen raised an upside-down American flag as a distress signal.

Various other mediators, including Bo Gritz, came and went over the course of the period from May to June. Finally, on June 10, the three-man delegation from CAUSE met with FBI negotiators and were allowed to begin negotiations with the Freemen. The CAUSE team, ideologically sympathetic to the Freemen and desirous of a peaceful ending, worked out a deal whereby Edwin Clark would be flown to Schweitzer's jail cell to seek the written approval of Schweitzer to end the siege. Schweitzer finally agreed to sign such a document on the condition that his files and legal library, all on the farm, would be safeguarded and taken into the custody of Republican Montana State Senator Karl Ohs to be used eventually as evidence for the Freemen's alternative legal theory and territorial claims. Thus, by dint of this agreement, which also included four other negotiated points (including the proviso that the Freemen who wanted lawyers could retain 51 percent control of their own case with the cocounsel and that the government would not oppose bond being posted for two Freemen to be released if their health deteriorated), the "standoff" ended on June 16 and was signaled to the outside FBI observers by the raising of a Confederate flag over "Justus Township." The Freemen were all taken into custody, though none, as per the agreement, was handcuffed.

In June of 1998, after a five-week trial of twelve members of the group and a prolonged hunger strike by six of them, a federal court jury convicted several of the Freemen leaders, including LeRoy Schweizer, Daniel Peterson, Rodney Skurdal, and Richard Clark, of various Federal crimes. Convictions included bank fraud, mail fraud, and threatening to kill a United States District Judge. Defense lawyers had argued that their clients had truly believed that they had formed an alternative government with the capacity to issue common-law liens and checks.

Tupac Amaru 1996–97

This 127-day standoff between the Peruvian (Cuban communism inspired) Marxist group Tupac Amaru and the military forces of Peru began with a commando-style assault by fourteen members of the group's "Commando Edgar Sanchez," on the residence of the Japanese Ambassador to Peru on December 17, 1996. Some 600 guests were inside the residence on that evening, at a party celebrating the birthday of the Japanese Emperor Akihito. The guests included many other ambassadors to Peru, many high-ranking military and civilian officials of Peru, several Supreme Court Justices and assorted businesspeople. They were all initially taken hostage by the Tupac Amaru guerrillas, several of whom had gained entrance in the disguise of waiters. Eventually, over the course of the four-month standoff, all but one hostage would be liberated (either through release by their captors or in the eventual rescue mission by the military forces). That one hostage, a Supreme Court justice, would be killed in the rescue mission. As well, all of the Tupac Amaru members who had occupied the house were killed in the final attack, including the operation's leader, former union organizer, Nestor Cerpa Cartolini.

The Tupac Amaru group designated this operation with the name "Oscar Torres Condesu," and, in its first of many communiqués, indicated that the official slogan of the operation was, "Breaking the Silence – The Peoples Want them Free." The slogan referred to the some 400 imprisoned members of their group (including Victor Polay, their most senior leader imprisoned since 1992) whom they sought to have released from some of Peru's most infamous prisons. In fact, the day prior to the assault on the Japanese Ambassador's house, hundreds of Tupac Amaru prisoners in Peru's jails announced that they were going on a hunger strike to protest the harsh conditions.

The Tupac Amaru commandos presented four demands for the release of their hostages: first, "That the government commits itself to change its economic course in favour of a model which aims for the well-being of the great majorities"; second, "That all prisoners belonging to the MRTA [Revolutionary Movement Tupac Amaru] and every prisoner accused of belonging to our organization be set free"; third, "Transfer of the commando that entered the residence of the Japanese ambassador together with all the c. [sic.] prisoners from the MRTA to the central jungle. As a guarantee, some of the captured persons, who will be selected correspondingly, will also come along. They will be set free when we have reached our guerilla zone"; and finally, "Payment of a war-tax".[42]

The Tupac Amaru group was founded in 1984 by organizations from the Peruvian radical left (though it had been conceptualized as early as 1982 in a document entitled, *Las Resoluciones del 1 Marzo: Sobre la lucha armada*"). The group takes its name from José Gabriel Tupac Amaru, the leader of a rebellion of indigenous people in Peru in 1780. After fighting for a year, Tupac Amaru was killed in 1781. His year-long campaign is commemorated as a great revolutionary movement in the history of Peru.

While sharing a certain similar leftist ideological historical profile as the Sendero Luminoso (Shining Path) group, it has never been as large nor as violent. Taking inspiration from the Cuban Revolution, they broke away from the legitimate political leftist party APRA which, in the 1980s, actually took power under President Alan García. The movement issued a foundational document in June, 1984, a "manifesto" comprised of twelve "platform planks." The group declared that its objective was to serve as the extraparliamentary arm of the political left. They also called on the United Left (an umbrella organization of the Revolutionary Socialist Party and the Popular Democratic Party) to join with progressive forces in the Church and the Shining Path organization. A hostage standoff and subsequent gun battle in late 1995 ended with the Peruvian police capturing several of the leaders of the Tupac Amaru. The group then entered a period of dormancy until the assault on the Japanese Ambassador's residence.

Through the years since its inception, the Tupac Amaru group has been responsible for repeated bombing attacks on American affiliated businesses (Kentucky Fried Chicken, Pizza Hut, branches of Citibank) among other high profile corporations. However, the current influence of the United States in Peruvian business and politics is not as dominant as that of Japan. Beyond the historical ties between Peru and Japan (with some 50,000 Peruvians of Japanese ancestry living in the country), recent Japanese political administrations have given $66 million dollars in direct aid to Peru and had just that year (1996) approved a $549 million loan to fund rural hydroelectric, sewer, and road development projects. As well, the current President of Peru, Alberto Fujimori, is himself of Japanese ancestry. Thus there was a political logic to the choice of the residence of the Japanese Ambassador.

After the initial takeover, which consisted of a series of explosions going off in the interior of the house, the hostages being taken en masse to lie down in the tent that had been erected for the party in the garden, and intermittent shooting between police and commandos, some hostages (primarily the women and children) were released that same night. All told, by the day of the final siege on the part of the Peruvian military, all but 72 of the original 600 hostages had been released for reasons of health, political symbolism, and interim negotiated settlements (including Fujimori's concessions of granting limited access of the commandos to the press and restoration of electricity after its earlier shutting off).

Fujimori designated his education minister, Domingo Palermo, as his chief negotiator (although the Tupac Amaru group had requested Peru's human rights ombudsman instead) and his efforts were mediated by the Canadian Ambassador (who had earlier been a hostage and was released), Bishop Juan Luis Cipriani, and a Red Cross official. On December 29, Palermo entered the residence and had his first direct contact with the commandos. While various concessions around media access and electricity were tendered over the course of the four months, and while Fujimori went so far as to meet with Fidel Castro to plan for a safe passage and exile in Cuba for the hostage-takers, there was never any concession made by the Peruvian government on the central point of the release of Tupac Amaru prisoners in Peruvian jails.

Despite the continuous dialogue, the frequent release of hostages, the generally civil atmosphere inside the residence (with the Red Cross representative bringing daily hot meals, letters from family members, music cassettes, instruments, and so forth), the standoff ended violently, with an attack on the compound by Peruvian military forces on April 22. The 150-member military assault group split into three parts – one group blasted the front of the house, another attacked from the rear, and a third operated on the roof. One hostage and two military personnel were killed as were all fourteen Tupac Amaru members. Japan commended Fujimori on the end of the standoff.

Republic of Texas 1997

This standoff between members of the separatist Republic of Texas group on the one side and the FBI, the Texas Rangers, and the Texas Department of Public Safety on the other, took place in late April and early May of 1997 in the southwestern Texas town of Fort Davis. It lasted for seven days and concluded with a "cease-fire agreement" between the contending parties. The standoff began when, in retaliation against the arrest of the Republic group's security chief, Bob Scheidt, on weapons charges (including the possession of an AK-47 automatic weapon), the group kidnapped and held hostage two neighbors, Joe and Margaret Ann Rowe.

At the time of the standoff, the Republic of Texas group had at least three factions, these factions disagreeing largely on questions of tactics. But all agreed in their interpretation of the history of Texas and where that history had brought them. Texas' independence from Mexico was delineated in an 1836 treaty and was assured in the 1848 Treaty of Guadalupe Hidalgo. Texas was officially annexed by the United States in 1845, an act that consisted in the breaking of an 1838 treaty, this one a boundary treaty between the Republic of Texas and the United States. It is this interim period between 1838 and 1848 that preoccupies the Republic of Texas group, a period during which there was some sense of Texas as an independent Republic, however fanciful. The group claims further that Texas legally withdrew from the union in 1861, and further that Texas became a captured nation after the Civil War. As partial proof, they pointed out that it was placed under military rule for several decades following the war.

In December of 1995, delegates of the Republic of Texas held a convention in San Antonio to form what was termed a provisional government, to elect a general council, and to anticipate a statewide referendum leading to a constitutional convention in July 1997. They reproduced a copy of the 1836 Texas Constitution with the names of all the original signers (including Samuel Houston). With this provisional action, the group commenced a series of so-called legal maneuvers to, as their "Open Letter to All Texas Sheriffs" indicates, "lawfully seize[d] all assets of the STATE OF TEXAS (UCC Statement #96-00021085, filed February 5, 1996) . . ."[43] Letters were sent to a wide range of public officials, including US Secretary of State Warren Christopher and Chief Justice William Rehnquist.

In a manner similar to that employed by the Freemen of Montana, the Republic of Texas group commenced a campaign of filing countless liens and other claims against state officials (including Texas Governor George W. Bush), and issued drafts for large amounts of money drawn on the Republic of Texas Trust. It wasn't until early 1997 though that this group began to receive much national attention.

The group was founded in 1995 by Richard McLaren, a Missouri native who moved to Texas in the 1970s. McLaren took the titles of Ambassador,

Chief Foreign Legal Officer, and Consul General for himself. By April of 1997, he and his wife Evelyn already had outstanding warrants against them for such things as conspiracy to commit bank fraud, mail fraud, and contempt of court for filing bogus liens. These actions were termed "paper terrorism" by the authorities, a phrase reminiscent, again, of the charges against the Freemen. As well, McLaren himself had an outstanding warrant charging him with burglarizing a neighbor's house. One of the Republic of Texas factions apparently began to feel that McLaren had gone too far and had "impeached" him on March 22. Other members continued to back him and set up their "embassy" at a cabin in a Davis Mountain resort complex.

As noted above, the standoff began on April 27 when McLaren, his wife, and several others (approximately seven all together) stormed a neighbor's house and took the husband and wife hostage in retaliation against the arrest of Bob Scheidt. The Texas Department of Public Safety put up road-blocks, and special weapons and tactics teams from the FBI were set up on nearby ranches. Members of the group put forward a demand that the United Nations become involved in their secessionist aims. By Monday April 28, with Texas Rangers engaging in phone negotiations with the group, an "exchange of prisoners" had been arranged – Scheidt and the Rowes were released. As the standoff continued into its fifth day, on May 1, members of the Republic of Texas group not involved in the confrontation issued a document which at one and the same time distanced them from McLaren and his actions and found Roger Erickson, their then Secretary of Defense, issuing a "notice of Alert to the Defense Forces of the Republic of Texas, placing them on Yellow Alert 1." By May 3, all but two of those involved in the standoff agreed to a "cease fire agreement," (explicitly avoiding the word "surrender") and gave themselves up to Texas officials. As part of this process, they engaged in a military-style ceremony of the laying down of arms, after which they were all arrested. The final two members slipped away from the cabin early on the 3rd and ran off into the Davis Mountains. One was subsequently shot and killed, the other captured and arrested. Police found rifles, handguns, 500–700 rounds of ammunition, twenty-four pipe bombs, eight to ten gasoline bombs, and a scrap iron shooting cannon in the cabin.

On May 11, after another Republic of Texas member, uninvolved in the standoff, was charged with contempt of court, Secretary of Defense Erickson placed the Republic of Texas Defense Forces on Orange Three alert status, "to provide for the influx of concerned patriots, as well as assistance from individuals with pathfinder, recon, and medical expertise."[44]

The cultural setpoints of standoffs

Whether the imaginative scheme is unitary or pluralistic and whether it takes its more elitist and systematic or more popular and contradictory forms, it exercises a retrospective stabilizing influence upon a social order. Any marked deviation by an individual from social norms begins to appear selfish and antisocial whatever its actual motives. Any conflict that defies the scheme seems to threaten civilization itself, if not in the large then in the small, in the detailed pieties by which people evaluate one another and in the implicit assumptions that sustain trust and permit communication.[45]

As should be clear, the standoffs forming the basis of analysis of this book all took place, with one exception, in the United States (though many of the standoff protagonists explicitly refute just such a territorial localization as they (re)claim their independence from the United States of America). While the 1996–97 standoff in Peru does figure in this analysis (and as such, will be of particular interest precisely for its cross-cultural interest[46]), the focus is on the cases that occur within the United States between those living in the US and the extant governmental authorities. This is so because the majority of the cases are located in the United States and the culture of the US is reflected in the particular themes of the stands taken in them. Thus, it is central to the study to gainsay the patterns in standoff "material" in contemporary America. This goal necessarily entails identifying culturally specific values and norms, because something *recognizably* transgressive – recognizable to a particular culture – must be "discovered" for a standoff to ensue. Obviously, there are specific events and interactions leading up to standoffs proper – and we will describe many of them as their intertwining tends in one or another direction. More proximally, there are surveillances, assaults, "dynamic entries,"petitions by neighbors (with their often attendant threats to vigilante action), arrests and incarcerations of other members of the relevant group, and the like. Local claims, with their temporal histories, intersect with authorized organizational missions and the situation begins to be labeled as a potential standoff. But the following section seeks to answer a puzzling question about the genesis of standoffs. Given the great number of individuals and groups in the United States operating at the margins of the law, strictly defined, and given the high incidence of violence in this country as well, why are certain individuals and groups the focus of so much official attention and others largely ignored? Clearly, something culturally charged is involved in what we might call the "discovery" phase of the standoff. As the standoff begins to emerge as the phenomenon it is known to be, it is inevitably in that "discovery" phase that the cultural norms and lines of cleavage triggering and triggered by the relevant actions most clearly reveal themselves. And I would argue it is precisely those cultural lines of cleavage that are the lynchpins of the standoffs.

Contemporary American culture reveals several thematic gravitational force fields that seem to attract official and media attention. These thematic clusters will be introduced below. Latent within each of these force fields are what I would like to term "set-points," points on a continuum of behavior associated with particular cultural forms and values. Behavior that strays from the culture's set-point of "normalcy" will, under the right, and certainly contingent, conditions, attract an exaggerated attention from the authorities. The contingency of these conditions works on at least three levels.

Starting at the most local level (the family, neighbors, the community) there are domestic interactions that occur between individuals and, as Alexander writes; "not 'the family,' 'the father,' 'the manager' but concrete and segmented versions of the same."[47] Here, the diverse characters respond to the actions of others only partly with script in hand. Someone has a "bad day" and responds more vehemently than usual. A neighbor calls in the "authorities," lodges a complaint – or doesn't. At the next level, there are interactions that occur between locally situated individuals and institutions as well as those among representatives of a given institution. In terms of the latter, even bureaucrats in the same agency may disagree with each other about the interpretation or application of particular rules in particular situations. As for the former, a classifier may, as the ethnomethodologists have so incisively demonstrated, hedge his or her bets and wait for a repetition of the complaint before filing a report or may simply fill out a prevaricating report on the situation. Harold Garfinkle's centrally important analysis in "Good Reasons for Bad Clinic Records" details the methods and motives for such preemptive report creation. Finally, as evidenced in the work of literary theorist Mary Poovey[48] among others, there are key historical moments in which competition for dominance among professions or disciplines creates a space of friction in which categories of behavior and social identity (the ill, the hysterical, the mad) literally come and go as the subjects watch the action.

With these levels of contingency in mind, I would propose that among the most highly charged cultural issues in contemporary America, those most apt to contingently trigger a standoff are: *family structure, religious practice, gun ownership, and political and territorial jurisdiction.* Here, a cultural comparison with the case of the standoff between the Tupac Amaru group and the Peruvian authorities reveals an altogether different set of contentious issues. As with many countries in which severe historical differences in social class have generated class-based political movements, this Peruvian case brings to light an image of "the dangerous classes," set on overturning the established order. This theme, along with that of under-development, more than family structure or gun ownership, strikes a cultural chord in many South American countries. While this study will focus on the American cases referenced here, comparisons with this "outlying" Peruvian case will provide a glimpse of an alternative conceptual cultural world.

Within the designated culture, for each of the identified charged fields, certain behaviors are tracked. For example, *family structure* encompasses issues of lifestyle (including residential location and source of income), gender relations, generational relations, sex across genders and generations, incest taboos, and so forth. *Religion* as a charged cultural theme foregrounds the difference between official and unofficial religions, normal and deviant practice (with excess piety bleeding easily into the deviant category). Thus the term "cult" has come to signify excessive religious belief or behavior. *Gun ownership* revolves around competing notions of function: defense, offense, militarization, and sport. Here, the American cultural take on capitalism and free market individualism can intertwine with the anti-statism of proponents of gun ownership in boundary-testing ways. For example, the Branch Davidian collection of weapons was alternately viewed as stockpiling for Armageddon or as a business investment: "Under new government regulations restricting gun ownership, the weapons were increasing in value and the community hoped to reap a profit when they resold the weapons."[49] Numbers and types of guns in individual's possessions play a huge role in determining whether one will catch the attention of authorities. The public is often aware of the irony of official targeting of specific individuals and groups that possess guns. For example, a *Detroit News* reporter was told the following by a resident of Jordan, Montana during the Freemen standoff "You're from Detroit . . . and you're questioning us about how many guns we have?"[50]

Finally, the question of *territory* looms particularly large in several of the standoffs under investigation. The members of the Republic of Texas group staked their entire raison d'être on the claim that Texas was not really a state in the United States but was rather its own separate jurisdictional entity. Similarly, the Freemen of Montana claimed that the 250 acre ranch on which they were encamped was an independent entity named "Justus Township" (note the significance of the spelling). The Oglala Sioux at Wounded Knee demanded that the Senate Foreign Relations Committee hold hearings on US–Indian treaty violations. (The United States Government's response to this was to call for a meeting between the Interior Department and the leaders of the American Indian Movement.)

Such claims to alternative jurisdiction have severe consequences for those attempting to assert them.

Mainstream American culture sometimes overtly and sometimes covertly identifies the normal and the appropriate behaviors relevant to all of these issues. Emergent designations are as much based on decisions about *degrees* of deviation as about *kinds* of behavior. When, for highly contingent reasons, the focused attention of authorities and media representatives is drawn to individuals and groups that have gone beyond the set points of contemporary cultural norms, the stage is set for a standoff. Case-specific processes by which an encounter between culturally deviant or antistate groups and the authorities actually gets "fixed" and categorized as a standoff will be discussed in the context of the schematic frames of the separate chapters. Here, some of the highly charged variations on these cultural themes will be examined in the context of the cases in which they appeared and of the general cultural frame of constructing an "America."

Who is an American[51]

The analytical framework of the "set-points" for normalcy also allows one to get at some self-understood national "essence." And indeed, there is often an overt preoccupation with, and discussion of, the meta-question "What/who is an American," throughout the course of the standoffs being analyzed here. During one of his last phone call negotiations with FBI agents, David Koresh asserted: "And we're also Americans. And I think – I think that America has a patronage – a very clear patronage of individual citizens who – who- who- have a breaking point."[52]

Against such claims to the rights and privileges of "being an American," those investigating the claimants often look for symbolic indicators of the falseness of those claims. During the Senate Judiciary Committee Hearings held after the standoff at Ruby Ridge, amidst a generally sympathetic series of questions directed towards Randy Weaver, Senator Diane Feinstein probed just such a claim in the following interchange: Senator Feinstein: "Did you possess any Nazi armbands?" Weaver: "I did not, no, never." Feinstein: "Did you possess any Nazi swastikas?" Weaver: "Swastikas, maybe. I had a – I have to go to the restroom really bad."[53]

Here, Weaver comes perilously close to falling off the map of "being American," a claim that is crucial to the way he construes his identity and the way he construes the irrationality of the agents of law enforcement who surrounded his cabin. Perhaps sensing the direction in which these questions will take him, he quickly exits the interchange and goes to the bathroom. After the break, Feinstein never comes back to the swastika question.

It is important to chart the paired designations of "normal" and "American" in much of the standoff discourse and to track the self and other assertions of American-ness on the parts of both authorities and anti-authority groups. Sometimes it is clearly good to be an American (a claim to legitimate one's actions). Sometimes, as in the case of the self-identity of the Oglala Sioux occupying Wounded Knee, Americans are represented as the offending others. But its centrality as a moral designation is always, if only eventually, explicit. One need only recall Philadelphia Police Commissioner Sambor's announcement over the loudspeaker in the early morning hours of the MOVE standoff: "Attention MOVE, this is America."

The key here is clearly a concept of community, both civic and political, that organizes our self-understanding in time and in space. In a manner reminiscent of Tocqueville's description of secondary organizations, and the way they link individuals to the state, anthropologist Carol Greenhouse writes about this notion of "community": "In the United States 'community' is always an ambiguous (and sometimes unintended) evocation of an element of the constitutional structure of government which links suffrage to place of residence . . . Thus the household, a family in place, is the smallest civic unit in the political organization of the United States."[54] The idea of "a family in place" is so strong and so normative for American culture, that families "out of place," transgressing literal and figurative borders, act like magnets for the attention of the authorities.

The family

"The right of the people to be secure in their persons, houses, papers, and effects, against unreasonable searches and seizures, shall not be violated, and no Warrants shall issue, but upon probable cause. . . ." (Fourth Amendment to the Constitution of the United States of America).

Since Phillipe Aries forced us to look transhistorically, and anthropologists have forced us to look cross-culturally at "the family," we have become aware of the widely variable and socially constructed nature of this social system. Pierre Bourdieu has written most explicitly about the kinds of assumptions that trail after this grouping in contemporary society. His assessment, which acutely links issues of place and time, deserves to be quoted at length:

Definitions of the family are seen as having in common the fact that they assume the family exists as a separate social universe, engaged in an effort to perpetuate its frontiers and oriented towards idealization of the interior as sacred, sanctum (as opposed to the exterior). This sacred, secret universe, with its doors closed to protect its intimacy, separated from the external world by the symbolic barrier of the threshold, perpetuates itself and perpetuates its own separateness, its privacy, as an obstacle to knowledge, a private secret, 'backstage'. One might add to this theme of privacy a third theme, that of the residence, the house as a stable, enduring locus and the household as a permanent unit, durably associated with a house that is endlessly transmissible.[55]

What Bourdieu doesn't say here (but does intimate later in his discussion), is that such privileges as privacy, stability and transmissability across generations can be revoked by the state if the family is determined to be, precisely, not a family. In several of the cases under examination here (MOVE, Ruby Ridge, Branch Davidians and, to some extent, the Freemen of Montana) claims to being a family by those in the standoff center were problematized and rejected by the encircling authorities.

What is it, exactly, that makes the determination of "family" begin to vibrate in contemporary American culture? As noted earlier, there are several key aspects of family life that take on a charged quality. Perhaps chief among these is the issue of sexual relations – who is having sex, in what manner, with whom. Sexual relations are typically acceptable only when they happen between legally married adults. David Koresh's claim that he had personally annulled the marriages of many of his followers and "married" the now single women was an issue for those investigating the Branch Davidians. As well, there was the information that he had had sex with girls as young as twelve. Thus polygamy, pederasty, and promiscuity were all cited in various investigations.

Children as a special figure in the family are assessed along many material and symbolic fronts – that of diet, of manners, education, of proximity to other families and to communities, of exposure to the stuff of modern, mass-mediated culture, of access to and familiarity with guns. The set-point approach is particularly useful here as a certain idea of "just the right amount" is exquisitely calibrated. For example, MOVE and Branch Davidian children were seen as not having had enough exposure to mainstream America's idea of kidstuff (television, sweets, hamburgers, etc.). In both of these cases, those children who escaped (from the burning house of MOVE) or exited (the still beseiged Mt. Carmel) their natal scenes were subsequently reported to be drinking sodas and eating junk-foods and watching television, all activities that were proscribed by their families. Inevitably, this sight was horrifying to those adults who were still involved in the respective groups and was reassuring to the authorities who felt they had brought the children back from the cultural brink. Isolated locations, such as Justus Township (the Clark ranch), Mt. Carmel, and Ruby Ridge, suggest cultural deprivation as well, as forests and wilderness and barren plains are felt to be too primeval a site for raising children.

Even with these separatist cultural forces at play, though, certain items, like milk (pace the late-career vegan exhortations of Dr. Spock) often strike antagonists on both sides as necessary and appropriate for children. The FBI's offer to send in milk for the Branch Davidian children if more children were sent out was accepted until Koresh claimed that they were down to his biological children, and thus at a kind of negotiating dead-end. In fact, FBI negotiators at Waco sought to establish their own "family credentials" based on biological links. Several negotiators made their own family videotapes to send into the Branch Davidian compound. On the tape, one negotiator states: "Gary mentioned that we're all family men. I'm proud of my family . . . I mean, we can show you pictures." Another negotiator adds, "I have a picture here of my son. You know, look at the picture. He certainly is his father's son."[56] Thus did the idea of children drinking milk, and appeals to a strict biological reading of family, appear to be accepted as appropriate norms on both sides of the barricades.

And then there are the children who are armed. MOVE children, the Weaver children, and the Freemen children all were described as carrying guns – and this is clearly transgressive. Certainly, in the wake of the recent schoolyard shootings, few would dispute the problematic nature of putting such powerful weapons in the hands of children. However, as we shall see in the section on guns as a cultural theme, just such refutations were tendered by adults who chose to arm their children. The image of a family in arms is a powerful one, no matter where one stands on the issue. One neighbor of the Weavers, Ruth Rau, who was not sympathetic to their lifestyle testified about Weaver's son Sam during the Senate Hearings: "Sam Weaver had been portrayed as an innocent little boy. He had become a skinhead more than 2 years earlier at age 12. He was a trained killer, a young skinhead, Nazi soldier and just as deadly and dangerous with a gun as any 200-pound man could be . . . It was very unfortunate that he was raised and trained this way and lost his life at such a young age. Randy Weaver has himself to blame."[57] On the other side, a friend of the Weaver family described the family scene to a *New York Times* reporter in August, 1992: "When she last visited them a month ago, all the Weaver children except the baby were armed," Mrs. Trochmann said, adding, "I'm proud of Randy and I hope he doesn't surrender."[58]

What could be more powerful than an image of an innocent baby surrounded by those who ought to be protecting it but who, instead, create a situation of danger by the collective taking up of arms? In this scenario, children become charged whether or not they have possession of guns. Such a

family cannot win, culturally speaking. I'm reminded here of a very evocative painting, "Quarto Stato," by Pellizza da Volpeda, a late nineteenth
century Italian painter. In this painting, a wave of angry men, most likely
workers in a northern Italian factory, recently displaced from their agricultural roots, are on the march under a stormy sky of roiling clouds. They
come straight at us as we look at the painting, almost pouring out of its
frame. They are dressed roughly, move excitedly, yet are clearly exhausted
and anxious. Leading them forward, in the front line are three figures – two
men and a woman. The men are slightly better dressed variants of the mass
behind them. They stare straight ahead and look altogether determined to
face the foe. The woman, on the far right side of this front line, marches at
an angle, almost as if she has just entered the frame and is on a different
planar trajectory than the men. She is barefoot and, with one outstretched
supplicating hand, gestures toward the two leaders. In her other arm, she
carries a naked, male baby. What are we to make of her appearance here? Is
she a part of the protest or is she pleading with the men to desist, to turn
home? Why does she bring the baby with her? Is she aware that by doing so
she puts him in danger? No matter, she is paid no heed by the men and one
imagines her either changing her angle of approach and joining the march
or, alternatively, turning away to return to the "backstage" of the home. This
painting, with all of its ambiguity of character and relationships, points to
a final subsidiary theme of the family cultural theme. Women and children
go together – Vicky Weaver holds her baby in her arms as she stands in the
cabin doorway and is shot by FBI sniper Lon Horiuchi, Ramona Africa
escapes from the burning MOVE house with the child Birdy Africa and the
two remain linked in the public mind as a kind of ersatz mother–child dyad.
Women, even more than men, are suspect when children are at risk.

Religion

"Congress shall make no law respecting an establishment of religion, or
prohibiting the free exercise thereof. . . ." (First Amendment to the
Constitution of the United States of America).

A recent family trip to Colonial Williamsburg, Virginia found us all in
the late eighteenth century – riding in a horse and carriage, visiting the royal
governor's palace, eating peanut soup. Each day in contemporary
Williamsburg represents a historically significant day in the earlier century
and, on one of the days of our visit, we noticed that we might visit the Gaol
to see and listen to James Ireland the dissenting Baptist Minister who, in
prerevolutionary Virginia, had been preaching against the established
order, and was, accordingly, thrown into prison.

In spite of the lauded religious tolerance and religious freedom that is one legacy of the Constitution, the United States has always had certain religions at its cultural margins – Mormons are a more recent example – that are suspect in the eyes of the majority. Many of these standoffs involved participants who made claims to be adhering closely to one or another marginal religion (MOVE, Ruby Ridge, Freemen, Branch Davidians) and whose adherence brought them into conflict with the authorities. Some scholars, such as John Hall and Catherine Wessinger, are centrally interested in the religious profiles of these groups. Alternatively, I am interested in discerning what it is about their religiosity that attracts the attention of the media and the state. Here again, the set-point schema is helpful. For I would contend that, along with cases of clear deviance from mainstream beliefs, excess and boundary transgression are the keys to this problem. The overly pious, the true believer, the person who views all of what others would term "secular life" through the lens of religion – this is the person whose religion will prove to be problematic. Contemporary processes of religious legitimation incorporate a deep understanding of moderation. Prophecy, resurrection, visible manifestations of a deity acting in the present, are all examples of things that cannot be unproblematically embraced by modern believers. Literalism of almost any stripe is often considered excessive. A neighbor of Randy Weaver, reflecting on Weaver's friend Kevin Harris, made the following telling comment to a newspaper reporter: "We have tried numerous times to get Kevin out of there. We believe Kevin has been brainwashed by his religious beliefs, which are *so extreme they are unbelievable.*"[59]

A similar skepticism about extremist religious positions broke through the surface of the negotiations between the FBI and David Koresh at Waco. Misinterpreting some of Koresh's comments as indicating that Koresh believed himself to be Jesus Christ, chief FBI negotiator Byron Sage burst out with: "David, my own personal commitment, my own personal faith – And I tell him that I am absolutely confident in my salvation and he's not in a position to challenge it. . ."[60]

Religious Studies scholar, Moshe Sokol, writes about the dilemma of immoderate true believers (Jewish believers in the case of his analysis) in modern society. He calls them the "cognitive minority," and writes that:

Since the plausibility of the religious world view depends upon a sound plausibility structure, that modern society's religious plausibility structure barely exists places a great burden on those in the cognitive minority. They must, in the end, either surrender; or protect themselves by self-isolation into a kind of sect; or engage in what Berger calls "cognitive bargaining" with modernity. This last tactic usually results in what Berger calls "compartmentalization," sealing off one's religious convictions from one's secular identity, so as to keep each as unimpaired as possible.[61]

An inability to bargain with modernity and compartmentalize will usually lead exactly to the kind of self-isolation of so many of the groups under examination here. Withdrawal is often read as rejection, however, and mainstream society may not rest easy with such a move.

Obviously, some of these groups hold beliefs that are just repugnant to most other Americans. Those groups adhering to some form of the Christian Identity Movement philosophy (in which white people from northern Europe are God's chosen people, Jews are the offspring of Satan, and African-Americans are subhuman "mud people"), such as the Freemen and, to a lesser degree, the Weavers, combine deviant beliefs with excess piety.

In all of the cases, however, there is a contingent quality to whether and in what manner the group will attract the attention of the authorities. Going beyond the set-points on the key cultural themes continua is one provocation. Even more important is that several themes ought to be co-present (guns and religion or territory and guns, for example),[62] and placed in relief. Finally, the interpretive processes of the protagonists can be engaged, as John Hall writes of the apocalyptically oriented Branch Davidians: "For groups that have not stabilized a heaven-on-earth, the play of events is especially contingent upon the interaction of the group with the wider social world."[63] In such cases, the charged interpretation of key texts will push the narrative of the group forward in a particular direction or another. Chapter 4 will take a close look at the role of texts and textual analysis in standoffs.

Gun ownership

"A well regulated Militia being necessary to the security of a free State, the right of the people to keep and bear Arms shall not be infringed" (Second Amendment to the Constitution of the United States).

Over the last two years (1998–99), we in the United States have witnessed an unprecedented wave of armed attacks by students against their school-mates and teachers in their own schools. Guns and home-rigged bombs have figured largely in the arsenals of these disaffected youth, setting off, as occurs intermittently here now, debates about guns more generally. In a country flooded with guns, there is a strange and persistent ambivalence about individual gun ownership in the United States and the issues raised are multiple. Clearly, some Americans – enough to have an impact on law –

think that individual Americans ought to be able to possess guns privately. Scholars debate the meaning and contemporary implications of the Second Amendment but, as Gaffney writes: "There is no scholarly consensus over whether the Second Amendment was enacted at least in part to preserve an individual right to keep and bear arms . . . or whether it was designed only to assure that the states would retain the right to an organized and effective militia."[64] Given this constitutional sticking point, many questions arise vis à vis gun ownership. What is the function of a gun? Is it to be used for hunting, for target practice, for defense against wild animals and dangerous people? Is it for criminal purposes of terrorizing potential victims? Is it for a military or paramilitary reason having to do with a kind of constitutional check on the legitimate militia raised by the state? Following upon issues of function, what kinds of guns ought to be available to individuals or private groups? What kinds of guns ought to be available to law enforcement agencies? Who ought to be allowed to purchase and use a gun? What features make a gun legal or illegal? How ought individuals to hold and carry a gun?

On this last point, the mode of firearm presentation was a key issue in several of the groups under investigation here. In May of 1977, an earlier standoff between MOVE and the City of Philadelphia was, after a long period of conflict, precipitated by members of MOVE appearing on the porch of their house holding rifles. Of these rifles one MOVE member, Janine Phillips Africa stated, several years later when appearing as a witness in the 1985 trial of Ramona Africa, that "I and all MOVE people call these [rifles] deterrents because they were inoperable, and the only reason why we had these that could be seen was the police believe in guns, okay?"[65] For his part, Police Commissioner Sambor, questioned at the MOVE hearings to give "proof" of the assertion that MOVE was a terrorist group, referred to those rifles as evidence: "pictures of the MOVE organization in 77–78 in uniforms and berets, with automatic weapons in an attack posture on the walls of Powelton Village."[66] In the case of the standoff at Ruby Ridge, much was made of the manner in which Randall Weaver and his friend Kevin Harris were holding their guns outside of their cabin during the period of heightened surveillance and confrontation. The issues involved whether they were actually pointing and getting ready to shoot or whether they were carrying the guns in a nonreadiness position. Further, there was considerable discussion of whether the specially formulated "Rules of Engagement" had actually provided for the FBI snipers to shoot anyone simply carrying a gun – regardless of the manner in which they were held (these "Rules of Engagement" will be discussed at length in Chapter 4). Finally, a government negotiator at Wounded Knee spoke most explicitly of the symbolic force of guns when, toward the end of the standoff there, he maintained that: "I can't get the President's representatives to come to

Wounded Knee as long as the guns are being pointed at Federal officials. I don't care if it's only symbolic."[67]

With all of these issues and qualms, it is still clearly legitimate for private citizens in the United States to legally purchase and possess guns and to keep them in their homes. The conceptual apparatus of the set-point poses the question of when that which is legitimate tips over into the illegitimate and, further, when such tipping brings forth the strong response of the law. One indicator has to do with the types of guns and their legal registration. As scholar Jayne Docherty writes in her dissertation on the Branch Davidians: "Thus, the *material* issue in the conflict was the Mount Carmel community's possession of particular types of weapons and munitions, their failure to complete the necessary paperwork for some of the weapons, and their alleged possession of (and intent to use) the parts necessary to convert legal (semiautomatic) weapons to illegal (fully automatic) weapons." However, "some of the problems in Waco may have arisen because the changes in gun laws were difficult to understand. Koresh at one point went to the Sheriff's office to ask about the legality of some of the weapons."[68] On the other hand, some guns, such as sawed-off shotguns, are clearly illegal and here the question becomes the proportionality between the crime of altering and selling legal guns and the discretionary interest of law enforcement agencies in prosecuting such offenses. Senator Kohl reflected on just such a decision during the Senate Hearings on Ruby Ridge:

So how did a man who was only charged with selling two sawed-off shotguns come to be the focus of such an enormous investigation and siege? Well, he failed to show up for a trial date and from then on became the target of three Federal agencies and countless local and State police. They subjected him to round-the-clock surveillance with high-technology video cameras. Before it all came to an end, more than $2 million was spent. And more than 200 law enforcement agents encamped in a meadow near his cabin were given rules of engagement that told them they "could and should" shoot to kill any armed male.[69]

Political and territorial jurisdiction

". . . The Congress shall have Power to dispose of and make all needful Rules and Regulations respecting the Territory or other Property belonging to the United States . . ." (Article Four, Section 3, the Constitution of the United States).

Breakaway republics have dominated the news recently, particularly in the wake of the disintegration of the Soviet empire. One cannot always predict how world opinion will view such claims to independence and autonomy. Sometimes the claims are universally accepted and officially recognized.

More often, they are contested both by those from whom the "republic" is attempting to break away, and by others with a stake in a certain map of the world. The conceptual line between riot, rebellion, civil war and independence movement is a moving one. Weber's classic definition of the state as consisting of those who hold the monopoly of the use of legitimate (i.e. considered to be legitimate) force over a given territory pares this matter down to its essentials. Of the standoffs analyzed here, those involving the Republic of Texas group, the Freemen of Montana group, and the Independent Oglala Nation at Wounded Knee, most centrally involved issues of political and territorial jurisdiction, as the groups asserted that they considered a certain territory no longer within the confines of the United States of America. To a lesser degree, the Branch Davidians represented their homestead as a separate entity. They claimed a biblical centrality to Mt. Carmel, flew their own flag, and anticipated the beginning of Armageddon there.

Such features as the changing of names (the "Republic of Texas" instead of Texas and the "Republic of Montana" instead of Montana are two examples), the hoisting of a flag other than that of the United States (or the hoisting of the US flag upside down), the refusal to pay state and federal taxes, the issuance of bills, writs, and monies, the references to Common Law, the assertion of new boundaries, all figure in the claims to territorial autonomy. Regardless of how realistic the threat to carry through with the assertion of independence – and in all of the cases under investigation here the threat was minimal, creating what anthropologist James Faubion calls a "hiatus irrationalis" between the threat and the official reaction – the mere fact of making such an assertion transgresses that cognitive boundary held intact by the Constitution. All of these territorial issues will be expanded upon in Chapter 3.

Conclusion

Senator Grassley: Do you have your own personal gun collection – and I don't mean one that you would use as law enforcement – a personal collection?

Mr. Johnson (former US Marshal, District of Idaho): I have guns, Senator, like most Idahoans; I've probably got more than what I need.

Senator Grassley: Have you ever had as many as 10, 20, or 30?

Mr. Johnson: At some times. . . .

Senator Grassley: Randy Weaver had 12 guns, two BB guns; he also bought and sold. Can I conclude that in Idaho, it is not unusual for citizens to own more guns, or as many guns as Randy Weaver had? . . .

Mr. Johnson: No; that's not unusual.[70]

Always, with all of the key cultural themes discussed above, the latent question is "what is usual and what is unusual?" Both prospectively, when investigators try to make a case against someone, and retrospectively, when committees and judges try to evaluate a completed operation, the struggle is to locate this moving line between the normal and acceptable and the abnormal and unacceptable. When, under contingent conditions, as in all of the cases examined here, a slide away from the normal set-point on clusters of cultural themes is discovered, action will be taken. It is the task of this book to make such themes, their normal set-points, the "discoveries" of their transgressions, and the subsequent action, visible and analyzable. The greater, more specifically theoretical aim is to develop an analytical language that can simultaneously chart the forms and transformations of such processes.

2

The times of standoffs

What constitutes the objectivity of the temporal indicators conveyed by language is that they are interpreted by means of facts which are not modified by the fluctuations of subjectivity. Whether these facts be of a natural order, such as the succession of days and nights, or of an institutional order, such as the succession of the months, makes little difference. The objective resides not only in what we suffer but also in what we build.

(Gonseth, *Time and Method*, p. 80)

Eternity is in love with the productions of time.

(William Blake, *The Marriage of Heaven and Hell*)

By their very nature, standoffs stop time in its tracks. A certain tension, an expectancy, marks their existence in and through time. Standoffs may reflect entrenched, long-term, serious disagreements of individuals, groups, communities, or nations. Yet the kind of crisis that precipitates itself into a standoff draws attention to itself as a temporal anomaly, something outside of the normal parameters of time. As I noted in the first chapter, standoffs are existentially contingent and thus, at least analytically, temporary – no matter how long they actually last. Everyone knows that the standoff will end, but nobody knows exactly when or how. Standoffs are expected to be broken and resolved, such that the idea of a permanent standoff is a narrative and political anathema. All involved wait for "something to happen" that will break the paralyzing spell.

Because the standoff, by temporarily stopping time, draws attention to our normal expectations for the passage of time, time weighs that much heavier on the participants. Everything that was unproblematically assumed before is now put into high relief as the clock (actually several clocks) start ticking. We know that we are in a state of waiting and that all action will be calibrated not only in terms of its intrinsic effectiveness or desirability or necessity but also in terms of its timing. This is why notions of patience, waiting, deadlines, and temporal intervals loom so large and, as we shall see, provide so much of the actual content of "standoff talk."

At any given time, we live at the intersection of many different kinds of time – seasonal time, the time of the week (as analyzed by Eviatar Zerubavel), the time of our age (as measured by our own number of years alive since birth plus a sense of our particular generation, as Mannheim taught us), menstrual cycle time for women, metaphysical time for religious believers, clock time for work and social appointments. In that sense of the multiplicity of times, it is fruitless to ask if we live in the short or the long run. Clearly we live in both simultaneously. But it is worth thinking about whether at any given time, we are more or less conscious of how our stances in the world (moral, political, aesthetic) reflect our emphasis on short-run notions of time or long-run notions of time. Do we live for eternity, immortality,[1] or for the sake of tomorrow? And how do we decide which time frame makes the most sense for any given situation?

Such time orientations can have a profound effect on the way in which any given action is viewed and on the ramifications of its implementation. For example, David Harvey highlights this impact in his description of the difference between the way the capitalist and the worker conceive of the worker's wage:

The former insists that a fair day's work is measured by how much time a worker needs to recuperate sufficient strength to return to work the next day and that a fair day's wage is given by the money required to cover daily reproduction costs. The worker replies that such a calculation ignores the shortening of his or her life which results from unremitting toil and that . . . wage looks entirely different when calculated over a working life. Both sides, Marx argues, are correct from the standpoint of the laws of market exchange, but different class perspectives dictate different time-horizons for social calculation. Between such equal rights, Marx argues, force decides.[2]

It is precisely because of the way that the standoff self-consciously poses these questions, with the specter of force always on the horizon, that it is so ontologically rich a site of human time-taking. It calls for a profound understanding of the relations of the temporary to the (seemingly) permanent, the short run to the long run, the time of practical action to the time of eternal verities. Decisions about action always have the various horizons of time in mind. Anticipating somewhat some of the larger questions about the ethics of standoff action, we might ask if an action aimed at defusing a self-consciously temporary situation needs to temporarily (pragmatically) abandon the longer time frame suggested or imposed by a concept of transcendent social and historical values, values that may even touch on ideas of good and evil? How does one weigh the relative value of decisions that are highly variable in their relevance to the short and the long term?

First though, we should begin with the question of how we calculate the actual difference between the temporary and the permanent, the short run and the long run? For example, conceptually Purgatory is represented as a temporary location, a place where all souls (except for the Virgin Mary) wait before they can move forward to Paradise. Yet by definition many are destined to spend literally thousands of years there (as well as to suffer their own Inferno-like punishments as those still alive pray and seek indulgences for their benefit). Purgatory is a kind of allegory of waiting and of the temporary. It generalizes waiting as a universal human condition. And it breaks up the narrative forward march of time, imposes a period of waiting, and requires a certain specific kind of effort to move the story to its next location. It has the conceptual structure of the interval – something that knows itself to be a break in the action. Something that few people realize is that Purgatory came into being in the Christian world in 1254, arriving at about the same time as the invention of the hour.[3] These temporal innovations can be viewed as a primer to the first mechanical clock that was invented in 1354 (the minute and the second held off until the seventeenth century). When the idea of waiting for a state of being to be over takes hold, along with a method for spiritually and practically intercalibrating action and time coordinates, time calculation must follow suit in order to allow its more and more precise accounting. The standoff, like Purgatory, is an archetypical situation of waiting, action, and of precise time calculation.

In terms of its grammatical stance, the standoff might be viewed as attempting to lock the present into a frozen state, where the opposed forces stop the flow of time by literally locking heads. The lack of movement seems to be its very raison d'être. However, as I developed the idea in the first chapter, it actually makes more sense to see the standoff as a situation in the subjunctive mood, anticipating the trajectories of a variety of potential moves. As such, the subjunctive might be described as the conceptual (and often subjective) meeting ground of past decisions, doctrines, and actions and as the launching pad of future transformed states. And it's not just the present subjunctive ("If I were to do x, then y") that shapes the standoff. The past subjunctive applies its own pressure as the standoff takes its fatal shape against an alternative past in which the confrontation might have been avoided. The besieged David Koresh claims as much in a phone conversation, made from Mt. Carmel in the early stages of the standoff, to Waco Sheriff Jack Harwell : "If you all had called us up and said you had a warrant for us, I'd have met you in town."[4] Randy Weaver claimed something similar in his testimony to the "Senate Subcommittee on Terrorism, Technology, and Government Information" when he declared that all the law enforcement agents had to do was to come up to his cabin with their warrant for him to go peacefully (the truth-claims of the past subjunctive must, however, always be immune from validation).

It is thus important to ascertain the specific types of time-consciousness and time-orientation that the particular protagonists bring to the standoff as they tend to assume different discursive tense formations and narrative temporalities. If, to use just one highly relevant example, some protagonists bring a prophetic discourse to standoffs while others bring the official discourses of their organizations (bureaucratic, legal, military, and so forth), these discourses will obviously be in conflict with each other over many issues[5] but one of the most fundamental is that of the perspective on time. Anthropologist William Hanks has analyzed the written texts produced by native officials in early Spanish-colonial Maya society in Mexico in order to chart the ways in which what we might call a colonial/indigenous population standoff worked itself out in the discursive improvisations of the Mayan officials who needed to communicate with the Spanish authorities. In comparing the *prophetic* Maya discourse with the *official* Maya discourse, Hanks writes the following: "Thus whereas Maya prophetic discourse apparently became historical fact by serving as a general guide for action, official discourse was designed to become fact by being accepted as a definitive record of specific actions performed under specific circumstances."[6] Thus, while both types of discourse must bring the past into colloquy with the future, the prophetic discourse is singularly oriented toward the future while the official discourse is singularly rooted in a specified and codified past. Such distinctions are extremely important for gauging the relative expectations regarding the temporal parameters of standoffs. They shape participant ideas about how long standoffs "should" last, according to what clocks they should be calibrated, and how much a role the past/present/future should play in making decisions about actions.

When radically divergent time horizons and time-reckoning frameworks meet and confront each other in a standoff, practical and epistemological complications are inevitable. When one group of protagonists is calibrating the situation according to an ultimate day of judgment and another group or agency is anticipating the impatience of a Congress already skeptical about their own continued funding (as was the case with the Alcohol, Tobacco, and Firearms Agency during the Branch Davidian confrontation), time spent in the standoff state will parse very differently for them. As well, culturally derived and developed ideas about the times of the

generic standoff will influence agents of the mass media and the generalized audience, watching the event from the, mainly mediated, sidelines.
Media observers attempt to "read" the actions of a standoff as indicators
of a narrative flow. A reporter for the *Los Angeles Times*, noting an increase
of movement by Red Cross officials and journalists into and out of the
Japanese Ambassador's house during the standoff in Lima, wonders what
this means about the times of the standoff itself: "The movement of Red
Cross workers and journalists back and forth into the grounds intensified
as the guerrillas permitted medical teams to bring in supplies and tend to
ailing and injured captives. The earlier tension appeared to have dissipated,
*but it was not clear if the increased activity heralded a breakthrough or merely
both sides settling into a rhythm of a siege.*"[7]

The idea of a recognizable "rhythm of a siege" indicates that standoffs
have their own times. Thus I want specifically to raise questions about temporal expectations in crises such as these. What does it mean to import into
these emergency situations our workaday notions of efficient use of time,
delay, deadlines, procrastination and the like? The nerve strains of waiting
also point to the emotional registers of individuals in stances of expectation. I was startled to come across the absolutely right and yet paradoxical
idea of the *tedium* of standoffs in a recent review of *Mad City*, a movie
about an unemployed postal worker who takes a building hostage to get his
job back. The reviewer writes, "Mad City . . . lumbers along, seemingly
determined to convey the tedium of a real-life hostage situation . . ."[8] With
lives on the line and actual or imminent violence, how is it possible to talk
of tedium? But in a manner perhaps analogous to the routinization of charisma, there is a routinization of the emergency. And so it is that, after a
certain amount of time, a kind of narrative boredom sets in. Think about
the very words that track the standoff through time – deadline, deadlock,
standstill, stalemate. These words evoke a certain attitude about time,
denying time itself or suggesting that time has overstayed its welcome, is
stale, and is running out. They also imply that time has an endpoint that
can be located by line or lock, after which time will be abandoned in favor
of time-defying action.

Variations on a theme of time

The analytical problem here becomes one of finding a way to excavate and
intercalibrate the varieties of time-consciousness subtending and carrying
forward the standoff. A linear notion of time[9] provides us with a reference
to past, present, and future as well as beginnings, middles, and ends. A
hypothetical and subjective temporal stance introduces the subjunctive

mood. Empirical highlighting and observations of the sun, the moon, the changes in temperature and flora give us the material of reckoning day and night, seasons and years. Social conventions provide us with the seven-day week.[10] Codified and transcribed memories provide individual, familial, and social historical legacies in the forms of calendars, history books, and holidays. Religions may intimate and even create road maps for eternity. Standoffs, as noted above, are understood to have their own distinctive rhythms as well. At any given time during the waiting, negotiating, or armed battles of a standoff, some or all of these inhabited ideas about time are engaged and provide indicators about what should happen when. Certainly, this is true as well for any interaction of social life. However, the stakes of divergent time-consciousness are that much higher and put into greater relief in a standoff and thus it behooves us to analyze them even more closely.

The linear, the cyclical, and the eternal

We may indeed both suffer and build the objective natural and institutional diacritical indicators of time's succession, as Gonseth claims. This does not, however, prevent us from developing radically different subjective orientations to this succession. Sociologist John Hall has developed a nuanced analytical schema by which to gauge these temporal orientations. This schema presents four distinct temporal types: the synchronic, the diachronic, the strategic, and the eternal. The types explicitly and implicitly incorporate ideas about the relative merit of linear and cyclical frameworks, about the relation of time to action, as well as ideas about the relationship(s) of the past, present, and future to each other. The schema can be particularly salient in thinking about the contingent elements in social situations, like standoffs, where the efforts moving the situation forward draw from diverse existential orientations toward time. Hall elaborates these four types in the following way:

1) synchronic – [the] Now is the locus of individual and collective attention . . .; 2) diachronic : de-emphasized the Now in favor of reproduction of the past and antic-ipation of the future . . . (conventions, norms, recipes) . . .; 3) strategic – goal ori-ented . . . the anticipated future defines the meaning and utility of action in the Now . . .; 4) eternal time – meaning from a "mythical" past . . . which precedes any frame of diachrony . . . [emphasizes the] abstract character of timeless re-creation.[11]

Hall's schema provides a useful template for thinking about the groups involved in the standoffs under examination here. Some of the groups obviously operated with a strong sense of the importance of the past for determining present action and future goals. For certain groups (the Branch Davidians is the clearest example), this past lay outside and prior to the legally codified past of socialized history. They moved with a sense of the mythical, the eternal, and thus downplayed all that had inserted itself between that mythos and the timeless time of the future. On the other hand, they may also have operated at various points during the standoff with the strategic sense of time, where specific action now pointed precisely to that eternal future. Representatives of legitimate legal authority paradigmatically typically operate with a diachronic orientation, following the codified norms and rules that set the precedents for action in all future situations. Alternatively, they might engage a more synchronic approach in which the compelling nature and idiosyncracies of the Now overtake the diachronic perspective and call forth new rules and norms (Chapter 4 will discuss one example of just such a triumph of the synchronic in the FBI's codification of "Rules of Engagement" in the standoff at Ruby Ridge). While the match of these examples with the different temporal orientations might imply a rather broad interpretation of Hall's schema, the overriding point is that any given protagonist might find these different orientations coming into and out of focus and relevance for themselves and their antagonists over the course of the standoff.[12] And with these alternations and intermixing of temporal orientations, the binary oppositions between the Now and the Later, the past and the future, the contemplative and the strategic, the linear and the cyclical, the historical and the transcendent begin to be broken down. Once again, the forms of Structuralism and the procedures of Pragmatism interweave to move the story along. In a later section of this chapter, the apparent historical "repetition" of a critical earlier event (as was proposed in the case of Wounded Knee), plays into the protagonist's understanding of the current standoff in ways that problematize the linear/cyclical dichotomy and that make the story of the standoff appear to live simultaneously in two different time zones.

Further, the resolution of certain standoffs can portend the breakthrough of one kind of a time over another. Political standoffs can speak precisely to such a hope of a temporal breakthrough. A recent example is the case of the long-term Italian standoff between the entrenched and corrupt political class, so long in charge of the continuously recycled centrist government, and the reformist jurists intent upon cleaning house. Italian sociologist Sandro Cavicchioli writes of this campaign against the corruption in the following time-sensitive way:

The activity of the "Clean Hands" pool [of prosecutors and judges] was perceived as a process capable of modifying the very temporal structures of Italian life. From the cyclical time of the crisis of government – the usual reorganizations, the same faces, and the same scandals – it seemed possible to change to a time charged with a direction, an orientation that allowed the identification of new beginnings and goals, a before and an after. Thus [it was also possible] to articulate a transformation that was not wedded to the old "*gattopardo*" adage: "everything changes so that nothing changes."[13]

Linearity breaks out of the confines of the cyclical and the transformed time frame poses the possibility of the new.

A variety of time frames attempt to stake out their territory around the standoff. Among those that have figured in the standoffs under examination here are: legal time, metaphysical or spiritual time, media time, and official time. These are broad and internally differentiated frameworks to be sure, so the categories must be somewhat overly generalized, but the aim here is to explore the way such time frames make themselves known over the course of the standoff and to play them off against each other.

Legal time

Time and the law intersect in many different ways before, during, and after a standoff. Neighbors and relatives may or may not turn to the law to solve their problems with groups they view as over- or undershooting the various cultural thematic set-points.[14] Legal investigations may or may not lead to the creation and serving of warrants. Warrants may or may not be considered to be timely in accurately reflecting a changing situation. In explaining the legitimacy of claims, protagonists on all sides of the standoff will appeal to a variety of historically foundational legal doctrines, codified and brought to the present in written texts or subsisting in collective memory as they stake their claims (Chapter 4 will examine the critical role of a variety of types of texts in the evolution of standoffs). The temporal reach of constitutions, treaties, and Common Law doctrine may set contradictory time frames for those on opposite sides of the barricades.

Warrants: the raw, the stale, and the rotten

A warrant makes a claim about the real in a particular temporal zone. It makes a "conceptual connection," in the words of Stephen Toulmin, between data and claims or conclusions reached about the data. And such connections are made over relatively shorter or longer periods of time. The serving of legal warrants for specified crimes is always contingent on situational and institutional factors. Legal warrants (of the search and arrest type) are actually described by lawyers, judges, and other agents of law enforcement as being "ripe" or "stale." On the ripeness side, the creation and serving of a warrant is revealed to involve a process of checking out various agencies to see if the evidentiary and political moment is right for drawing these specific conclusions into this specific form. Sometimes, as in the case of the long drawn-out process leading to the MOVE standoff, it is, for a long while, determined not to be. Philadelphia Assistant District Attorney Eric Henson recounted having been in contact with the Parole Department in the summer of 1984 (one year before the 1985 standoff) to see if they wished to proceed with the parole violation warrant against MOVE member Frank Africa: "I think that gives the history of our sub-junctive mood . . . with regard to the warrant." And District Attorney Ed Rendell spoke of the fact that a "memo did not ripen into arrest warrants" at that time.[15] One waits for a warrant to become ripe.

Several remarkable things are happening here in these statements about the timing of warrants. Mr. Henson's characterization of the city legal department's mood as subjunctive reveals the exquisite sense of timing, of contingency, that surrounds legal action scenarios. Here the drawing of the warrant appears as the hinge to a particular future and Henson's feeling out of the Parole Department tests the water of that future. Retrospectively, the long time spent in the subjunctive mood contrasts with the ultimate rapid-ity with which the several arrest warrants were finally drawn up and served on May 12th and 13th of 1985. The fact that it was nearly impossible to peaceably serve the warrants so drawn up and embedded in the neighbor-hood evacuation plan, showed how warrants can go from ripe to rotten in rapid order.

Warrants can thus, once codified, exert a kind of temporal pressure on a situation. A Department of Justice report on the Ruby Ridge standoff ties the existence of a bench warrant to the temporally extended actions of law enforcement: "Although some may question the expenditure of manpower and resources by the Marshals Service during this 18 month period, we believe that institutional pressure created by the existence of a bench warrant and an indictment, left the Marshals Service with little choice but to proceed as it did."[16] Warrants thus live on either side of a "probable cause" threshold, revealing that not only space, but time as well has deline-able thresholds. As well, the case of the warrant against Randy Weaver reveals how difficult, if not impossible, it is to drag a warrant back over that temporal threshold once it has been approved. During the Senate Hearings on the raid on Ruby Ridge, Former Director of the US Marshals Service, Henry Hudson, describes his unsuccessful attempt to have the bench warrant drawn up against Weaver temporarily withdrawn – an attempt to essentially go back in legal time. He stated,

Senator Specter, when I was first briefed on this case in March 1992, they gave me the overview of Mr. Weaver's background and what plans they were thinking about at that point. And I concluded, fairly readily, that this would be a very dangerous mission for the Marshals Service and for any law enforcement agency. I began to see whether or not we could use non-confrontational approaches . . . My plan was to ask the US attorney for the district of Idaho, to ask Judge Ryan to withdraw the bench warrant. To have it reissued, and place it under seal and to allow a period of time to go by – a cooling off period. I felt that Mr. Weaver would eventually come down off that mountain and we could arrest him in town, without his family present.[17]

As to the possibility of warrants going stale, in describing some of the main constitutional problems of the Branch Davidian standoff, Edward McGlynn Gaffney, Jr. maintains that:

there is the staleness problem. This is related to the reliance upon former members of the community, whose recollections of life at Mt. Carmel went back months or even years before the time of the search warrant . . . The general rule is that information submitted to a magistrate must be based on recent information that supports the conclusion that the item sought in a search warrant is probably still in the place to be searched.[18]

Thus warrants are inserted into the temporal time frames of situations and are calibrated, at least partially, on the basis of their relative freshness or their delinquency. Once a standoff has begun, however, warrants, like so much else, are put into a state of suspended animation. Nothing goes stale because linear legal time (during which crimes secrete their evidence and then the evidence can dry up) is stopped.

Common Law versus constitutional and statutory law

When standoff protagonists claim an existential basis for the stands they have taken, it is often the case that they will appeal to legal principles embodied and embedded in particular constitutions, charters, treaties, statutes, or Common Law doctrines. Such appeals formulate specific temporal connections between the past and the present, with the past being conjured as alternately bound up in historically codified documents or residing in a kind of suspended animation in a transcendent Common Law. Several of the standoff protagonists examined here referred explicitly to past treaties between their natural or chosen ancestors and the government of the United States and claimed that these treaties had been transgressed by the US government and that they ought to have contemporary validity. Among these groups were the Oglala Sioux at Wounded Knee (staking their claim on the Fort Laramie Treaty between the Sioux and the United States

Government of 1868), and the Republic of Texas (referring to the Boundary Treaty of 1838 between the Republic of Texas and the United States). In a statement released during the standoff at Wounded Knee, the leaders of the occupation make explicit demands regarding the reinvigoration of the Fort Laramie Treaty: "Let it be known this day, March 11, 1973, that the Oglagla Sioux people will revive the Treaty of 1868 and that it will be the basis for all negotiations. Let the declaration be made that we are a sovereign nation by the Treaty of 1868. We intend to send a delegation to the United Nations as follows: Chief Frank Fools Crow; Chief Frank Kills Enemy; Eugene White Hawk, District Chairman [of the Wounded Knee District Council]; Meredith Quinn, international advisor; Matthew King, interpreter . . ."[19] In addition, the Freemen of Montana referred explicitly to the pre-Civil War Constitution and prestatehood Montana county codes to validate its claim that Montana should be considered an independent country.

At the same time, some of these groups also argued for a more ancient and, to some extent, timeless idea of the Common Law or biblical laws as bolstering their contemporary claims. The Freemen, the Republic of Texas, and the Branch Davidians all made claims that incorporated transcendent ideas about the law and that looked back to a past beyond the establishment of the legitimate government of the United States, a past codified in such ancient documents as the Magna Carta and the Old Testament. More than simple, desperate, combinatory eclecticism is operating here as groups point both to very specific, dated treaties and to more timeless ideas about rights. Carol Greenhouse understands the contemporary resonance of common law tradition as identifying a space of legal and temporal indeterminacy. This indeterminacy is, I would claim, precisely exposed in such existential moments as standoffs, where the time lines are confused and vibrating. She writes:

In the symbolism of the modern liberal tradition, the common law in effect stands at the border between the two great themes of Indo-European myth: the human made . . . and the god made . . . One implication . . . is that the symbolic fonts of the judiciary's cultural legitimacy are nourished in the discursive space created by the indeterminacy of the distinction between events in linear time (politics) and the significance of time itself (justice) in some larger scheme of things . . .[20]

When worldviews are played off against each other, as they are in the standoffs here, the "larger scheme of things" is always in contention. Thus Greenhouse's identification of that discursive space provides a useful image of the narrative stage of the standoff as it grapples with questions about time and the law.

Metaphysical, spiritual, and ritual time

The transcendence of the concept of the common law over the time-bound law of statutes and constitutional amendments points to an even more timeless framework of metaphysics. Decrees and predictions about time's beginnings and endings are at the center of religious cosmogony. When standoff participants choose their temporal frameworks, they may indeed situate themselves within a cosmogenic cycle and anticipate the connection between what happens during the standoff itself and some final end. Other time frames are still active in such scenarios – people still wake up in the morning, cook meals during the day, and eat dinner in the evening. And these "normal" time frames can even be utilized by those on the other side of the barricades in preparing an "emergency" plan. For example, the ATF gathered detailed information about the daily routines of life in the Branch Davidian compound in order to prepare for the "dynamic entry" of the Special Response Team. That configuration was: 10 a.m., just after morning services, women doing chores in the kitchen and watching the children while the men were working in the pit that was under construction outside the main building.[21]

Yet a conscious prioritizing of time frames where the metaphysical takes precedence over the culturally routine can itself determine specific, instrumental decisions over the course of the standoff. The time of the standoff, from this perspective, must be viewed as part of the in-between-time of life on earth (earth life variously configured as fallen time, waiting time, and so forth). As David Harvey writes:

The Christian awareness of "time as drama" in which "earthly life and the whole of history are seen as the arena of a struggle between good and evil" rendered the moment of internal freedom of choice as critical to the historical process. Nevertheless, such acts could not be abstracted from daily routines. The result was a variety of spatio-temporal conceptions deriving from different modes of experience (agricultural, political, ecclesiastical, military, etc.). But these disparate spatio-temporal conceptions were subordinated to an overarching Christian conception.[22]

The religious beliefs of the protagonists necessarily inflect their navigation through both time and space. In an instance that dramatically brings the variety of temporal and spatial dynamics into play in ways that highlight the contrasting frames of the antagonists, the Weaver family "birthing house" was made the focal point of the US Marshals' plan at one point in their eighteen-month long surveillance of Randy Weaver and his family. According to the testimony of Randy Weaver's lawyer during the Senate Hearings:

One of [the Weaver's] beliefs is that, according to the Old Testament, the women of the household were required to go to the birthing house during their menses, and the marshals, by their surveillance, discovered when Sara went to that house and their own written documents here will attest to the fact that they intended to kidnap Sara and the other children when they came to visit Sara in an effort to apprehend Randy Weaver.[23]

Here menstrual cycle time intersects with spiritual time in ways that literally remove Weaver's wife from their cabin. The US Marshals apparently attempted to make strategic use of their knowledge of this alternative spatio-temporal framework, though they never actually carried it through.

It was clearly the case in the standoff between the Branch Davidians and the FBI that an apocalyptic conception of time absolutely dominated the actions of David Koresh. Having decided that Mt. Carmel was a likely location for Armageddon, Koresh could not but believe that a final end-time could happen there. On the other hand, he continued to press his claim that he had the prophetic power and the historical obligation to actively interpret biblical scripture (particularly the Seven Seals of Revelation). As such, all attempts at negotiation with the encircling authorities were calibrated according to how long Koresh needed to complete his hermeneutical acts. Recorded segments of the telephone dialogues between various law-enforcement agents and David Koresh point up the discrepancy between time calculated according to an apocalyptic time frame and time calculated according to the official "rhythms of a siege," as well as the requirements of bodies here on earth. The following is a stark example of this disjuncture and comes from the earliest of communications, the 911 phone call David Koresh made to the local Deputy Sheriff on the day of the original ATF assault, February 28, 1993:

Koresh: What reward did Christ receive in heaven? He received a book with seven seals. Now in the prophecies. . . .
Deputy Sheriff: All right. Let me – can I interrupt you for a minute?
Koresh: Sure.
Deputy Sheriff: All right. We can talk theology, but right now. . . .
Koresh: This is life and death.
Deputy Sheriff: Yes, sir.
Koresh Now, you need to learn Deuteronomy 32.
Deputy Sheriff: Okay. But let me ask you this. The present situation – one idea this morning is to take their injured troops out of your area . . .[24]

The Deputy Sheriff is focused on the life and death activity of rescuing the stranded and wounded ATF officials. His time frames address the here and now of the standoff. Koresh too views the situation as one of "life and death." And yet his approach to such extremities of human existence sends him to the Bible and the prophecies. The question of what exactly constitutes action here, the removal of wounded troops or the exegesis of the Bible, is contested as the time frames for action expand and contract.

In many of the standoffs analyzed, Bible time, ritual time, and holiday time present alternative temporal schemas to the participants. Both officials outside the perimeter of the standoff and those in its center reveal intermittent sensitivity to such symbolic times. In the MOVE confrontation, the date for the serving of warrants was purposely shifted when it became clear that the original date chosen would fall on Mother's Day. Even the Marxist Tupac Amaru group made a symbolic overture to the Christian religious calendar in the release of over 200 hostages on December 23, 1996. A statement by the group indicated as such when it called the release "a gesture of ours for Christmas."

Ritual events held over the course of the standoff insist that, counter to assumptions of paralysis, time is not frozen after all. Transformations in status occur and are marked as temporally discontinuous events in a variety of ways. Two salient examples come from the Wounded Knee standoff – a wedding and a funeral. In April of 1973, in the second month of the standoff, notices went up around the town of Wounded Knee that stated the following: "On this evening, the twelfth day of April, the forty-fifth day of freedom for the residents of Wounded Knee, Independent Oglala Nation, the first ceremony of matrimony, between a man, Noo-ge-shik, and a woman, Annie Mae, will take place in the trading post."[25]

Several ways of calibrating time are evident in the notice. Months and days of the month derive from a calendar common to those inside and outside the occupied zone. The idea of the forty-fifth day of freedom is a contested conceptualization of time that is justified by the contentious assertion of a real, extant Independent Oglala Nation. The first ceremony of matrimony points to origin myths and a beginning of a history of a nation when various "firsts" are recorded for posterity. The wedding, then, is situated at the intersection of various time zones, only some of which are shared by all participants in the standoff.

Also at Wounded Knee, a public period of mourning, set to last four days, was established after one of the occupiers, Frank Clearwater, was killed in a firefight with the authorities. People at Wounded Knee entered this four day period of mourning for Frank Clearwater on April 25, 1973 and, after a contested debate about where he was to be buried (see Chapter 3 on Space for a discussion of this debate), a representative of the occupiers, Crow Dog, responded on April 27 that "no negotiations will continue until Clearwater is buried properly." The rhythms of negotiation are thus made dependent on the ritual time frameworks of mourning and burial, where life and death point beyond the practical calculations of standoff negotiations.

Media time

Reporters, journalists, editors and producers never directly control the times of standoffs. They do, though, influence the timing of some of the actions of the participants as well as assert a certain pressure on establishment officials to resolve the standoff in a "timely" fashion. Communication scholars Daniel Dayan and Elihu Katz have analyzed the "time-out" quality of certain critical and choreographed events in the life of a nation (royal investitures and marriages, geo-politically critical signings of peace treaties, political assassinations and subsequent funerals) during which entire nations turn to organs of the mass media to watch the event ritually unfold and time seems to stand still. Standoffs certainly garner their share of media attention, but the uncertain and unpredictable duration of them makes sustained media attention problematic. Antisystem groups will often actively avail themselves of whatever media coverage they can get during a standoff. During the fifty-five days of the kidnapping of former Italian Prime Minister Aldo Moro, the Red Brigades issued their several official communiqués specifically on the days when they knew that major newspapers had the highest circulations. At some level, the axiomatic media story about the standoff is simply that the standoff is still going on and has been going on for a certain number of days. However, reporters need more than a simple count of numbers of days so far to make a story that will interest an audience. Sometimes, journalists will be granted access by both the authorities and the anti-authority group to the inside of the standoff where interviews and photographic images can report back to those on the outside what is happening within. Timing plays a crucial role here though, as the permission to enter can be temporally constrained. Such was the case at Wounded Knee when, after almost a month of occupation of the town, reporters who had previously had full and daily access to the occupiers began to have that freedom rescinded. One measure of that constraining action was around the question of timing: "Then, on March 21, the Government began to tighten media access once again. First, reporters were ordered to leave the village by 4:30 pm each day, which prevented them from observing the nightly meetings and firefights."[26] Once the "rhythms of the siege" begin to take their shape, it becomes more and more possible to predict the times when crucial decisions will be taken or when violent action is more likely. Participants of a standoff can then use this knowledge to extend or deny media access to such things and, in so doing, inevitably shape the standoff narrative that is being communicated to the public.

Media coverage of both the standoff and the stands being taken can be extremely important to those on the inside hoping to get their message out. Standoff negotiators can play on this desire for coverage by implementing a temporal calibration of "airtime" and reciprocal action. David Koresh was keen to have his apocalyptic sermon reach a large audience. Thus, one negotiating move was to trade airtime for release of children from Mt. Carmel: "The negotiators begin to bargain with Koresh. They offer him airtime to broadcast his message on the radio in exchange for kids. He agrees to send two children out every time his two-minute sermonette is read on the air."[27] Two children for two minutes – a precise, if fairly horrifying, calibration of the value of time.

Official time: time-telling and intervals

Officials charged with "handling" the standoff are constantly calculating the time. They enumerate time "spent thus far" in the standoff state, the numbers of times and durations of phone calls into or out of the standoff center, the number of times and durations of face-to-face talks, the number and duration of gun battles, and so forth. Official time must be quantified and filled in with the content of calculable standoff action. Seconds, minutes, hours, days, weeks, months – all are noted as the record is constructed. Patterns are discerned as phone calls "normally" last a certain number of minutes. This stop-watch stance toward calculating the phone and face-to-face sessions of negotiation becomes excessive in its precision. In a typical Associated Press release regarding the Freemen standoff, the media, reflecting law enforcement's preoccupation with time quantification, exercise their stop-watch muscles: "The morning meeting lasted two hours and 15 minutes, followed by an afternoon session of 45 minutes."[28] Any changes in such patterns are noted and observers seek to draw conclusions about the state of the negotiations from them. The Reuter Information Service noted such a pattern change in the timing of talks during this standoff and wondered aloud about it: "After a brief meeting Monday morning, no talks were held in the afternoon . . . they have usually held both morning and afternoon sessions."[29]

Clearly this official, time-calculating temporal orientation must draw its strength from instrumental reason which, in the words of literary theorist Susan Wells; "establishes the world as an object of control, thus circumscribing it, excluding from thought both mythical and mysterious discourses, the traditional discourses of religion."[30] Of course, we have just seen how powerful a role these religious discourses about the world played in several of the standoffs being examined. Secular officials of law enforcement do not operate with the time frame of the millennium. They count minutes and rely on a fundamental concept of cause and effect to calculate a "reasonable" amount of time between one standoff action and the anticipated, concomitant reaction.

For example, negotiators at both the Wounded Knee and the Freemen of Montana standoffs found a way to promise these two groups that a series of hearings and trials committed to engaging the larger historical and metaphysical issues raised by the antisystem groups would take place if they would stand down and leave their standoff redoubts. Once having made such promises, the eventual agreements always indicated a specified period of time at which the surrenders or laying down of weapons would occur. On this point, the Branch Davidian standoff once again demonstrates how the contrasting temporal frameworks of the FBI and David Koresh made such an agreement impossible. On April 16, 1993, the FBI negotiator, in a last-ditch effort before what was to be a final assault on April 19th, was attempting to extract a time frame from Koresh on the phone, contingent on Koresh's being able to finish his interpretive manuscript on the Seven Seals, and was frustrated by his inability to do so:

FBI negotiator: But I'm getting from you – I'm asking you, When that [manuscript on the Seven Seals] is finished, are you then telling me that you are coming out the next day, or two hours after you send that out or what?
Koresh: Oh, I'll probably – when I – when I bring it out – see – my attorney is gonna get the – get the copy.[31]

The negotiator needs an exact time because the pressure of official time-telling and record keeping demands that the future be known. It's ironic that knowing the future is precisely the goal of David Koresh as well, as he labors to interpret the meaning of the Seven Seals. Indeed it is difficult to live with the narrative uncertainty of an open-ended future, a kind of Borgesian "Garden of the Forking Paths" lived in real time. These imperatives to know the times of the future lead to such things as the codification of the "ten-day rule," so complacently articulated by FBI commander Jeff Jamar, even in the face of evidence to the contrary. Thus not only the past, with its charters, treaties, constitutions, and immemorial laws, exerts a pressure on the standoff, but the future does as well.

One way to think about the desire to fix the amount of time between a standoff action and its anticipated reaction is to think in terms of temporal intervals. The Structuralist view of such intervals is best represented by the binary model of Edmund Leach as he elaborates a theory of a pendulum swing with repeated oppositional pairs: "The sequence of things is discontinuous; time is a succession of alternations and full stops. Intervals are distinguished, not as the sequential markings on a tape measure, but as repeated opposites, tick-tock, tick-tock . . . The essence of the matter is not the pendulum but the alternation."[32] Here, even the conventionalized ticktock sounding of the clock figures in our interval-forming repetitive sense of time. And this model is particularly useful in grasping the essential interdependency of linear and cyclical time as the repetitions are only repetitions at one perceptual level.

We can also think about the alternations and the full stops as the continuous and the discontinuous. In Eviatar Zerubavel's terms, the continuous is unmarked time when "nothing" is happening but the passage of time itself. The discontinuous is marked time when time temporarily draws itself together to take the shape of a transformative action. Thus: "There is no time without alternations between marked and unmarked times."[33]

There are, of course, cultural variations in the determination of how long an appropriate interval between pendulum swings should last. Issues of power, deference, appreciation, respect, and so forth lie at the base of the action–reaction timing. Bourdieu has written on the social meaning of gift-giving and has paid specific attention to the period of time between the gift and the return, or counter-gift: "It is true that the lapse of time interposed is what enables the gift or the counter-gift to be seen and experienced as an inaugural act of generosity, without any past or future, e.g., without calculation . . ."[34]

In the standoff, participants can be viewed as giving each other the gifts of time itself. Looked at from this perspective, the FBI negotiator's "gift" to David Koresh of time to finish his prophetic interpretation of the Seven Seals was forced to reveal the naked calculation behind its apparent generosity as Koresh refused to indicate when the counter-gift of his surrender to the authorities would be forthcoming.

A sensitivity to the power of intervals also highlights the inevitable times during a standoff in which "nothing is happening." Beyond raising the issues of the role of patience and waiting during a standoff (to be addressed below), such characterizations of time point to the irony of stalemates embedded within standoffs. The Freemen standoff was particularly replete with long intervals in which, according to journalists and local residents in Boundary County, Montana, nothing was going on. The FBI and the Attorney General, still feeling the fallout from the tragic consequences of action during the Ruby Ridge and the Branch Davidian standoffs, made a conscious decision to lie low during this newest siege. The narrative press of time going by, with an overload of long intervals and without the requisite alternations of full stops led to perplexed and not entirely satisfied comments from protagonists on all sides. Indeed it is very difficult to switch the perceptual valences and read the unmarked intervals themselves as the full stops. In other words, it is hard to accept that doing nothing is a form of action. For example, as a reporter for *The Detroit News* covering the Freemen standoff put it, when describing a news conference held by the right-wing founder of the paramilitary group, the Michigan Militia: "[Norman] Olson settled for giving roadside news conferences to journalists eager for diversion *after days without action at the Freemen compound.*"[35] And the ubiquitous Bo Gritz, standoff negotiator-at-large, reflected somewhat paradoxically (given his sustained critique of the law-enforcement agencies over the years): "It's an entirely different FBI from what I've seen." But at the same time, Gritz criticized the FBI for inaction. "They need to do something. The way it is now it is bad for the country because the FBI *counts away the days* until something violent happens," he said."[36]

Deadlines, waiting, and patience

Standoffs are full of deadlines, most more honored in the breach than the observance. Both those on the inside and those around the perimeter can issue deadlines. The word, "deadline" indicates a line of time or action that goes nowhere, that comes to an end. Deadlines are, however, always accompanied by ultimatums – do this by a certain time, or else pay a precise consequence. Thus are time and action contingently coordinated to move the story along with action providing a narrative escape hatch. Sometimes, the consequences are explicit – meet the demands by a particular time or x number of hostages will be killed. Sometimes the consequences are implicit but hang heavy in the air. In his prepared statement, to be read at 5:00 a.m. on the morning of the MOVE standoff, Philadelphia Police Commissioner Sambor indicated a precise deadline for the voluntary evacuation of all occupants of the MOVE house, but left the consequences of not doing so unarticulated: "All occupants have 15 minutes to peaceably evacuate the premises and surrender. This is your only notice. The 15 minutes start now."[37]

There is always the question of how seriously one should take a deadline. If deadlines come and go without the demanded response and without the threatened consequences concomitant upon noncompliance, are deadlines really the temporal rupture they claim to be? There were several deadlines set and ultimately bypassed by the Tupac Amaru group during the standoff in Lima, with their fatal consequences continuously elided. The *Los Angeles Times* noted one such occasion: "In Lima, earlier in the day, a guerrilla leader had threatened to shoot Peruvian Foreign Minister Francisco Tudela if negotiations did not begin by noon. That deadline though came and went without incident."[38] Such interrupted causal chains can have interesting perceptual and strategic consequences. As one Western diplomat put it: "I think any threat is serious, but we've seen deadlines set before and pass. If I were a terrorist, I would set deadlines constantly and keep everyone on edge and push the negotiations."[39] Of course, such repetition of threats and deadlines with no immediate or concrete consequences may engender very different responses to the state of being kept on edge. In a way, humans demand that time goes forward, whatever the consequences, as endless repetitions of a dead-ended time promote an existential claustrophobia. We may find that we have lost our patience.

If impatience, and thus anger, unfold over time, what does it mean concretely to be at the limits of one's patience? As we have seen in the last chapter, A.J. Greimas poses this question in semiotic terms with patience and impatience as the binary oppositional pair. Sometimes specific, clearly demarcated events will move us from a state of patience to one of impatience – a clerk that had been handling all of the transactions in a particular line at the bank seems suddenly to go on a coffee break just as you reach the head of the line. Sometimes, the transformation will occur in a more ambiguous, gradualist manner in which it will not be really possible to say if there was a single event that pushed us over the threshold from a state of patience to a state of impatience.

Recalling Greimas' claim that impatience "introduces discontinuity into the midst of duration," we are once again thrust into a segmented temporal order with intervals, alternations, and stopping points where we gather our ideas and emotions together and examine them for changes. This scrutiny of the continuous, where the very state of patience is made analytically interesting, calls for a more process-focused analytical language, where patience is understood as a process enacted over time rather than as a state of being at one or several points of time. As well, understanding patience as the simple opposite of impatience becomes just one of several ways of parsing its meaning. Patience can be calibrated along several axes with adjunct concepts – waiting, being calm, being in a hurry, accurate or inaccurate calibrations of the amount of time required for things, relative degrees of commitment to such calculations, and so forth.

The acts of waiting

"I am presently being permitted to document, in structured form, the decoded messages of the Seven Seals. Upon completion of this task, I will be free of my 'waiting period.' I hope to finish this as soon as possible and to stand before man to answer any and all questions regarding my actions" (excerpt from April 14 letter of David Koresh to his attorney, Dick De Guerin, quoted in Wessinger, *How the Millennium Comes Violently*).

Patience, and the act of waiting, are critical features of standoffs. Since much of the actual "action" of standoffs is waiting itself, the phenomenological experience of time pulsates in uneven tempos. There are long periods of waiting and then quick moments of hostage release, or gun battles, or negotiated exchanges. In the action-oriented culture of the United States, there is an exaggerated *horror vacui* – the horror of nothingness, of doing nothing – that exerts pressure on the standoff.. Nobody wants to do nothing. And standoff resolutions have been generally understood to require active crafting rather than simply to happen in their own way and time. Officials charged with dealing with standoff situations are keenly aware of this, even when they are mired in a case in which patience has been determined to be the order of the day. Apropos of such a case, the Freemen of Montana standoff, where all law-enforcement officials took a purposely low-pressure approach, Senator Ernest Hollings told Attorney General Janet Reno, "*Law enforcement just can't sit around waiting for a peaceful settlement.*" "I know," was Reno's response.[40]

The combination of an action orientation with the necessity of waiting reintroduces the issue, addressed at the beginning of this chapter, of the chosen time frame. If the day or the week is the relevant period of time, waiting for a standoff to resolve itself is absurd. If one opts for the *longue durée*, however, certain kinds of standoffs will indeed inevitably work themselves out (though obviously not without potentially doing great damage to the antagonists). As Susan Hunter writes in the book *Intractable Conflicts*: "Seemingly intractable conflicts sometimes simply go away. In some cases, a redefinition of the problem . . . may be all that is needed. Time ameliorates many conflicts as well. Children grow up and end custody disputes; a species becomes extinct and removes the object of contention; or parties begin to see advantages in friendship, as in the current [1989] Soviet Union/US Summit initiatives."[41] What is important to grasp in Hunter's proposition is that, to a large extent, the standoff participants choose a time frame in which to understand the meaning of waits of variable lengths.

The few analyses of waiting developed by sociologists have alternately stressed the role that power plays in situations where someone waits for someone else to pay attention to them and their needs (Barry Schwartz), or a sense of purposefulness or timing that inheres in certain attendant postures (Paul Corcoran).

The question of who has the greater situational power (clearly, the representatives of the state, with their superior arsenals and personnel have a much greater *absolute* power in all of the cases under examination here) is a key one in tracking the dialectics of standoff interactions. One way of gauging that power is to identify who is waiting for whom, with "waiting", in Schwartz's (1974) terms, providing an index of deference, dependency, and status differentials. An interesting and strange question comes up in standoffs regarding the uneven distribution of time among the protagonists. The question is: Whose side is time on? Some expert managers of standoffs claim to be able to answer this seemingly metaphysical question with apparently empirically derived responses. Writing the Foreword to Bureau of Indian Affairs Superintendent Stanley Lyman's personal recollection of Wounded Knee, Alvin Josephy, Jr. reflects back on the official time-consciousness emanating down and outward from the President and the Justice Department during the standoff. Josephy recalls that the sense was that time was on the side of those on the *outside*. He calculated this differential meaning of time for those on the inside and those on the outside when analyzing the combined effect of public opinion and past experience. If his words are read carefully, what at first appears to be an essentially pacific and patient official stance is revealed to also harbor the more clearly strategic goal of exhausting the opponent:

The orders went down through the Department of Justice for a peaceful solution. Aware of the sympathy for Indians that had been newly aroused among the media and the general public, the President did not want an Indian Attica. *Extreme patience, moderation and tolerance, the tiring out of the occupiers of Wounded Knee,* and adopting the policies followed successfully at Alcatraz and at the takeover of the BIA building [in DC] – these were the official prescription.[42]

Alternatively, R.J. Craig, a member of the FBI "Hostage Rescue Team" sent to Waco to deal with the Branch Davidians, made the following assertion: "The first couple of days belong to the negotiators and you got to give them their shot to do it. But the longer the tactical people wait, the less chance they have of being successful. Time is on the favor of the people *inside*."[43] Time's favor, though, is calibrated not according to some overarching theory of the relative strengths of centers and peripheries, insides and outsides. It is here tellingly represented as intimately bound up with the intraorganizational competition between the negotiating wing and the tactical wing of the FBI.

Even with the waiting-indexed power differentials between those on either side of the barricades and between those on the same side of the barricades, the very fact that anyone in a standoff is waiting for anyone else (however obviously coerced) indicates that there is some attempt at achieving an existential overlap of temporal systems. Thus the link with the other sociological view of waiting – waiting as a purposeful, existentially legitimate stance in specific social situations. Lurking behind such an analysis is the question of how we *use* time. Do we use it productively or do we waste it? How do we calculate the meaning of such things as "down-time" or "waiting someone out?" Former FBI analyst at Waco, Farris Rookstool, expressed the sense of wastefulness and futility that can accompany a kind of interloping mundane time that inserts itself into an emergency-time situation: "There's a lot of down time in these situations where we would sit over coffee and go, 'Jesus Christ!' You know, 'God damn! This is just' you know, 'Where is this going?'[44]

Beginnings, middles, and ends

Beginnings

At a certain point in time, standoffs are understood to have begun. Spatial dislocations and reconfigurations play a significant part in determining these beginning points, as the following chapter on the spatial parameters of standoffs will show. Particular actions, such as the threat of vigilante neighbors, the firing of the first shot, the taking of hostages, or the serving of an arrest warrant, also act as diacritical markers of the beginning, and the actions of standoffs will be analyzed at length in Chapter 4. Here, I'm interested in the role that time and time consciousness plays in determining beginnings.

As both Leach and Zerubavel would agree, beginnings are grounded in a distinctively discontinuous conception of time. Time is broken up into befores, durings, and afters. The beginnings of standoffs often stand out in a time continuum that is alternately characterized as being filled with delay, restraint, reluctance, patience, haste, or speed. As agents of law enforcement develop their legal and/or military strategies vis à vis a particular group, they and others will intermittently evaluate the appropriateness of the timing of specific actions as they do or do not move the standoff narrative closer to its "once upon a time" opening salvo.

Regardless of how violent subsequent action may have turned out to be, many of the standoffs under examination here were typically and self-consciously slow to get started. We saw an Assistant District Attorney in Philadelphia looking to generate arrest warrants against members of the MOVE group a full year before the ultimate standoff. Investigators from the Texas Child Protective Services began and ultimately dropped an investigation of child abuse at Mt. Carmel, Waco, two years before the ATF raid. And, as John Hall (1995) notes, the FBI was originally reluctant to get involved when former members of the group presented affidavits of statutory rape, immigration violations, food and water deprivation, and the like against the Branch Davidians. In the case of the Freemen of Montana, the *New York Times* reported that: "Montanans had grown increasingly impatient with the reluctance of state and local law-enforcement officers to arrest the fugitives. In a poll conducted in December for the Billings Gazette, 60 percent of respondents disapproved of the go-slow tactics. Only 24 percent of the 817 voters polled approved."[45] Finally, in the case of the Republic of Texas group, an April, 1997 CNN report noted that Republic of Texas leader, McLaren, "has accused officials of seeking a 'total military assault' against his group, even though state officials have *been reluctant to enforce a warrant* for McLaren's arrest issued in December accusing him of contempt of court for filing bogus liens."[46]

All this reluctance and delay seems ill-fitting in action stories of sieges, raids, gun-battles, and extremism. But the play of reluctance against the inevitable speed of movement when the antagonists initially engage each other reveals the difficulty with which the narrative tempos of confrontations and standoffs attempt to sustain some kind of measured, even pace. The beginning always announces itself as a breach in time.

Middles

"A source familiar with the FBI strategy said the highly publicized arrival of the armored vehicles and helicopter was not a sign that authorities plan to move on the Freemen immediately. 'They're sending a message that we are prepared,' said the source, who spoke on the condition of anonymity. '*Nothing is imminent*.'"[47] While beginnings are characterized by the temporal preoccupations with the binary opposition between reluctance and haste, middles pose their own issues of progress, stasis, and duration. This between-time, when the situation has been characterized as a certain kind of event, the protagonists identified and defined, and when it must live its situational life, is variably calibrated according to a perception of how much progress is being made and how close it is to the end.

Negotiators are actually constantly asked whether or not they think "progress" is being made. How is such progress calculated? Certainly, material transactions are one measure – x number of hostages freed, exact terms of antagonist demands revealed, a formula for surrender codified. Transactions that are less tangible (though still, interestingly, quantifiable) can also count as progress – x number of telephone calls to negotiators or relatives, x number of minutes of talks. Here again, though, different indicators of the existential nature and temporal parameters of progress create discrepant readings:

David Koresh: Everyone in the tanks – everyone in the tanks out there is playing.
FBI: No, nobody is. People just want to see some progress.
Koresh: Look, some progress is being made. You don't realize what kind of progress is being made. There are people all over this world who are going to benefit from this book of the Seven Seals. You don't seem to understand.
FBI: And what you don't seem to understand is – is that the people here want to see that kind of progress, but [also] other kind of progress.[48]

With all the other markers of progress, the key to creating a sense that something is happening in a standoff seems to be the presence or absence of "talks." The very act of communicating gives some reassurance that progress is being made toward resolving the crisis. A hyper sense of stasis is associated with talks being "on hold" as was perceived during the Freemen standoff: "With talks between the anti-government Freemen and outside intermediaries on hold, one negotiator said he doesn't believe the two-week old standoff with the FBI will end anytime soon."[49] The middle of the standoff is thus the time of the *durée*. And the linguistic cognate of endurance captures the subjective sense of the duration. As the ten-day rule reveals a kind of wishful thinking on the part of the FBI (and even more fanciful is the consequence of turning off the electricity after ten days – rather like putting a cloth over a bird cage to trick the bird into thinking it is night; those in the standoff center are expected to surrender when it goes dark), the actual length of time of the standoffs examined are widely divergent. To reiterate – the standoff at Wounded Knee lasted seventy-one days, the 1985 MOVE confrontation lasted one day, that at Ruby Ridge, Idaho lasted eleven days, the standoff at Waco lasted fifty-one days, the Freemen of Montana standoff lasted eighty-one days, that of the Tupac Amaru, 127 days, and the Republic of Texas standoff lasted seven days. Not only does such discrepancy problematize the bureaucratic rules that chart the time/action coordinates of authorities, it also is set against a backdrop of highly variant statements about subjective impressions of how long is too long to wait for the standoff to end.

The case materials reveal radically different estimates of the "how long is too long" question, irredeemably relativizing any organizational claim to designate such a figure. At the lowest end is MOVE, of course, which involved just one day of siege and standoff. There, the question put was more "how short is too short." In fact, one of the "organic mediators," Novella Williams, actually asked the Mayor during her phone conversation with him why all of this had to take place in the prescribed time frame of twenty-four hours (residents of the Osage Avenue block had been told that they would be back in their houses in twenty-four hours – of course all of their houses burned down in the ensuing fire). His answer to that question, as to so many posed to him about the specifics of the plan to serve the arrest warrants, was that experts had determined this to be the right time frame. Next up from the minimalist duration of MOVE was that of the standoff at Ruby Ridge and here we get a glimpse of the problematized perceptions about length that internally cleaved the FBI. Former FBI negotiator Frederick Lanceley testified at the Ruby Ridge Hearings:

I think there was a certain amount of frustration after 10 or 11 days, yes . . . When I left that evening I was expecting the possibility that there would be an armed assault on Mr. Weaver's cabin. And I said to the SAC [Special Agent in Charge, Portland, Or. FBI], Robin Montgomery, who was at the top of the mountain with us, I said, "Robin, some day you are going to have to sit in court and you are going to have to tell the court why you assaulted, why you felt it was necessary to assault on day 11, but it wasn't necessary to assault on day 2 or 3. Why now, Robin? Why has the situation become more compelling? Why is it more dangerous now? Why are we considering this now?"[50]

At Waco, the negotiation team began to defer to the tactical team during the third week of the standoff, when the equation of radio airtime for children began to break apart. Explaining this sense that things had gone on long enough, former negotiator Byron Sage justified signing on to a plan to recommend inserting tear-gas into Mt. Carmel by saying: "I mean, this is kind of a radical departure for a negotiation team to recommend tear-gassing, but we're now what, 20, 23 days into a siege. Haven't had a child out since the 5th of March."[51]

The eighty-one day Freemen standoff, during which law-enforcement officials consciously decided to adopt a stance of waiting, not cutting off electricity to the ranch until the seventy-first (as opposed to the tenth) day, also generated "long enough" talk. As early as the second day of the standoff, officials were already comparing this standoff to the one at Waco and were projecting the effect of this wait on the Freemen themselves, speculating when they would find it had lasted long enough. What is interesting in this statement though, is that the fifty-one day mark refers to the frustration of the FBI officials, not the Branch Davidian's frustration, at the length of the Waco siege:

Acording to Mr. Freeh's current plan, Federal agents positioned themselves at a building out of sight of the ranch, leaving the group's leaderless followers to decide how long they would remain inside. Law enforcement officials said that so far negotiations have been fruitless, but said that if the group refuses to surrender, the FBI is prepared to wait them out and send most of its agents home. "Let's see what happens after they've been there 51 days," said one official, referring to the siege at Waco that ended when exasperated FBI officials declared negotiations at an impasse and ordered tanks to spray tear gas into the ramshackle compound.[52]

The standoff at Wounded Knee, chronologically prior and significantly longer than that at Waco (though for interesting reasons that will be discussed in the last section of this chapter, on standoff genealogies, the memory of Wounded Knee doesn't surface in the "how long is long enough" talk regarding subsequent standoffs), finds even sympathetic interlocutors expressing frustration with the duration of the occupation of the town. Assistant Attorney General Kent Frizzell,

threatened that if a disarmament was not arranged soon, more drastic measures would be taken. He told the Oglala negotiators, "I can't keep all the hotheads held off that long. I'm not talking about your side – I'm talking about my side. I'm talking about people on the outside who say, 'sixty days is too long for them to hold the Government at bay!'"[53]

Ends

"He [Koresh] resisted their talk. He laughed at their tactics. And finally, he lured them to a course whose obvious dangers they could not see. Perhaps the FBI's greatest failure was that they let him write the final act."[54]

The story of the standoff is precisely about the suspense of not having an end to the story, a final act. The end, like so much else, is held in suspended animation with everything – identities, lives, liberty – at stake. Chapter 5 will examine the various forms that standoff endings can take: deals and disarmaments, surrenders, violent battles. Here I simply want to consider the narrative ordering of the standoff ending, coming as it does after the beginning and the middle. Perhaps it is simply obvious to state that most standoffs come to an end at a specific point in time after the beginning and the middle (sometimes, in the cases of the long-term intractable conflicts that Susan Hunter mentions, this end point is only discerned retrospectively). With the erection of that temporal boundary, in the manner of Paul Ricoeur's analysis of time and narrative, the whole event is emplotted on, and sectioned out of, a linear concept of time.

When considering endings, it is useful to return to the question of media-time(s) and the way that organs of the mass media tell the stories of standoffs. Writing about the structure of news stories in both television news programs and print media, communications scholar Justin Lewis argues that: "The main point of the story does not come at the end, but at the beginning. It is like being told the punchline before the joke . . ."[55] If Lewis is correct that we get the end before we get the details and history of the beginning and middle of the story, media reports of ongoing standoffs must constantly have to backtrack to undo the story of the day before, where an ultimately false end had previously been asserted. Thus does the end keep getting bumped up in time.

Such narrative recursions raise the question of historical genres: is the standard story of the standoff archaic, realist, modern, or postmodern in nature? The uncertainty of the end, the strange temporal dislocations involved with the beginnings and the middles, the time-stopping pugnaciousness of the situation itself, all push against easy characterization of its brand of narrativity. The contingency of its trajectory resonates with that which Michael André Bernstein characterizes as either archaic or postmodern narratives: "both archaic and postmodern narratives show that stories need not have a single beginning and a single end; indeed, they need not even have a single, chronologically ordered series of actions."[56] On the other hand, all of the standoffs here do eventually come to an end, though the end can be more or less gratifying to the various parties. Herrnstein-Smith writes about that narrative gratification that comes with conclusions:

We tend to speak of conclusions when a sequence of events has a relatively high degree of structure, when, in other words, we can perceive these events as related to one another by some principle of organization or design that implies the existence of a definite termination point. Under these circumstances the occurrence of the terminal event is a confirmation of expectations that have been established by the structure of the sequence, and is usually distinctly gratifying.[57]

It is noteworthy that those standoffs that did not reach generally gratifying conclusions (for a variety of reasons) had endings that were apocalyptic in nature: the total destruction by fire of two residential city blocks in the case of MOVE, the total destruction by fire of Mt. Carmel, the killing of all Tupac Amaru members in the Japanese ambassador's home and the eventual razing of the complex to the ground. When the story cannot find the principle of organization or design that it needs to reach a gratifying end, it is as if the story must cancel itself out.

The time-lines of history

Recent studies in collective memory have illuminated the ways in which the past lives in the present. Contemporary group identities are shaped, sustained, and even transformed as past incarnations of the "same" group are recognized, commemorated, and deployed. In some contemporary conflicts, the past is a belligerent participant acting as a kind of symbolic trump card in any discussion. As Susan Hunter writes about two such cases: "In both the Northern Ireland and Israeli cases, the contemporary territorial symbolism (and associated rituals and language) serves to perpetually cast the present in terms of the past. This process puts the territorial claims embodied in the symbolism outside society and into nature."[58] Reaching back to a less ancient, more recent historical past, several of the groups involved in the standoffs here asserted the importance of what I want to call a historical time-line. These time-lines were construed as linking the extant groups to predecessors and to values, laws, and documents of that past. This three-dimensional past thus acts to legitimate the actions taken in the present, including actions that will be viewed by outsiders as illegal. Earlier in this chapter I examined the power of constitutions, treaties, and the common law in buttressing the legal claims of the standoff antagonists. In Chapter 4, the proliferation of such ur-texts will be analyzed for the specific role they play as texts in the "writing" of the standoff narrative. Here, I am interested in the way that such documents are represented as playing a trick with time, a way of claiming that the past not only provides a template for the present or should be remembered in the present, but actually lives in and displaces that present. The present society is shown to be nothing more than an interloper or a pretender, masquerading as the legitimate representative of the desires of the people. Real representation will not be possible until the past triumphs over the present.

Of course choices about which past and what things from that past will inevitably be made. For two groups, the Oglala Sioux at Wounded Knee and the Republic of Texas group, specific events in the nineteenth century and the legal documents that emerged from them focused their claims about their present actions.

For the Oglala Sioux, the 1868 Fort Laramie Treaty that set up the Great Sioux Reservation and granted the Native Americans the right to self-government was the defining document. This is clear in almost every exchange between the occupiers of Wounded Knee and the government negotiators. One such exchange between Independent Oglala Nation representative Dennis Banks and government negotiator Kent Frizzell reveals, among other things, the Sioux demand that any legal acts that occurred in the intervening, middle, period between the Treaty and the present, be rescinded. It also demonstrates the government's qualified acknowledgement of the arguable validity of the Treaty as its representative offers the possibility of Congressional hearings:

Banks: With the advice of the chiefs and after consulting with Mrs. Lamont, we're agreed that the 1868 Treaty must be the continuing foundation for all discussions . . . this proposal: 1. The 1868 Treaty has to be reopened and discussed. Set up an agenda immediately for the Treaty Commission during the third week of May. 2. Rescind the 1934 Howard-Wheeler Act. 3. The chiefs and headmen will govern the Teton Sioux. There will be an immediate pull-back of arms when this is guaranteed.

Frizzell: I do have authority to insure that the government of the United States, certainly the White House, and probably Congress, will discuss anything with your chiefs – anything and everything you want to discuss about the 1868 Treaty. I think there will be Congressional hearings into the 1868 Treaty.[59]

On the other hand, the Oglala Sioux were careful to point out that while their historical time-line demanded the reopening of discussion about the 1868 Treaty, they were also explicit that the past was not the only, nor necessarily the dominant, temporal period in their protest and occupation of Wounded Knee:

Our armed defense at Wounded Knee is then both defense of life and defense of Treaty. However, it is not a protest born of the hates and hurts of history, as, more immediately, it was made necessary because the present experience of hundreds of Sioux Indian families is too frequently that of fear – while our country and our communities have fallen under a reign of terror . . .[60]

There is, of course, another moment in history that played a large role in the Wounded Knee standoff. In some ways this moment, the massacre of approximately 375 Sioux men, women, and children by the United States Army at Wounded Knee in 1890, was more instrumental in setting the spatial parameters of the 1973 standoff. Its spatial imperatives will be examined in the next chapter. Here, it will be taken up in the next section of this chapter on time, when questions of historical genealogies are addressed.

In "An Open Letter to All Texas Sheriffs," written by their Secretary of Defense, Archie Lowe, the Republic of Texas group wrote its own history:

In 1836, Texas was free, independent, and established as a sovereign nation among the nations of the world. When the United States violated the terms of the unlawful annexation resolution of the 1845 Congress in 1861, Texas lawfully withdrew from that union. After the Civil War, Texas became a captured nation and was placed under military rule, where it remained for many decades.[61]

Thus, according to this group, Texas was not actually a state in the United States of America – it was and should be its own republic. A subsidiary time-line has to do with the much diminished role of the sheriff in the so-called state of Texas: "Under military law imposed since 1865 and subsequent corporate law imposed in 1933, the federal government of the United States has relegated the sheriff's office to one of servitude."[62] Thus, once again laws, resolutions, and secessions from the nineteenth century are presented as determining the legitimate boundaries of sovereign and sovereignty in the present.

While less specific about identifying one ur-text as its historical center-piece, the Freemen of Montana did make a similar claim about the illegitimacy of present laws and the relevance of the past. They referred often to the Declaration of Independence, the pre-Civil War Constitution, and pre-statehood Montana county codes. For all these groups, to a greater and lesser degree, these assertions about historical time-lines are really assertions about the predominance of the past over the present. There is, in their stubborn insistence about the contemporaneity of the laws and social arrangements from various points in the nineteenth century, something of a feeling that the standoff is actually occurring between those who inhabit this world and time travelers from another era. Such confrontations between parallel universes provide yet another manner of temporal disjunction in the standoff.

Finally, historical time-lines can be cast not only into the direction of the past, they may also point to a vision of the future. Certainly the Branch Davidians lived in a future that was not determined by the instrumental reason of empirical calculation of probability, extrapolating from the present. Nor did it count on the continuity of social structures and arrangements that the modern, secular world had at one point imagined into being but that were now naturalized through habit and organizational sedimentation. The future of the Branch Davidians was one of apocalypse and Armageddon and the only question was when. Thus was David Koresh so taken with the project of interpreting the Seven Seals in order to predict the time and place of these cosmic events. The past and present only made sense in terms of this future.

At a more mundane level, the Republic of Texas group also looked to the future, when Texas was once again a free Republic of Texas:

You and I have an opportunity unique in history, one that will surely not occur again in our lifetimes, to leave to our children and to all future generations a freedom few have ever had in this world. Let us do that which is right and proper for the peace and dignity of the Republic, and as Texans, build together what we have been given: a government based on law, truth, and integrity; a true government of the people.[63]

What is key in any formulation that claims that the present is really the past or the future or that, as in the Republic of Texas formulation, the future is the recuperated past, is the idea that the ongoing, transformative aspects of linear time are irrelevant and meaningless. The present is evacuated of meaning because it is only an empty container for the past and/or the future.

Genealogical dimensions of standoffs

An alternative conceptualization of the relationship of the past to the present is one where connected points along a time-line create a lineage of ancestors. To say that today's standoff (or protest, strike, or revolution)[64] understands itself as being in a long genealogical line of standoffs conjures an image of time as a series of repetitions. At one level we are back to Edmund Leach's intervals between pendulum swings and repeated phrases as a way of tracking time. At another level, we are reminded of Jeffrey Alexander's appeal to the act of typification, an act requiring that we make an effort to match a current object or person with a category of objects or persons with which we are already familiar. Thus typification is a creative act of repetition, one that requires recognition of family resemblances. Anthropologist Evans-Pritchard's conceptualization of the time of genealogies emphasizes the construal of relationships. Thus, lineage time is : "not a continuum, but a . . . relationship between two points," with a "constant number of steps" between ancestors and living groups of persons. Because it is noncumulative, engaging a limited set of nonprogressive positions rather than an incremental movement, the genealogical grid creates only an immobilized "illusion" of time."[65] Such seeming immobility, however, does not necessarily ultimately undermine the linear notion of time. For, as Nancy Munn writes: "so-called 'circular' (repetitive) time does not logically exclude 'linear' sequencing because each repetition of a given 'event' necessarily occurs later than previous ones."[66]

What does it mean then for participants in a standoff to claim that they are taking up the mantle metaphorically passed to them by another group whose own standoff predates them in time? As well, what does it mean for observers and analysts of a given standoff to say that it reminds them of an earlier standoff, the tragic conclusion of which they do not want to repeat? Finally, what does it mean for standoffs that took place at an earlier time *not* to be referred to as an ancestor, to be forgotten or genealogically orphaned?

The answers to these questions have wide-ranging ramifications. They have much to say about religious, racial, and ideological clusterings of identity. They also have a direct bearing on the practical decisions of law enforcement, as we shall see, as agencies develop strategies for dealing with each subsequent standoff.

The most obvious and, in many senses, the most reasonable case of genealogy-making involved the standoff at Wounded Knee. The very developmental course of the 1973 standoff, with the Oglala Sioux Civil Rights Organization and the American Indian Movement deciding to stake their claim at the site of the 1890 massacre, linked the past confrontation to the one of a century later. This was an active decision to claim the mantle of the earlier event and to draw parallels between past injustice perpetrated against the nineteenth-century Sioux with present injustice perpetrated against twentieth-century Sioux. The story of the 1890 massacre also involved a journey, or pilgrimage (the relevance of pilgrimages generally to the examined standoffs will be analyzed in the next chapter on spatial parameters), by the Minneconjou Sioux under the leadership of Chief Big Foot. The crucial incident is described in the 1993 report of the United States Senate subcommittee on Public Lands, National Parks, and Forests:

They traveled from the Cheyenne River Indian Reservation to the Pine Ridge Indian Reservation on the invitation of Chief Red Cloud to help make peace between Indians and non-Indians. The journey of Chief Big Foot and his band of Minneconjou Sioux occurred during the Ghost Dance period when extreme hostility existed between Sioux Indians and non-Indians residing near the Sioux reservations, and the United States Army assumed control of the Sioux reservations; Chief Big Foot and his band were intercepted on the Pine Ridge Indian Reservation at Porcupine Butte by Major Whitside, and surrendered unconditionally under a white flag of truce and were escorted to Wounded Knee Creek where Colonel Forsyth assumed command; on December 29, 1890, an incident occurred in which soldiers under Colonel Forsyth's command killed and wounded over 300 members of Chief Big Foot's band, almost all of whom were unarmed and entitled to protection of their rights to property, person and life under Federal law (see 19 Stat. 254, Art. 8).[67]

While there are obvious structural differences between the past event (not really a standoff *in stricto sensu*, as a surrender to authorities preceded the massacre), the similarities in characters and plot are more than evocative. The seizure of control of the Sioux Reservations by the US army in 1890, the subsequent massacre of Sioux men, women, and children, the general undermining of the 1868 Fort Laramie Treaty, all bring the past into active play in the present as the modern-day Sioux occupy the town of Wounded Knee to protest the abrogation of their rights by what they read as a corrupt and dominating US Government. Thus are 1868, 1890, and 1973 linked along a genealogical time-line.

Not everybody was similarly inclined to make these connections. A singularly telling aspect of the transcripts and reports of the Senate and

Congressional Hearings in 1991 and 1993 on the creation of a Wounded Knee Park and Memorial to commemorate the 1890 massacre is that they make absolutely no mention of the 1973 standoff at Wounded Knee. Obviously 1890 figures large in those documents and the 1934 Indian Reorganization Act is a subsidiary referent. But it is as if 1973 never happened. The 1973 standoff at Wounded Knee is dropped out of the genealogical time-line.

It's one thing for a group to claim a patrimony from a predecessor group that observers common-sensically accept as an ancestor (though, as we've seen, there is no guarantee that these observers will accept the entire patrimonial repetition narrative of analogous circumstances). It's another thing for a group to claim familial connections to apparently unrelated individuals or groups. As John Hall explains this process: ". . . narratives are particularly important when the meaningful content shifts, when the narrative moves from one source to another, when affinities develop between the narratives of two individuals or groups, and where the incorporation of a received narrative rearranges other meanings for an individual or group."[68]

The rearranged narratives linking one group to another include certain things and exclude others. The claims of ancestry most often rest on the assertion of ideological or religious identification and/or the fact that these previous groups found themselves in similar structural situations with respect to the opposing government agencies. For example, a newspaper reporter covering the local reactions in Jordan, Montana during the Freemen standoff, wrote: "People here talk a lot about Waco and Ruby Ridge. As in: 'We don't want another Waco.' Or: 'Remember what happened at Ruby Ridge.'"[69] In the same vein, Republic of Texas leader Richard McLaren articulated his own sense of predecessors: "Evoking comparisons to fatal standoffs at Ruby Ridge and Waco, McLaren has accused federal and state officials of conspiring to destroy his group and silence his claims."[70]

Both of these quotes reflect a quite common construal of ancestry – Ruby Ridge to Waco to Freemen to Republic of Texas. News articles reflect public linkings of these cases, actual standoff participant linking of these cases, and, ultimately, governmental linking of these cases. In the case of law-enforcement officials, genealogical consciousness directly affected subsequent strategy. As reported in the *New York Times*, officials involved in the Freemen standoff, "had delayed moving against the group because of the backlash from two earlier incidents involving militant separatists: the so-called Ruby Ridge case in Idaho, in which an FBI sniper shot and killed a woman during a siege, and the 1993 siege of the Branch Davidian Compound near Waco, Tex., which ended with the deaths of more than 70 people."[71]

Looking at these four standoffs, the commonalities among them seem obvious at one level. All four groups could be characterized as ideologically conservative, even right-wing. All four view the United States government as either illegitimate or as not the final arbiter of law (either family law, firearms law, territorial law, or laws regarding religion). On the other hand, while a deep form of religiosity animated the Branch Davidians, the Weaver family, and the Freemen (however extremist in nature), this was not the case for the Republic of Texas. As well, while territorial legal jurisdiction formed a central core of the Freemen and the Republic of Texas standoffs, this was not literally the case with the Branch Davidians or the Weaver family (though it is true that creating a separate spiritual domain was key to these latter two groups). Finally, the Weaver family and the Freemen of Montana were explicitly committed to a platform of white supremacy and racial separatism. As well, the legacy of the original Constitution of the Republic of Texas, which codified the extension of the system of slavery there upon achieving independence from Mexico in 1836 and forbad free African-Americans from residing in Texas, was only briefly dealt a correction in the 1990s version. At the very end of the Republic of Texas group web page reproducing of the 1836 Constitution, a tag-on line at the end states: "Also see the Amendments that remove all references to race, sex, religion, national origin, etc." While white separatism was not a focused platform issue with the group, neither was it seeking to radically overturn its historical stance toward African-Americans. With its multiracial membership, the Branch Davidians were clearly not participants in any Christian Identity movement ideology about racial superiority or white separatism. Given these very variable ideological stances, it is clear that some of the dominant genealogical mapping is logical, and some of it clearly reflects the partiality of the active and tendentious connecting of case to case.

What becomes really interesting here though is both this presence of linking new cases to specific prior cases and the absence of linking to other, structurally similar, but ideologically variant cases. Whenever the chronologically later Ruby Ridge, Freeemen or Republic of Texas standoffs' discourse displays such linking behavior, neither Wounded Knee, nor MOVE are ever mentioned. They play no role in any of the later protagonist's self-understanding nor do they play any role in the government's reflections or self-recriminations about past actions during standoffs. The absence of Wounded Knee might be partially explained by the relative distance in time from the early seventies to the early nineties. The MOVE standoff in 1985 was more temporally proximal. But the fact that both the standoffs at Wounded Knee and that in Philadelphia involved groups composed entirely of racial minorities makes such genealogical elision more culturally comprehensible.

It is clearly easier for the majority American public and government officials themselves to embrace, or at least feel the shadow of, groups that had suffered from botched or overzealous official involvement in such culturally and ideologically loaded standoffs if these groups are not predominantly composed of people of color. One clearly chooses one's ancestors.

Most standoff genealogies are voluntarily chosen by those who would profess a certain pride in the association made to the predecessor. Some genealogies are foisted involuntarily on the latter-day group and are anathema or, at best, perplexing to it. For example, it is difficult to know what to make of the showing of the John Birch Society film *Anarchy* about black "riots" during a hiatus in the impeachment trial of the contentious Chairman of the Pine Ridge Reservation Tribal Council, Dick Wilson. During this trial's hiatus then, the Sioux activists aiming to impeach this official with charges of corruption and thuggery were shown this right-wing propaganda film. Many of these activists would be soon thereafter occupying the town of Wounded Knee. Was this film supposed to serve as an admonitory lesson about how the establishment views minorities who get active around civil rights? Was it meant to link the Sioux activists with the concurrent black power movement and their actions with the inner-city riots of the sixties and early seventies? Was it meant to deter them from doing the same thing?

Another case of involuntary ancestral linkage involved the articulation by government officials during the standoff at Waco that the Branch Davidians were similar to those followers of Jim Jones at Jonestown and that they were thus prone to the same decision to engage in mass suicide. Here the commonalities asserted were those of strongly believing followers blindly accepting the decisions of a charismatic leader. Officials at Waco would later claim that their decision to make the final assault with tanks and tear gas grew largely out of this fear that the Branch Davidians would commit mass suicide rather than surrender. Hall writes: ". . . because of our failure to learn from Jonestown, cultural opponents could take narratives about mass suicide from Jonestown and bring them to bear on the Branch Davidians in ways that proved central to how the tragedy at Mt. Carmel unfolded."[72] Finally, there are a few exceptions to the general rule of broad-stroke ideological and racial alignment. And they are as interesting as the rule itself. In the case of the Waco standoff, frustrated by the lack of progress in negotiations, the Branch Davidians hung a banner from the windows of Mt. Carmel. In all of its strange but ultimately embracing meaning, it articulated a very different line of ancestry than any other we have seen. Referring to the African-American motorist chased and beaten by several Los Angeles police officers, the banner read: "Rodney King, We Understand."

3

The spaces of the standoff

The bridge indicates how humankind unifies the separatedness of merely natural being, and the door how it separates the uniform continuous unity of natural being.   (Georg Simmel, "Bridge and Door," p. 9)

Senator Specter to Randy Weaver: So would you please walk over to the mock-up and point out where your home is located and where that door was located?
Mr. Weaver to Senator Specter: . . . That all looks pretty good. This is where my son was laying, in this shed here. This is what we called the front door. That door opened like this on that front porch – closed – open –   (Senate Hearings on Ruby Ridge, p. 63)

Just as there is a need to situate the standoff in time, so there is a need to locate it in space. The practical and symbolic imperatives of space provide a multidimensional map for the participants. As well, as anyone who has ever found themselves in a competition for a parking space knows, conflicts over space itself can lead to standoffs. Again in this as in previous chapters, I will carry forward the project to develop an analysis of the contingent elements of standoffs. Here, the goal is to analyze both the *binarism* of the wealth of dyadic oppositional terms linked to the spaces of standoffs as well as the *interactional qualities* of the mediating terms and concepts that travel back and forth between them.

The standoff, understood as a system comprised of discrete terms, establishes boundaries within and around itself. There are insides and outsides, and the symbolic elements comprising the spatial frame combine and recombine to represent and reproduce forces of opposition, mediation, and alliance. As well, the idea of *spatial displacement* (analogous perhaps to that of *temporal anomaly*) sets so many standoff narratives in motion. This form of a first mover cannot be accidental and we can turn to Structuralist literary criticism for a clue as to why.

In developing his diachronic analysis of the morphology of the folktale, Vladimir Propp identified several absolutely fundamental "functions" that appear in all folktales. Among these functions, the very first to be presented after the establishment of the initial situation is: "One of the members of a family absents himself from home."[1] The actual departure gets the story moving. Additionally, and importantly for understanding the narrative of the standoff, this "absentation" is eventually revealed to have taken place after an interdiction has been laid down – and typically this interdiction is precisely not to absent oneself. Thus, fraught or illegitimate spatial dislocations are the first movers in that fundamental narrative form of the folktale where the absentation sets off a series of challenging events that the hero must deal with before he or she can successfully return home. Propp's analysis provides a model then for the centrality of spatial configurations and spatial dislocations in all stories, of which the standoff is one variant.

Following upon Propp's delineation of the importance of spatial dislocations and relocations is Algirdas Greimas' bare-bones semiotic program to provide foundational coordinates for human beings in space. Considering such things as displacement, orientation, and support, Greimas thinks quite literally about the figure–background interplay of bodies in space. He recommends an analytical model that can "recognize behind the visible figures, the existence of a categorical vision of the natural world, of a grid made up of a limited number of elementary categories of spatiality, whose combinatory arrangement produces visual figures and also accounts for functioning of the visual expression code."[2] The spatial features of the standoff – perimeters, insides and outsides, doors and bunkers – emerge, recede, and combine in ways that can indeed be made meaningful when Greimas' categories of spatiality, in tandem with other, perhaps more metaphorical and allegorical spatial categories, are taken into account.

In the standoffs examined here, individuals and groups are, put simply, not where they should be. They are, in Mary Douglas' immortal words, "matter out of place." They have left civilization and set up in the wild, or they have illegitimately established themselves on someone else's land (thus displacing the rightful owner), or they have spatially transformed their domicile in such a way that it no longer existentially fits with the other domiciles around it. In a significant sense, they have left home.

Spatial binary oppositions

Once occurring, these spatial dislocations are processed by participants and the public alike through a series of grids of binary oppositions. This is where the more synchronic mode of Structuralist analysis becomes relevant. At any given point in time, the binary calculus of standoff spaces includes the following oppositional pairs: inside and outside, near and far, open and closed, permeable boundary and impermeable boundary, ingress and egress, offense and defense, wild and civilized, safety and danger, public and private. These binaries provide a static, frozen sense of the opposing forces of this archetypically static situation. As well, they are all culturally and morally inflected as various protagonists will view one or another member of each pair as the positive or negative position.

For example, from the point of view of the authorities, the *inside* of the space of standoffs is the space of evil or corruption, inhabited by incorrigibles and, often, their "hostages."[3] Those holed-up in the now militarized standoff center are the enemies who must be simultaneously contained and extracted from their base. Thus we are encouraged to think about the insides of such places as similar to military posts – always on the alert, always in combat mode, where nothing of the domestic or the pacific can survive. Given this, as noted in the first chapter, it is disconcerting to discover that the Tupac Amaru members holding the hostages in the Japanese Ambassador's house allowed for the division of internal space into smoking and nonsmoking "sections." Internally variegated spaces, with rooms for cooking, for smoking, for playing guitar, complicate a vision of a heart of darkness. Smoking and nonsmoking sections are associated with more domestic spaces – restaurants or airplanes – and undercut the notion of a strictly militarized space.

From the point of view of those inside the standoff center, the authorities circling and surrounding them are the incorrigibles. They may be characterized as heathens, as invaders of privacy, and as suppressors of liberty. They almost certainly always represent the hegemonic power of the state.

The larger society and the representatives of the legitimate state institutions view themselves quite differently. For them, *outside* the space of the standoff are the "normals" – law abiders and law enforcers alike. We have seen in the first chapter how the concept of the normal in American culture circulates through several cultural themes. Those most relevant to standoffs have been ones involving family structure, religious belief, territorial jurisdiction, and gun ownership. The set-point schema developed here relies on a sense of a continuum with the extreme positions representing "overvaluing" and "undervaluing" these key themes and the relationships relevant to them, to use Lévi-Strauss' terminology. Normals know where to locate themselves and others on these thematic continua. The notion of literal location demonstrates the relevance of this schema to a discussion of the spatial parameters of standoffs. For example, in terms of family structure, a Structuralist sensitivity to the way meaning is created and engaged through symbolic oppositions and combinations can view the various readings of adult–child and male–female relations inside the compounds by those on the outside as attempts to emphasize the negative poles of these characterizations. As described in Chapter 1, we culturally recognize bad parents and bad husbands and there are cultural consequences for over and undervaluing existential family relations.

Another of the binary pairs, offense and defense, becomes relevant as the spaces themselves come to be described in these terms. It makes quite a bit of difference whether a given standoff structure (be it termed house, compound, or fortress) is characterized by authorities as offensive or defensive in nature. An *offensive* structure is bad for society and threatening in its very presence. The decision of the federal government in 1997 to literally pick up and transport the two-window shack of the Unabomber, Theodore Kaczynski, from its original siting in Montana to a warehouse in Sacramento reveals the degree to which the very physical structures of a standoff, even a standoff that could not be literally located in space while it was in progress, come to have great symbolic and legal meaning. The shack was to have served as evidence in Kaczynski's trial, a trial cut short by his guilty plea.

On the other hand, a structure defined as *defensive* can be simply misguided, in the eyes of the authorities, or can be absolutely necessary, in the eyes of the members of the anti-authority group inside. Groups anticipating some incursion by the authorities of the law may significantly alter the shape and bearing of their home/base in order to be prepared for any attacks.

During the inquisitional hearings that were held in Philadelphia after the MOVE confrontation, a police officer involved in the operation was repeatedly asked whether the boarded-up MOVE house represented an offensive or a defensive structure. He prevaricated in his response by saying both that, "If you watch any war movies, you know that is a defensive structure," and that "That house, in its construction . . . was a threat. I've never seen anything like it in my life."[4] A similar preoccupation with ambush and offense plagued the investigators of the Branch Davidian conflict. The opening paragraph of the Treasury Department Report claims that; "On February 28, 1993, near Waco, Texas, four agents from the Treasury Department's Bureau of Alcohol, Tobacco, and Firearms were killed, and more than 20 other agents were wounded when David Koresh and members of his religious cult, the Branch Davidians, *ambushed* a force of 76 ATF agents" (emphasis mine). In this rendition, the Mt. Carmel complex was clearly an offensive structure, capable of actively ambushing those on the outside, even those whose very approach toward the stationary house could be said to constitute an assault in its own right.

On the other hand, echoing the Branch Davidian's language of defense, Dr. Phillip Arnold of the Reunion Institute in Texas expressed his opinion that:

They definitely had religious reasons [for accumulating weapons], in order to protect themselves when the prophecy would one day be fulfilled that they would be attacked. It was not an attempt to go on the offensive and go to war against people, but all the prophecies that they quoted [during the 51 days of negotiations]... *they were not intending to have those weapons in order to go to war but to defend themselves when they were attacked*.[5]

Those on the outside, the governmental authorities, also have their own locations and spatial configurations characterized as offensive or defensive in nature. The former Assistant Director of the FBI, Larry Potts, made such a claim when explaining the meaning of the presence of the Hostage Rescue Team at Ruby Ridge. He testified that:

I can tell you categorically that the HRT was sent on a defensive mission. In brief, the HRT's mission was to contain the situation so that they, along with other elements of the FBI, could bring it to a peaceful resolution. The anticipated first step in carrying out that mission was to secure a perimeter that would both contain the situation and promote safety for the negotiators.[6]

This defensive position leads Potts to assert the necessity of the perimeter. A similar stance leads to the opposite strategy on the part of Janet Reno confronting the Freemen standoff: "The government continues to try to resolve this matter peacefully. We will do so in every way possible. It intends no armed confrontation, no siege and no armed perimeter."[7] Spaces clearly have personalities. It makes a big difference if that personality is characterized as offensive, aggressive, and assaultive or merely defensive, prepared for aggression from the outside. As will be evident, standoffs constantly generate such opposing characterological pairs, with all of the attendant consequences for action.

Mediations across spaces

Along with the spatial binary oppositions that provide a kind of architecture for the standoff, there are crucial mediating terms, concepts, and real individuals that literally and figuratively travel back and forth between them. Terms relevant here include: messenger, supplier, mediator, negotiator, bridge, road, door, communication. These are all things that move, or provide for movement, in the theoretical sense and in so doing aim at breaking the stasis facilitated by the binary oppositions. Some things (including gestures, symbols, spatial rearrangements) or persons must create the possibility of interaction across the barricades. They must bring the wild into colloquy with civilization; the safe into colloquy with the dangerous; the inside into colloquy with the outside and so forth. And in so doing, these mediating terms aim at undermining the apparent mutual exclusiveness of the protagonists' categories.

Another way of analytically characterizing the combinatory model I am attempting here is to think in terms of intercalibrating the stationary (binary pairs) and the mobile (mediators). Reflecting back to the first chapter, this is analogous to combining the *Iliad* and the *Odyssey*, or a largely synchronic mode of Structuralist analysis with a process-oriented Pragmatist theory of symbolic interaction. An illuminating example of just such a combining comes from a real-life event that has been studied by the anthropologist Abner Cohen. Cohen developed a historical and ethnographic analysis of the often politically and racially charged Notting Hill Carnival in London, England, an event that has undergone many changes over the several decades of its existence. A centerpiece of this largely Afro-Caribbean festival is the music of the bands that play each year. Some of the bands have big sound systems and they set up as stationary structures in the carnival, attracting crowds to stand and listen. Other bands, including the mas (masquerade) bands are mobile and attract crowds that would follow them as they made their route. As Cohen writes about the 1981–87 period, during which both types of bands figured in the carnival and during which the government was attempting to gain more control over the ever-more politically charged event: " The carnival was thus an integrated unity of mobile and stationary sections . . . It was why, during the following four years, the police concentrated on completely separating the two sections, smashing the integrated unity."[8] Cohen neatly shows how there is not only an analytical advantage to a combinatory conceptualizing of both the stationary and the mobile aspects of social systems, but also an actual strategic advantage to colonizing space in this way.

Government agencies have shown themselves to be exquisitely sensitive in the past to the difference between populations that move and those that stay put. They like to keep tabs on where people are and their very administrative census categories can reflect this preoccupation. One clear case of this is recounted by Ian Hacking in his book, *The Taming of Chance*:

When we examine the excellent yearbooks published by the Prussian statistical bureau throughout the latter half of the nineteenth century we find the first division in the population: military on the left, civil on the right. You were first of all civil or military, then you were male or female, servant or master, Mennonite or Old

Catholic. There was of course an unstated rationale. People were counted, as they still are, by geographic area. The civilian population stayed in one place, while the military were mobile and in garrisons. Military and civil were different aspects of the national topography.[9]

The standoffs under examination all involve antisystem individuals and groups who have not stayed in one place and who have made an ostentatious point of moving somewhere else. And along with everything else suspect about them, this must certainly be one. Mobility, as in the Prussian case, ought legitimately to be the exclusive purview of the law-enforcement agents that get sent from crisis to crisis, from standoff to standoff.

Nevertheless, even with this categorial opposition between people who move and people who stay still, real people navigate among different spaces in ways that allow them to both move and come to full stops. As well, these navigations can act to both separate spaces and to bring spaces into contact with each other. In a short, brilliant essay, "Bridge and Door," Georg Simmel laid out the fundamental theoretical template for this idea of connecting and separating and for the key role of human-made spatial features that make these things possible. Focusing on the central images of the bridge and the door as those features of the human-made environment that connect the separate and separate the connected, Simmel writes: "Path-building, one could say, is a specifically human achievement; the animal too continuously overcomes a separation and often in the cleverest and most ingenious ways, but its beginning and end remain unconnected, it does not accomplish the miracle of the road: freezing movement into a solid structure that commences from it and in which it terminates."[10] Of course, and this is Simmel's deepest point, spatial separations and connections are truly in the eyes of the beholder and the navigator. This is even more exaggeratedly true in a standoff than in everyday social life. Mediations across situationally recognized borders, perimeters, barricades and the like are always fraught and potentially dangerous. As we shall see, the opening and closing door to Randy Weaver's cabin is just one of several points of frozen and melted movement that shape the action of the narrative of the standoff.

Codifications of space

It is thus important to establish a typology of spaces in the standoff and to theorize their interactions. We need to consider literal spaces where geography, proximity, territory, and tactics combine to influence the emerging map of the standoff – looked at from both inside and outside. Here, perimeters, roadblocks, the state of the terrain (rocky, forested, mountainous, inhabited, uninhabited) all set parameters for action. As well, we have to analyze the symbolic spaces of the standoff where contestations over the very names of the places occupied, divergent views as to the sacred or secular valence of a given space, and aesthetic characterizations of a space all affect the stances of the protagonists.

Literal spaces: perimeters and spatial alterations

One of the first things to happen at the outset of a standoff is that a perimeter, or a series of perimeters, gets established. Establishing a perimeter involves imagining a central point of containment and a circular area 360 degrees around it. The action of creating a perimeter attempts to answer a question analogous to one of the key questions raised regarding the times of a standoff, "How long is long enough?" The positioning of a perimeter, then, asks, "How close is close enough?" Perimeters control ingress and egress into and out of the standoff center. They determine and are determined by issues of visibility and audibility. Law enforcement agencies are the primary agents of perimeters, setting up surveillance equipment and staffed posts around the space where the "*out*laws" (aptly yet ironically named here, as the outlaws are so much creatures of an inside) are holed-up. Other participants have their own perimeters, including those in the standoff center and including representatives of the mass media. The standoffs proceed as people move into position along these perimeters, move across them, and move the perimeters themselves as the center grows and shrinks.

Sometimes, the authorities are reluctant to establish a perimeter. The reasons are various and beget different policy decisions about action. In the Treasury Department's report on the Branch Davidian standoff, it is reported that the original decision of the ATF to implement a siege with a perimeter was overturned and that they opted instead for a "dynamic entry." The stated rationale for this change refers to the nature of the surrounding terrain: "After the planners saw the terrain . . . which offered little cover from the dominating Compound, and after considering the injuries that could be inflicted with the long-range, powerful .50 caliber weapons the planners thought Koresh possessed, they began to reconsider this option. Even if a perimeter could be established, they reasoned, it would have to be quite large and therefore difficult to maintain."[11] Ultimately, of course, the intial raid of the ATF failed in its mission to arrest David Koresh, and the FBI ended up establishing a perimeter even in the face of this tactically challenging terrain.

With alternative motives, the Freemen standoff was explicitly characterized as one in which there was to be no establishment of a perimeter. Here, it was the goal of Attorney General Janet Reno to essentially deny that a standoff was occurring and part of the way of doing so was to hold back from implementing the conventional actions that mold the spaces of the standoff. Reno's statement on this matter is quite clear, as we have seen: "'The government . . . intends no armed confrontation, no siege and no armed perimeter,' she said at her weekly news briefing in Washington."[12]

With the exception of the Freemen standoff, all of the others had active, self-conscious perimeters that set physical boundaries around the standoffs. Talk about the perimeters involved issues of their establishment, their distance, their permeability, and their occupancy (who should be allowed to approach the perimeters and to position themselves there). Obviously, agents of law enforcement asserted their rights to a perimeter, but agents of the mass media also sought to claim their own perimeters. As well, those in the standoff centers often established their own perimeters that, they claimed, laid out the boundaries of their territory. Thus several terms were used to designate this circle around a center – perimeter, border, boundary, barricade. Each term has a slightly different connotation revealing that the pressure for the line drawn comes either from the inside or the outside and that its goal is either to keep something in or to keep it out. In a way, these terminological distinctions are analogous to the difference between a factory lockout and a strike. These two actions are diametrically opposed in meaning, even though they effectively do the same thing spatially – keep people out of a factory.

The first thing that needs to happen in the spatial realignments that signify a standoff in the making is that the perimeter must be established. There's often a real military sense of conquering a hostile space and holding it against the enemy. Most importantly, perimeters signify control. Reflecting on the disappointment and frustration felt by the FBI when the Branch Davidians failed to exit Mt. Carmel at the designated time (because David Koresh began, at the last minute, to pray), the FBI agent in charge of operations, Jeff Jamar, told the *Frontline* interviewer: "God told him to wait. Okay. Well, now, where are we? We're – now we have to get a perimeter. They're not coming out, so we had to get control. We had to get a perimeter and we had to get our people in place safely. That's what led to our appearance of greater control. We built, you know, fake sniper positions."[13] With control as his goal, Jamar puts his finger on the complex relation of appearance and reality in the establishment of a perimeter.

Further, there is often a sense of trepidation and uneasiness about the ability to maintain this perimeter control. Practical considerations are obviously articulated. For example, the FBI commander in charge of the standoff at Ruby Ridge stated that: "I was extremely fearful of sustaining casualties while attempting to establish a perimeter at the crisis site, since the subjects possessed every tactical advantage."[14] On the other hand, the logical reluctance to enter and take a space of danger is open to the normative critique that one is not living up to one's reputation as bold, courageous, and in charge. During the Senate Hearings on Ruby Ridge, a former FBI negotiator took issue with that reluctance to get hurt:

And we didn't have a perimeter around Randall Weaver's house until sometime Sunday, a perimeter through the night. And I was shocked by that. And I said, Why don't we have a perimeter? And I was told because it's wet, it's dark, and we're afraid one of our guys is going to twist an ankle up there on that mountain. All the time – and I truly believe that the FBI's hostage rescue team is the best team of its kind in the world. But, on the other hand, we don't have these guys deployed; we don't have a perimeter around the house because they're afraid they're going to twist an ankle? I was appalled by that.[15]

What's doubly interesting here is not just that the law-enforcement agents seemed to have been fearful of harm, but that the harm should come not from Randy Weaver et al., but from the very terrain itself. This is just one of many moments, as we shall see, where the protagonists and the space they inhabit seem to infect each other with the physiognomy of malevolence.

Once established, the perimeter must be set at a particular distance from the center. Obviously this will vary depending upon the terrain, the surrounding structures, the roadways, and the assumed "firepower" of those on the inside.

At Wounded Knee, the town of Wounded Knee was located at the intersection of four roads that could be viewed as consisting of an X. Initial roadblocks were actually erected by the occupiers themselves on each of the four roads leading to the center of town. At the beginning, these roadblocks were places of picketing with people allowed in and out. Following the ensuing exchange of gunfire, the US Marshals created a larger concentric circular perimeter surrounding the Oglala Sioux roadblocks, and arrested all Oglala Sioux who were attempting to exit. Thus the two perimeters nestled within each other, creating a demilitarized buffer zone between the inside and the outside. They also reflected radically different senses of the meaning of the lines themselves. The sense of a territory conquered and reclaimed led one of the occupiers to claim: "We no longer have a perimeter – we have a border."[16] Perimeters, like standoffs themselves, are existentially temporary, a product of a state of mobilization. Borders stake their claim on the *longue durée* of the life-spans and seeming naturalness of nations. Standoffs that have territorial jurisdiction as a central theme will inevitably get caught up in such debates over spatial terminology and names as geography is politically reconfigured over their course.

The outer perimeter around Wounded Knee undulated in a wave-like manner over the course of the standoff, moving in and out as the tactical and negotiation processes announced that greater proximity or more distance were necessary. Early on, the FBI and the US Marshals announced that they had established a perimeter at a distance of five miles out from the center. Announcing this at a press conference a few days into the standoff, the official government spokesman was contradicted by journalists who claimed that, "There are those of us that have been to that checkpoint that overlooks Wounded Knee last night. And there is no way your people are five miles away from Wounded Knee."[17] Gradually, the outer perimeter of the law-enforcement agencies was understood to stand at one mile from the center but then, as negotiations with the governmental representative, Harlington Wood, seemed to break down, ". . . the US forces tightened their perimeter. Two of their road-blocks were moved in until they were virtually on the edge of the village. There were firefights nearly every night . . ."[18] In standoffs there are constant calibrations of the actual distances of the perimeters: five miles to one mile at Wounded Knee, three miles at Ruby Ridge,[19] three miles for the outer perimeter and 300 yards outside the compound gates for the inner perimeter, both manned by the FBI Hostage Rescue Team at Waco (interestingly, the FBI negotiators at Waco were five and a half miles away in an airplane hangar), two miles from the Republic of Texas redoubt in the Davis Mountains. Obviously, the perimeter is never stationary in reality. It moves in and out and it is breached by those trying to go in and those trying to get out. It provides intermittent openings for negotiators or media representatives or carriers of physical or spiritual sustenance.

Nevertheless, the perimeter is typically represented as a solid, stationary line around the standoff center, the mission of which is to literally surround the core. The approximately 700 law-enforcement agents brought to the scene in Waco, the 500 Philadelphia Police officers brought to the block on which the MOVE house was located, the 400 agents brought to Ruby Ridge, the 200 Texas State Troopers and officers of the Texas Department of Public Safety all attest to the desire to make literal the concept. Testifying at the Senate Hearings on Ruby Ridge, US Marshal Michael Johnson makes precisely this point:

Senator Craig: At the time that you were there and involved, observing and watching and participating, did you ever question that kind of buildup?

Johnson: Senator, when you looked at the geographical area that we were trying to – and I guess the word is "surround" – to protect both law enforcement that were there, people trying to come in, either supporters or people that were against either side, it was a mammoth undertaking to try to do some type of perimeter as you would in any type of situation like that.[20]

Finally, as we have seen that there may be two perimeters in any given standoff (one established by law enforcement, one by those in the barricaded center), there is often yet another one specifically set up for the press and onlookers. At Waco, the 75 or more media agencies sending their representatives positioned themselves around the three-mile out roadblocks. This was the closest they could get to the center. This perimeter actually generated a small city-like organism of its own named, appropriately enough, "Satellite City." With food vendors, trash service, and even a symbolic "mayor," this small-scale society trafficked specifically in a Branch Davidian-oriented market economy.[21] Thus can the perimeter come alive in its own right.

Beyond the establishing of perimeters, standoffs are replete with several other kinds of literal spatial alterations and reconfigurations. On the parts of law-enforcement agencies, these changes usually include evacuations of houses and businesses in the area of the standoff (MOVE and Republic of Texas), the clearing away of constructed or natural structures to create cleaner lines of vision and movement (Waco, Ruby Ridge), the creation of openings in buildings that they occupy or hope to occupy in order to insert listening devices or explosives or tear gas (MOVE, Waco, Ruby Ridge), and the actual tearing down of the standoff structure at the conclusion of the standoff (MOVE, Waco, Tupac Amaru).

The clearing of the scene is often represented by law-enforcement officials as a way for them to get reoriented in space. One example comes from Ruby Ridge, a setting in which the heavily forested mountain on which Randy Weaver's house was located played such a strong role. An FBI sniper/observer noted:

None of us had been on the ground before, of course. We only had aerial photographs to use to orient ourselves. And aerial photographs can be very deceptive as far as the relief of the ground . . . I moved down about 10 yards in front of the two of them, and began to try to set up a better position where I would be able to see. I had my clippers out and I was clipping some branches away that were in front of me. . . .[22]

At the Branch Davidian compound as well, the FBI moved in with tanks specifically to clear and remove all cars, motorcycles, and trees that interfered with their being able to see and gain access to the buildings.

Those on the inside usually reshape their spaces as well. They build structures on the tops of their homes or compounds, structures that often resemble, and are named as, "bunkers" (MOVE, Ruby Ridge). They create slits in walls as in medieval castles, out of which to see and, sometimes inevitably, out of which to shoot (MOVE, Waco). Alternatively, they board up the openings of their structures (doors and windows alike). The Tupac Amaru group placed land mines around the yard of the Japanese Ambassador's house during their occupation. The Branch Davidians buried an old school bus in the ground around Mt. Carmel. Thus are closed spaces opened and open spaces closed.

It is possible to claim that the emergence of a standoff necessarily involves some type of spatial metamorphosis. Spaces are no longer innocent or fairly unselfconscious about issues of access and ingress and egress. Houses, yards, streets, and bridges all undergo critical transformations. Both of the opposing camps set out to to reconfigure the spaces of the standoff in order to have fuller, easier access or to cut such access off. No one can deny the practical elements of such action, at least at first blush. If one is aiming a gun, one has to be able to see the target. But the vehemence with which much of this action of spatial reconfiguration occurs suggests that more is going on here than a simple clearing of a road. In the most extreme of cases (the MOVE standoff, in which the MOVE house and the two surrounding city blocks were burned to the ground, and that at Waco, where the entire compound of the Branch Davidians was similarly burned in a consuming fire, are certainly two) this zeal to restructure the space approaches the delirium of the "Burn a village to save it" mentality that emerged from Vietnam.

Symbolic spaces of the standoff – the moral, the political, and the sacred

While the literal spaces of buildings, forests, mountains, towers, and roads seem to map the practical and tactical alignments of foes across the standoff barricades, such spaces also simultaneously reverberate with symbolic power. Standoff spaces are intermittently stages for dramas of good and evil, innocence and victimization, strength and weakness; they are settings for moral and spiritual claims (in essence, sacred spaces), and they are political territories with contested "monopolies of the legitimate use of force," in Weber's words. Spaces of standoffs can either be chosen for their traditional sacredness, as in the case of Wounded Knee, or they can become sacred after the fact of the standoff. The latter is indeed the case with places like the Federal Arsenal at Harper's Ferry or the Alamo. In fact, as Kenneth Foote writes about the Alamo:

Visitors are asked to remove their hats as they enter the shrine, and silence is enforced rigorously by guards. When rock-music star Ozzy Osbourne urinated on the Alamo in 1982, he was not just convicted of public indecency but banned from performing again in San Antonio until he made a public apology and a $10,000 donation to the Daughters of the Republic of Texas, which he did in 1992.[23]

There is obviously not always consensus about the meaning of a so-called sacred space. Standoffs are often, precisely, rooted in the contradictory meanings generated by the same space, as antagonists plant literal and figurative flags staking their claims. This sense of the multivalent nature of space is echoed by Roger Friedland and Richard Hecht in their work on sacred centers. Friedland and Hecht argue for the interdependency of territoriality and the formation of collectivities. They write: "The implication of our work is that spatialization and the formation of sacred centers may be critical to the formation of collectivities of all sorts . . . Ritual rights depend on property rights, sacred space being a property, like any other, which cannot internally produce the conditions of its reproduction."[24] Standoffs are often precisely about the conditions of the production and reproduction of spatially centered ritual and property rights.

Yet even as the majority of standoffs and standoff spaces analyzed here are geographical and physically expansive in nature, it is analytically important to recall that an object as small as a memo can constitute the space of a standoff (with its textual evidence that the parties have either resolved the conflict or remain unreconciled). Recalling the space of the academic journal article that was cleaved by a runaway footnote (the "Agnes" article by Garfinkle and Stoller discussed in Chapter 1), it is clear standoffs leave their textual traces. The idea of "occupying" space in a publication of the mass media became key in the long-running standoff between the Unabomber and the US law-enforcement agents trying to track him down. Thus, an interim negotiating demand of the Unabomber was that he be able to publish his many-paged manifesto in several major national newspapers and that if he were so able, he would desist from wounding and killing people with his mail bombs. Finally, it is interesting to follow the path of spatial contractions of standoff conflicts as they move from geographical space to the mere graphical space of texts. Ian Hunter's analysis of the nineteenth-century combined struggle of population administrators and Sunday School proponents to control the volatile English working class reveals such a process. Targeting working-class children, the reformers first established the opposition between the ungoverned, immoral space of the street and the moral space of the playground. Then, with the introduction and ultimate curricular hegemony of the teaching of English literature, that moral space contracted even further. As Hunter writes, "In fact, the history of English is in large part the history of the contraction of the morally managed space of the school into the landscape of the literary text. . . ."[25]

At the most general level, the standoff space operates as a kind of theatrical stage, with the perimeter(s) functioning as a proscenium. The "action" of standoffs will not be visible to all participants and observers at any given moment. Those in the standoff redoubt cannot see what is going on in the backstage of the law-enforcement agents. Those staffing the perimeter cannot see into the standoff center. Representatives of the mass media and interested onlookers may often be restricted to sites at some remove from the central space of action. Nonetheless, all know that there is a kind of magic circle that is produced by the combined (if oppositional) efforts of the antagonists inside and outside.

Sometimes, those who are only tangentially implicated in the standoff dynamics (the press, the sympathizers, the public) find themselves creating alternative spaces, beyond the perimeters, that are similarly symbolically charged. "Satellite City," outside the Branch Davidian perimeter was one, with its own circus atmosphere. Christian Identity movement members clustered around the perimeter in Jordan, Montana. In Peru, the more traditionally street-oriented public actually held a march in Lima calling for a peaceful settlement of the standoff. The movement of the march through the streets was in direct contrast with the paralysis of the standoff at the Japanese Ambassador's house. And the public attempted to create alternative symbolism as well, waving Peruvian flags, carrying and displaying religious ornaments, and even bringing along pet doves. Nation, religion, and universal symbols of peace all appeared in the street to create a space of contrast with the occupied house.

The spaces of standoffs, like the spaces of scaffolds,[26] provide a ground for the enactment of the self. There may be a kind of paradoxical clarity that comes from being so trapped, so locked into a space of antagonism, so much beyond in this no-man's land. One way to understand this strange freedom is to refer to the idea of a convergence of spatial and moral orientation. Charles Taylor, in his philosophically profound analysis of identity, describes this convergence:

To know who you are is to be oriented in moral space, a space in which questions arise about what is good or bad, what is worth doing or not . . . I feel myself drawn here to use a spatial metaphor; but I believe this to be more than personal predilection. There are signs that the link with spatial orientation lies very deep in the human psyche. In some very extreme cases of what are described as "narcissistic personality disorder," which take the form of a radical uncertainty about oneself and about what is of value to one, patients show signs of spatial disorientation as well as moments of acute crisis.[27]

Thus, an alternative theoretical model for understanding the standoff is one that views it as a situation of hyperorientation. Literal space and moral space coincide to refine the contours of identity. Ultimately, this may or may not be a good thing for providing opportunities to improvise one's way out of the standoff.

Space names

Just as the *longue durée* of undifferentiated time is broken up by human-kind into such things as years, weeks, weekends, holidays, seasons, and so forth, so is the wide expanse of undifferentiated space divided into named and bounded territories. It is thus not incidental that in the exquisite self-consciousness of the standoff situation, the very names of the places occupied by the antagonists become charged and contested. Place names of streets, cities, counties, states, and nation are typically put into high relief during the standoffs examined here. These names often reflect the key themes and axiomatic worldviews at their roots. A host of symbolically res-onant names emerge when one actually maps these standoffs. The sheer number of biblical and value-laden names, for example, cannot be coinci-dental. These include: "Jordan" and "Justus Township" in Montana, "Boundary County" in Idaho, and "Palestine," "Mt. Carmel," and "Ranch Apocalypse" in Texas.

Some of these names can be found on official maps (Jordan, Boundary County, Palestine), some are the creations of the antisystem groups assert-ing their own symbolic spaces (Mt. Carmel, Justus Township), and some are creations of the media and the law enforcement agencies (Ranch Apocalypse, the "Compound"). Thus some names that are in common cir-culation (common to all protagonists in a conflict) already intimate that they designate a zone of contestation or symbolically charged demarcation. For example, the Ruby Ridge standoff occurred in "Boundary County, Idaho," signifying a space that harbors what one might call a predilection for territorial contestation. Jordan and Palestine[28] are clearly names that derive from ancient, biblical precursers, and it cannot be an accident that standoffs with religious principles in contention circulated around precisely such places. At some level, these various names reflect a broader demarca-tion of the space of the nation into zones of modernity and civilization, zones of premodernity, and zones of primitivity and wilderness, with some of the antisystem groups gravitating toward the premodern and the prime-val side of the dichotomy. We will examine this symbolic reading of geo-graphical space below.

Some of the charged space names do not appear on any official maps.

They are the creations of the standoff protagonists. As noted earlier, the Freemen called their redoubt "Justus Township." By contrast, the federal officials called it the Bliss Ranch after the name of a man who had legally purchased the ranch the year before. All of the paraphernalia of national territorial law (maps, passports, flags) were placed in high relief and drawn into the standoff as the Freemen declared the area around the ranch to be sovereign territory. Writing in the magazine *Soldier of Fortune*, James Pate made ostentatious moves in the direction of "recognizing" the alternative territorial map:

Clutching a press card and an expired passport in one hand, and a white handkerchief tied to a stick in the other, I stepped around the barricaded farm gate at the end of a Garfield County dirt road, 35 miles northwest of tiny Jordan, Montana. Signs posted on the gate by the farm's occupants warned that I was entering the realm of a "sovereign" and could be "imprisoned" for up to a year for trespassing.[29]

Similarly, the Branch Davidians called their place of residence "Mt. Carmel." The authorities called it the Branch Davidian compound. The members of the Republic of Texas claimed the name of "The Republic of Texas" for their territory. The United States authorities called it the State of Texas. The Oglala Sioux occupying the town of Wounded Knee renamed the area of the town, up to the FBI-manned perimeter, "The Independent Oglala Nation." Here it is significant to recall that among the initial demands of the occupiers was that they be able to meet with the Senate Foreign Relations Committee to discuss some 371 treaties negotiated over the course of US history between the United States and various Native-American nations. Among the responses to these initial demands was one that spoke to the issue of jurisdictionally contested space: Harlington Wood, head negotiator for the Justice Department, proposed that the occupiers actually meet with the Interior Department. The juxtaposition between Foreign Relations Committee and Interior Department couldn't be clearer. The government was insisting that the town of Wounded Knee was still part of the United States.

Finally, there are some provocative names that hover around the edges of the standoffs examined. These names do not figure directly in the confrontations but they may indeed indirectly give shade to their meanings. For example, the MOVE house was located on a very small street in West Philadelphia comprised of row homes but bordered by a large park. Recalling that MOVE's mixed and hybrid philosophy contained elements of vegetarianism, back to nature, antitechnology, it was always somewhat ironic that MOVE persisted in living in the heart of urban Philadelphia. And indeed, MOVE was very self-conscious about this decision.

Nevertheless, given these philosophical tendencies, and given that the group was ultimately characterized by neighbors and politicians as wild and primordial, it must be noted that the street on which they lived was named "Osage Avenue." A reminder then, of the Native American predecessors who once occupied land upon which contemporary urbanized Americans have built their cities. MOVE is thus indirectly linked to these more primordial Americans.

A last literary example comes from the Tupac Amaru standoff in a very exclusive neighborhood of Lima, Peru. The Japanese Ambassador's residence, the site of the occupation, was a large, majestic white house built to model exactly Scarlett O'Hara's house, "Tara," from the movie *Gone with the Wind*. Thus did Cuban-inspired Marxists from Peru hold Peruvian, Japanese and other international politicians, businessmen, and diplomats hostage in the residence of the Japanese Ambassador to Peru in a house inspired by southern, pre-Civil War, slave-holding North Americans. Given the previous attacks against United States-owned businesses by the Tupac Amaru group, the coinciding symbols of the Peruvian government, the Japanese government, and United States culture represented by this latter-day "Tara," became the perfect standoff site.

Spatial narratives of America – outside space

There is an old saying that Europe is the continent of time and America is the continent of space. Thus does history create the palimpsest of European cities, with layer upon layer of civilizations buried in any given spot. Thus does history create the migration trail of the American continent, with only the thinnest of traces of multiple pasts in settled spaces.

Certainly, the possibility of movement away from the centers of civilization was a historical option for heterodox religionists, adventurers, and criminals alike in the early centuries of American colonization by Europeans. Religious scholar Catherine Wessinger contrasts the situation of early religious movements with that of what she calls "New Religious Movements" (NRMs) today. She refers, in particular, to the Mormons, who "were fortunate that the American frontier provided space for them to move very far away from their oppressors in mainstream society, and thus they succeeded in building their own society in which their church was dominant . . . Today however, members of NRMs . . . do not have the space to flee their opponents in society."[30]

Thus it makes sense that groups like the Branch Davidians and the Freemen of Montana, and individuals like Randy Weaver may inevitably try to find any residual spaces "far from society" wherein they can practice their heterodox religions. The mountains of Idaho, the sparsely populated plains of Texas, the big-sky ranches of Montana, all make sense as spaces of settlement for these groups. Symbolically, however, much more is at stake in such localizations than just the mere fact of their distance from urban centers or their geographical inaccessibility. Traditionally there is a distinct tension in the ways that Americans have envisioned the wild and forested spaces to which so many have migrated. Simon Schama speaks of the way that the first generation of white, native Americans saw the forests as either the wild place of godlessness and Indians or as a providential, natural tabernacle. Of the latter view, he writes:

> It is from this primordial vegetable matter, celestially sanctified and unspoiled as yet by the touch of man, that America was born, so the writers and painters of the first native generation proclaim. In so doing they self-consciously turned their back both on the classical contempt for woodland barbarism and the long Puritan legacy that equated the forest with pagan darkness and profanity.[31]

And yet, the ambivalence about such wild spaces remains within the American mind. Witness the melodramatic and evocative ways in which some of the spaces of the standoffs under examination here were described in newspapers, books, and academic prose alike. Clifford Lindecker, author of the book *Massacre in Waco*, recalls the Wild West historic legacy of the town Waco, Texas to describe its (not very similar) contemporary feel:

> Shootouts were so common in the streets, saloons, and whorehouses that stage-coach drivers called the rowdy cowboy town "Six-Shooter Junction" . . . The daring feats of the Rangers soon became a good yardstick against which to measure the worth of other hard-riding, hard-shooting, lawmen whose stamina and courage helped tame the Wild West. The old-time lawmen and their professional descendants are memorialized in Waco by the Texas Ranger Hall of Fame and Museum at Fort Fisher.[32]

The *Philadelphia Inquirer* used very similar phrases and images to describe the town of Jordan, Montana, site of the Freemen standoff: "The town [of Jordan] is in the middle of the Missouri Breaks, the rough country used more than a century ago by stagecoach robbers, renegade Indians fleeing reservation life, and even Butch Cassidy and the Sundance Kid, who hid in the gullies that crease its surface."[33] A final example comes from the *Los Angeles Times*, covering the standoff in Ruby Ridge, Idaho: "In the dark and brooding mountains covering the long panhandle of northern Idaho, Randy Weaver – survivalist, racist and fugitive from the law – chose his fortress well."[34]

All of these descriptive passages traffic in the melodramatic language of overwrought romantic verse. Mountains are brooding, towns are rowdy, gullies crease the surface of the earth. Clearly, these descriptions of the settings of the standoffs are meant to bring the environment into alignment with the actors and the actions involved, or, in what comes to the same thing, to explain the actions in terms of the predetermining environment. In Kenneth Burke's terms, we must pay attention to these act/scene/actor ratios where everything lines up a bit too neatly. And so it shouldn't be surprising that a few voices would seek to conjure up an alternative vision of these wild spaces, either disclaiming their wildness or extolling its very wild virtues.

The former tack was taken by Senator Larry E. Craig, US Senator from Idaho, who began his opening statement at the Senate Hearings on Ruby Ridge with the following recitation:

Thirty-six months ago, north Idaho's image began to be viewed by the world as something different from what it is. In August 1992, on a small town known as Naples, national media focused with a spotlight. This is a small community of independent, peaceful, and hard-working citizens in Boundary County, our furthest county in the State, bordering Canada. It is not a community of gun-toting outlaws ... North Idaho's deep clear lakes, tall green mountains ... The people of Boundary County are attracted by the natural beauty, the good-natured residents, and the opportunity to live far from the madding crowd.[35]

The evocation of Thomas Hardy in Craig's statement is unconsciously apt, as the virtues of rural life are indeed often intertwined with its cruelties. Craig's praise of Northern Idaho rests on his sense of the good-natured simple folk who choose to live there. A friend of the Weaver family, talking to a *Los Angeles Times* reporter, gave a different spin to the rugged individualist temperament cultivated by this area: "[Carolyn] Trochmann, one of the minority who grew up in the area, said that perhaps the most important aspect of the mountains is not their isolation, but the hardships they pose. Only the strong and pure will stay, she said, and if the land breeds a certain harsh defiance, that's the way it should be."[36]

Given the heightened American sensitivity to the moral, political, and religious valences of space, and given the varied characterizations of it, is useful to ask the question: why did the antisystem groups involved in these standoffs decide to locate themselves where they did? What was at stake symbolically for them?

Agents of law enforcement have their own ready answer as to why groups go where they do and, typically, their explanations run more in the direction of the strategic than the symbolic. Richard Garner, chief of the ATF Special Operations Division testified before the Senate Appropriations Committee during hearings on the ATF Branch Davidian raid:

I have been in law enforcement for 23 years, and I know that there have been similar types of situations involving survivalists or cults, if we define them further, that put their zeal above the law; that they will take any violent means and attack the government forces for whatever cause they feel is appropriate. As you look over the years, a lot of these are in rural areas. A lot of them have strategically located hideouts or places that add additional complexities to the law enforcement problem.[37]

The groups themselves, however, often have a different type of answer. The Oglala Sioux stopped purposely to pray at the site of the 1890 massacre cemetery and decided to stake their claim there in that charged space. This eventual overlapping of spaces, the 1973 standoff on top of the 1890 massacre, is rendered visible by a literal palimpsest of graves. At the cemetery at Wounded Knee, a fairly large memorial inscribed with the names of those warriors killed in 1890 looms over two smaller gravestones marking the burial sites of two Oglala Sioux killed in 1973.

Some groups claimed explicitly religious rationales for their locations. David Koresh ultimately came to believe that Armageddon could and would begin at Mount Carmel, rather than in Israel. The Freemen of Montana would claim that their god, Yahweh, had protected Justus Township with an invisible barrier surrounding them on all sides (their own form of sacred perimeter).[38] Randall Weaver obliquely linked his religious belief in racial segregation to his decision to move into the almost exclusively white mountains of northern Idaho. Out of over 8,000 people in the county, only three were African-American. Here a form of "voluntary" apartheid maps the external space. During his Senate Hearings testimony, Weaver attempts to explain his position:

Number 1, I am not a hateful racist the way most people understand that, but I believe that if there is separation of the races, scripturally speaking, that is what I believe is right. It sounds like an impossible task and most likely is, but I believe that people of every race should be proud of who they are and what they are.[39]

Other groups make decisions based on an ideological position that is not exclusively religious in nature. The Tupac Amaru group chose the Peruvian "Tara" in the heart of Lima precisely for its ambiguous nationality and jurisdiction (technically Peru had authority over the house of the Japanese Ambassador but the Peruvian government was theoretically duty-bound to ask permission of the Japanese for any operation they initiated there). However, the decision here to purposely set off a standoff in the midst of civilized Lima is directly contrasted with the group's normal locus of activity, that being the Peruvian jungle. When the initial negotiating demands of the Tupac Amaru were published in their Communiqué #1, the third demand insisted on the return of all group members, those currently imprisoned and those involved in the takeover of the Ambassador's house, to the jungle: "Transfer of the commando that entered the residence of the Japanese ambassador together with all the . . . prisoners from the MRTA to the central jungle. As a guarantee, some of the captured persons, who will be selected correspondingly, will also come along. They will be set free when we have reached our guerilla zone."[40] The self-chosen localization of the group in this nondomesticated zone is re-emphasized in several other communiqués. In Communiqué #13, responding to some government actions against civilians in the Peruvian hinterland who had been accused of sympathizing with the MRTA, the group writes: "These actions against the civilian population cannot be excused. The army knows full well that Tupac Amaristas do not stay in the homes of the campesinos, rather out in the woods."[41]

MOVE wanted specifically to remain within the heart of the city of Philadelphia, even, and especially, with their antimodernity, antitechnology stance. This became clear in the earlier 1978 standoff during which a group of local members of the Society of Friends attempted to convince MOVE to relocate to a farm in the predominantly Amish-settled Lancaster County (the Amish themselves are known to be radically opposed to modern technology), several hours outside of Philadelphia. Apparently paradoxically, MOVE refused to resettle in the more rural location. The Republic of Texas group chose to make their stand against government interference in a cabin in the Davis Mountains, in Fort Davis, Texas, an area in the south-west corner of the state near the Mexican border. This bit of Texas land jutting off of one side of the state reveals a proximity to the land away from which the Republic of Texas originally broke in its civil war against Mexico. Thus it too, in a manner similar to "Boundary County," evokes notions of boundaries, borders and limits.

Flags: where the outside meets the inside

"We cannot hope for a preacher who will walk through cities and towns telling allegorical tales which will make clear the original guiding principles of the Constitution. All we have are symbols – the flag being the most recognizable of these, the flag being the one we all seem to endorse."[42]

Flags mark the point of contact and connection between the outer spaces and the inner spaces. "We" are Americans if we fly the American flag on our house, school, or business. Flags typically are flown on the tops of roofs, staking their territorial and symbolic claim by being both planted on solid ground and airborne simultaneously. As the standoff perimeter divides the tactical space of the normals from the space of the transgressors (looked at from either the perspective of those inside the standoff center, believing that they themselves are the normals, or of those outside the standoff center, who believe the same about themselves), flags flown in standoffs divide the symbolic spaces of those with opposing claims.

While the proximal focus here is on literal flags of nations or other collective entities, it is important to clarify that "flag" may be understood in a more metaphorical as well as literal way. Typical flags made of cloth with symbolic colors, mottos, and symbols on them were in abundant evidence in several of the standoffs examined. However, we might even understand the tiny and seemingly insignificant footnote or endnote number that appears in superscript above a word to be a kind of standoff flag. Recall the curious footnote in the text of the article on Agnes by Garfinkle and Stoller, wherein the text is seemingly doubled and then split. The reader is stopped in his or her tracks by the little number flown over a line of the main text and is pointed to the extended footnote or endnote below. The number, planting itself in the midst of things as it does, accomplishes a spatial divide in the text where a new, alternative, emergent territory begins to show itself below.[43]

More conventional flags of nations and armies have always been important in battle and in territorial claim-staking, but they haven't always been important in the same way. Carrying the colors in military battles has been important and, as Stuart McConnell writes about the Civil War, it has always generated intense emotions: "The regimental flag symbolized home and hearth, and in battles during the war it was guarded with an appropriately intense loyalty."[44] At the time of the Civil War, however, the national flag had not yet achieved that level of abstraction and pluralistic meanings that it has today. Particular flags that had lived through a historic event were revered metonymically, as the place and the actions of the event left their literal traces on the flags in the forms of jagged rips, holes, or place names of particular battles sewn on after the fact. By the 1890s, however, after a period of growth in patriotic organizations such as the Sons and Daughters of the American Revolution, and the development of patriotic rituals like the Pledge of Allegiance,

The flag was not only spoken of more abstractly, but it also began to be treated ritually as an object of transcendent significance. Although "flag etiquette" is largely a product of the twentieth century, the 1890s saw the writing of the pledge . . . the adoption by veterans' organizations of flag codes, and, most important, the elaboration of the ceremony of flag presentation established during the Civil War.[45]

Thus, the flag became a more synecdochic symbolic creature – it was a highly condensed part standing for the whole of the nation. And thus, no particular, individual flag was necessary; any stars and stripes would do.

As noted above, several of the protagonist groups in the standoffs studied here had flags of their own design or purposely altered the national flag and flew it in this altered form. These were often displayed on the roofs of the houses/compounds/bunkers or on flagpoles nearby. The Branch Davidians had their own blue and white "Star of David" flag, which they flew on a tall flagpole next to the main building at Mt. Carmel. The Tupac Amaru had a red and white flag with the face of Tupac Amaru, a star, and a rifle on it. The Freemen of Montana first flew the United States flag upside down, and then as they began their standing-down ceremony (in lieu of an actual "surrender") they lowered that and raised a Confederate flag.

The Freemen were particularly preoccupied by rather arcane symbolism relating to the meaning of gold fringe attached to the American flag. In his "The Montana Freemen: Patriot Reactions" web page, Ted Daniels recounted some of the articles in a negotiating document drafted by the Freemen that had to do specifically with flags and with what we might call their own "marginal notes":

Others [articles] insist that the flag is "red, white and blue." This stems from the common right-wing belief that flags with a yellow fringe are military and that actions carried out in their presence have the force of admiralty law, not constitutional law. Since the latter is the law of the land, it follows that other laws are the law of the sea. The gold fringe has the arcane power of automatically suspending all constitutional rights.[46]

Beyond the groups designing and raising their own flags, it is important to note the ultimate reactions of the law enforcement agencies to these flags in the final moments when the standoff is coming to its end. The antisystem group's flag is always either replaced or responded to by that of the authorities. Catherine Wessinger reports what happened to the flag of the Branch Davidians: "The fire burned the Branch Davidian flag flying on a flag pole near the building . . . By the time that fire trucks had chilled the building's ashes, a new and victorious banner was flying in its place – someone had raised the flag of the ATF."[47] In fact, the film documentary, *Waco: The Rules of Engagement*, reveals that the ATF flew two flags, one on top of the other. One was red and white with a large star on it. The other, underneath, had the letters "ATF" emblazoned on it. As well, videotapes of the final FBI assault reveal that the tanks themselves had the United States flag mounted on a small flagpole. At the end of the Tupac Amaru standoff, the triumphant soldiers of the Peruvian military who assaulted the Japanese Ambassador's residence were shown on television ripping down the Tupac

Amaru flag and raising the Peruvian flag. In all of these cases, the symbolic point was to erase that spatial divide between outside and inside that the alternative flags marked and made.

Spatial narratives of the home, the compound, the reservation – inside space

Just as outside spaces are symbolically aligned and realigned over the course of the standoff, so too are the inside spaces. Law enforcement personnel, mass media representatives, onlookers, supporters, and occupiers /inhabitants themselves have great curiosity about, and interest in, the layout of the standoff center. Obviously, there are tactical reasons for wanting to know who and what is where inside the sealed-off space of the standoff center. As I noted in the last chapter, the ATF made much of their knowledge of the location of women, children, and men in the Branch Davidian compound at particular times of day, so that they could plan their "dynamic entry" in such a way as to limit harm to the women and children and to know where men with guns might be. Inside spatial alignments also speak to issues of identity and morality, in terms more similar to Charles Taylor's ultimate questions about spatial orientation than to those of the ATF. Further, inside spaces represent, in however fraught a manner, the sphere of the private where secrecy and intimacy are considered to be conditionally legitimate. However, as I sought to demonstrate in my discussion of the set-point theory of key cultural themes, the symbolic and the strategic are cheek to jowl when it comes to decisions about legal interventions in particular cases. If, for example, one discovers that men and women, known to be legally married to each other, are sleeping in sex-segregated quarters, and that the women intermittently sleep in the only single bedroom of the complex, as was the case with David Koresh and the Branch Davidians, the symbolic weight of that discovery can flow into the very legalistic channels that create arrest warrants and seige tactics. In fact, the Treasury Department Report on the Branch Davidian raid refers to the detailed ATF investigation of sleeping quarters and sleeping arrangements at Mt. Carmel. Women and men were not where they "should" have been located.

Gender and familial relations were also revealed by spatial alignments in Randall Weaver's mountain home. As mentioned in the last chapter, a detached shed stood near the main cabin in which Weaver, his wife and children, and his friend Kevin Harris lived, a shed that they called "the birthing house." The adult and teenaged women in the family repaired to this house when menstruating or giving birth. During his Senate Hearings testimony Randall Weaver refers to this "birthing house"and to the children visiting his wife, Rachel, there when she was menstruating. This categorization and separation of the "pure" and the "impure" women is not uncommon in orthodox religions or pre-industrial small-scale societies, but it nevertheless struck investigators as one more thing proving the cultural marginality of the Weaver family (and as one strategic avenue for assorted plans by the US Marshals to kidnap the women while they were separated from Randall Weaver). In the tragic days of the standoff, after the original shoot-out, the body of Weaver's son Sam was placed in this "birthing house."

Hygiene, and its power to signify and construct the opposition between the wild and the civilized, was spatially resonant during the period of time that led up to the first (1978) and the second (1985) MOVE standoffs. With their communal homes in Powelton Village and on Osage Avenue, MOVE members activated a certain civic mystery about the organization and hygienic dispositions of the interior of their yards and houses. As animal-rights activists who included cockroaches in their pantheon of protected species, MOVE members did not infuse their urban row homes with insecticide. With their reconfigured kinship structure (all members, including the founder John Africa, taking the last name of Africa), they had no separate quarters for biological parents and children. Finally, as the windows of their Osage Avenue home had been boarded up with wooden railroad ties, no one could even glimpse the disposition of the internal part of the house. Were there separate rooms for separate functions? How clean was it? John Africa's niece, Sharon Sims Cox, represented MOVE's Powelton Village quarters as having been precisely the opposite of what hygienic-minded accusers and detractors claimed:

MOVE wasn't filthy like people said. There wasn't feces all over. When the kids who didn't have diapers on went to the bathroom, mostly it was outside and we'd dig a hole and cover it like cats do . . . We were the cleanest people in Powelton Village. We constantly cleaned because we had so many dogs and children. We washed windows; we mopped and scrubbed floors every day.[48]

In the case of the standoff in the Japanese Ambassador's residence in Lima, there were several overlays of internal spatial categorization. I've already noted the separation of smokers from nonsmokers, a category based on health and aesthetic needs. As well, after two days of occupation, journalists reported that the hostages had been divided by nationality into different rooms. This move indicted a sensitivity to geopolitics and intimated diverse attitudes of the Tupac Amaru group to different countries. Later, during a visit to the residence by journalists and photographers, there were reports that the most important, highest ranking, most politically charged hostages were kept on the upper floors of the house with the less significant hostages below. This may have suggested a tactical decision to keep the "key" hostages in a position where they could be even further sequestered if the Peruvian forces somehow managed to break into the residence on the ground floor. While not allowed to visit these upstairs rooms and hostages, journalists were able to report that the downstairs rooms looked "disheveled and bare," and that along with the expected furniture stacked against the windows, there were several tables with medications lining the rooms. Obviously, aesthetic distinctions, infirmary-like divisions, and geopolitical distinctions live uneasily together and may have even conflicted in terms of locating any given hostage. But the exquisite sensitivity to a kind of spatialization of worldview and politics reveals the inevitable intertwining of the symbolic and the strategic.

Finally, while not as focalized as a home, compound, or residence, the Native-American reservation can be understood as an internal social space of conditional privacy. At the time of the Wounded Knee standoff in 1973, the literal ownership of the Reservation land was put "in trust" and held by the US government so that it could ostensibly look out for the best interests of the Indian population. Thus, in a way that was somewhat structurally analogous to the ambiguous jurisdiction of the residence of the Japanese Ambassador to Peru, the Pine Ridge Reservation did and did not "belong" to its inhabitants. As we have seen, the ambiguity of property rights (let alone any worldview divergences in conceptualizations of land as property) was woven through the entire pre-standoff and standoff narrative of the tension between the federal government, in the figures of the Bureau of Indian Affairs and the Justice Department on one side, and the Oglala Sioux on the other.

In terms of the internal spaces of the Reservation, one of the most sacred and intimate categorical spatial decisions is that determining where the residents are ultimately buried. Cemeteries are spaces with profound symbolic resonance. In fact, we need only recall that it was the decision to stop and pray at the site of the cemetery created after the 1890 massacre, that halted the pilgrimage to Porcupine and triggered the beginning of the 1973 standoff. As well, over the course of the standoff, several occupiers were wounded or killed. The dead needed to be mourned and buried. After the death of one of them, Frank Clearwater, on April 24, as the occupiers began their four-day period of mourning, they learned that their age-old antagonist, Tribal Chairman Dick Wilson, had refused to allow Clearwater to be buried in the cemetery on the Pine Ridge Reservation land. Independent Oglala Nation representative Crow Dog responded that no negotiations would continue until Clearwater was properly buried. On April 30, a compromise was reached between Wilson and the Justice Department – Clearwater's body would be taken to an adjacent reservation some twenty miles from Wounded Knee, the Rosebud Reservation. The Independent Oglala Nation leaders and the US Government representatives then needed to work out an agreement that would allow the Oglala occupiers to attend the funeral. As recounted by the participants,

The Independent Oglala Nation had understood that [their] "dispossession of arms" before the funeral would involve a "pullback" – with the [government] Armed Personnel Carriers and Federal personnel retreating from their positions, and the Indians giving up their illegal weapons, evacuating their bunkers and "laying down" – but retaining – their legal arms within the village. But [the government's] idea was that the ION would turn all its weaponry over to the Government, and that Federal forces would then enter Wounded Knee and remain there to oversee the "open" funeral.[49]

Thus the symbolic and the (now) strategic spaces of the reservations were alternatively configured, as the gestures of pulling back (expanding the space) and laying down (thus domesticating the space) mapped the meaning of the land. In this way, the spaces of both the living and the dead shifted their symbolic alignment over the course of a standoff.

Prisons and jails: standoff annexes

While the dominant hot-zone of the standoff is the standoff center-perimeter complex, there are often auxiliary spaces that play key roles in the ongoing narrative. In several of the cases examined either civilian or military jails acted in this capacity. The Freemen of Montana, the Republic of Texas group, the MOVE group, and the Tupac Amaru all had members of their groups in jail at the time of their respective standoffs. And in all of these cases, it was that very fact of having jailed members that acted as one of the proximal triggers to the standoff itself. For example, MOVE members had met with Mayor Goode several times over the course of the year preceding the 1985 confrontation precisely with the goal of arranging a new trial, or an overturning of the convictions, of other MOVE members serving long prison sentences for the killing of police officer Ramp in the 1978 conflict. MOVE also as much as admitted that they had inaugurated their bullhorn-on-the-side-of-the-house reign of harassment against their neighbors on Osage Avenue in order to force the authorities to respond to their demands regarding those imprisoned. In the case of the Tupac Amaru group the hundreds of Tupac Amaru members held in Peruvian prisons had announced that they were going on a hunger strike to protest the harsh prison conditions one day before the assault on the Japanese Ambassador's house by their free comrades. Subsequent demands of the occupiers of the house included the release of their imprisoned fellow members. As well, an interim settlement of the standoff involving the Republic of Texas group involved the exchange of the two hostages held by the group for the imprisoned Republic of Texas security chief Bob Scheidt, who had recently been arrested on weapons charges.

There are several ways in which jail cells can be understood as structurally analogous to the standoff center. They are both spaces of moral and physical isolation, both spaces of unreconstructed enmity and alienation from the enforcers of the law. With their severe limitations on movement and their hyperactive regimes of surveillance, standoff centers and jail cells approximate each other structurally. They differ, of course, in the ways in which those in the standoff center attempt to assert an alternative moral and geographical map, and in the ways the inhabitants feel a solidarity with each other. Neither feature is necessarily the case for those inside of prisons, though there have been many recorded instances of politically inspired prisoners in jails in countries like Italy and Ireland proselytizing and engaging in political education/recruitment. Despite these possible similarities and differences, it is theoretically useful to think about the prison cell more generally as a kind of antispace, a space that simultaneously sucks the normal energy out of situations that require action and movement and as a space that can have its own kind of moral energy. One need only think of the hundreds of people who visited John Brown in his federal prison cell as he awaited execution for his role in the standoff at the Harper's Ferry Federal Arsenal, or of the famous letter written from prison by Martin Luther King, Jr., or Antonio Gramsci's "Prison Notebooks," to understand the complex form of moral authority that imprisonment and the place itself provides.

Movement across space

All of the binary oppositions that have thus far been highlighted in this discussion of the spaces of standoffs (inside/outside, enforcer/incorrigible, offense/defense, wild/civilized, and so forth) must be connected or mediated by terms, things, or people who move. The issue of transit becomes salient as we seek to explore what kinds of object move across the literal and metaphorical spatial boundaries of the standoff and in what manner they do so. Thus it is important to gauge the degree of permeability of the standoff space. In the relevant cases here, everything and everyone from journalists, negotiators, hostages, "hostages," rock music, tear gas, tanks, milk, and bullets moved back and forth across the barricades. The analytic frame being developed here encourages a narrative consciousness of messengers and messages coming and going into and out of the space of the standoff. We need to ask what stories are told by the types and frequencies of visitors into the very center of the standoff action/in-action? Are they stories primarily about power, about filial piety, about charity? We can recall the spatial displacements and journeys of the Proppian functions here as heroes, villains, magic helpers, magic objects literally move so that the folktale itself can move. Beyond the spaces of center and perimeter, we also need to ask if there are intermediary and adjacent spaces where meetings and interactions occur and of what these actions consist. The next chapter will focus exclusively on the actions of standoffs. Here, the fundamental role of space in framing and formulating these actions will be the focus.

Social and political events that are enacted across an extended geographical terrain establish a kind of resonant spatial map of meaning, analogous to the historical mapping of genealogies. Here, the movement across space and the various stopping points of action can be intercalibrated to develop a narrative logic of an event's spatial development. Kenneth Foote indicates as much for the American Civil War when he writes: "Nowadays it is possible to point to Harpers Ferry as the prelude to war, Fort Sumter as the war's actual beginning, Appomatox Courthouse as its end, and Washington's Ford Theatre as the tragic coda of the conflict."[50] The implication here is that the war moves in two dimensions simultaneously, time and space, and that the stopping points along the spatiotemporal way congeal into narrative hinges of meaning and action. As well, event-journeys across spaces take on different configurations, both literal and figurative. Literally, they can be linear or circular. Figuratively, they can take the shapes of pilgrimages, exiles, quests, or returns.

The literal shape of the spatial trajectory can be meaningful in and of itself. Partly this has to do with the relation of the trajectory to the natural and/or constructed environment encompassing it. Partly it has to do with the variable notions of beginning, middle, and end points. A line appears to have a more predictable beginning and end than does a circle, though the exact middle of an unfolding line is contingent, and thus fraught. As well, no one knows in advance what, if anything, will occur along the way and whether such structurally significant places as the middle will take on particular importance. Circles present their own form of uncertainty and power. Writing about the politically charged marches of the Argentinian Madres and the antinuclear weapons protesting women at Greenham Common in England, Jennifer Schirmer analytically draws out the meaning of the shapes of the marches:

One interesting aspect of the actions by the Madres and the Greenham Common women is the recurrence of encirclement to counter the grid patterns of government plaza and the military base. Interestingly, rather than marching in a straight line through the plaza up to the steps of the Casa Rosada, as many political party and trade union demonstrations in Buenos Aires have done, the Madres, in twos, arm-in-arm, circle the monument.[51]

The endlessness and organicity of the circle are in direct contrast, then, with the finitude and angularity of the line.

One of the first things one notices in surveying the spatial histories and trajectories of the set of standoffs here is that almost all incorporated some form of journey or pilgrimage. These journeys, based as they are on movement itself, are analytically contrasted with the locked-in paralysis and stasis of the standoff itself. Writing specifically about the phenomenon of the pilgrimage, anthropologist Victor Turner referred to its experiential threshold quality and to the liminality of the pilgrimage situation itself, "an interval between two distinct periods of intensive involvement in structured social existence out of which one opts to do one's devoirs as a pilgrim."[52] Pilgrimages take one out of "normal" time and space.

The journey of the Oglala Sioux comes the closest to constituting a pilgrimage proper; that being a journey having an intent to start from a "home," or "familiar place" (in the terms of the ethnographer and folklorist Arnold Van Gennep) to travel to a far-away unfamiliar place of sacred or otherwise symbolic significance, and to return home in some kind of changed state. For reasons both practical (to find a larger hall to meet together with representatives from the politically activist American Indian Movement, themselves involved in their own "Tour of Broken Treaties" pilgrimage) and symbolic, the disgruntled residents of the Pine Ridge Reservation set forth on a journey that was to take them to a meeting hall in Porcupine and back home again at the meeting's conclusion. Of course, they never arrived, stopping off to pray at the cemetery at Wounded Knee and staking their claim to autonomy there. As noted in the last chapter, the degree to which this modern-day pilgrimage mirrors the 1890 pilgrimage of Chief Big Foot and his group of some 375 Minneconjou Sioux men, women, and children setting out to meet and make peace, in tandem with Chief Red Cloud, between Indians and non-Indians, is impressive. Both events anticipated journeys, meetings, dialogue, and symbolic actions. Both journeys were interrupted: that of 1890 was interrupted by the interception of the group by Major Whitside of the US Army, that of 1973 was interrupted by the decision to stop the pilgrimage at the intermediary site of

Wounded Knee. So one might call both of these events thwarted or transfigured pilgrimages.

Other groups examined here incorporated other kinds of journeys in the periods temporally adjacent to their standoffs. Some journeys took the forms of exile and return narratives. This was certainly true for David Koresh and his particular followers in the years prior to his ascension as the collectively recognized leader of the group. We recall that Koresh (then still named Vernon Howell) was exiled from Mt. Carmel by George Roden in the mid-1980s, that he then moved to Palestine, Texas, and that he returned to Mt. Carmel in the late 1980s, transformed into David Koresh and taking his place as the acknowledged leader. The MOVE group, as well, experienced a form of involuntary exile after their Powelton Village house was razed to the ground following the 1978 standoff with the Philadelphia Police. MOVE then regrouped and found a new house on Osage Avenue in West Philadelphia. Finally, the Freemen of Montana also went through a form of exile-return journey. A member of the group having lost his ranch in a fore-closure some time prior, a large group of Freemen gathered in the Fall of 1995 in the town of Roundup and formed a caravan of six vehicles to drive some 150 miles at night to Jordan in order to reoccupy the controversially named Bliss Ranch/Clark Ranch/Justus Township. As noted, the Freemen claimed a kind of spiritual presence that protected this newly reclaimed and renamed territory.

The force and impact of exile and return/recombination should not be underestimated. Recalling Charles Taylor's comments about the impor-tance of spatial orientation, it is obvious how critical it is for a group to feel that it is where it ought to be. Arriving at a new location after the destruc-tion and/or loss of the old one or returning to a place from which one was forcibly exiled are experiences that are strongly felt and swept along in a kind of moral energy of literal movement.

Finally, there is the structurally voluntary quest. Randall Weaver and family seemed to be on some kind of quest. Some time prior to the standoff, they had moved from their rented house in the more highly populated Naples, Idaho, a house equipped with all of the modern amenities, includ-ing a satellite dish in the back yard, to the much more rustic cabin in Ruby Ridge. Weaver's aim was to leave the corrupting detritus of civilization behind and to find a purer place in the mountains.

All of these journeys could be said to set the stage for the eventual standoffs. Each of the groups examined had experienced a definitive kind of "arrival" at the place where the standoff would occur. None were where they were by accident.

Transit, transgression, and trespass

Regarding the attempt on April 18, 1973, by 35 women and children to walk
   through the government Roadblock 5 to get into Wounded Knee. Transcript of
   radio conversation between government and occupiers:
Red Arrow (government): Be advised there are several people attempting and have
   attempted to sneak into Wounded Knee by flanking RB-5. They will be arrested
   and will be detained. And they violate our perimeter.
Wounded Knee occupiers: Is it your perimeter or ours that they are violating? I
   don't think they are violating yours. Your perimeter is outside. If they are coming
   into our perimeter they are not violating our perimeter. (*Voices from Wounded
   Knee*, pp. 180–181)

Transit

While a certain kind of movement stops once a standoff locks itself and its
participants into place, other kinds of movement are actually made possible
by the erection or identification of standoff spatial features. Without perimeters, there could be no movement across perimeters. Without concepts of
territorial boundaries, there could be no forms of trespass and transgression. As mentioned above, there have been many kinds of things and
persons moving back and forth across the boundaries of the standoff, and
many ways in which they have done so. As well, there have been many
motives underlying the transit. Some messengers have brought food, others
basic supplies, and spiritual sustenance to those in the standoff center (the
Red Cross representative and the priest in Peru are the most singularly
notable examples of these functions). The food messengers don't seem at
first glance to have any impact on the narrative flow of the standoff, appearing as neutral, merely a conduit. However, absolute neutrality affords a
glimpse of an area of partial existential overlap between the two sides. Food,
especially hot meals, speak a language of domesticity and nurturance. Even
if, as in the case of the Tupac Amaru, the food was primarily aimed at the
hostages, the permission of both sides to its sustained delivery could be
viewed as acting as a kind of "open-line" across the barricades. Other food
deliveries may have had mixed motives and messages. The milk delivered to
the Branch Davidian children had small listening devices hidden inside of
their packaging. A distant narrative kin of the poison apple, this apparently
most innocent of foods is inserted in a tactical plan. Koresh himself, we'll
recall, had his own form of transit-based strategy. He agreed to send out two
children for every time that his radio sermon was aired.
   It is also key that spiritual messages, either in the form of a priest or in
the form of a sermon, can make the journey across the standoff lines. The

reference to some absolute deity, and the belief that deities know no human-made boundaries can provide another area of existential overlap, even for groups, like the Tupac Amaru, ideologically disdaining of metaphysical religions.

Beyond these figures of absolute neutrality and absolute transcendence, standoffs provide for the transit of a number of other types of characters as well, revealing a certain permeability of the perimeters and of the standoff centers. In the case of Wounded Knee, Ruby Ridge, Waco, and the Freemen of Montana, sympathetic visitors managed to go in and out of the standoff center in the pre-standoff periods of surveillance and in the early stages of the standoffs themselves. As the *New York Times* reported the situation in Ruby Ridge, "The Federal authorities have kept the cabin under surveillance hoping, they said, to arrest [Weaver] without a confrontation. They did not stop visitors, who regularly brought in food and other supplies."[53] Sometimes the law-enforcement authorities were cognizant of such "breaches" of the perimeter and actively tolerated them. Other times, as in the case of the breach of the FBI perimeter at Waco by two Branch Davidian supporters, the authorities were embarrassed to have been less than vigilant. After these incidents, the perimeter was made more concrete and more dangerous with the addition of razor-sharp concertina wire.

Journalists and photographers from various mass media organs also made transit across the perimeters and into the standoff centers. Journalists visited the Tupac Amaru occupiers and their hostages at several points in the early stages of the Lima standoff, taking pictures and doing interviews. Often, though, the authorities try to keep journalists far away from the standoff "action." This was the case at Wounded Knee:

International attention was focusing on the confrontation. But from the first, Government policy was to keep the press as far away as possible. The Marshals' log for Feb. 28 read, "Do not let newspaper personnel in the Wounded Knee area . . . No TV coverage of the Wounded Knee area, authority [of] Attorney General [Kleindienst] . . . No photos of [US Marshal Service personnel] . . . " Reporters who sought to cover the story had to hike into the village over the hills, while the only "official" source of information was the daily press conference in the Pine Ridge BIA Building.[54]

The ability of these reporters to hike over the hills into the town revealed the inevitable permeability of the perimeters and the influence of the terrain on the transit.

During the Freemen standoff, everyone involved, including the journalists, were doing their best to lie low. Nonetheless, even their fairly distanced outpost was deemed too close by the authorities who were at pains not to declare the situation a standoff. For their part, the Freemen drew a categorical distinction between the press spatial etiquette and that of the law-enforcement agents: "Journalists Wednesday vacated under court order a hill that offered them a good view of a remote ranch ... The Freemen later left a press release at a gate outside the compound, saying members of the press had been 'courteous and maintained a safe distance throughout the entire time of the FBI *trespass* upon the men and women of Justus Township.'[55]

Friends and family members of those in the standoff center also manage to send messages across the lines even when they themselves cannot physically make the journey. However, as the authorities typically control these messages, they are often broadcast with the sole intention of persuading those left inside to surrender. Appeals are made to family loyalty and love. At Waco, the FBI provided broadcasted recorded pleas from family members to the Branch Davidians to give themselves up, as well as messages from those who had already exited Mt. Carmel. These latter contained assurances to their fellow Davidians that they were being treated fairly on the outside. Similarly, officials at Ruby Ridge used bullhorns to play a series of tape-recorded messages from the relatives and friends of Weaver and Harris. With the valence switched and the permission for transit coming from those in control of the standoff center, the hostages of the Tupac Amaru received letters from family members on the outside on a regular basis.

Bullhorns and public address systems generally are interesting channels of communication in these tense situations. If the perimeter is in place and if it is to have any military and symbolic meaning, it cannot be completely permeable. Thus even intimate and sentimental messages of love and hope may have to travel across wide spaces. Indeed, looked at semiotically, there is a distinct discrepancy between the channel and the message here. Bullhorns, with their amplification and publicity, seem a most inappropriate channel for messages that are private and emotional. On the other hand, it makes all the sense in the world that announcements of arrest and search warrants should be made over a public address system, as they were in the cases of MOVE and the Branch Davidians. As much warnings as announcements, these messages were made just prior to some form of military action. For their own part, MOVE members consciously played on the sense of the bullhorn as destroyer of intimacy when they shouted sometimes very personal critiques of politicians and neighbors alike through the bullhorn mounted on the side of their house in the months prior to the 1985 standoff. Analytically, I might suggest that when the channel and the message are radically out of alignment, the situation is better characterized as one of transgression rather than as one of transit.

Along with bearers of transcendent meaning, figures of ultimate neutrality, family members, friends, and sympathizers, there are other categories of messenger. One important one, of course, is the negotiator who transports, codifies, and reconfigures messages (texts) of various kinds back and forth. The work of the negotiator will be a central focus of the next chapter. Another figure in transit is that of the go-between, more a bearer of messages of others than a negotiator *per se*. Go-betweens are a bit like the Helper function of the Proppean folktale analysis. They almost inevitably have something of magic about them, if only for the simple fact that they safely traverse the dangerous territory of the standoff center and perimeters. Their modes of transit tend to be low-tech – they walk in and out or, as in the case of former President Jimmy Carter shuttling between Anwar Sadat and Menachim Begin at Camp David, they ride bikes. As Marc Howard Ross writes of that mild, but potentially problematic, standoff between the two political leaders:

In fact, after the third day of the thirteen-day talks, Begin and Sadat never met face-to-face because of their intense dislike of each other. Carter then moved to a common-script strategy in which he carried a single document, often on his bicycle, to Sadat and Begin and each party, in turn, made suggestions until both were in agreement.[56]

Another "magical" go-between was the Canadian Ambassador to Peru who, along with the Red Cross representative and Father Cipriani, made frequent transit into and out of the Japanese Ambassador's house in Lima. What made him magical was that he had actually begun his life in the standoff as a hostage inside the house. After his release, with his experiences of the two worlds of the standoff – captivity and freedom, inside and outside – he was able to go back into the residence in a transformed categorical state. Traversing this space he embodies a kind of narrative progress in the seeming stasis of the standoff – he was a hostage, he is now a go-between. Even without any direct involvement in codifying protagonist demands or negotiation policy, he signifies the ongoingness of the situation.

Finally, the ubiquitous Bo Gritz made appearances at both Ruby Ridge and "Justus Township." Gritz derived his standoff situational legitimacy for the authorities from his military past in the Green Berets and for those in the standoff centers from his commando-style raids into Vietnam to rescue individuals he claimed were still missing in action from the Vietnam War. Gritz moved in and out of these spaces with ease and seeming invulnerability.

Of course, safe transit across the boundaries is not always granted to go-betweens, even the most apparently benign of them. One might assume that priests and other religious leaders, representatives of the Red Cross and other neutral aid organizations, and medical professionals would unproblematically be allowed to traverse the lines. However, such was only intermittently the case at Wounded Knee, as the negotiator Harlan Frizzell recounts what happened. In an attempt to persuade Tribal Chairman Dick Wilson to allow a new, replacement medical team into Wounded Knee in anticipation of the departure of the first one, Frizzell remarks that, "I motioned him over and I explained to him that this was the relief team for the medical team that would be coming out. Did he have any objection? He said, 'Yes.' I said, 'Mr. Wilson, this is not going to add or detract from the population in Wounded Knee, it's just going to be an exchange.' 'No.' [said Wilson]"[57] At another juncture of the Wounded Knee standoff, on April 17, 1973, sympathizers of the Sioux managed to airlift 2,000 pounds of food into the occupied town, food that would not have been allowed to make legal transit by any other means.

Transgression and trespass

While transit denotes a free and open passage, transgression and trespass signify movement across boundaries that think themselves to be impermeable. Permission is precisely not granted to transgressive forays across codified space, transgressive understood from either of the antagonist's points of view. In standoffs, transgressions take many forms. Certain objects, when hurled across contested space, are by their very nature transgressive. Bullets, tanks, and tear gas are a few of the more obvious interlopers, moving, as they do, in both directions and capable of causing damage and death. Other, perhaps less predictable, things act in a similar, if less immediately destructive, manner. At both Waco and the Japanese Ambassador's residence in Lima, the surrounding authorities blared high decibel recordings of rock music outside of the standoff centers in an effort to psychologically wear the occupier/inhabitants down. Also at Waco, the FBI played recordings of Tibetan chants, Nancy Sinatra, Barry Manilow, screaming rabbits, squawking birds, sirens, crying babies, Christmas music, and bugle calls twenty-four hours a day.[58] The Branch Davidians responded by turning David Koresh's powerful speakers outward with Koresh and his fellow musicians playing their own rock music for several hours. This mixture of popular culture, sounds of nature, and religious music reveals a kind of wild eclecticism at the heart of contemporary American life, where the sounds of modernity can easily be lassoed together to create an astonishing psychological weapon. At a certain point, sound was supplemented by light as bright lights were shone directly into Mt. Carmel in the middle of the night.

Obviously people engage in transgressive movement across boundaries too. As we have seen, the whole question of privacy and property rights is woven into the very existential make-up of the standoff. Randall Weaver, the Freemen, the Branch Davidians, and MOVE all asserted an ultimate right to do what they wanted on their "own" property/territory. In such a world of strict and contested border-mongering it is inevitable that the efforts of law enforcement officials to deliver warrants would run up against claims of sovereignty. As well, as an analysis of the historical background of the debates over the meaning of the Fourth Amendment reveals, the right to be secure in one's home and the actual warrant of the word "search" in search warrants, often butt up against each other. Legal scholar Clark Cunningham details the semantic history of the term "search" vis à vis search warrants, and refers to Patrick Henry's speech warning of the government's power to "go into your cellars and room" at the Virginia convention on the adoption of the federal Constitution. Clark notes the implications of Henry's speech: "The forced entry and subsequent ransacking affected one's home particularly because a house that could be so searched had lost to a degree its sacred character."[59]

On the phone to Sheriff Harwell, David Koresh asserts such a claim in the initial period of the standoff after the AFT raid. He says: "Well you can tell these agents that as an American citizen, somebody has stepped on my property and there's going to be some butt whupped over this . . ."[60] With people dead and wounded on both sides, it might strike one as odd that an assertion of the American rights to private property should be the grounds of Koresh's protest here. Yet the sanctity and inviolability of the home is precisely at the core of American self-identity. As Edward Gaffney notes, writing about the core constitutional issues at stake in the Waco conflict, this case involved a transgression of overlapping constitutional themes, privacy and religious freedom: "This [residual] grief [over the Branch Davidian tragedy] stems in part from the failure of the government to pay enough attention to the reasons why the sanctities of the private home and of the religious community require the government to be careful when they contemplate entering either, especially with such destructive force as they did at Mt. Carmel."[61] Randy Weaver was another standoff protagonist who continued to assert his "sanctity of the home" prerogatives. For Weaver and for his friends and followers, the whole tragedy of the shootings outside his home would not have occurred if the US Marshals had not "trespassed" on his property in the first place. On the other hand, Weaver later asserted during the Senate Hearings that he would have been more than amenable to receiving an arrest warrant were it to have been hand-delivered to him in the preceding months. ATF Special Agent Herb Byerly was asked specifically about such an alternative decision, a question that aims at its target in a manner that evokes Bernstein's notion of "sideshadowing." Senator Abraham asks Byerly the following question: ". . . Was any thought given at all to simply going to Mr. Weaver's home and simply attempting to arrest him with a warrant at the door?" Byerly answers: ". . . We realized that this residence was up on the top of a mountain, one way in, one way out. There was really no way to get enough support people up there. Considering the number of kids, considering the isolation, knowing that he did leave the residence, that he did go into town . . ."[62] Thus the ATF, clearly believing that the Weaver house constituted what we are calling an "offensive structure," made the decision not to engage in transit. Whether one chooses to believe Mr. Weaver or not when he claims that such peacefully delivered messages or their messengers would not have been greeted in an offensive manner, the phenomenological difference between trespass and transit is clearly key.

Other apparently thwarted transit/transgressions had similar tragic consequences. Accusations were made in both the standoff at Waco and the MOVE standoff in Philadelphia that in the final fiery moments, when the standoff centers were engulfed in flames, that occupants of these structures attempted to exit, only to find their ways blocked by gunfire and/or detritus-swamped doors. As well, on the thirty-seventh day of the standoff in Lima, CNN reported that, "an open archway at one corner of the compound was barricaded in an apparent attempt to keep it from being used as an escape route. As police armed with automatic rifles crouched in position cover, workers using wooden planks boarded up the archway entrance."[63]

The door

". . . life flows out of the door from the limitation of isolated separate existence into the limitlessness of all possible directions."[64]

Doors are especially charged spaces of standoffs. Many things happen in and around doorways: conversations, exchanges of participants and hostages, entrances and exits of negotiators, exchanges of supplies, deliveries of documents, exchanges of gunfire, and so forth. Clearly, whatever flow is possible in this situation of paralysis will occur through and around doors, windows, and other openings. Many things might have happened in doorways that didn't; David Koresh, Randy Weaver, and MOVE members alike expressed regret that authorities hadn't simply "come to the door to deliver the warrant." Even if the regret is sincere, it is certainly impossible to know in any of the given cases what might have happened if the authorities had gone that normal route in approaching the respective dwellings.

One of the most vexed and preoccupying refrains in the examination of various witnesses at the "Federal Raid on Ruby Ridge" Senatorial Hearings, was that of the disposition of the door of the Weaver cabin on the day that Kevin Harris was wounded while on his way back into the cabin door and, simultaneously, Vicky Weaver was shot to death as she stood inside that doorway holding a baby in her arms. Randall Weaver, Kevin Harris, Weaver's daughter Sara, and various sniper/observers of the FBI who took part in the raid were all questioned extensively about the visibility, positioning, and occupancy of the doorway and the area of the cabin porch around it.

Much of the questioning and testimony revolved around the line of vision of the actual FBI shooter, Lon Horiuchi, at the moment he shot Kevin Harris and Vicky Weaver. With a mock-up of the cabin porch, door, and window in the Senate Hearing room, questions also involved characterizing the way that the front door opened, whether it was opened all the way, who was on the porch, who running into the house, when the door was opened, who was holding the door open, and so forth.

The actual shooter, under possible indictment at that point for the death of Vicky Weaver, did not testify at the Senate Hearings. However, the Senators did have a transcript of testimony that Horiuchi had given regarding the event. What Horiuchi claimed was the following:

When I fired the shot, I knew the cabin door was standing open, but I believed even though the subject at whom I fired was on the porch at the door, that my shot would not impact the cabin itself. As the shot impacted, I believe that I saw the male subject at whom I fired flinch, and I believe that I had hit him low, around the hip area.[65]

Here it is the very cabin itself that takes on the life of a potential subject or target of a gunshot. As well, that ultra-bureaucratic word, "impacted," employed with the passive tense, muffles the sense of a shot or a hit that can actually kill someone.

For one of the other sniper/observers of the FBI who was on the scene with Horiuchi, the door, and the very day itself, seems to take on an even more animate and mysterious existence as he struggles to claim both that the door was obscure and the day was raining and cloudy, but that Horiuchi had a clear line of vision anyway. His description begins after Senator Craig sets up his answer with the following:

Senator Craig: That shot has now been fired. Apparently by that time people are now running back to the cabin . . . you stood before the chairman and looked at the door, and you were discussing the door itself, referring to it being very dark; you couldn't tell if there was a window in it. You used the words, I believe, "very dark." Is that not correct?

Mr. Monroe: That is correct . . .

Senator Craig: Mr. Horiuchi testifies that the visibility is good and that it is good enough for him to take a shot.

Mr. Monroe: I don't refute that testimony, Senator, because he did take the shot before the individual went behind a door, a solid door. The individual was still in the open and was just stepping onto the porch . . . It was – there was no sun. It was overcast and raining intermittently, and it was extremely dark . . .[66]

In the end, Monroe ends up in the clutches of a tautology – our training is such that we only take shots when visibility is good, Horiuchi took his shot, thus visibility was good – in order to explain his way out of the dark day and the darker door.

How different is Sara Weaver's description of her mother's position behind the curtained window of the cabin as the others tried to run back in out of range of the FBI snipers. Sara's very reference to curtains brings domesticity into jarring contact with the bellicose:

Senator Specter: How long would you say your mother was standing there in that position in the door?

Ms. Weaver: The whole time it took us to run from that shed to the house . . .

Senator Specter: And do you think she was visible through the glass at the time?

Ms. Weaver: I do believe she was . . . Because I remember the curtains. I remember having to close them. I remember, we gotta get the curtains in the house closed, all the curtains in the house . . . because the night before, we hadn't been worried about anyone looking in our house or trying to take shots at us. We were just all in such shock.[67]

4

The action of standoffs

10:20 – An informant of established reliability in a position to know, advises that he was informed by American Indian Movement leadership that there would be a meeting at Calico at 15:30 this date and that *this is where the action will be.*

> (From a US Marshal's log, February 23, 1973, quoted in *Voices*, p. 29, italics mine)

We arrive, finally, at the action of the standoff. But in announcing that "finally" I do not necessarily mean to privilege action over temporal and spatial coordinates. It is just that action seems to be where "the action is." Of course, action is infamously difficult to account for or even to describe. Scholars seek to do it by drawing such distinctions as that between structure and agency or by tracking transformations in things as they take shape and develop in the context of cause/effect and means/ends chains. When one attempts action's actual description, though, time and space immediately move once again onto center stage. No action can be described without them. The simplest physical movement can only occur in ways that are both enabled and constrained by time and space. Such epistemological conundrums return us to the problem articulated in the first chapter of this book: how is it possible to track or trace the present, that time during which action is emerging and has not yet taken definitive (i.e. retrospective) shape? Perhaps the most precise way of articulating this emergence, where spatial and temporal parameters have not yet congealed, is to describe it as the point at which the subjunctive mood hands a bit of reality over to the present.

And just to add to the epistemological challenges, we must further grapple with the paradox of charting the action of a situation that emphatically declares its own paralysis. A standoff makes the existential claim that it can actually halt action in its tracks. While the standoff continues, action is precisely that which should *not* occur. Nevertheless, a series of action chains secrete themselves into the interstices, literal and figurative, of the times and spaces of the standoff. Things happen at night and during the day, at the perimeter and in the standoff center. People and things move across the boundaries and barricades. Certainly the concept of effort, the hinge element of Alexander's discussion of action in his "Action and its Environments" essay, must play an enormous role here, greater than is normally the case in social life. The effort taken to act during a standoff involves not just the necessary carrying out of typifications and strategizations, but requires a constant recognition that any action launches itself directly in the face of the situation-defining stasis of mutual threat and the hovering spectre of violence.

As noted above, social scientists have been trained to think about action in terms of structure and agency, cause and effect, or means and ends. Because the goal here is to theorize the very contingency of action, I want to focus on an alternative conceptualization that has been emerging over the course of the book. This approach draws upon a variety of literarily, dramaturgically, and semiotically derived tropes and concepts suggested by the respective acts. These are the classic tropes of metaphor, metonymy, and synecdoche. And, as Hayden White put it so clearly in his now-classic study of the narrative styles of historical writing, they are "paradigms, provided by language itself, of the operations by which consciousness can prefigure areas of experience that are cognitively problematic in order subsequently to submit them to analysis and explanation . . . Metaphor sanctions the prefiguration of the world of experience in object–object terms, Metonymy in part–part terms, and Synecdoche in object–whole terms."[1]

Thus metaphor is a term describing the process of analogizing, of identifying things and individuals in the world according to their similarities and differences to other things. Metaphoric action takes particular configurations of participants and events as similar to others that have already occurred. We have seen examples of such metaphoric action in the chapter on the temporal parameters of the standoff, when current standoffs were analytically linked to others that had taken place in the past. Metonymy entails substitution of one thing for another, either things that follow each other in time or in space, or things that are read as causes of other things and that are linked together in this causal manner. Readers of literary narratives and observers of social narratives often read contiguity as causality. Social life doesn't admit of a kind of laboratory experimentation with controls and variables. So indeed we are often left with a kind of Humean ultimate understanding of cause/effect relations that perceives a kind of magical transmission of energy from an initial thing to its neighbor in time and in space. Indeed, it is useful to think with the notion of metonymy when figuring the symbolic role and narrative placement of all of the literal neighbors of the various standoff protagonists. So we will pay particular attention to neighbors below. With synecdochy, one part of something is taken to characterize the whole. Thus when certain authorities focused on a vision of David Koresh as paradigmatically a creature of hypersexuality, they set the stage for such synecdochic situational navigation.

For purposes of this study which, unlike White's, aims to track the contours of ongoing situations as opposed to the stylistically tendentious histories written by historians, these tropes help us get a handle on the pulsating relations between process and crystallization, the ongoingness of the event and the stopping points along the way. For action is forever starting and stopping. Another useful literary distinction, in the context of this attempt to intercalibrate the Structuralist and the Pragmatist projects of analysis, is that between *stories* and *chronicles*. Writing about the difference between these two terms for narrative structure, White writes that, "stories trace the sequences of events that lead from inaugurations to (provisional) terminations of social and cultural processes . . . Chronicles are, strictly speaking, open-ended. In principle they have no inaugurations . . . and they have no culminations or resolutions; they can go on indefinitely."[2] I think we need to think of standoffs as both stories and as chronicles. They have emplotted temporal and spatial boundaries that consist of crystallized and congealed movements (placements and displacements). But, while they are in progress, they are adamantly open-ended, leading, it sometimes seems, nowhere at all. Stories are what we know of and say about situations retrospectively. Chronicles are how we recount them to ourselves while we are still in them.

Finally, I will continue to draw upon the dramaturgy of Kenneth Burke and the semiotic program for human action of A.J. Greimas in order to assess the characterizations of standoff scenes and the actions that take place in and around them.

Configuring action narratives

What then concretely comprises action in and of the standoff? A first approximation of broad categories might divide standoff action into linguistic acts and extralinguistic acts. Linguistic acts include messages that are spoken as well as those that are written. And meta-level interpretive linguistic acts are constantly being generated and fed back into the situation to move it along. Take, for example, the persistent presence of comments that aim to characterize the situations themselves. When individuals on either side of the standoff divide communicate with each other, it is meaningful to find out how such communication is labeled. It might be termed conversation, ultimatum/response, discussion, or negotiation, with different ramifications for how seriously such communication is to be taken and what actions subsequently follow.

Not only speech, but written texts play an enormous role in the forging of the standoff narratives of action. We've already begun to explore the role of warrants in standoffs. But texts of all types are hauled out, referred to, interpreted, and deployed. I will want to differentiate between two analytically distinct types of texts which I will term "ur-texts" and "texts-in-action." Ur-texts are foundational documents that establish world views and principles. Participants almost always frame and justify their actions in terms of deep values embedded in chosen ur-texts, such as the Bible, the Magna Carta, the US Constitution, John Africa's "Guidelines," the Tupac Amaru's Manifesto, and so forth. Necessarily partial and overtly interpretive readings of these texts participate in the generation of texts-in-action of which arrest warrants, negotiating decisions, and plans for assault are some examples. Texts-in-action strategically enable and constrain the action of the standoff. I will discuss these various texts at length in a later section of this chapter.

Extralinguistic action runs the gamut from physical gesture (hand shakes, bodies in motion, guns lowered and raised, hand signals, hostage and "hostage" releases, flag wavings), to the deployment of equipment, large and small (tanks, cameras, robots, fire engines), to outright violence. This chapter will pick up the issue of transit again, first introduced in the preceding chapter on space. It will do so in order to track the meaningful physical movement through and across the spaces of the standoff as bodies, natural objects, and artifacts of culture interact.

All situations are constantly asking the question "What am I?" Some begin with a very well delineated sense of self: "I am a criminal trial," "I am a wedding," "I am a telephone conversation between friends." And we can be confident that most such situations sustain their existential commitments to such identities as they proceed through time to their conclusions. Other situations have a more ambiguous self-identity. One might imagine a sidewalk encounter between two people who know each other. The situation might evolve into a conversation consisting of small talk. It might become an argument. It might become a legal consultation. As long as the two people didn't actually plan to encounter each other in a specified way and at a specified time for a specified purpose beforehand, the situation's sense of self is necessarily more amorphous and contingent. But even those events that seem the most clearly bounded by predetermined roles and tasks constantly threaten to evolve or devolve into something else, or to become several things simultaneously. A wedding can become a hostile family encounter. A criminal trial can turn into a shouting match and a brawl. This perspective on situations and their identities recapitulates the sense behind my earlier statement that all situations work to ward off their transformation into standoffs because virtually all parties to virtually all situations want to eventually exit the situation intact. And standoffs cut off the escape routes.

What actually makes a situation what it continuously is? Clearly the identities of the various participants play a major role. In the case of standoff identities, we need to ask how any given participant comes to be characterized. Is their orientation to the situation primarily one of neighbor, hostage, antagonist, religious figure, military personnel, mediator, and so forth? How convincing, effective, and sustained is any particular role? As well, modalities of operation must be established in order fully to understand what a situation is. Are there standard operating procedures with which participants are familiar for moving through certain situations? In a wedding, codified religious rituals, documented legal formats, and familiar cultural customs of celebration constitute the standard operating procedural framework within which the wedding creates itself. However, it is also the case that situations may want to expand beyond the formulaic moves of standard procedures. A couple may want to be married in an orchard rather than in a religiously consecrated building. They may want to write their own vows. Thus, within the constraints of the absolutely bedrock necessary standards, improvisation stamps situations with their own idiosyncratic character. If all situations can be said to consist of some ratio of standard operating procedures and some ratio of improvisational moves, the important thing is to distinguish the two from each other and to analyze the meaning of the proportion and quality of the improvisational actions.[3]

There are obviously standard operating procedures implemented by the representatives of law and law enforcement in standoffs. Texts, identities, and extralinguistic acts are all co-active in the carrying out of these procedures. Institutions have rules and preset plans for dealing with "these kind" of situations. Such plans encompass rules about negotiation tactics, the use of deadly force, the evacuation of surrounding areas, the treatment of hostages. We will look closely at some of the many plans that were brought to bear on the standoffs under investigation here. But we will also look at the gaps, slippages, and ultimate limitations in these plans that belie the smooth application of them to the emerging, contingent situations. Sometimes, the gaps are downright grammatical, with tense formations coming and going. Sometimes, as when the standoffs end in fiery conflagration, we are bearing witness to the paroxysm of a plan imploding on itself.

Improvisation, as an alternative to the strict application of standard operating procedures, will be explored in the next chapter. The degree to which improvisation is warded off or, alternatively, embraced in the standoffs indicates much about exactly how comfortable any given participant is with the highly contingent nature of the situation, and the degree to which they want to work with that contingency. The introduction of improvisation also meaningfully encourages thinking about the aesthetic dimensions of standoffs and standoff action. Here ideas about harmonic variations and transformations provide a useful and innovative vocabulary for action.

Setting off the standoff

In Chapter 1, I identified several culturally specific themes that resonate strongly with law enforcement and political officials when decisions are made about official intervention into the lives of individuals and groups. The transgression of the assessed setpoints of the "normal" for each of these themes constituted a provocation for official attention. In Chapters 2 and 3 we saw how standoffs get temporally and spatially marked off from their nonstandoff backgrounds. Proximal triggers include arrest warrants that are codified and delivered, with all the attendant plans for dynamic entries, spaces of operation that are reconfigured, flags that are raised. Thus the standoff takes its shape. Additionally, neighbors complain to authorities that they are fed up with the relevant group and that they will soon be taking things "into their own hands." Finally, first shots are fired. These series of typical actions generally culminate in the actual naming of the situation as a standoff.[4]

The above pattern generally holds true for most of the cases under examination here. To some extent, Wounded Knee, the Republic of Texas, and the Tupac Amaru cases diverge from this model. In those cases, an active decision to precipitously and forcibly occupy a particular place activated the standoffs. Nevertheless, we might view the other four standoffs as emerging at the end of a gradual and successively more and more forcible occupation of a place. Convinced, as they were, of government hostility toward their ideas and actions, these groups reacted by fortifying their chosen domiciles. For all of the antisystem groups in the standoffs analyzed, however, there is an essential existential feeling of being trapped. The diverse initial moves reveal that this feeling can occur in the context of either a defensive or an offensive posture, either "at home" or "abroad."

Inevitably, a warrant to search a place or to arrest an individual is drawn up and served (or attempted to be served). I've considered earlier the issue of the timing (ripeness or staleness) of warrants. Here, I want to look at the way that spatial coordinates combine with the temporal ones to give shape and reason to the standoff-initiating act of serving the warrant.

Criminological studies of the process of the decision to arrest or not to arrest an alleged malefactor, reveals the lineaments of such contingent moves. As one study puts it,

The police officer at the street level is the first judge and jury for a potential arrestee. An individual may be ignored, merely warned, taken to the station for a "talk," or arrested. The officer's decision is not made in a vacuum, but rather depends upon a variety of factors including the availability of witnesses, the existence and credibility of a complaining party, the attitude of the suspect, the egregiousness of the offense, and the location.[5]

It is easy to read these criteria through the grid of the standoff model here being constructed. The very ability to locate a given individual who has met the criterion of falling off the map of the normal *vis-à-vis* identified cultural themes can indeed tip the balance in deciding who to arrest. Trying to get a handle on why Randall Weaver had been so specifically and disproportionately targeted for arrest, Senator Grassely asked Michael Johnson, former US Marshal of the District of Idaho, the following question: "If there were some [other outstanding arrest warrants for other people in Idaho], were they acted on, and why did Weaver seem so much more important?" This question elicited the following dialogue:

Mr. Johnson: It wasn't the importance of Weaver as much as we knew where he was at all times, Senator.
Senator Grassley: And you're saying you didn't know where the othere were, maybe?
Mr. Johnson: One of the jobs of the US Marshals Service is to apprehend fugitives and people where felony warrants, misdemeanor warrants are on those individuals, and you know, at all times, we are always tracing down leads to find those individuals. Mr. Weaver's circumstance was unique for the fact that we knew exactly where he was.[6]

A similar sense of perplexity has motivated the broad discussions of the decision to serve arrest and search warrants on the Branch Davidians. If one were to adopt a straightforward approach to analyzing the priorities of law-enforcement organizations such as the Bureau of Alcohol, Tobacco, and Firearms, one would be hard pressed to explain the attention paid to the Branch Davidians. As Edward Gaffney has written:

the Government Accounting Office has prepared a comprehensive analysis of the priorities that BATF has established for recommending cases for federal prosecution (Firearms and Explosives 1993). Koresh and his followers actually fell pretty low on this list of the BATF's priorities, for no narcotics were involved, Koresh was not a career or violent criminal, and he was not using the firearms for other federal offenses such as bank robbery or acts of organized crime or terrorism.[7]

Only an analysis, such as the one being developed here, that is precisely concerned with moments of excess (and its opposite, neglect) can make sense of such decisions. Clearly, the assessment by these agencies of the Branch Davidians, and especially of David Koresh, prominently featured their reading of the group's transgression of a number of culturally charged taboos. In the chapter of the *Report of the Department of the Treasury on the BATF Investigation of Vernon Wayne Howell, also known as David Koresh*, entitled, "The Decisionmaking Process Leading to Forceful Execution of Warrants," a sustained preoccupation with characterizing who they were dealing with took the place of what might have been the more likely cataloguing and matching of Davidian offenses with ATF priorities. And thus the organizational priorities for recommending cases for federal prosecution were effectively overridden by a stronger cultural thematic.

As the standoff is precipitated out of the chaos of the actions associated with the attempts to serve warrants, first shots inevitably are fired. First shots are always diacritically marked and become the subject of much subsequent debate. Catherine Wessinger reports that,

According to Davidian testimony, the first shots fired in the ATF raid came from the helicopters. However, another possibility was that the first shots were fired to kill five dogs (pets) – by ATF agents arriving in cattle cars at the front door. ATF agents in this team testified that when they first heard shots, they assumed these were being fired by the agents assigned to take out the dogs.[8]

Frequently, the ultimate reports issued about the standoffs include lines to the effect that no one can say with certainty who fired the first shot. Indeed, this is the case with the Ruby Ridge standoff, as described in the US Department of Justice Report of the Ruby Ridge Task Force:

With regard to the responsibility for the deaths that occurred at the Y, the marshals assert that Harris initiated the fire fight when he shot Deputy Marshal Degan while Weaver and Harris claim that the marshals fired the first shots. After a thorough review of all of the evidence made available to us, we have been unable to determine conclusively who fired the first shot during the exchange of gunfire.[9]

Even with the usual lasting uncertainty about who did fire the first shot, the focused attention to the question reveals a desire to blame someone for the standoff by way of locating a very specific initiating act. The first shot is, then, put into high relief as both signifying the responsible party and as constituting the proximally causal agent setting off the standoff.

Neighbors who express annoyance with groups and their lifestyle and who threaten to become vigilantes themselves play a role in several of the standoffs. Their spatial contiguity to the standoff protagonists give them a kind of metonymically inflected appearance of causal power. Their very sympathies move back and forth across the terrains of solidarity motives, fealty to the law, privacy needs, and territorial prerogatives. As well, cultures often place great import on the moral policing power of neighbors as residents characterize each other along a continuum of similarity and difference. Jeffrey Alexander has laid out the various options here as cultural members differentiate among those others who are: 1) Somewhat like us, 2) Very much like us, 3) Not like us, and 4) Too much like us.[10] By gauging the moral valences of behaviors that are public and semiprivate (as behaviors in neighborhoods often are), neighbors determine appropriate degrees of acceptance, tolerance, ostracism, and rejection of each other. Such processes of evaluation are exacerbated when the neighborhood itself has been chosen for highly specified purposes (such as those detailed in the previous chapter on standoff space). And they are clearly placed on alert during standoffs themselves. Sympathies and even strong identifications with certain others can shift dramatically as a consequence of specific boundary-transgressing actions. As reported in the *Detroit News*: "[Pat] Mournion [a bankrupt wheat farmer] said he stopped short of joining the Freemen because the group violated a basic tenet of the cowboy code: 'They screwed their neighbors. Hell, some of them even passed bad checks on their own family members.'"[11]

Authorities sometimes refer to extant neighbor problems as goads to their own action and to neighbors as victims. These authorities have also sometimes been negligent about actually doing anything concretely to restore neighbors' "domestic tranquillity." In their focus on the standoff protagonists, they bring in heavy equipment and vehicles, they evacuate people from their houses for long periods of time, they make noise (sometimes of the same type that the standoff protagonists themselves have made and of which the neighbors have complained), and they have also been known to allow neighborhoods to burn down. Neighbors are thus often in the peripheral vision of the authorities as they inevitably get assigned the role of supporting character.

On the other hand, vigilante neighbors are frequently cited as proximal causes for law enforcement action. Neighbors of MOVE on Osage Avenue went through literally years of feeling harassed by MOVE members and by the MOVE house itself. They had attempted on-the-block talks with MOVE members, had written to various politicians, had even contacted the media. The May 1985 confrontation snapped into place very soon after the neighbors sent a final notice to local political figures, threatening to do something themselves. Some of Randall Weaver's neighbors in Ruby Ridge also had complained to authorities that the Weavers had been engaging in harassment. Former Director of the US Marshals, Henry Hudson, testified at the Senate Hearings about this neighbor dynamic:

There was another factor here. Toward the early part of August 1992, we began receiving phone calls from the neighbors, the Raus, who suspected that the Weavers may be stealing some of their property, may be harassing them. They continually called and said that if the marshals do not come out there and do something about it, that they were going to take it into their own hands and do something with Mr. Weaver.[12]

Some neighbors of the Freemen of Montana threatened to cut the group's telephone lines and close the road to the Clark farm near the end of 1995. And, of course, the Republic of Texas group went so far as to kidnap their surely frustrated neighbors, the Rowes.

The action of the antisystem groups vis à vis their neighbors, along with the obsessive search of the authorities to determine who fired the first shot, both point to the critical issue of whether a given action is represented as being offensive or defensive. We saw how such antitheses play themselves out spatially in the last chapter, as houses/compounds get characterized as either defensive and ready for an attack or offensive and assaultive in nature. The issue looms large again here in the consideration of action. In the chain of events that lead to and through the standoff, participants are constantly claiming one or another of these stances for themselves and for their antagonists. Ultimately, these determinations of self and other offensive or defensive stances and actions, along with kindred determinations of being in control or out of control, are used for justificatory purposes. Such determinations are particularly salient in situations where lives and property are at stake. Thus are all of the actions of the authorities and the anti-authority groups interpreted through the normatively inflected perceptual and cognitive grids.

Charles Goodwin makes this point both theoretically and empirically in his study of the organizational strategies for representing the beating by police officers of Rodney King. The beating of this African-American motorist who had been stopped by Los Angeles police officers led to two consecutive trials of the officers themselves, the first of which came out with a verdict that precipitated the Los Angeles riots of 1992. Goodwin develops a careful analysis of the courtroom presentation of the video tape taken by a bystander of that beating. The defense attorneys attempted (in the first trial successfully so) to prove that Rodney King was actually continuously aggressive and in an offensive posture for the duration of his beating by the several police officers. As Goodwin writes:

To rebut the vision proposed by the prosecutor, Sgt. Duke uses the semantic resources provided by language to code as aggressive extremely subtle body movements of a man lying face down beneath the officers. Note for example not only his explicit placement of King at the very edge, the beginning of the aggressive spectrum, but also how very small movements are made much larger by situating them within a prospective horizon through repeated use of "starting to". The events visible on the tape are enhanced and amplified by the language used to describe them.[13]

Thus it was that, in the face of common sense, a videotaped rendering of a single man lying on the ground being beaten by several other men standing up could be interpreted as the deployment of necessary force against a persistently attacking predator. Note here a less egregious but nonetheless analogous reasoning at play in the characterization of the sending of FBI agents to Ruby Ridge as a defensive act. Larry Potts, former Assistant Director of the FBI, told Senate committee members that, "I participated in the decision to send the Hostage Rescue Team to Ruby Ridge. I can tell you categorically that the HRT was sent on a defensive mission. In brief, the HRT's mission was to contain the situation so that they, along with other elements of the FBI, could bring it to a peaceful resolution."[14]

There is almost something oxymoronic about being sent on a defensive mission. Defenders stand their ground, they do not journey to new ground to seek out aggressors. Because common sense is so undercut by these alternative readings of defense, there must be a powerful epistemological force at work (the jury in the first Rodney King trial was convinced). Goodwin finds that epistemological base in the concept of "coding schemes," world-shaping schemes that act as grids through which discrete events are read. Further, and importantly for this study, such schemes have organizational roots: "In so far as the coding scheme establishes an orientation toward the world, it constitutes a structure of intentionality whose proper locus is not the isolated Cartesian mind, but a much larger organizational system, one that is characteristically mediated through mundane bureaucratic documents such as forms."[15]

As suggested above, standard operating procedures, both formal and codified and informal and assumed, get activated as soon as situations take even minimal shape. Goodwin's coding schemes draw our attention to the impact of such frames on our very perceptions. The world is simply unknowable without them.

Standard operating procedures

As regards the dramatistic tautology in general, an act is done by an agent in a scene
. . . The scene is motivational locus of the act insofar as the act represents a scene–act ratio (as, for instance, when an 'emergency situation' is said to justify an 'emergency measure').   (Kenneth Burke, "Terms for Order," p. 287)

The area is now a crime scene.
  (Jeff Jamar, Special Agent, FBI at a news conference to announce the transfer of
      authority from the ATF to the FBI in the Branch Davidian standoff)

The present of regularity or habit is but a weakened case of the present of the rule, the norm, the law, persistence, invariability, perenniality, fatality, necessity, eternity, and unconditional existence.   (Ferdinand Gonseth, *Time and Method*, p. 117)

Organizations confronting unknown and volatile situations and individuals have a particular reflex action to turn to their standard operating procedures. In a sense, these procedures are the only familiar elements at play in an emergent and still inchoate situation. Standoffs are often born when some group has transgressed the boundaries of the acceptable and the known. Their marginality is a necessary given of the situation.

Obviously, there is a certain irony in applying standards to the marginal and the unusual. What's implied is an immediate normalization of this errant reality. Standard operating procedures implies a match between event, participants, categories, and moves. Such matching action brings literary theorist and social commentator Kenneth Burke's Pentad to mind. Kenneth Burke thought about all situations in terms of the relations among the following five terms: act, scene, agent, agency, and purpose. Absent a utopian moment out of time itself, Burke proposed that there was inevitably going to be some friction among the terms, as reality never precisely coordinates in all of its aspects. This is what gives situations their energy and their impetus to change and develop. For our purposes, the attempts to impose and implement standard operating procedures in an errant situation inevitably calls forth some readjustment of the terms themselves and of the procedures of implementation. The resistant reality recognized by Pragmatists and other social theorists continuously eludes schematic representation and intervention. Some analysts, such as Cornelius Castoriadis and Hans Joas, have stressed the creativity necessary to take on this resistant reality. Others, such as Jeffrey Alexander and Roger Friedland and Robert Alford, have stressed the normative dimensions of this effort. Creativity and normativity constitute a kind of motivated action (however consciously identified as such). As motives, they are combined with a kind of habituated social "instinct" that is another way of understanding acts of typification. Friedland and Alford acknowledge that the process of matching rules to contexts is one consisting of a mixture of motives:

Ethnomethodological studies of microinteractions in both interpersonal and organizational settings have shown that people are highly sensitive to context in rule use. Under some conditions, they are artful in the mobilization of different institutional logics to serve their purposes. Sometimes rules and symbols are internalized and result in almost universal conformity, but sometimes they are resources manipulated by individuals, groups, and organizations.[16]

The point here is to highlight the mechanisms by which such bridging actions connecting rules, symbols, and contexts (or scenes) are accomplished and to articulate the mix of creativity and normativity that, mediated as they so frequently are by complex institutions of authority and control, figure in the process.

In the standoffs examined here, institutions of bureaucracy, law, and law enforcement are intimately involved in defining and managing the situations. These institutions come replete with their arsenals of rules, structures, roles, and plans. The degree to which such game-plans are considered essential is revealed when a former advisor to the United States Ambassador to Japan states that, "the Japanese response to previous terrorist attacks has been 'to be frightened and run around like chickens with their heads cut off because they don't have any policy, and in the end, they cave in and do whatever the terrorists want.'"[17] Most organizations of social control thus live on the terra firma of standard policies and standard operating procedures.

Organizational imperatives

"The institution is a socially sanctioned, symbolic network in which a functional component and an imaginary component are combined in variable proportions and relations. Alienation occurs when the imaginary moment in the institution becomes autonomous and predominates, which leads to the institution becoming autonomous and predominating with respect to society." (Cornelius Castoriadis, *The Imaginary Institution of Society*, p. 132.)

In a key sense, standard operating procedures are the calling cards of organizations. We recognize the stamp of particular organizations in them, whether they consist in the deployment of armed troops and weapons, or the deployment of forms (such as those of the internal revenue service with its various "schedules"). Thus these recognizable procedures become synonymous with the organization and the organization becomes literally unthinkable without them. What begins as specific choices, imagined up out of a universe of possible items and combinations, becomes naturalized in ways that come to be termed "rational." Organizational domains and issues are expressed as solvable problems of means and ends. Recent studies of institutions have focused on their self-understanding as "rational" structures, and have simultaneously critically analyzed that very rationality. As Meyer and Rowan write:

modern societies are filled with rationalized bureaucracies for two reasons. First, as the prevailing theories have asserted, relational networks become increasingly complex as societies modernize. Second, modern societies are filled with institutional rules that function as myths depicting various formal structures as rational means to the attainment of desirable ends . . . Once institutionalized, rationality becomes a myth with explosive organizing potential . . .[18]

It is often the case that only societal crises or situations that command comparative analyses allow the clients and publics of these organizations to see the arbitrariness of the rules, roles and procedures by which they live. In his book, *The Taming of Chance*, Ian Hacking performs a simple, yet revealing, act of comparison when he notes the existentially key differences among juries in different countries and different legal systems. He asks,

How many choices are open to the jury? In the English system of criminal trials, there are two choices, guilty and not guilty. In the Scottish there are three, namely guilty, not guilty, and not proven. Secondly, what shall be the size of the jury? A traditional English jury is twelve in number. The Scots have fifteen jurors. Thirdly, by what majority shall the jury decide? The English jury had to reach a unanimous decision (today a majority of ten suffices).[19]

Such differences will matter a great deal in cases where ambiguity plays any significant role. Opening up the categorical options puts all standard operating procedures in a new light.

In a crisis such as that provoked by the emergence of a standoff, many organizations are called into action, and some are imagined into being. These organizations operate and emerge on both sides of the standoff divide as the antagonists reckon with the new situation. While it is virtually a reflex action to think of law-enforcement agencies arriving at the scene to handle the standoff, it is also true that those inside of the standoff center rely on and, at times, imagine up their own organizations to deal with the crisis. For example, as the chronicler of the Wounded Knee standoff recalls:

In the first two weeks of the take-over, a community developed spontaneously as people worked together to set up sleeping quarters, bunkers, and communal kitchens. Then, after the affirmation of the Oglala sovereignty on the weekend of March 11, the newly-formed provisional government of the ION established committees on housing, medical care, food supply, customs and immigration, internal security, information, and defense . . .[20]

New organizations can be born on the outside as well as, for example, a unit called the "Guarantor Commission" was devised to act as the official negotiators for the Tupac Amaru standoff.

Several analytically distinct kinds of imperatives operate to create and sustain these organizations: *internal imperatives, external imperatives,* and *contingency imperatives.* All of these organizations have internal imperatives, having to do with their senses of self-identity. These imperatives come in the forms of standardized rules, roles, relationships, and chains of command for designated action. We assume, or soon learn, that law-enforcement agencies such as the FBI, the ATF, and the US Marshals have codified job descriptions that divide their personnel into investigators, SWAT-team members, hostage negotiators, and so forth. We further assume that these roles will appear in specified, hierarchical relations to each other. Finally, we assume that action taken by these organizations will literally embody the meaning and missions of these organizations. Thus, after word that the Peruvian military had prepared a plan to storm the residence of the Japanese Ambassador was leaked to the press, a *New York Times* journalist was told the following by an official of the anti-terrorist police:

"The existence of a military plan to free the hostages should not come as a surprise," said an official of the antiterrorist police. "In fact, the public should be worried if we did not have one." . . . The report of the plan comes at a time when the Government and the guerrillas are in delicate discussions to end the two-month standoff . . . Under the plan, commandos would descend upon the Japanese residence using ropes from a helicopter, amid the chaos of loud military music and the sounds of helicopters and airplanes projected from speakers that have already been set up near the compound.[21]

The official's point is the obvious one that a military should develop a military plan, even and especially in a moment of heightened negotiation activity. But this obviousness should startle us, as it reveals the naturalized quality of embedded organizational imperatives.

There are also external imperatives that anticipate and respond to a sense of how the organization is perceived by those outside of it. Issues of legitimacy, authority, and publicity come into play here. In the original raid of the ATF on the Branch Davidians, there was an exquisitely attuned sensitivity to how this event would and should portray the ATF agency to the larger public. The public relations officer of the ATF had actually tipped off journalists in advance of the raid that "something big might be happening" in Waco, Texas. A publicity center was set up with telephones and fax machines to report what was anticipated to be a triumphant episode in ATF history. As Shupe and Hadden report, "In tipping off selected media agents about a vague but imminent law enforcement event, the BATF clearly anticipated favorable publicity that would aid their own pursuit of legitimacy. There were approximately a dozen members of the press, including a television cameraperson, present to witness the raid and ensuing gun battle."[22] Ultimately, the event played out very differently than anticipated, however, with significant damage to the agency's legitimacy.

Finally, when an organization is on the move, as it must be when a crisis constitutes its environment, it must make an even greater effort to remain true to itself through actions that assert consistency and predictability. Thus, in the terms of this study, there is a simultaneous confrontation with and denial of the contingency of changing contexts of time and space.

Predictability in such situations is problematic because interactions with an emergent and contradictory other can never simply count on compliance with norms and rules. As well, it is empirically, if not theoretically, the case that standard procedures come replete with organizational breakdowns. We will see many examples of such breakdowns in this chapter. Often, these breakdowns come in the form of lost or broken or absent equipment and plans, or in breakdowns in communication.

Standoff scenes and their equipment

The actual scenes of the standoffs exert an enormous gravitational pull on these institutions. One of the first standard operating moves is to bring personnel and equipment onto the scene. I will address the nature of personnel characterizations later in the chapter. Here, I am specifically interested in what Burke would call the agency/purpose ratio or what, in lay terms, might be termed the match between the equipment and the purpose for which it was sought. The machines' purposes reveal themselves through the actions they take on.

Certain pieces of equipment seem logical when they appear at the scene of an emergent standoff: law-enforcement vehicles with identifying names, initials, and flashing lights on them; firearms of various sorts on both sides of the barricades (these include automatic weapons, shotguns, and antitank weapons); long-range visioning equipment, such as binoculars; defensive equipment, such as gas masks. They represent the specter of violence that hangs over these scenes, regardless of whether any actual violent act has occurred up to that point. It is important, though, to disentangle the practical and the symbolic logics of such equipment. One assumes that the state will respond to violence or to the threat of violence with violence. After all, the state is the wielder of the "monopoly of legitimate force" over a given territory. Only a far-flung and oxymoronic imagination might conceive of a Ghandian state, where nonviolence is the response to incipient violence. Nevertheless, the example of the response of law-enforcement authorities to the nonstandoff standoff with the Freemen of Montana points in exactly that direction. They brought no "standard" equipment with them to the "scene" itself. The nearest such equipment was, as the following Associated Press statement reported it, positioned 30 miles away: "Two armored vehicles, bearing prominent 'FBI' signs on their sides, were unveiled for reporters and photographers on Friday, and a third was delivered Saturday. But the vehicles remained at the FBI command post at the Garfield county fairgrounds, 30 miles from the ranch."[23] At some level, this establishment of a kind of sideshow exhibit was precisely to assure the mass media reporters and photographers that the normal steps were being taken. They, as much as the Freemen themselves, were deemed worthy of such communication. But at another level, the symbolic provocation of such equipment was acknowledged by a law-enforcement team that had determined to resist turning this scene into a "scene."

At the other end of the spectrum, several of the standoffs saw law-enforcement officials bring specifically military equipment to the scenes. Armored personnel carriers were driven around the wealthy residential neighborhood of Lima where the Japanese Ambassador's house stood, for the duration of the Tupac Amaru standoff. Similar tank-like vehicles drove onto the yard of Mt. Carmel during the Branch Davidian standoff in order to flatten the terrain (by crushing or removing all vehicles and trees in the area) and eventually to insert tear gas into the building. Wounded Knee occupiers claimed that Air Force planes were used for surveillance purposes during the period of the standoff in 1973 (some thirteen years later, a federal court ruled that Alexander Haig and other former government officials could be sued by the occupiers for allowing the military to intervene in a situation of domestic unrest). The National Guard also flew surveillance flights over the Branch Davidian buildings. Police helicopters were used in the MOVE standoff (to drop a satchel of explosives onto the roof of the MOVE house) and in the standoff at Ruby Ridge. These vehicles, with their impermeability or their great mobility, move across the various borders of the standoff. In doing so, they attempt to assert a story of control and ubiquity, as if their particular point of view transcended the assumed stasis of reciprocal threat.

But the equipment that interests me the most is the equipment whose function is ambiguous. I refer here specifically to fire engines, video cameras, and generators.[24] Fire fighters, like doctors, are traditionally healers and saviors, not aggressors. Only in the most distorted scenarios, like that of the novel *Fahrenheit 451* for fire fighters, and like that of the concentration camp Nazi "doctors," would these roles be transmuted into something destructive and evil. The fire engine itself normally represents machinery at its most gleaming, benign, and helpful. It is the stuff of child-hood fantasy. Yet in several of the standoffs studied, the fire engine lends itself to acts of offense and to acts of neglect. In the MOVE standoff, the fire engines of the City of Philadelphia were brought to the scene in the early morning hours of May 13, 1985. They were not brought to Osage Avenue in order to fight any eventual fire. Rather, they were brought to point their powerful "squirt" hoses onto the MOVE house in the attempt to literally flush the MOVE members out. These hoses were then shut down at 11:15 a.m., having been unsuccessful in causing the residents to exit. At the end of the day, after the satchel of explosives had been dropped on the roof of the house, the helicopter pilot reported seeing flames on the roof. This was at 5:49 p.m. Only at 6:32 were the squirts turned back on, this time in order to fight the fire that was now beginning to burn the MOVE house down (and would subsequently burn down two entire city blocks of homes that night). Full-scale, conventional fire fighting would only commence at 9:30 p.m. How is it possible to explain this delay, particularly given the on-the-scene presence of the fire engines and fire fighters? Instrumental expla-nations would take into consideration the diminished water pressure in the hoses (as the earlier use had depleted them). They would also consider the claim that the police wanted to make sure that no officers were on the roof of the house when the fire began, with consequent danger of any water spray reducing their visibility. Symbolic explanations might move into the deeper terrain of considering what it meant for the fire-fighting machines and personnel themselves to have to fight a fire that wasn't supposed to happen (the police asserted that the tear gas dropped onto the roof was nonincendiary) and to have to make a switch in character in the middle of the story – from aggressor to rescuer.[25] Symbolic gears are often as difficult to switch as practical gears.

The standoff of the Branch Davidians also experienced a strange *lapsus* in its relation to fire fighting. Unlike the scene of the MOVE standoff, fire engines were nowhere to be found at the FBI perimeter at Mt. Carmel. In the over 500-page final FBI assault plan involving the insertion of tear gas into the Branch Davidian building by tanks, there is no mention of what to do in the possibility of a fire. And yet, a fire did indeed break out. As Catherine Wessinger reports:

A small flame appeared there at 12:07. By 12:08 a large fire was seen in the dining room. At 12:08 another fire was seen in the gymnasium where the roof had collapsed. The separate fires quickly escalated to consume the building. At 12:13 FBI agents called the fire department. Tanks continued demolishing the building as it burned. Fire engines arrived at 12:34, but were held back by FBI agents . . . At 12:41 the fire fighters were permitted to begin putting out the fire.[26]

The FBI agent in charge of the Branch Davidian conflict, Jeff Jamar, was asked during the 1995 special Senate Hearings whether the FBI had a plan indicating what to do in the case of fire. He answered: "We held the fire trucks [at the perimeter]. So that was our fire plan."[27] Fiery conflagrations have been a fairly consistent theme in the "resolutions" of such standoffs – MOVE and Waco are just two cases (the standoff between police and the Symbionese Liberation Army in the 1970s is another example). There was also a fire in one of the buildings in the town of Wounded Knee during the Oglala Sioux's occupation; that building burned down because of the lack of available water. Certainly, with so many wooden structures in the United States, fire is always a possibility when incendiary actions are at play, and fire engines might be considered fairly standard equipment at such scenes. But their role has proven to be a confused one, strangely analogous to that of negotiators (whose role we will explore later in the chapter). One might expect fire engines to be the Red Cross of the vehicular world and yet their neutrality is often traduced.

Video cameras also seem to be benign and domesticated technology, used in recording the family vacation and ballet performances. And yet video cameras are also involved in surveillance operations and have been recently showcased as unanticipated interlopers in such "private" scenes as the police capture and beating of motorist Rodney King. Video cameras appeared in the standoffs at Ruby Ridge, Waco, and MOVE in a variety of ways. At Ruby Ridge, two video cameras were set up around the Weaver cabin in the months before the US Marshals' actual approach to the cabin that resulted in the first gun-fight. Weaver's friend, Kevin Harris, testified during the Senate Hearings that they had actually found and dismantled one of the cameras. Harris claimed in the following question-and-answer section of the transcript that he had interpreted the presence of the cameras as indicating that no actual individual would make the trip in person to approach the cabin:

Senator Specter: Now the question I have for you, Mr. Harris, is in the context that you knew that Mr. Weaver had not responded to the pending court charges and that the video camera was up to observe what was going on, didn't you have some sense that some Federal law enforcement officers might well come into the area to take Mr. Weaver into custody so that they could compel him to stand trial?

Mr. Harris: No. When I – I assumed they didn't want to be in the area. And so that's why they used their video camera thingy they had up there if they didn't want to be up in that area.[28]

Thus the presence of video cameras can be read semiotically as the replacement of the actual eyes of actual agents and as a signal of the agents' avoidance of the scene. Such a reading was, in fact, a misreading in this case. Other video cameras used in standoffs operated in the more traditional manner of "home movies." The FBI negotiators at Waco both made their own home movies to show the Branch Davidians that they, too, were family men and had the Branch Davidians make home movies of life inside Mt. Carmel. The reciprocal exchange of home videos attempted the transmutation of the situation into one where the domestic rules of gift-giving and familial recognitions take precedence. However, at the end of the Branch Davidian standoff, when the final FBI assault was in progress, another video camera taped this moment at the antipode of domesticity. Interestingly, when the Congressional subcommittee investigating the Branch Davidian confrontation requested the tape, it was revealed that the tape was blank.

The presence of a running video camera in one of the police surveillance posts across the street from the MOVE house led to much questioning of the police in the subsequent MOVE Commission Hearings. A short bit of the tape, played repetitively during the hearings, showed the MOVE house in flames (the camera was set up in the second story window of the posthouse) and the audio part of the tape reverberated with police laughter and a voice saying, "I guess they're never going to call the Commissioner a motherfucker again." Such a scene constitutes the moral inversion of the home movie, and has nothing in common with it save the technology.

Generators and their product, electricity, represent another machine of vexed communication. The continuous flow of electricity into a place of habitation signals particular temporal cycles, and their overcoming. Night can be inhabited, and the coldness and the darkness of it suppressed, because electricity warms and illuminates the space. Food can be preserved beyond what might be naturally expected of it because it can be refrigerated. So we may not be surprised to learn that among the most frequently implemented of the standard operating procedures in the standoffs under examination is the cutting off, and intermittent restoration, of electricity to the standoff centers. This occurred during the Branch Davidian standoff, the Tupac Amaru standoff, and the Freemen of Montana standoff. Such a move makes sense if one of the goals of the authorities is to break contact between the inside and the outside, because electricity is, along with being a lifeline in intemperate weather and a way of keeping the corroding aspects of nature at bay, also a form of symbolic communication. Electricity keeps people hooked into society. Cutting off electricity also means pushing the natural paralysis of the standoff to further extremes. Movement is literally frozen in the cold and the dark.

On the other hand, several of the standoff centers were equipped with their own generators. These generators signaled an attitude about electricity and its vicissitudes, but it also signaled an attitude about society. The fact that, among others, the Weavers and the Freemen had their own generators ready to go were the electricity to fail, indicated that these groups had already begun to cut themselves off from the symbolic media linking them to society at large.

The rules of engagement

The collision between standard operating procedures and an exaggeratedly contingent reality is best exposed in actual codifications of new or amended rules. These rules have as their purpose the task of dealing with the flux of an emergent situation. But they must do this in such a way as to be consistent with established organizational imperatives. So right away there is an existential contradiction – how can you be both consistent with the past and allow for adaptation to the future. These are truly moments when the subjunctive takes over and tries to preempt or bridge such transformations. Rules of Engagement are fairly common features in military-type operations in which there is an assumption of a high degree of risk of physical harm. For example, law-enforcement assaults planned for both the Waco and the Ruby Ridge standoffs included some form of Rules of Engagement. At Waco, the plan for the final assault of the FBI, which included the insertion of tear gas into the compound, also provided for the escalation of the assault in the case of the Branch Davidians firing on the tanks. The decision to escalate would rest with the on-site commanders. Thus do Rules of Engagement represent moments of hypersubjunctivity. They traffic in hypothetical reactions to hypothetical reactions to proposed actions. As such, they are "texts-in-action" (a category of texts that I will explore below), texts of contingency that insert themselves into a superficially metonymic narrative of simple cause and effect, action and reaction. In doing so they reveal the many possible forking roads.

Here, I want to examine closely one case of codification and implementation of Rules of Engagement – that being the Rules of Engagement at Ruby Ridge. These Rules were drawn up for the FBI sniper/observers who were sent to the scene in the aftermath of the shooting deaths of Sammy

Weaver and US Marshal William Degan (see the chronology of the Ruby Ridge standoff in Chapter 1 for a review of the sequence of actions leading to the FBI taking over the operation). On August 22, 1992, the day after these initial shootings, members of the FBI "Hostage Rescue Team" were deployed to the scene. They brought with them the specifically formulated "Rules of Engagement."

The Rules themselves were actually handwritten by FBI agents in charge of the operation, and were based on an in-flight telephone conversation between Special Agent Richard Rogers (who was on the plane to Idaho) and Larry Potts, Former Assistant Director of the Criminal Investigation Division who was in Washington.[29] As the handwritten version reproduced during the subsequent Senate Hearings on the Federal Raid at Ruby Ridge had it, the Rules were the following:

If any adult in the compound is observed with a weapon after the surrender announcement is made, deadly force can and should be employed to neutralize the individual. If any adult male is observed with a weapon prior to the announcement, deadly force can and should be employed if the shot can be taken without endangering the children. If compromised by any dog the dog can be taken out. Any subjects other than R, V, & K presenting threat of grevious [sic] bodily harm FBI rules of Deadly Force apply.[30]

Operating under these rules, FBI sharpshooter, Lon Horiuchi, fired and hit Randy Weaver as Weaver stood outside the building near the cabin called "the birthing shed." A second shot was fired at Kevin Harris as he was retreating into the Weaver cabin. It seriously wounded him and killed Vicky Weaver who was standing inside, behind the cabin door, holding a baby in her arms.

The shooting death of Vicky Weaver and the injuring of Kevin Harris were among the most controversial actions that were retrospectively assessed in investigations of Ruby Ridge. During the many internal and external investigations of the standoff, the FBI Rules of Engagement received focused attention, for they seemed to many to have set the stage for just such shootings. For one thing, the Rules seemed to modify the constitutionally ratified Deadly Force policy of law-enforcement agencies. As delineated in *Tennessee v. Garner*, that policy is understood in the following way: "Where the officer has probable cause to believe that the suspect poses a threat of serious physical harm either to the officer or to others, it is not constitutionally unreasonable to prevent escape by using deadly force."[31] In this 1985 Supreme Court case, the Court found that the common law doctrine permitting police officers to use deadly force to arrest any escaping felon was unconstitutional under the Fourth Amendment.

Only in the case of a significant threat of death or serious injury to the officer or others could such force be used. Beyond seeming to override the Deadly Force policy, the Rules seemed to have placed too much power in the hands of the individual FBI sniper/observers.

Thus the Rules of Engagement, assessed by some, including FBI director Freeh,[32] as unconstitutional, were considered a situationally specific adaptation and expansion of the Deadly Force policy. They indicated that the mere holding of a weapon by an adult at the scene of the standoff could constitute justification for the use of deadly force. Further, it allowed that any other individual beyond those specified by the initials, R, V, and K who presented a threat to bodily harm to FBI agents could have the conventional rules of Deadly Force applied to them. These other individuals, the only other people at the scene, would necessarily have been the Weaver children. By dividing the universe of potential antagonists into the nominated "R, V, and K" and the minor others, these Rules of Engagement present a kind of split-screen image of the scene. Different rules apply to different participants in the same situation.

And yet such splitting is not the most significant or the most phenomenologically challenging aspect of the Rules of Engagement. Rather, what is most challenging here is the manner in which free will, situationally specific thinking, standard operating procedures, chains of command, and applications of rules are all mixed together and vie for dominance in the interpretation of the meaning of these Rules. As FBI agent Larry Potts testified: "These [rules] were established to assist the HRT personnel in making a determination regarding what constituted a threat to them in this extraordinary circumstance. The [rules] were not intended to supersede the FBI standard deadly-force policy. The final determination regarding such implementation of deadly force must always remain with the individual . . . and each individual must make an individual, final determination of threat."[33] In a further clarification, Danny O. Coulson, Former Deputy Assistant Director of the Criminal Investigative Division of the FBI stated that:

An understanding of the relationship between rules of engagement and the FBI's deadly force policy is essential. The policy – which permits deadly force only when necessary to protect oneself or another from death or grievous bodily harm – is taught to every FBI agent, from new agents at the FBI Academy to seasoned agents like HRT personnel. This policy is the ultimate guide with regard to the use of deadly force. Rules of engagement are meant to heighten agents' sense of awareness of the seriousness of the threat or to give a specific instruction. Rules of engagement cannot substitute for individual judgment. Regardless of how rules of engagement are crafted, the use of deadly force is always limited by the FBI's deadly force policy.[34]

Such official interpretations of the Rules of Engagement represent significant attempts to locate these Rules somewhere on a continuum between a constitutionally delineated Deadly Force policy and something called "individual judgment." Thus for any given interaction one has, first, one's own individual reading of the moment, a reading comprised of a mixture of instinct, moral judgment, trained reflexes, and causal reasoning. Next, impinging upon this bundle of associations and reactions, are the codified Rules of Engagement (that are the acting rules for navigating the situation). And capping off the whole lot is the covering law of the FBI deadly force policy. How then is it possible to understand any given action in a situation with so many embedded and abstract parameters? How are we to understand blame and responsibility when rules hit a living situation – all as mediated through individual actors? One way to approach such questions is with a notion of a grammar of procedures.

Operational grammar

From the beginning, this study has been concerned with understanding the standoff as an exemplary moment of contingent social action. As such, the subjunctivity of hypothetical calculations has been foregrounded as most accurately capturing the mood and the narrative pulse of such events. As we look closely at the grammar of the event's actions, such as that entwining the Rules of Engagement, we can see this subjunctive mood, and the provocations and controversy it contingently generates, most clearly.

To briefly recapitulate the sense of the subjunctive – it is a grammatical mood in English that expresses speculations tinged with emotions of a certain sort (doubt, hope). Subjunctive statements come in the form of "if X were to occur, then Y." Thus, the subjunctive can be linked grammatically with the conditional tense or the imperative form. So, one has the following set of possibilities: "If it were to rain, you would carry an umbrella" (subjunctive/conditional); "If it were to rain, you should carry an umbrella" (subjunctive/imperative). The latter can be alternately written as an out-and-out command, "If it rains, carry an umbrella!" As Greg Urban writes, in his study of the role of imperatives in contemporary American culture, the linguistically imperative form

typically involves characteristic marking of the verb, with special treatment of the second person subject. In English, the verb is minimally marked as true present (i.e., not a progressive) and the second person subject is deleted: "[you] answer the question, Colonel." Second, however, the imperative form must also be a functional command within the on-going stream of discourse, and be recognized as such by the interlocutors.[35]

It is this last claim, that the imperative form must be recognized as an imperative to function as such, that is key for an analysis of the Rules of Engagement. For the linguistic calibrations above become much more than an academic parsing when they are considered in the light of what, exactly, linguistically, the Rules of Engagement allowed the FBI sniper/observers to do.

First we need to understand the nature of the subjunctive reasoning of the Rules, as they seek to anticipate and provide for the unpredictable. The focus of the Rules is the possible appearance of "any adult with a weapon," with separate sentences for what should happen if such an appearance is made before or after a surrender announcement.[36]

Recall that the standard Deadly Force policy does not base itself on the appearance of adults with weapons, but rather on the appearance of suspects who are actively threatening the life of the pursuing officers or of others. The mere possession of a weapon is not sufficient to trigger the use of deadly force by the officer. The Rules, then, seem to lower the threshold for the use of deadly force.

Aware of the problematic nature of such a lowering, the various FBI agents involved in the confrontation sought to justify the actions they took by angling around the actual words and the less obvious meanings of the Rules. For example, FBI sniper/observer Christopher Whitcomb suggested in his testimony that the concept "appearance with a weapon" could be and had been further subdivided into "mere possession of a weapon" and "possession of a weapon that signified its imminent use." Toward this end he stated:

I saw three individuals run out from the front of the cabin with, what appeared to me to be, shoulder weapons, long guns, rifles. Could not tell what caliber, and they were carrying them, as Special Agent Wenger indicated, in port arms, or a position you would carry a weapon in *if you were going to use it*, they were not slung over their shoulder.[37]

Here Whitcomb actually maps the subjunctive on to the ongoing scene through his reading of the position of the weapon.

But, for the FBI agents called to testify after the fact, activating the subjunctive in one's description of an imminent event is different from engaging in self-conscious speculation about the subjunctive. Even as the Senators push them to do so, they resist. When asked by Senator Thompson about the threat – real and potential – of Randy Weaver and Kevin Harris standing outside of their cabin, FBI sniper/observer Dale Monroe answered with: "Senator, I don't want to get into hypotheticals. I know what I saw. I know the threat that was administered by the two adult males. That is what happened, and those are the conditions that met the requirements of the deadly force." Senator Thompson responded, "Well, rules of engagement, you know, have to do with hypotheticals. That is what they have to do with, a lot of potential things that could happen."[38]

But of all of the words and implications in the Rules, the ones that caused the most trouble for the FBI agents involved in the raid were "can and should." These words appeared in the handwritten version of the Rules that became the "official" text. This "can and should" appeared as the phrase that linked the appearance of adults with weapons and the use of deadly force by the FBI agents. Thus: "If any adult in the compound is observed with a weapon after the surrender announcement is made, deadly force can and should be employed to neutralize the individual." The question then was: did this phrase, "can and should" really constitute not just a permission to use deadly force (in allowing the officers on site to make individual and contingent decisions) but an actual command to use deadly force? In other words, did it constitute an imperative? The Senators on the Judiciary Committee pushed the testifying FBI agents on precisely this point. To a man, none of the FBI agents were willing to interpret the "should" as having constituted an order.[39] Rather, they took pains to linguistically and legally parse the terms. For example, as Monroe put it during his questioning by Senator Arlen Specter:

> Mr. Monroe: . . . the deadly force policies that states, we are authorized deadly force only in the event that an individual threatens the life or grievous bodily harm of us or another, myself or another, is the overall umbrella of the policy. I took these rules of engagement only as a means of focusing to us what the potential, the highest potential threat to us would be. They were, in no way a directive. They were not an order to exercise deadly force because -
> Senator Specter: Well, without being an order, were they permission for you to use deadly force?
> Mr. Monroe: They were an authorization to use deadly force only as long as the requirements for the overall policy was met. That is, and that is that a threat has been shown to myself or another and a threat of grievous bodily harm or death.[40]

Permission, order, authorization – all of these labels imply slightly different ideas about organizational mandates and individual autonomy. And these implications spoke to the particular self-identity of FBI agents who clearly were portraying themselves as autonomous agents, making their own decisions on site, rather than as automatons programmed to kill. The organizational complexities of this self-portrayal clearly had to do with the issues of the constitutionality of the Rules themselves, and the ongoing investigation of the agent who had shot Vicky Weaver. Nevertheless, the assertions hinged on exquisitely sensitive lexical distinctions and a rejection of the imperative form. Special Agent Edward Wenger was among the most adamant:

When we were given the rules of engagement, as I am sure all of us here have heard for the last 3 years, words to the effect – or the words "could" and "should" were used. I can't speak – like Special Agent Whitcomb said, I can't speak for everyone, but I can certainly speak for myself, and I do believe in my heart that all of us feel the same way here. Could means just that – could. It lets me exercise my judgment as a sniper/observer, as a special agent of the FBI. Should, granted, is a little stronger wordage than could, but it still lets me justify or use my – I just lost my train of thought – my judgment on a matter. And the bottom line with that is I don't care who you are, anybody – and I do mean anybody – can talk to me until they are blue in the face telling me I could and should. It never said must.[41]

Indeed it is easy to lose one's train of thought in the verbal forest of could, authorized to, should, can, and must. At some deeper level, these agents are all pointing to the contingent preeminence of the situation in determining action. Such insights are similar to those of Pragmatists, sociolinguists, and even such situationally sensitive methodologists as Ferdinand Gonseth who, in his almost mathematical exploration of the verb, admits the following: "What may be surprising is the complexity of the role of the context and of its inexhaustible capacity to modulate the function of the verb even for tenses as simple as the present and the future."[42] In the case we have been exploring, two existential contexts – that of the scene of action and that of the Rules of Engagement themselves – intercalibrate and, sometimes collide, wreaking havoc with the proffered verbs.

Scenes and their agents : standoff identities

The scene

Naming, analogizing, and typifying are processes at the heart of all action. Not just individuals and organizations, but situations as well are named and entered into a kind of situational typology. Sometimes this naming is literal, as when a military assault is given a code name, and the situation becomes a veritable individual. The process and art of naming situations seems to phenomenologically reinforce their boundaries, to give them a definite shape in time and in space, to anticipate their trajectories. It can also reverberate with the sense of self-understanding of the organization that is responsible for the naming.

In the standoffs under examination here, several of the military-type operations were named, on both sides of the standoff divides. For example, the US Marshals called their reconnaisance/assault on Ruby Ridge "Northern Exposure," reflecting the sense of a perilous trip to a marginal and unpopulated place (it may also have referred ironically to the popular television show that explored the (largely benign) ongoing eccentricities of the inhabitants of an isolated Alaskan town). The ATF, in their preparation of the initial plan to utilize a "dynamic entry" to serve warrants on the Branch Davidians, termed their project "Operation Trojan Horse." Here the concrete reference was to the covered cattle-cars in which the agents were to be hidden and driven to the Mt. Carmel compound. The metaphorical reference was to the ancient story of the Trojan horse and the manner in which the Achaeans insinuated their soldiers into the heart of Troy, hiding them in the gigantic wooden horse. Finally, the Tupac Amaru group itself designated the takeover of the Japanese Ambassador's residence with the name, "Operation Oscar Torres Condesu," a reference to one of the founders of the group.

All of these operations suggest, as do all such named military forays, that there is an underlying narrative sense of the meaning of military action. As I noted above, such naming gives a shape to what otherwise might be viewed as an amorphous series of military advances with guns, grenades, and the other weapons. It also gives the situation a personal identity, such that it elicits a certain mental, psychological, and aesthetic attachment.

One step down from the absolutist and all-encompassing action of naming is that of making explicit analogies between the situation at hand and others, that have already been characterized elsewhere. In Chapter 2, we saw such analogizing at work across temporal periods, setting up similarities between current events and ones that have already occurred in the past. As well, we saw how event-genealogies are thus established and how their modeling action works backwards and forwards in time. Here, we encounter processes of concurrent analogizing as when the attorney for the Wounded Knee Legal Defense/Offense Committee,[43] Ken Tilsen, claimed that:

The best analogy [to Pine Ridge] is South Viet Nam. There are a lot of similarities. Most obviously, there is a corrupt government of "natives," who are set up, supplied, financed, propagandized for, and maintained in power by the US Government. Richard Wilson, whom the Government and the press repeatedly style "the elected leader of the Pine Ridge Reservation people," plays a role like that of Thieu and Ky in South Viet Nam – ruling and repressing people of Pine Ridge in the interest of a foreign power – and in the interest of personal gain.[44]

Here, not only is the situation referred metaphorically to another, obviously vexed, situation and characterized accordingly, but specific individuals are also matched. In matching Tribal Chairman Richard Wilson with Thieu and Ky, Wilson's narrative persona takes on greater depth and clarity.

The next step down in framing the scene is essentially a synecdochic one – the scene is characterized by one of its many aspects. These acts are responses to the basic and ubiquitous question: what kind of a situation is this? The answer comes from the available repertoire of situation types. Perhaps the situation is an emergency, a war, an occupation, an assault, a dynamic entry.[45] Obviously, such characterizations not only act to epistemologically capture the scene, they also set in motion whole series of repercussive actions that logically derive from them.

It is often the case in standoffs such as those studied here, that the anti-authority protagonists attempt to characterize their actions, and those of the authorities, as being part of an ongoing war. When war is posed as the scene of action, a certain legitimacy comes to inhere in any violent, or potentially violent, maneuver. In Burkean terms, the scope of the scene is widened.[46] Thus, looking back over the whole episode at Wounded Knee, several of the former occupiers of the town issued the following statement from their jail cells: "One thing this Government better realize is that what came down at Wounded Knee was real in every aspect, and as far as calling it an occupation . . . They are completely wrong in every way. It was a war where people died and people got shot, where any second you had the chance of being shot by the Government forces . . ."[47] Similarly, the Tupac Amaru group asserted that its actions were part of a larger, nationally ramifying war. In their Communiqué #7, Point 3, they wrote:

Neither Tupac Amaru nor MRTA initiated the war in Peru, and even less the violence; rather we have been, and continue to be, its victims. Here we stand refusing to accept that violence be institutionalized. The approach of taking over an embassy might not be right, since it does not correspond to our tradition, but then again, that tradition has been violated a million times. There is no other way to be heard in a country where people who operate basic needs programs in the communities, such as soup kitchens and milk-for-the-poor programs are arrested . . .

For their part, the law-enforcement agencies typically engage in a narrowing of the scope of the scene. They will call it a "crime scene" as did FBI agent Jeff Jamar at Waco, effectively dismissing any legitimation claims of those on the other side of the barricades. To give validity to their own often military and seemingly precipitous actions, law-enforcement agents will also employ a characterization of the situation as an "emergency." This can be explicit or implicit as in the following statement explaining the elaborate steps taken to attempt an arrest of Randall Weaver during the standoff: "'Because of the terrain, because of the weather, because of the wife and kids, we are taking every step possible to arrest him without hurting anyone,' said Gene Glenn, the FBI's special agent in charge of the Salt Lake City office, who is heading the federal effort here. 'It is not a routine arrest.'"[48]

What is meant here by the notion of a "routine arrest?" The assertion seems to suggest a minimal amount of complexity of operation and a minimal amount of risk of physical harm. At a common sense level, it might seem almost oxymoronic to think of a routine arrest (similar, in its way, to thinking about "normal accidents" in Charles Perrow's term). Arrests come at the culminating point of specifically nonroutine behaviors, relationships, and interactions. Resistance to being taken into custody seems highly probable, if not inevitable. Perhaps, though, the idea of a "routine arrest" is likely to signify some degree of resistance and some degree of acquiescence on the part of the person being arrested. A complete ontological relaxing into voluntary surrender is as analytically distinct from the "routine" as, in its own way, is armed resistance to arrest (such as that of the Branch Davidians to the original ATF dynamic entry mode of serving warrants). Such a relaxing into arrest seems almost mythical, and indeed there is a distinctly mythical quality to the past subjunctive assertions of Randall Weaver testifying in the Senate Hearings about his own hypothetical stance to an arrest-style that was never attempted:

Randall Weaver: But if one – at no time did any law enforcement official come up there in uniform with a badge, walk in my yard, says, "Weaver, I have got a warrant for your arrest." If they had done that, you know, what? I respect courage and I would have trusted that man.
Senator Abraham: Does that mean that you would have peacefully surrendered?
Weaver: That is right.[49]

Gestures of the scene

"Traditionally work on gesture in interaction (and deixis in linguistics) has drawn a bubble around the perimeters of the participants' bodies. The body of the actor has not been connected to the built world within which it is situated."[50]

The extralinguistic world of gesture subtends and complements the spoken and written linguistic texts that move a situation along its existential path. Gestures are extremely difficult to grasp analytically, to insert meaningfully in a narrative analysis of human interaction, even to simply describe. Semiotician A.J. Greimas comes the closest to developing a systematic analysis of gesture. He focuses on the points of intersection between the human body and spatial environment in which the body operates. For

Greimas, the background environment is, perceptually, epistemologically prior and human movement within it can only be described accordingly: "The human body moves within a spatial context that for reasons of description must be categorized before the human volume filling it, situated in it, or moving in it can be. Three types of criteria will be retained: displacement, orientation and support."[51]

As we have seen earlier, displacement, orientation, and support are concepts that can be applied to people and to the objects that people maneuver in their environments. Doors and windows come to mind when thinking with these criteria. We can recall here the focus on the Weaver cabin door, with salient issues of whether it was open or closed and whether people were running into or standing behind it, at Ruby Ridge. Similarly, the front door of the Mt. Carmel compound in Waco became a key marker of law enforcement power and competence and of the compound's existential stance toward the world (offensive or defensive). It is important to note here that individual Senators on the joint Congressional subcommittee holding hearings on the Branch Davidian confrontation specified that they had requested the front door for examination but had been told by the FBI that the front door was missing. Such specific maneuvers with and around doors must reverberate with the key orientational feature of buildings having "front doors" and of the meaning of people entering buildings through these front doors. Here, what Greimas calls the "mythical gestural praxis" (or what sociologists might call simply, the symbolic) intertwines with the "practical gestural praxis" (or, alternatively, the instrumental) to doubly endow any action with meaning.[52]

Gestures in standoffs are usually self-conscious symbolic gambits that can both reflect deeply held values and constitute strategic actions. We have already referred to several of the conventional extralinguistic standoff gestures – the raising of flags,[53] the imagining and constructing of a perimeter, the subdividing of hostages into distinct existential categories, the cutting off of electricity. There are many hybrid gestures as well – ones that contain elements of both a linguistic and an extralinguistic nature.

The hanging out of banners is one such hybrid gesture and constitutes what I am calling "texts-in-action." Banners hung on the outside walls of the standoff center have an explicit communicative purpose and constitute an attempt to make an end-run around the standardized channels of communication across the barricades – those generally being telephone conversations between the antisystem groups and law-enforcement negotiators, and bullhorn announcements of arrest warrants and incipient military advance. Banners were hung at both Mt. Carmel and at the Japanese Ambassador's residence during these respective standoffs. The Branch

Davidian banners consisted of large sheets on which were written messages of various kinds. One, previously noted in an earlier chapter, read simply: "Rodney King, We Understand," a metaphorical linking of the Branch Davidian travails with the agencies of law enforcement with Rodney King's beating by the Los Angeles police. Other banners constituted a kind of plangent plea with practical implications: "God help us, we want the press." This banner was answered by one hung up by members of the media which read, ironically, "God help us, we are the press." A final category of banners had distinctly pragmatic communicative purposes, such as the one that stated: "FBI broke negotiation: We want press."

The banners of the Tupac Amaru, in a manner consistent with their various communiqués (sixteen of which were released and subsequently posted on the Internet over the course of the standoff), affirmed their political stance, directly addressed Alberto Fujimori, and tracked the situation's progress. The phrases on the banners included the following: "Mr. Fujimori, with arrogant declarations and without dialogue, there will never be a solution"; "Mothers, wives and children of our prisoners are also waiting for their freedom"; "Today's Peru – 13 million Peruvians in extreme poverty. Where is the progress?"

Other extralinguistic gestures of symbolic import in standoffs involve the movement (orientation, placement, motility) of bodies in and out and around the standoff scene. While we've already addressed the spatial issues of ingress and egress, the ways in which bodies coming and going constitute standoff action of a gestural nature remain to be analyzed. Several such action nodes are relevant: the timing and nature of release and reception of hostages and "hostages" from the standoff centers; the literal structures of meetings and the proximity of bodies to each other and to the perimeters in negotiations; the entrance and exit into and out of the standoff center by journalists and intermediaries; and the introduction of objects (food, clothing, medical supplies, musical instruments, stones, listening devices, tear gas, and so forth) into the standoff center.

Taking the above gestures in turn, we begin with the expulsion of hostages/ "hostages" from the standoff center. In the cases under investigation, there were clear sets of hostages in two cases, the Tupac Amaru standoff and that of the Republic of Texas. In the Republic of Texas standoff, the two hostages (a neighboring married couple, the Rowes) were released early in this brief standoff in exchange for the release from jail of Republic of Texas member, Bob Scheidt. Phone negotiations with the Texas Rangers arranged this "exchange of prisoners," a terminology that was made symbolically acceptable to all parties.[54] This exchange suggests a certain symmetry of movement, a simultaneity of prisoner crossing of boundaries from inside to outside. In the Tupac Amaru standoff, a much more rhythmically complicated system of hostage release developed. Partly due to the sheer numbers of hostages (600 party guests at the outset of the occupation of the Ambassador's house), partly due to the symbolically charged nature of the hostage population (politicians of various nationality, diplomats representing a broad array of countries, business executives, religious figures), the Tupac Amaru were presented with rich possibilities for "working with" the hostages to develop a narrative of purpose and ideological motivation. At the outset of the standoff, many hostages were released for "humanitarian" reasons – they were the women, the aged, and the infirm. So from the beginning, the Tupac Amaru sought to exhibit their essential respect for human life and their compassion. Over the course of the long standoff, a steady stream of hostages were released. Often, these hostage groups included ambassadors from other countries and a smattering of business executives and Peruvian legislators. We need to recall the exquisite sensitivity to categorization evidenced by the architectural dividing of the hostages into more important upstairs, less important downstairs and into distinct nationalities in separate rooms. Looked at from the larger theoretical framework of this study of contingency, we might view these groups of hostages released at particular time points as representing crystallized harmonic meaning deriving from metaphorical choices along the synchronic axis of hostage types (nationality, occupation, political importance). Then, as they are inserted into a diachronic (metonymic) narrative of other hostage releases over time, they tell an evolving story of the meaning of hostage release in this event. Thus, to refer back to Lévi-Strauss' dictum, the story constitutes a work that apprehends the continuous and the discontinuous in total fashion.

In this case, as the hostage release continued, humanitarian messages were mixed with other messages, often articulated by the released hostages themselves. On December 21, 1996, for example, when a group of hostages were released, the *New York Times* reported their statement about the progress of negotiations: "The released hostages included the Ambassadors of Brazil, South Korea and Egypt, as well as business executives, journalists and a Peruvian legislator. Five of those freed said they were being released to communicate the hostages' concerns about the lack of progress in negotiations as well as poor conditions in the residence."[55] Sometimes, these messages were less tied to the ongoing standoff situation and its progress and more tied to the international political scene and to the Tupac Amaru's desire to weigh in on political transformations occurring elsewhere. For example, Uruguay Ambassador Tabare Bocalandro Yapeyu was freed on December 24th after a Uruguayan court refused to extradite two

Tupac Amaru members who had been imprisoned in, and then released from, Uruguayan jails. As well, their December 26th release of the Ambassador of Guatemala was reported in the following way: "While today's release was insignificant in number, the rebels appeared to make a symbolically rich gesture by liberating Jose Maria Argueta, the Ambassador of Guatemala. Mr. Argueta said that his release 'was an acknowledgement of the historical accomplishments of Guatemala reaching a peace agreement to be signed on Dec. 29' that will end a 40-year-old guerrilla war."[56]

It is important to reiterate here the somewhat unique narrative possibilities afforded the Tupac Amaru by the international and occupational range and importance of the hostages they held. But it is also important to note the corresponding aesthetic improvisations of the Tupac Amaru in the way they attempted to infuse meaning into their hostage releases. It should be clear, though, that such sensitivity does not always reflect higher moral ground or translate into strategic success. I will return to these larger questions in the section on standoff improvisation in the next chapter.

The gestural analysis of the movement of "hostages" is analytically murkier than that of hostages. "Hostages" are those individuals in standoff centers who, for various reasons, are viewed by law-enforcement officials as not being entirely free to determine their own fates. Often, "hostages" include children and women, and the very old. As Senator Lantos put it in the joint Congressional subcommittee hearings on the Branch Davidian confrontation, there were "children, women, and other innocents."[57] Sometimes, the "hostages" include all those in the standoff center but the leader of the group and his or her main subordinates. In a later section of the chapter, I will examine the phenomenological profile of "hostages." Here I will just note that there were "hostages" at the following standoffs: Wounded Knee, MOVE, Ruby Ridge, Waco, Freemen of Montana.

A pervasive ambivalence greets the outward movement of "hostages." Those on the inside of the standoff center understand their exiting to be, perhaps, necessary, but also emotionally painful for the group as a whole. Those on the outside understand their release as partially constituting an act of rescue and partially constituting an act of criminal apprehension. In the fiery finale of the MOVE confrontation, only two of the eleven MOVE members emerged from the house. One woman, Ramona Africa, was taken into custody immediately. The other, Birdy Africa, a child, was taken to the hospital and fed a hamburger later that day, a dish that in being cooked violated MOVE's dietary law. Thus was Birdy immediately reclaimed for "America" (to use Police Commissioner Sambor's term). During the early phases of the Branch Davidian standoff, several elderly adult "hostages" exited from the Mt. Carmel compound, only to be gesturally reconstructed as apprehended criminals. As reported by Wessinger, "Every adult Davidian who exited Mount Carmel was made to put on an orange prisoner's jumpsuit and was led away in front of television cameras in handcuffs and leg chains."[58]

Other extralinguistic gestures incorporate literal structures of support and orientation, in Greimas' terms. In the chosen cases, these turn out to consist of a fairly broad repertoire of structures, including buildings, tables, fences, tipis, and school buses. Many types of conversations, with a variety of ramifications, attempt to move the standoff to a conclusion. These may consist of casual contact across the barricades or they may be formal negotiations. Regardless of the specific nature of the contact, the agents in the scene need some place at which or in which to hold the conversations. For pupposes of this section's analysis of gesture, it is revealing to look at some of these places of converse and ways they themselves speak semiotically.

The standoff of Wounded Knee tracked a long list of charged places of interchange: from the Bureau of Indian Affairs building on the Pine Ridge Reservation where the original protests against Tribal Chairman Dick Wilson were held, to Wilson's impeachment hearing in Billy Mills Hall on the reservation, to the cemetery at Wounded Knee, to the town of Wounded Knee itself. Symbolism of the contemporary relationship between the Sioux and the US government and of the historical relation between them is manifest in these loci of action. Drawing this symbolism out even further during the standoff proper, as talks began on March 4, 1973 between the Justice Department and the Independent Oglala Nation leadership, a tipi was brought out of the village of Wounded Knee into the "demilitarized zone" between the two perimeters. The selection of the tipi as the chosen structure of support for the talks clearly resonated culturally, as the tipi asserts the historical specificity of Native American culture. It also resonated across time, for the original deliberations of the historic Fort Laramie Treaty Commission were also held in a tipi. A photograph reproduced in the book *Voices from Wounded Knee, 1973: In the Words of the Participants*, reveals that in those meetings in 1868, the Sioux are sitting on the ground and the representatives of the United States Government are sitting on overturned wooden boxes at the opening of the tipi. Another photograph, this one reproduced in Bureau of Indian Affair's Superintendent Stanley Lyman's first-hand account of the 1973 occupations, reveals *all* of the occupants of the contemporary negotiation tipi, including government negotiator Kent Frizzell, sitting cross-legged on the ground.[59]

On April 3, 1973, the meetings moved back into Wounded Knee itself and an initial disarmament agreement was signed at an outdoor table in front of a sacred tipi. The standoff did not end with this signing, however, and further talks got underway in May. Unlike the previous meetings, these were held in two school buses in the demilitarized zone. In one bus were the "military" discussions. In the other bus, the discussions were categorized as "political." Thus, a semiosis of gesture would claim that the rectangle supersedes the circle, and an explicit military/political division of negotiation labor supersedes the all-encompassing discussions of April.

During the Freemen standoff, the fence gate stood in for the tipi and the school bus. It provided both the physical support for conversations across the standoff divide and the symbolic resonance of an open channel of communication. And it should not surprise us to learn that the structural support of the fence gate symbolically anticipated another gesture, this time one of gestural orientation, the handshake:

Two unidentified FBI agents, accompanied by Colorado State Senator Charles Duke, drove up to a cattle gate on the edge of the ranch. They were joined there minutes later by four Freemen and a discussion began, with the militants talking directly with the FBI agents, reporters at the scene said. After a few minutes, both sides shook hands as they stood under the drizzle . . .[60]

Hands actually do a lot of the gestural work in and around standoffs. They shake, they wave, they point, they salute, and they are cuffed. Working with Greimas' natural semiotic program's "morphological disarticulation of the body," we note the displacements and reorientations of the hands of standoff antagonists and mediators. The Branch Davidian members exiting their compound during the standoff were all handcuffed and led away by awaiting law enforcement officials, the Freemen were specifically not handcuffed at the conclusion of their "standoff" and Randy Weaver was almost handcuffed, as indicated in the following statement made by intermediary, Bo Gritz, during the Senate hearings on Ruby Ridge. As well, it is important to note that Gritz refers to something he does with his own hand during the exiting from the Weaver cabin. He delivers a particular salute to some right-wing "skin head" bystanders who had written a letter to Weaver during the standoff. Because the Nazi salute had come up earlier in the hearings (an undercover informant for the ATF testified that Weaver did make the Nazi salute during a meeting he attended of the Aryan Nations organization), Gritz is careful to point out that his hand is not making the Nazi salute. Rather the salute constitutes a particular, secret communicative gesture:

As we trailed out of the cabin a federal marshal started to handcuff Weaver. Upon my appeal to Dick Roger, Weaver was allowed to proceed in dignity with what was left of his family. At the bottom of the hill, media and vigil rushed forward. I spotted the skin heads toward the back. Raising my hand (not in a Nazi salute) to gain their attention, I told them Randall had asked for me to give them a special salute, they would know what it meant (referring to the help their letter had been), no one else knew of their contribution.[61]

Clearly, hands can make things happen – practically and symbolically. This sense of their immanent power to move and effect change across boundaries helps explain the need to handcuff even those who are defeated and surrounded by agents of the law.

Finally, other important scenic gestures include the introduction and exit of other people and objects into and out of the standoff center. I've already approached such movements as spatial transmissions and transgressions in the last chapter. Here, I am interested in such actions as they symbolically communicate meaning and practically push the standoff in particular directions.

Many individuals and objects make the crossing from outside to inside and from inside to outside: statements and declarations (both written and oral), food, water, medical supplies, musical instruments, cameras, listening devices, stones, tear gas, and bullets are all represented in the repertoire of moving objects. Mediators, journalists, religious figures, and Red Cross workers are typically included in the set of people in transit across the boundaries (these ideal typical categories of standoff personages will be examined more fully in the following section on the participants of standoffs). Sometimes, permission is necessary for these people and objects to make their journey – permission by those on the outside and/or permission by those on the inside.[62] Sometimes, the objects are unwanted and warded off.

At first blush, the group of objects enumerated above appears easily divided into categories of benign and malign or peaceful and war-like. For example, when the authorities send medical supplies, water, food, and milk into the standoff centers (this occurred intermittently at Wounded Knee, at the Branch Davidian standoff, and at the Tupac Amaru standoff) the gesture seems obviously humanitarian in its motives and goals. However, sometimes these very innocent objects become employed in more strategic campaigns and incorporate other, less benevolent objects in them. The milk cartons sent into Mt. Carmel for the Branch Davidian children, and the guitar sent into the Japanese Ambassador's residence in Lima, both contained listening devices that allowed the authorities to hear the conversations inside these standoff centers. Innocence and experience can be inextricably linked:

Paradoxically, it may have been a guitar requested by the hostages on behalf of the guerrillas and taken into the compound by the Red Cross that hastened the rebels' undoing. At least, that is what one Peruvian newspaper reported. It said officials had reported that a pin-sized microphone placed inside the guitar had helped military and police intelligence officials to monitor the guerrillas' movements inside the mansion.[63]

Thus does irony enter the standoff compound.

Another strategic action in the standoff is the halting of the flow of people and objects, once such a flow has been initiated. This takes the form of stopping an ongoing release of hostages from the standoff center, cutting off the supply of essential materials into the center (electricity, water, food, medical supplies, and so forth), refusing further permission to intermediaries and journalists to re-enter the standoff center. Journalists were alternately afforded and then denied permission by specific parties (inside and outside) to enter the standoff centers in the cases of Wounded Knee, Freemen of Montana, and Tupac Amaru. When materials such as water and medical supplies are held hostage (an illuminating use of the term given the centrality of the hostage concept here), the situation often reaches a state of extremis rather quickly. This is evidenced by the following from Wounded Knee:"We need medical supplies in here badly, like for colds. We have no cough medicine or antibiotics or drugs for guys that are really in pain. The last few days they've cut off even bandages and things like that, that people have sent from all over the country."[64]

A different kind of holding hostage consists of holding information hostage. Such things occur when particular messages, in various formats, do not get communicated to the anticipated audiences. This can occur on either side of the standoff divide. An interesting example of this decision occurred when, as noted above, the FBI had sent a video camera into the Mt. Carmel compound in order that the Branch Davidians might make a video of themselves talking and going about their "normal" activities. The resultant video, sent back out to the authorities, was not shown to any individual or media organization. The reason for this, it was subsequently revealed, was that the authorities were concerned that it might portray the Branch Davidians in too sympathetic a light.

One of the last communiqués sent by the Tupac Amaru group during the standoff in Lima provides a list of objects that, in their enumeration, gives a feel for an atmosphere of objects swirling around and through the standoff, sometimes halting in their trajectories, sometimes flying with force across the boundaries. It also gives a sense of the way these objects in motion and in suspended animation act to pitch the standoff now in one direction, now in another:

4. The government has repeatedly shown its desire to resolve the conflict militarily:
- water, electricity, and telephone communications have been cut off;
- stones and branches were thrown into the residence grounds;
- the guerrillas were issued an ultimatum to surrender and hand over their weapons;
- the national and international press have been harassed and told to stop reporting, to limit their reports and their approach, and to participate in the regime's disinformation campaign;
- the area around the residence has been sealed off by armored vehicles and the military;
- strong loud speakers have been installed;
- there was a parade of military mine sweeping vehicles and police units with heavy weaponry in front of the residence;
- overhead flights by military helicopters.[65]

Dramatis personae, syntactically speaking

"I am concerned that the option I represent – to negotiate a settlement not involving force – has come to an end. The United States is in control of the situation, but not in control of the people." (Assistant Attorney General, Stanley Pottinger, April, 1973, referring to Wounded Knee)[66]

In a profound way, it is indeed true that "people" make a situation. They make it by the roles they take on, by the ways in which they interact with each other, and the ways in which they interact with their environment. But what are people? And how is it possible to differentiate them, in the way that Assistant Attorney General Pottinger does, from the situation itself?

At the beginning of the chapter, I argued that institutions and organizations are key players in standoffs and that among the wares they ply are standard operating procedures, rules, and roles. At the most obvious level of analysis, a standoff is divided into two main opposed camps, the antagonists metaphorically staring each other down across the determined perimeters. Typically, in the cases examined here, these two camps are the legitimate government and the antistate groups. But there are all sorts of shadowy figures who also populate the standoff dramas. We have been introduced to many of the following already, listed here in the manner of Proppean functions: neighbors, religious figures, mediators, experts, hostages, "hostages," journalists, supporters, and bystanders.

In categorizing standoff participants in this way, it is easy to gain the impression that identities are fixed and stable. However, as the ongoing analysis of the times, spaces, and actions of standoffs has begun to reveal, such stability of role or identity is not always the case. Former hostages of a standoff can become negotiators, members of anti-authority groups can be labeled "hostages," former law enforcers can become both mediators and state antagonists, and so on. There is clearly a practical and narrative investment in the idea of stable roles, particularly in situations where the stakes of identity are so high. Yet social reality is unremitting in its presentation of sliding and multiple identities.[67]

The tension between stability and instability of individual identity might seem to be simply a matter of semantics, engaging us in a process of applying and removing specific labels (hostage, negotiator, antagonist, authority) to and from specific individuals. In itself, this coming and going of semantic identity would be confusing. But this tension plays itself out dialectically in the action of standoffs in ways that are more akin to a kind of situational syntax than to semantics. As indicated above, in the section in which the action parameters of the scene of the standoff were characterized, the verb is the key to understanding the standoff's propulsion through time and space. And it is the task of the verb, as Gonseth characterizes it, to integrate the temporal aspects of language with its other aspects, including those of action.[68] And yet, verbs must attach themselves to nouns, or agents, of action. And it is in this necessary connection to movers that identity becomes as much, or more, a matter of syntax as of semantics. A sentence, inserted into a series of sentences, building up into a full-fledged narrative (even, and especially, ongoing narratives) sustains identity through patterns of verb/noun connections. Assessing such linguistic strategies, Gonseth sees syntax necessarily overstepping its prerogatives:

Does not grammar transgress its rights by calling into syntactic existence a person to whom it lends the unreal quality of remaining identical with himself? . . . In order that a real person should not have the feeling to be somebody else from one day to the next it is necessary that something should persist in him which is profoundly characteristic for this person; the syntactic person is a theoretical form of this "something."[69]

Protagonists on both sides of the law

While there are several categories of persons whose ability and/or desire to sustain identity over the time(s) of the standoff is problematic, there is one analytical category of identity that is particularly interesting and salient here. This is a category of identity with a deepened sense of history and its transformations. The category encompasses all those standoff protagonists who have been, at one time or another (before, and then during the standoff) on both sides of the law. These *dramatis personae*, among whom Ruby Ridge antagonist Randy Weaver, Freemen leader Rodney Skurdal, and mediator Bo Gritz figure prominently, have all represented the armed wing of the legitimate power of the state and have taken up positions (armed or otherwise) against that state.

Two standoffs in particular, that of the Weaver family and that of the Freemen of Montana, were populated with protagonists whose identity vis à vis the law had reversed course. Randall Weaver had been a Green Beret in the US military and had even run for county sheriff in 1988. Ronald Skurdal was a former marine. Bo Gritz, like Randall Weaver, had been in the military's Special Forces and then,

became a hero in right-wing circles when he staged several unsuccessful commando-style forays in Southeast Asia in the 1980s to search for POWs. His activities were curbed after US authorities charged him with using a passport under a false name. Based in Nevada, he later became a lecturer on emergency preparedness, self-sufficient living and homeopathic remedies. As a Populist Party presidential candidate in 1992, his slogan was "God, guns and Gritz."[70]

Among all of the standoffs under examination, that of the Weavers and the Freemen were the most explicitly right-wing, antifederal government, and antilaw-enforcement agencies. It is interesting then, to find these two standoffs full of protagonists who at one time actually represented and fought for this very government. Vietnam may provide the historically contingent key here. As James Aho writes:

The four protagonists in our story – Weaver, Gritz, Degan, and Cluff – all accessed American paramilitarism through their association with the Special Forces. Like Beam, each in his own way brought Vietnam home – in a sense refighting the war, this time on Ruby Ridge, with Weaver and Gritz on one side and Degan and Cluff on the other. Not until the siege was well under way did they come to recognize their shared paternity. By that time they had become deadly enemies.[71]

While Vietnam, and its vexed historical legacy for the generation of men who fought there,[72] helps to explain the singular appearance of reverse-image protagonists in these two standoffs, the very analytical possibility of such a category is critical to our exploration of identity and its emergence in and through action. The *possible* presence of such characters points up the way that standoffs place contingent readings of actions in high relief. Again here, literal and figurative gestures, comprised of orientation, displacement, and support, map the contours of the standoff protagonists in action. The recognition that, were the antistate protagonists to be standing on the other side of the perimeter, facing inward rather than outward, leaning against the perimeter on one side rather than the other, they would be state-representing protagonists instead, is made most powerfully when the empirical possibility of individuals having "switched sides" is proven. Even when standoffs do not harbor side switchers, the phenomenological possibility of such mirroring hovers over this situation so existentially dominated by images of symmetry.

Agents of the law

When looking to track the involvement of law-enforcement agencies and agents in standoffs, an empirically key question concerns the issue of who has jurisdiction? While in a larger, more metaphorical sense, these standoffs are all poised between a given antistate or anti-authority group and something like "the state," or "the government," in concrete terms of who ends up facing whom across the barricades, particular law-enforcement agencies and their representatives are usually the chosen synecdochic part standing in for that larger whole.

As with general standard operating procedures, there are institutionally devised ways of slicing up the law-enforcement map. As former Director of the US Marshals Henry Hudson put it when referring to the confrontation at Ruby Ridge: "One thing I might note, Senator – and I am sure you are aware [of] this – is that once a Deputy US Marshal is killed, the FBI has jurisdiction of that case."[73]

The appeal here is to a series of predictable contingencies that indicate to given agencies what their relationship to particular transgressions are and what their relationship is to other agencies. But there are other, less rationally calibrated contingencies that present situations where it is precisely the conventional claims to jurisdiction that are being contested. For example, when members of the Republic of Texas group found themselves in a standoff in their "embassy," they communicated to the authorities that the only extant law-enforcement agency they recognized was that of the Texas Sheriffs. Thus do history and geography and the overlays of maps and time lines insert themselves into the questions of particular agency jurisdiction.

Once jurisdiction has been determined, a "Who's Who" of the many agencies of law enforcement that have taken responsibility for the standoffs analyzed here would include everything from national military forces to local sheriff offices. A typology of agency levels would range from local police and sheriff officials, to state-level law-enforcement agencies, to federal law-enforcement agencies, to national military forces. The only standoff to have overt, formal military participation was that in Peru, where the Peruvian military took charge of the operation from the outset. As was noted earlier in this chapter, the National Guard flew helicopters over the Mt. Carmel compound in the Branch Davidian standoff and the Air Force was widely believed to have flown over the occupiers at Wounded Knee.

Many national agencies of domestic law enforcement have been charged with responsibility for standoffs. In terms of sheer ubiquity, the FBI has accumulated the largest portfolio, having been involved in the Freemen, Branch Davidian, Ruby Ridge, Wounded Knee, and Republic of Texas standoffs. The ATF and the US Marshal's Service have also seen multiple service; the ATF was centrally involved in the Branch Davidian and the Ruby Ridge standoffs and the US Marshal's Service was at Wounded Knee and Ruby Ridge. Other national level enforcement agencies, including the Immigration and Naturalization Service (Branch Davidian) and the Bureau of Indian Affairs (Wounded Knee) have been involved when issues deemed relevant to their mandates have been central to the themes of certain standoffs. State-level agencies also participate in standoffs, both during the phases of standoff emergence and while the standoff endures. These agencies include the Texas Rangers, the Montana Highway Patrol, and the Texas Department of Public Safety. Finally, at the local level, the Philadelphia Police were in charge of the MOVE standoff and various local sheriff offices were involved in several standoffs (Branch Davidian, Ruby Ridge, and Freemen of Montana).

Most of these agencies of law enforcement were internally divided into units that, metaphorically or morphologically speaking, we might call the head, the heart, and the hands. The head consists of the top-level adminis-trative unit and, in a standoff, is usually decapitated in the sense that most of its incumbents are far away from the scene and sending and receiving reports from the field. This is particularly true for national level law-enforcement agencies like the FBI, the ATF, the BIA, and the INS. Communication between the head and the hands and the heart often takes the form of memos and telephone conversations. Practitioners of the hand (in a nice alignment with the expression "hands-on"[74]) are potentially the most physically involved of those dealing with the standoff. They are the tactical elements, anticipating or engaging in acts of physical force and dis-placement of various sorts. The heart, or the negotiating and community relations units of law enforcement, can be physically present at the scene of the standoff, moving into and out of the standoff center, operating at the borders of inside and outside. Or the heart can be found at some distance from the scene (as they were at Waco) and only in contact with the antag-onists by way of mediated communication.

This division of labor is quite clear to members of law enforcement agen-cies. As Jayne Docherty writes: "An oft repeated aphorism among police negotiators is, 'Negotiators do not command and commanders do not negotiate.'"[75] These divisions seem to make organizational sense, and yet, when confronted with a situation in which the normal meanings and

sequencing of actions is precisely what is being put in suspended animation, such instrumental bureaucratic rationality is often counter-produc-
tive. As well, these situations of heightened uncertainty exaggerate
intra-organizational rivalries and hostilities. This is almost always the case
between the tactical and the community relations wings of local police
forces. Such a rivalry played itself out in an extremely asymmetric manner
in Philadelphia during the MOVE conflict. Police Commissioner Sambor
was very explicit in choosing only members of the Bomb Disposal Unit,
and other strategic units of the police department (including a sharpshooter and a pistol instructor) to develop the police plan to deal with the
MOVE group. None of these officers were members of the more commu-
nity-oriented Civil Affairs Division. Hostilities were also in evidence
between the tactical and negotiating wings of the FBI in the standoff in
Waco. In that standoff FBI negotiator Byron Sage claimed to have come
upon a bit of acerbic graffiti about himself on a door in the tactical team's
site that said, "Sage is a Davidian." Analyzing the sentiment behind such
graffiti, a former FBI analyst, Farris Rookstool explained:

If you ask a Hostage Rescue Team guy what he thinks of the negotiators, they
would see them as a bunch of pussies. The negotiators might look at these guys
as something a little disturbed, in the sense that these guys, you know, want to get
up in the morning and want to you know, breach a door and want to, you know,
drive a tank and, you know, there's something kind of a little unusual about a
person who – who gets some sort of a charge out of wanting to do those kinds of
things.[76]

Given these intra-agency tensions, unit names are as significant as all
other names that circulate in and around the standoff scene. The unit
alluded to above by Rookstool, the "Hostage Rescue Team," offers a
benign and focused identity – their job is to rescue hostages. But in truth
this tactical unit is often deployed in situations where there are no hostages
(though as we will see soon, there may be "hostages") and thus no one to
rescue. Something of a syntactic mystery then opens itself up when rescue
names the role and the situation provides no one to rescue. What exactly
are members of the HRT to do? Recounting the historical evolution and
deployment of the HRT, Senator Grassley evokes some of the contradictions in the hybridizing of venues (military and domestic), tactics, and
purposes, and in inverting the normal priorities of negotiation and
assault:

First came the rescue – or the creation of the Hostage Rescue Team, or HRT, as it
is known, and this was in the early 1980s. This is supposedly a crack tactical outfit
that trains with the military special forces at Fort Bragg. It is headed by a former

armored tank officer in the US Army. Its mission was to rescue American hostages overseas. Suddenly, the Hostage Rescue Team was deployed domestically, and the FBI increasingly relied on aggressive tactical solutions rather than on negotiations. This is said to have first occurred in the mid-1980s in Arkansas. It was a standoff involving a group known as the Covenant, the Sword and the Arm of the Lord. The case was handled peacefully in the final analysis, but it was the first time the upside-down strategy was employed.[77]

While law enforcement's role in negotiations will be addressed in a later section on standoff talk, the general and more specifically tactical role of law enforcers takes on certain predictable contours and purposes. As one African-American citizen of Philadelphia put it after the MOVE confrontation, "It's the responsibility of a Black elected official, who has responsibility over the police force, to ask the questions that whites don't ask, and to make certain that the . . . Commissioner of Police doesn't simply manifest . . . a police mentality."[78]

That one can say something as broad and unspecific as "police mentality" and expect to be understood indicates an assumption about a common view of the police. According to Daniel Swett, the police (and, with variations in education, training, and worldview, one can also indicate other law-enforcement agencies) represent a unique subculture. Swett writes that "the police . . . are more than a group of individuals organized into a bureaucratic, paramilitary structure to perform technical missions. Entry requirements, training, on- and off-duty behavioral standards, and operational exigencies and goals combine to produce a homogeneity of attitudes, values, and life ways such that members of police forces constitute a distinct subculture within their societies."[79]

This sense of a tightly knit subculture lends credence to a suspicion voiced by Senator Kohl during the hearings on Ruby Ridge that law-enforcement agents react with particular vehemence when one of their own is wounded or killed, and that such occurrences ratchet up the stakes in situations such as those presented by standoffs. Kohl is interviewing Henry Hudson, former Director of the US Marshals:

Senator Kohl: You know the impression that people can get listening to this conversation [regarding the question of why the FBI charged up the hill to Weaver's house so soon after Degan was shot, with their "Rules of Engagement" in hand] is that when deaths occur in our society, if the deaths occur to a US marshal or to an FBI agent, or to a cop, that the response by law enforcement will be more vigorous and more determined than if the deaths occur to a civilian. Do you want to make that statement?

Mr. Hudson: That is, in fact what occurs, Senator Kohl, whether I like it or not, sir, that is what happens in law enforcement when something like this happens.[80]

Finally, clothing constitutes a significant gesture of identity for law-enforcement officials. Decisions about whether to be "in uniform" or "out of uniform," to be dressed for camouflage and/or combat, to be easily identified as an agent of one or another of the various agencies of control or to go incognito, all act as arrows pointing to the self-in-construction in situational action. In an earlier study of the social drama of terrorism,[81] I described the manner in which various articles of the Geneva Conventions required insurgent combatants to identify themselves as such in their clothing, and the way in which such requirements conflicted with the *modus operandi* of insurgents seeking to hide themselves among the "civilians." An analogous issue affects law-enforcement officers who, seeking at once to reveal and conceal their identities in situations of high stakes and immanent violence, have vexed decisions about what to wear. This is true even for those not explicitly involved in undercover operations. In an already highly contingent situation, such as is the standoff, the ramifications of clothing choice is doubly contingent on the various ways such clothing is read by other participants *in media res*.

One example of contingent, and dangerous, reading comes from the standoff at Ruby Ridge. The first law-enforcement agents to approach the Weaver cabin (and, fatally, to attract the attention of the Weaver dog), were dressed in camouflage with stocking caps and were subsequently described by Weaver and his friend Harris as not being immediately recognizable as agents of the law. As Senator Feinstein seeks to get a clear image of what the US Marshals were wearing, or should have been wearing, on the day of the operation, she engages with former US Marshal, District of Idaho, Michael Johnson, in a question and answer session:

Senator Feinstein: Now the operational plan also says that the uniform and equipment of all units will be per unit SOP, which I take is standard operating procedure. What is standard operating procedure for the uniforms and equipment of the US Marshals in this situation?
Mr. Johnson: Senator, as far as normal uniform and equipment, you would have a side arm, handcuffs, you have extra ammunition ... They were wearing black type fatigues, bulletproof entry-type vests with "police, US Marshal."
Senator Feinstein: On top of the uniform?
Mr. Johnson: On top of them, right in front ... And a black type of kevlar helmet that our current US military carries. And goggles, gloves, you know, military type boots, different types of firearms ...
Senator Feinstein: Did Marshal Degan have that uniform on?
Mr. Johnson: Not to my knowledge, Senator ...[82]

By contrast, the federal and local agents sent to deal with the Freemen of Montana standoff were given explicit instructions to play down their usual military presentation of self. One of the ways this was accomplished was through clothing. As opposed to such combat-ready uniforms as that described by Johnson, the full range of personnel at the Freeman scene, from negotiators to SWAT teams, wore civilian clothes.[83]

Antagonists

"David, we are facilitating you leaving the compound by enlarging the front door. David, you have had your fifteen minutes of fame . . . Vernon is no longer the Messiah. Leave the building now."[84]

Negotiators often end up being on a first name basis with their antagonists, after so many hours or days or weeks of talk. But the combining of first-name nominalization "David," with the reference to Andy Warhol's claim that everyone in America has fifteen minutes of fame, with the sarcastic reference to Koresh's original and rejected name, Vernon Howell, with the final misapprised assault on the religious validity of the Branch Davidian doctrine (Koresh never precisely claimed to be the Messiah), reveals how high the level of frustration and anger had grown for those negotiating at Waco. And of course, we cannot ignore the importance of the threat/boast to enlarge the door, that symbolic portal of the standoff.

In the seven standoffs under examination here, there are a variety of different types of antistate antagonists, with different ideologies, backgrounds, and modes of organization. There are literal, biological families that constitute the groups either in whole, or in part (Ruby Ridge, Waco, Freemen). There are self-styled "families" that claim, through renaming and other strategies, to be a family (recall that all MOVE members took the last name of Africa). There are groups whose main claim to organizational raison d'être is religious (Freemen, Waco) or political (Wounded Knee, Republic of Texas, Tupac Amaru). There are antagonists who are ideologically right-wing and separatist (Ruby Ridge, Freemen of Montana, Republic of Texas) and antagonists who are left-wing and revolutionary (Tupac Amaru). And there are those whose politics are salient but less easy to categorize along the left/right continuum (MOVE, Wounded Knee, Waco). While several of the antagonist groups had been extremely disruptive of community relations and/or government administrative transactions, and a few of the groups had actually threatened or engaged in some kind of violent actions, none were large enough or well-equipped enough to constitute an actual, material threat to the prevailing governments in the respective cases.[85]

Despite the ideological and organizational differences among the groups of antagonists, they can all be analytically captured by the term "antisociety." An antisociety, according to Halliday, is, "a society that is set up within another society as a conscious alternative to it. It is a mode of resistance, resistance which may take the form either of passive symbiosis or of active hostility and even destruction."[86]

Names of such groups tell a story themselves about the groups' senses of transformed and refocused identity: MOVE, Freemen of Montana, Republic of Texas, Branch Davidians, Tupac Amaru, Independent Oglala Nation. But of course identity emerges at the sites of interactional matrices where acceptance, rejection, recognition, substitution, and acknowledgement are just some of the possible responses of others to identity claims made by the self. One group (Branch Davidians) claimed to be organized around religious precepts; law-enforcement agencies rejected that claim and argued that it was a cult. Another group claimed to be a separate republic (Republic of Texas); the state maintained that they were a group of terrorists and renegades. In the case of the Wounded Knee standoff, the members of the Independent Oglala Nation claimed to be comprised of warriors asserting the rebirth of a nation:

The American Indian Movement sees itself as a new warrior society for Indian people . . . To white persons, the warrior is the armed forces. It's the guy that goes out there and fights and kills for his people. But Indian people have never had hired killers. Warrior society to them means the men and women of the nation who have dedicated themselves to give everything they have to the people. A warrior should be the first one to go hungry or the last one to eat.[87]

The US Government rejected this claim and counter-proposed a complex, confused, and unstable identity for the group. Secretary of Interior Rogers Morton stated that:

Their demands are vague and change from day to day. They do not represent a constituted group with whom the Government can contract or serve . . . There is one thing of which I am very sure. Nothing is gained by blackmail. You cannot run this Government or find equitable solutions with a gun at your head or the head of a hostage. Any agency of government that is forced into a fast deal by revolutionary tactics, blackmail, or terrorism is not worth its salt. These are criminal operations and should be dealt with accordingly.[88]

Key images and identities in Morton's statement collide and commingle. The Sioux are blackmailers, revolutionaries, terrorists, and criminals. They are and are not a bona fide, constituted group. In fact both their perceived amorphousness and their revolutionary bandedness work against them – they are either not organized enough or too organized for the government to deal with. Of course, the synecdochic "gun at the head" image is the clearest and most centering one of all for this characterization of the antagonists and the situation of the standoff.

Images at odds with each other can be based on several aspects of identity. The relationship between agent, agency, and purpose reveals much about the assessed moral valence of any given protagonist/antagonist. Alberto Fujimori spoke explicitly to such identity/morality links when, in a statement to a Spanish news agency on January 1, 1997, he called the Tupac Amaru group (along with the Shining Path group) "terrorists." According to the *New York Times*, "He also rejected proposals to legalize the group, saying it would set a 'harmful precedent for other outlawed organizations who disturb law and order to legalize themselves.'"[89] For its part, the *New York Times*, along with several other news outlets, did not refer to the Tupac Amaru group as terrorists and such a demurral angered the Peruvian government.

As always, the antagonist group seeks to characterize itself and often explicitly refutes its characterization by others. The Tupac Amaru spent a good part of several of their Communiqués in rejecting the terrorist label and proposing the "guerrilla" alternative:

Communiqué #3: A. We lament that some political and journalistic personalities insist on labeling us as a terrorist and genocidal band, which is absolutely false, since there are no facts that sustain it. B. We don't accept that we continue being compared with Shining Path, an organization that we have repeatedly condemned for the use of an irrational violence that affects the people itself.

Communiqué #6 : We are a guerrilla that is open to dialogue. We have always been open to dialogue, with the organizations of the people, with the rest of civil society, with journalists, even with police and soldiers . . .

Some might see such category-mongering as splitting hairs. But labels matter, as any given group sees its perceived legitimacy and ability to act wax and wane. This sliding legitimacy is a function of the abilities of the participants to make particular labels stick over time and/or to dislodge extant labels. In the standoffs under examination, we find all of the variations on a theme: revolutionary, terrorist, guerrilla, rebel, warrior, zealot, insurgent, blackmailer, criminal, fanatic, extremist, cultist, and so forth. Each of these terms has a different historical etymology and a different contemporary inflection. While there is considerable overlap in the ways that the actions of, say, terrorist and fanatic, are envisioned, there is enough difference to slightly shift the expectations of the political and law enforcement authorities, the media, and the public as the terms come and go.

It is useful to recall the culturally specific standoff themes introduced in the first chapter as we seek to calibrate the antagonist identities. The four key themes (family structure and sexuality, religious orientation, territorial jurisdiction, and gun ownership), provide an apparently reliable grid for the authorities and the public through which the actions of specified groups can be gauged. Thus David Koresh's dictum separating men's and women's sleeping quarters at Mt. Carmel, his wedding and having sex with several very young women, and his fathering children by different women, were all read as actions in a state of excess and transgression. Thus the grid allows certain behaviors to be foregrounded and others to be elided in processes of description and characterization. As well, highlighted cultural themes and characterizing labels (labels here tendered by the authorities) tend to be coupled: sexual excess and unorthodox family structures tend to appear with labels of "cult"; association with guns (buying, selling, stockpiling, using) is connected to "terrorist," "revolutionary," "insurgent," and "extremist"; religious excess and heterodoxy appears with "cult," "zealot," and "fanatic"; and territorial ambition is linked with "rebel," "terrorist," "extremist," and "revolutionary."

Violence is read into some of these terms more explicitly than others, but it is always there, hovering in the shadows of the projects of labeling and responding to perceived cultural threats. Thus the question: "Is this individual/group dangerous?" This question is posed at every point as a group is identified by law-enforcement agencies, as warrants are developed, as arrests are attempted or made, as the standoff takes shape, and as the retrospection takes place in legislative hearings, judicial trials, and administrative reports.

As already noted, many attempts are made to answer this question as authorities and journalists read the gestures of antagonists as they transform structures, raise flags, display weapons, and issue statements. Sometimes, though, the gestures of law-enforcement officials themselves reflect an awareness that the answer must confront the situational contingencies of the activation/demonstration of dangerousness. In a certain sense, no one and everyone is "dangerous." The labeling of someone as dangerous is a probabilistic enterprise – someone either does or doesn't endanger someone else. Before the actual endangering occurs, the most that can be said with certainty is that a person has endangered someone previously or has threatened to do so. Law-enforcement officials (like mental health professionals and school administrators) must traffic in such probabilistic evaluations all the time. And yet standoffs emerging at the sites of the transgressions of culturally thematic set-points seem to encourage particularly contradictory and vexed characterizations of their antagonists. Officials must deal with people who are religious, but too religious; with people who believe strongly in family but are too expansive in their definitions of family; with people who take the constitutional right to bear arms too seriously; with people who transmute the constitutional right to privacy into a right to secede from the union, and so forth.

Because there is often a sense of dealing with antagonists who transmute a good into a bad by tipping it over, taking it to extremes, rather than with antagonists who are simply amoral, these contradictory images sometimes manifest themselves in strategies of interaction (interaction understood as, for example, apprehension and negotiation). The clearest example of this can be seen in the strange and complicated way that agents of the ATF arranged to serve Randy Weaver with an arrest warrant many months before the standoff. As Senator Arlen Specter recounted it during the subsequent hearings:

There was an elaborate procedure for your arrest where they [ATF agents posing as a family with car trouble] pretended to have a breakdown on the road. And when you were trying to help them, they took you into custody, which showed concern of theirs as to using that elaborate ruse, instead of simply coming and serving a warrant of arrest. We will try to find out what it was for law enforcement to undertake that kind of an unusual procedure.[90]

A strange series of assumptions undergirds this action. First, Weaver is assumed to be dangerous enough that a "routine arrest," providing for agents to go to Weaver's cabin and knock on the door and serve the warrant, would be too hazardous and should be avoided. Next, an apparently conflicting reading of Weaver, as a person decent and neighborly enough to stop his truck and attempt to assist this "family" that had a broken-down car on the road, was critical to the plan. So in one and the same plan, Weaver is both extremely dangerous and extremely friendly. It is easy to see how such contradictory readings can short-circuit any standard operating procedures and is likely to instigate impulsive and disjointed actions instead.

Hostages and "hostages"

If a standoff sets up a situational paralysis, where the opposing sides stave off each other's action through some kind of mutual threat, the "hostage" is often the character around whom that threat circles and on whom the threat hinges. This is in alignment with the *American Heritage Dictionary* definition of a hostage: "A person held by one party in a conflict as security that specified terms will be met by the opposing party." On the other hand, at a certain analytical distance all standoff participants can be viewed as being held hostage to the situation. And finally, if all situations are understood as possessing some kind of will to existence, and thus, to movement and development, we can look at the standoff from a metatheoretical perspective on situations. From that perspective, the very narrative of social life is being held hostage by the time/space/action freezing imprint of the standoff. Standoffs hold the social narrative hostage.

Thus at every level, the figures and concept of hostages insinuate themselves into the very essence of the standoff, even where there are no hostages in the literal sense. The figure of the hostage sets up alternative narrative programs, that being either the hostage's annihilation/sacrifice or his or her rescue. This is so because the hostage is typically understood as having no autonomous agency by which to effect action. The hostage waits for others to act.

Two of the standoffs examined here, the Tupac Amaru standoff and that of the Republic of Texas, had literal hostages. We have already discussed the way in which the staggered hostage releases in Lima created a rhythmic language of symbolic politics. In the Republic of Texas case, there was a symmetrical release of an imprisoned member of the group when they released the two neighbor hostages.

But the most interesting and analytically complex way that hostages appeared in the standoffs was as "hostages." That is, all of the other five cases examined contained participants whose status as hostages was claimed by some, but was contested by others. As well, even those making the claims that these participants were hostages often reversed course and declared them to be antagonists as well. From the children of the MOVE members in the house on Osage Avenue in Philadelphia, to the children and some of the elderly adults in Mt. Carmel, to the children of Randy Weaver, to some white residents of Wounded Knee, to the children of the Freemen of Montana, to various women in various standoffs, there were "hostages" in abundance.

What could one surmise about the existential and semiotic (orientation, displacement, support) stance of a hostage? First, one would assume that such an individual would want to leave, would choose to leave the epicenter of the standoff if so permitted. Second, one would assume that such a person would be in a relationship toward the standoff antagonists that was primarily defined by hostility (controlling here, of course, for the now mythical "Stockholm syndrome"). Finally, one would assume that the hostage would prefer to be in the literal and figurative embrace of the authorities and would share the worldview of these authorities more than that of the anti-authority group.

While certainly logical, these parameters of hostage action and attitude were precisely contradicted by the "hostages" in the remaining cases. For example, in the standoff at Wounded Knee, eleven white residents of the town were originally characterized as hostages by the authorities. As such, the two South Dakota US Senators, George McGovern and James Abourezk, flew to Wounded Knee in order to secure their release. To their surprise, the residents stated that they did not want to leave the town for the duration of the occupation. In both the Ruby Ridge and the Branch Davidian standoff, the law-enforcement units sent to the sites of conflict were units set up to deal with hostage situations. According to James Tabor, by the time the FBI had taken over the operation in Waco from the ATF, the situation had been classified as a "Complex Hostage Barricade Rescue Situation," but it was never entirely clear who, if anyone, was a hostage. Sometimes the Branch Davidian children were considered hostages, as were the elderly members. However, this characterization implied that the Branch Davidian adults would harm these other members, including their own offspring, in some calculated strategy. And it was clear that they would never do this. A similar ambiguous state of hostage identification occurred at Ruby Ridge, where the Weaver children were viewed as both hostages and potential armed antagonists. Thus, on the one hand the *New York Times* could report that: "[the FBI agents] said they did not want to storm the cabin for fear of harming the children. Mr. Glenn said he considered the Weaver children 'hostages' to their father, an Army veteran."[91] On the other hand, the authorities were well aware that the Weaver children knew how to shoot a gun and were potentially armed (as fourteen-year-old Sam Weaver proved to be during the original shooting at the Y), two pieces of information that undercut their hostage status.[92]

As Senator Thompson reflected, responding to the testimony of Henry Hudson, former director of the US Marshal's Service: "And well, just from the name of the team, one would conclude this is not the typical kind of case that the Hostage Rescue Team would be brought into either, because there were no hostages involved in the normal sense of the word."[93]

Hostages "in the normal sense of the word" is really the key here. In the case of children, and sometimes in cases of women and older adults, the mixture of filial piety, social and political innocence, spousal loyalty, religious belief, ability/inability to fight offensively or defensively, led to contradictory characterizations of them and conflicting orientations toward them on the parts of the authorities. A clear case of this categorical confusion and slipperiness emerged during the testimony of the former Managing Director of the City of Philadelphia during the MOVE Commission Hearings. Former Director Brooks was asked about a memo that had been sent from the District Attorney's office to the mayor during the period in which the city officials were planning the operation to arrest some of the MOVE members living in the house on Osage Avenue. The memo had referred to the MOVE children in some detail, and it was to this mode of referral that the MOVE Commission lawyer referred in his question:

Q: Do you recall any discussion at this meeting on May 7, 1985 concerning this statement that the police believed that MOVE would use their children as hostages?

Brooks: And I do recall [a] discussion which says great care must be used as pertains to the children . . . I might add that the use of the word "hostages," when put in quotations to some degree, and I don't know to what degree, colors the use of the word "hostages." Had the word not been put in quotations it might, might have made some difference to what somebody did. But I don't know that that did or didn't.[94]

Finally, hostages have a shadowy and precarious social existence (matching the precariousness of their physical existence). They are and are not who they once were, even who they were just a day ago, before their being taken hostage. They have been contaminated through proximity (contiguity) to the antagonists,[95] and they become as much a liability to the authorities as a subject of desired rescue. A particularly dramatic action of Peruvian President Alberto Fujimori revealed this tenuous and drifting hold on identity that hostages have during standoffs. On January 3, 1997, after only two weeks of what was to become a three-month long confrontation, Fujimori peremptorily replaced the president of the Supreme Court and six police generals, all of whom were among the hostages, in what one diplomat referred to as a "brutal" message to the rebels. Perhaps the message to the hostages was more brutal than that to the Tupac Amaru group, namely, you are no longer who you think you are.

Minor roles

There are a series of other *dramatis personae* who people the standoff dramas. Some, such as the symbolically strategic neighbors, have already been discussed (see this chapter's "Setting off the standoff" section). Others, specifically those involved in the crucial processes of negotiation (official negotiators, intermediaries, experts, mediators) will be analyzed in a later section on standoff speech acts. There are, however, other participants with incidental but significant roles, and these include law-enforcement informants and undercover agents.

Informants and undercover agents were used in both the Ruby Ridge and the Branch Davidian standoffs. Randy Weaver had originally been contacted by an ATF confidential informant, Kenneth Fadeley, who was attempting to infiltrate meetings of the neo-Nazi "Aryan Nations" group and saw Weaver there. It was Fadeley who ultimately convinced Weaver to sell him the two sawed-off shotguns that set everything in motion for Weaver's arrest and subsequent actions. Part spy, part seducer, part federal officer, Fadeley's actions reverberate across the boundaries of the legitimate and the illegitimate, the innocent and the corrupt. According to Gary Marx, in his book, *Undercover: Police Surveillance in America*, informants are the weak links in undercover operations. They have the greatest proximity to law breakers and thus, in such close quarters with corruption and illegality, they are susceptible to going over to the side of corruption themselves. In the case of Fadeley, he provides us with a sense of what some of the initial resistance to the role feels like, particularly when immersed in a world of political extremism and racism. Talking about his initial attendance at the Aryan Nations meetings, he recalls: "For instance, when the conference gets started, Butler gets up, makes a few words, and then everyone, which is – and I will just add this. The first time I had to do it, I mean, it was terrible. You raise your hand in a Nazi salute, and you yell, 'Hail, Victory.' Mr. Weaver also did that."[96]

Finally, there are always bystanders, groups of people who are positioned at various permissible distances from the standoff centers. Literal bystanders function as watered-down versions of the Greek chorus, lamenting man's fate, craving and decrying the potentially violent action at the same time. Bystanders might be a mixture of friends, relatives, supporters, and neighbors of those in the standoff center (antagonists and hostages and "hostages" alike). In the case of modern standoffs in mass-mediated societies, the larger group of bystanders are sitting in their living rooms watching the drama unfold on their television screens as a media event.

The situational lives of texts

Texts play a crucial role in naming, and thus creating, a standoff and in moving it through its phases toward its end. In the standoffs analyzed here, every state adversary has what I'll call an Ur-text, a foundational document that sets out the most transcendent terms of a particular worldview. Over the course of a standoff, these Ur-texts move in and out of focus. But regardless of how explicit any particular act is in its referencing an Ur-text, the Ur-text underwrites action for its adherents.

Ur-texts

For the Independent Oglala Nation at Wounded Knee, during the 1973 standoff with the authorities of the United States, the Ur-text was the Fort Laramie Treaty between the Sioux and the United States Government of

1868. As such, the ION issued the following declaration during the standoff:

Let it be known this day, March 11, 1973, that the Oglagla Sioux people will revive the Treaty of 1868 and that it will be the basis for all negotiations. Let the declaration be made that we are a sovereign nation by the Treaty of 1868. We intend to send a delegation to the United Nations as follows: Chief Frank Fools Crow; Chief Frank Kills Enemy; Eugene White Hawk, District Chairman [of the Wounded Knee District Council]; Meredith Quinn, international advisor; Matthew King, interpreter . . . [97]

MOVE members self-consciously referred their actions to *The Guidelines*, the doctrinal writings of founder John Africa. For David Koresh, leader of the Branch Davidians at Waco, the Ur-text was the Bible, particularly the books of Revelation, Zechariah, and Ezekiel.[98] For Randall Weaver at Ruby Ridge in Idaho, it was the inflammatory treatise, *The Protocol of the Learned Elders of Zion* (a hybridized document that mixes a plagiarized novel by a German government clerk and an anti-Napoleonic tract by a conservative French lawyer).[99] The Freemen of Montana claimed the Bible, the Magna Carta, the Declaration of Independence, and the pre-Civil War American Constitution. The Republic of Texas group referred to the Boundary Treaty of 1838 as the legitimate document determining Texas' and their future. Finally, the Tupac Amaru group put their own "Manifesto" forward as a foundational document and, in a bid to achieve a certain political legitimacy, also claimed the Geneva Conventions (specifically those Articles referring to insurgent movements); Communiqué #4 said:

The MRTA has respected and will respect the Geneva Convention on internal conflicts; in that sense the persons who are inside the residence are treated with respect appropriate to their situation as human beings and prisoners of war. They don't receive the same treatment that the Peruvian government gives to the political prisoners, who are subjected to a slow extermination in the prisons of Peru.

One thing to notice about the various Ur-texts cited is that each antagonist group, not just David Koresh, was selective about the particular passages or portions of the texts on which to focus. This will become theoretically significant shortly. Here it is important to note that religious scholars, such as Moshe Sokol, view such selectivity vis à vis religious texts as being essentially modern. He writes: "It seems to me that one of the distinctive characteristics of modern religious interpretations of texts is the extent to which the interpreter both self consciously selects out those texts which he wishes to interpret, as well as – and this is perhaps the critical point – considers such selectivity to be legitimate."[100]

But it is not only the anti-institutional protagonists in these standoffs who rely on and deploy an Ur-text. So do the authorities. Here secular texts function just as well as do sacred ones – the Pennsylvania State Criminal Code can be deployed with as much authority as the Bible in such situations. And sometimes all of the protagonists claim the same Ur-text, albeit with radically different interpretations. In one such case, it seemed that there was a significant Ur-text overlap between the FBI and the Branch Davidians – with the Bible and the Constitution being claimed by both sides. FBI Special Agent Byron Sage recounted that, at a crucial face-to-face moment in the negotiations with the Branch Davidians, he had been asked by a Branch Davidian member named Wayne if the Constitution had been suspended. Sage's response is telling. He says, "There are two documents that I would give my life for. One is the Constitution and one is the Bible and I would give my life to defend both of them."[101]

From the list of standoff Ur-texts above, it is clear that some are explicitly written and read as religious texts and some as secular, political texts. But the mythical power and world-shaping quality of such foundational statements is not limited to the clearly religious texts. As Carol Greenhouse writes: "It is tempting to consider that the ideas of fixed sacred texts and the instantaneous inscription of order on and in the world are not only ancient ideas but also modern ones, appropriated from the orality of priests and claimed for the literate mythos of law."[102] The authority and air of fatalism with which representatives of the legitimate governments involved in these standoffs deploy their often secular, chosen Ur-texts testifies to such power.

Agent Sage's statement above also raises several problems associated with what we might call text management in any standoff: 1) that of antagonists sharing the same Ur-text; 2) that of a given protagonist simultaneously embracing two (or more) Ur-texts; 3) that of orienting oneself to two potentially or actually conflicting worldviews; and 4) that of drawing on a sacred Ur-text to provide foundational principles in a secular world.

The idea of declared adversaries sharing the same foundational Ur-text may seem paradoxical, if not impossible. But it is both the inevitable fate and the prerogative of all Ur-texts to live lives of instantiation. Ur-texts need interpreters – they cannot live without them. They cannot reproduce themselves wholesale and are thus spoken or (re)written in bits and pieces and in different voices with different registers and intonations. Thus, Ur-texts are continuously and inevitably transformed into what I call "texts-in-action" as they encounter each other *in media res*. As such, the same Ur-text, interpreted, highlighted, and reorganized by different actors, can speak very different messages. One actor may interpret an Ur-text to be counseling unrestrained battle; another actor might read the same Ur-text as allowing history to take its own course, or to be out of the hands of human beings and only in the hands of a deity. Actions can thus derive from or attach themselves to Ur-texts in a variety of ways. On the other hand, the fact that there is a shared Ur-text opens the door to a new *situationally* derived reading that could, theoretically, be shared by the adversaries. Critiquing conventional approaches to conflict resolution, Emery Roe offers a similar approach: "Thus while conventional evaluation frequently undertakes the well-nigh impossible task of establishing common ground between opposing parties whose very definition of themselves excludes a common ground, intertextual evaluation ratchets up the analysis one level by searching instead for a shared intertext that is grounded in the very polarization observed."[103]

For protagonists who simultaneously claim two or more Ur-texts, there are problems of potential cross-text conflicts, even when the worldviews are not overtly contradictory. One solution to such a problem is to create a kind of text hierarchy, but even this must be situationally determined. When, for example, Byron Sage must choose between a particular reading of a specific passage of the Bible and a particular reading of a passage of the US Constitution (as might occur when negotiating with the singular text exegete, David Koresh), readings which may indicate very different actions, how is he to decide between them? Other standoff participants seem more certain of text hierarchy, as indicated by Carolyn Trochmann, a friend of the Weaver family at Ruby Ridge; "Here we don't roll over," Trochmann said, "Biblically, it's wrong whenever we allow the government to take another law from God."[104] Conditional obeisance to the US Constitution and civil and criminal codes is nevertheless easily trumped by the law of God as detailed in the Bible.

Trochmann's statement raises the final problem of Ur-text management, that of cleaving to a sacred text in a secular world. The Branch Davidians, the members of MOVE, the Weaver family, and the Freemen all, to some extent, encountered this problem over the course of their respective standoffs. As we have seen, excess piety acts as one proximal trigger to standoffs, and a literalist interpretation of a sacred Ur-text (to the detriment of adherence to secular, society-organizing Ur-texts) is a signal of excess piety. The complexities of a modernist religious hermeneutic are laid out by Moshe Sokol. Describing what he calls the "redemptive," the "reflexive," and the "constructive" characteristics of this hermeneutic, he writes: "Each modern religious person seeks in his own way to embrace the secular claims of modernity together with the claims of religion . . . Will he read the text only as a great work of art, for example, or only as God's word, or as both? . . .: the interpretation reflects back onto, and has an impact on, the interpreter's whole modern religious consciousness."[105]

Thus do all of the protagonists of a standoff pick and choose among Ur-texts and create hierarchies of authority for them. The Ur-texts provide the existential ground for all principled arguments that subsequently emerge. References to, and interpretations of, Ur-texts function as a warrant for the situational arguments of standoffs. According to Stephen Toulmin, the warrant is a "general, step-authorizing statement . . . a license to argue from grounds to a conclusion."[106] And therefore Ur-texts circulate throughout the standoff in this interpreted and referential manner. Thus are working texts, the texts-in-action, generated and take the forms of negotiations, conversations, memos, "Rules of Engagement," communiqués, manifestos, interviews, and journalistic accounts. They all talk the event into life.[107] These texts generated during a standoff are, by my mode of framing, sites of heterogeneity – the (usually) involuntary simultaneous cohabitation of a variety of textualized discourses, relying on and referring to different foundational Ur-texts. On the one hand, participants may have their own scripts in their heads or in their hands. They might even be able to anticipate what the scripts of the other participants will be. On the other hand, there is also the fact that the participants can't know in advance what new texts-in-action will emerge as the diverse scripts interact with each other. Emergent messages are inevitably complicated and contradictory. They enter a world already reconfigured by prior texts. As perceived by protagonists and/or mass-mediated audiences they necessarily open themselves up to interpretation.[108]

From Ur-text to text-in-action

To illustrate the process by which an Ur-text generates and disseminates texts-in-action, it is useful to look at one specific Ur-text, the Constitution of the United States. A broad range of standoff participants explicitly claimed the Constitution (or some historical version of it) as a foundational statement for their group or agency or self. The list includes the Branch Davidians, the FBI, the Freemen of Montana, the US Justice Department, and the Republic of Texas group. Each protagonist had an interest in laying claim to the principles and ideas of this document to explain and justify their actions. But the Constitution, like all Ur-texts, can only be applied piecemeal and in situations. It doesn't really live in a glass case. As well, the principles and worldview standards of the Constitution are often thought to provide broad rather than specific indications for proceeding through life. As Senator Thompson put it, in trying to get a handle on the organizational imperatives of law-enforcement agents stuck in a perilous and unpredictable situation, and having only a text-in-action, the Rules of Engagement, to explicitly refer to:

You are presented with these rules of engagement. You are not supposed to be practicing lawyers. *You are not supposed to carry around the Constitution in your pocket.* You are told what to do by your superiors. Your superiors give you these instructions. And I would encourage you – you know, you can say that you disagree with them or, yes, they were there and we chose not to follow them or whatever . . . but you are all trying to avoid the clear truth that you were told that anybody outside that cabin with a weapon was fair game, and you were encouraged to shoot them. I mean, that is the only interpretation of this document.[109]

You are not supposed to carry around the Constitution in your pocket. Indeed not. Life isn't an exegetical exercise of text hermeneutics – or is it? Certainly one of the things we can say about a good number of the standoff participants is that they took this particular vision of life very seriously. The Freemen of Montana produced a series of documents detailing their understanding of the Constitution, including to whom it should be applied (primarily white males), and which parts of it were legitimate and relevant. In a manifesto written during the standoff, the Freemen laid out their interpretation of the Constitution and challenged the government to disprove the lawfulness of that interpretation. An excerpt from that manifesto reads: "All things in law are timely. Article Three (3) [of the Constitution] is the Supreme Rule of Law, and the USA Land." A year earlier, Rodney Skurdal, a leader of the Freemen group had published a twenty-page manifesto describing the Christian Identity Movement beliefs and had filed it in a Montana county courthouse. The Constitution appears in this document as well: It called on people who would be "free" to sever ties to government, by not paying taxes and shunning Social Security cards, marriage licenses and building permits. The document describes two categories of citizens: "We the People," or white males, subject to "God's law," the Constitution and its first ten amendments; and other racial groups, enfranchised only by "man's law," the 14th Amendment's guarantee of equal protection."[110]

Certainly such a representation of the Constitution reminds us of Sokol's point about interpretive selectivity, here applied to a secular rather than a sacred text. Time lines are twisted and bent back on themselves in choosing an older version of the Constitution and applying it to some, but not all, United States citizens. But the point here to be made about the exegetical work being done with Ur-texts is that it results in a series of event shaping texts-in-action. The Constitution generates manifestos, reports, Rules of Engagement, and negotiation discussion points.

The action of texts-in-action

Like the gods on Mount Olympus, the Ur-texts send down lightning bolts in the forms of texts-in-action. Just listing all of the ones that shaped and carried the identified standoffs forward is a mammoth task. There are bench warrants, arrest warrants, search warrants, citizen's warrants, affidavits, federal, state, and local criminal and civil codes, Field Manuals, Rules of Engagement, writs, letters, declarations, communiqués, liens, claims, operation and assault plans, summonses, memos, petitions, statements, and reports, to name some of them. The power of these texts-in-action to change lives and property relations should not be underestimated. Clearly, they exert a pressure on people to act, as evidenced in the Department of Justice Report of the Ruby Ridge Task Force to the Office of Professional Responsibility: "Although some may question the expenditure of manpower and resources by the Marshals Service during this 18 month period, we believe that institutional pressure created by the existence of a bench warrant and an indictment, left the Marshals Service with little choice but to proceed as it did."[111]

One could actually describe an event such as a standoff by way of identifying the various emergent texts and the paths they took. For example, the Branch Davidian standoff presents several chains of texts, spawning new texts and moving the situation to its deadly finale. Beginning with the two noted Ur-texts, the Bible and the Constitution, we see the Bible used to produce David Koresh's radio sermons broadcast during the standoff as part of the negotiation agreements. As well, Koresh was working with the book of Revelation to write a manuscript interpreting the Seven Seals and said he would exit the Mt. Carmel compound once the text was finished. Right before the final FBI assault, he claimed to have finished the first chapter of this manuscript. The Bible also generated several statements made by the FBI negotiators themselves, as we have seen, in which they profess their own belief and adherence to its principles. The Constitution spawned various legal criminal and civil codes that make possible ATF affidavits about illegal guns, that make possible Western District Court search and arrest warrants, that make possible assault plans (568 pages in the case of the FBI plan), that make possible task force reports (Treasury Department and Justice Department), that make possible dedications at the beginning of such reports (the Treasury report is dedicated to the memory of the "four courageous ATF special agents"). As well, the Constitution provided for Koresh to be represented by a lawyer who helped him draw up a signed legal agreement indicating that he would exit upon his manuscript's completion.

Thus it is that in this one case, the textual trails are complex and meaningful. Such a process of tracking the texts could be performed for each of the standoffs analyzed here. The point is that texts make actions thinkable and doable. Like footprints, they metonymically leave their traces on a situation. The activation of particular texts becomes critical for protagonists claiming their legitimacy and relevance. Thus they enable action, but they can also be used to constrain action. When the government negotiator at Wounded Knee, Kent Frizzell, was told by the Sioux occupiers of the town that they wanted a treaty commission to be formed to resuscitate the Treaty of 1868 (their Ur-text), Frizzell referred to a text-in-action to explain why this probably would not be possible:

It's very doubtful [a treaty commission] would have the authority to implement or negotiate articles and provisions of the 1868 Treaty . . . I'm talking now from Citation 25, US Code 71, which is entitled "Future Treaties with Indian Tribes": "No Indian nation or tribe within the territory of the United States shall be acknowledged or recognized as an independent nation, tribe, or power with whom the United States may contract by treaty. But no obligation of any treaty lawfully made and ratified with any such Indian nation or tribe prior to March 3rd, 1971 shall be hereby invalidated or impaired."[112]

Some texts-in-action, like the standoff itself, are meant to stop ongoing action. The "paper terrorism" that the Republic of Texas group, the Freemen of Montana, and, to a much smaller degree, Vicky Weaver practiced is a case in point. The Republic of Texas and the Freemen of Montana groups printed and submitted to local, state, and federal courthouses and sent to a wide range of government officials a vast number of "official" documents intended to clog the wheels of normal judicial administration: letters, declarations, Common Law writs of Quo Warranto under the Law of Nations, notices (e.g., the "Notice of Disqualification under the Law of Nations of all Courts Operating on the Soil of Texas in the Name, Signature and Character of the "STATE OF TEXAS," was appended onto the "Open Letter to All Texas Sheriffs"of April 15, 1996).

The fact that this action largely takes the form of surreal textual excess doesn't mean that its capacity to terrorize is less real than if the actions were taken with guns. As a news release about the Freemen of Montana put it:

"The Freemen have over the past three years offered a $1 million bounty for the arrest of several local officials, issued a flood of real and bogus legal documents and written millions of dollars in phony checks, the officials say. Anytime any public official said 'no' to them for any reason, they were put on this hate list and would receive these harassing intimidating and I think terrorizing documents," Garfield County Attorney Nick Murnion said.[113]

Vicky Weaver's "paper terrorism" took the form of several letters she sent to various law enforcement authorities after Randy Weaver's initial arrest by the ATF. In these letters, which she signed with the moniker of "Queen of Babylon," she stated that her family would "live or die on the mountain." The authorities interpreted these letters as threatening a violent reaction to any attempt to bring Randy in for a trial.

It isn't just the main protagonists of a standoff who traffic in texts. Texts-in-action are the coin of the realm for minor characters as well. Neighbors, intermediaries, supporters, and opponents all submit their texts for consideration in the situation. While we have seen that the actions of neighbors can often be taken as a proximal trigger for the standoff, their own textual products don't usually have an independent force. The neighbors of MOVE on Osage Avenue had written to every politician they could think of in the year leading up to the May, 1985 confrontation. They had developed petitions, written letters, formulated statements for press releases. But it was only at the point at which they threatened their own vigilante (nontextual) action that the authorities took moves to codify the arrest warrants. A similar scenario unfolded in Montana, where a reporter noted that: "More recently, about 80 men signed a posse agreement against the Freemen, an indication that the FBI's arrival may have been timely."[114] Meanwhile, other local residents who were more sympathetic to the Freemen were circulating their own petition urging the Freemen to leave the house and end the standoff.

The ubiquitous Bo Gritz went a step further during the standoff at Ruby Ridge. In a gesture worthy of Martin Luther, he served a citizen's warrant on several government agents and administrators. Recounting the narrative of his arrival at Ruby Ridge during the Senate hearings, Gritz indicates that he was both invited and ignored by the authorities:

Mr. Gritz: However, when I arrived, I requested on Wednesday and Thursday repeatedly to see Gene Glenn, the special agent in charge, and was refused both days. I have commanded special operations units . . . and I am fairly familiar with special operations procedures under these kinds of circumstances. So I made a citizen's warrant arresting William Sessions, the head of the FBI, Henry Hudson of the Marshals Service, Gene Glenn, the special agent in charge, and also Governor Andrus of the State of Idaho based on the felony deaths of Marshal William Degan and Sammy Weaver. This resulted in my being allowed behind the police line and ultimately my arrival up at the top of the hill . . .
Senator Specter: Whom did you take into custody?
Mr. Gritz: Well, I didn't take anyone into custody . . . No one came forward, and so like the marshals would serve you with a warrant, I simply nailed it on the door, except in my case I put it across the police line with a rock on top.[115]

Finally, there are the texts-in-action that go AWOL, the ones that are written or miswritten, the ones that are lost or destroyed, or the ones that are ignored, or never delivered to their intended recipient. Randy Weaver ignored the various letters and summonses he received from federal authorities during the eighteen months leading up to the shooting incident on Ruby Ridge. On the other hand, several of the court documents sent to him during this time indicated the wrong date for him to appear for trial. For its own part, the FBI shredded many documents relevant to the standoff in its aftermath. The MOVE Commissioners, investigating the 1985 standoff in Philadelphia, were surprised to learn that the Philadelphia Police had lost its own internal critique of the previous MOVE standoff in 1978. No one could locate it in the police files (it had also clearly not been available during the period in which the 1985 plan for serving the arrest warrants on MOVE members was being developed). Recall as well the blank video tape of the final FBI assault on the Branch Davidians in Waco. In many ways, texts-in-action are the lifeblood of complex social situations. They can be clogged, moved along, or leaked – all with consequences for action.

Standoff talk

As the texts-in-action get drafted into existence and drafted into service over the course of a standoff, the standoff becomes littered with memos, warrants, letters, and plans. Along with this river of texts, and intermingled with it, is a river of talk. Talk is perhaps the single most important activity of human beings in the making, breaking, and sustaining of society. This is no less the case in a standoff, where an existential paralysis must nevertheless make itself known through speech and gesture.

Talk, and its opposite, silence, are key features in moving the standoff along its eventful path. The presence (or absence) of talk has been found to be critical in efforts to make a complex situation intelligible and manageable. In his analysis of processes of sensemaking in catastrophic situations, Karl Weick assesses the minimal amount of talk during the Mann Gulch fire tragedy, and the dangers in such minimalism. He writes: "It is striking how little communication occurred during the three and a half hours of this episode . . . The minimal communication is potentially important because of the growing evidence that nonstop talk, both vocal and nonverbal is a crucial source of coordination in complex systems that are susceptible to catastrophic disasters."[116]

For the talk that does occur during a standoff, it is possible to indicate certain common types of speech and speech acts. These include threats, demands, ultimatums, promises, requests, and pleas. As well, a typology of kinds of speech situations can be discerned. Thus, one usually finds participants engaged in and referring to conversations, discussions, and negotiations. Here the essential theories of conversation analysts and ethnographers of speaking focus our attention on the ways that "native taxonomies for the communicative event inform the [analyst's] analysis of talk and vice versa."[117] Much of the talk of standoffs consists precisely of statements characterizing the nature of the talk. In fact, determining the category of any given speech act is as much a part of the action of the standoff as the message of the speech act itself.

Participants typically will attempt to characterize their own speech as well as that of their adversaries. Whether something is a proposal or an ultimatum, a conversation or a negotiation, makes a great deal of difference. Proposals can be met with acknowledgments, counterproposals, rejections, or agreement. Ultimatums seem to have a more restricted set of options for their recipients – accept or reject.[118] Thus a good part of standoff talk is the apparently subsidiary talk about talk, with different participants attempting to lay claims on different swatches of speech.

The following long excerpt from the book *Wounded Knee – 1973: A Personal Account*, by then Superintendent of the Bureau of Indian Affairs, Stanley Lyman, reveals this jockeying for classificatory dominance at a critical point in the standoff:

On Saturday afternoon, March 17, Harlington Wood met Dennis Banks and Ramon Roubideaux at the main federal roadblock outside Wounded Knee and delivered a sealed envelope containing twelve copies of a *comprehensive proposal* from the government. Wood said the document was not to be regarded as an *ultimatum* but as the government's *best offer*. . . . The proposal offered a detailed plan for ending the confrontation. As a *compromise solution* to the Indians' *demands* that Marvin Franklin confer with them at Wounded Knee, the proposal stipulated that a meeting would be held between Franklin and AIM leaders in Sioux Falls. The AIM leaders would receive safe conduct to the meeting and would submit peacefully to arrest afterward. As that session in Sioux Falls began, all weapons at Wounded Knee would be laid down in one location, identified for future recovery by their owners. All occupiers would go to a roadblock for identification and processing, and those with warrants against them would submit to arrest. Federal agents would not cross the perimeter into Wounded Knee for three hours after the laying down of arms . . . The next day, Sunday, March 18, a press conference was held at the trading post inside Wounded Knee, and the government's proposal was denounced as *"total capitulation and submission to arrest and disarmament"* . . . The response from the militants came on Monday, March 19, in the form of a *counterproposal* that they termed their *"final ultimatum"* to the United States.[119]

In this excerpt from Lyman's account we find a fairly wide variety of ways of characterizing the government's speech act and the occupiers' response. The government presents a comprehensive proposal, a best offer, a compromise solution, an ultimatum, and a "total capitulation and submission to arrest and disarmament." The Sioux response is a counterproposal, more demands, or a final ultimatum. Obviously, it makes a big difference if a series of ideas and terms are understood as an ultimatum or as a compromise solution. An ultimatum anticipates responses of either acceptance or rejection and is coercive in its existential stance. A compromise solution seems to be emerging at the end of a process of reconciliation and interaction, and is experimental in its existential stance.

One of the most important of the categorical decisions is that of invoking the term "negotiations." So much is implied by that invocation: that the parties are somehow recognizing the presence and centrality of each other; that they are engaged in serious dialogue; that all are working toward some kind of commonly agreed upon resolution to the crisis; that some compromises in actions and values are within the realm of the thinkable, and so forth.

In several of the standoffs being studied here, the question of the nature of certain interchanges was raised in a manner that can only be described as diffident. In the Tupac Amaru standoff, government officials, wary of appearing to be in a posture of appeasement, expressed a preference for the term "conversations" over "negotiations," to describe designated interlocutor Domingo Palermo's talks with the Tupac Amaru group.[120] The Branch Davidian standoff experienced a similar diffidence. In describing the terminology used in the Justice Department Report, Mark Hansen notes: "Although the Justice Department Report is wary of calling their [the members of the Critical Incident Negotiations Team from the Strategic Information Operations Center in Washington, DC] phone conversations with the Davidians 'negotiations' – they felt the calls were more adequately referred to as 'discussions' due to the Davidians' refusal to negotiate on their terms – they did persist in calling the negotiators 'negotiators' (not discussants or conversationalists)."[121]

Finally, Bo Gritz, in his active role as interlocutor in the Freemen standoff, demonstrated his usual nonacquiescence to standard terminology, when he "described Sunday's negotiations as 'verbal judo all day,' a reference to what he called the 'legal mumbo-jumbo' spoken by the Freemen. He said he would return to the compound Monday."[122]

Negotiation talk

Much has been written about negotiation in the fields of conflict analysis and dispute resolution. Typically, such scholars are either also practitioners of dispute resolution themselves or are writing for practitioners. Distinctions are made in these fields between such things as negotiating on the basis of positions and negotiating on the basis of interests, between narrowing the set of disputed issues and expanding them. While such matters are indeed key to analyzing and formulating negotiation strategies within extant organizational and disciplinary paradigms, the interest in negotiation here is different.

Given the predominant theoretical preoccupation here with contingency, I want to focus less on the standard formulations and conventions of negotiation and more on the situationally specific, idiosyncratic shapes that negotiations take in states of paralysis. The key is to track that contingency over the course of these standoffs. One avenue of approach is to identify and reflect upon the kinds of self-consciousness about the nature of standoff speech acts, as developed in the preceding section. There we found a form of categorical hedging about whether participants were, in fact, actually "doing negotiation" when they spoke with each other across the barricades. As well, I am interested in the "who" of negotiations – the determinations of legitimate, quasilegitimate, and illegitimate negotiators. In the following subsections on intermediaries and experts we will explore the way these decisions are made. Relevant here as well is the nature of the relations between the negotiators and their administrative superiors and between negotiators and members of the tactical team. Finally, time and space become foregrounded here again. Issues of the pace and rhythm of negotiations intersect with the emergence of contingent temporal parameters in the standoff. Are negotiations experienced as continuous, intermittent, or stalled? And what do such experiences have to do with the sense that something, or nothing, is happening? In terms of spatial parameters – are negotiations taking place over the phone, via bullhorns, face to face, in the standoff center, in another "neutral" building, or at the fence/gate/wall/roadblock of the perimeter? Is the space of the standoff expanding, contracting, or transmuting as a result of the presence or absence of certain kinds of negotiations?

Symbolic interactionists, those sociologists who, following from the Pragmatist theoretical legacy, focus their analyses on the day-to-day negotiations that occur in all social structures, are interested in every kind of social unit, from dyads to the international system of nation states, with bureaucratic organizations like hospitals, businesses, and schools residing somewhere between these two extremes. They point to certain features of the organizational environment that give shape to these continuous negotiations about roles and actions:

> the number of negotiators and their relative experience; whether they represent themselves or a collectivity; whether the negotiations are sequential, repeated, one-shot, or serial; the respective stakes in the negotiations; the relative visibility of the process; the number and complexity of the issues; the options available to the negotiators and the relative balance of power of the participants in the negotiations.[123]

Scholars and practitioners of the particularly charged and highlighted negotiations that occur in crises of the standoff type are given the more precise task of mapping the specific activities that ought to constitute negotiations in these crises, and of articulating the (usually) contending worldviews that subtend the respective speech acts of the participants in them.[124] This is of a piece with the understanding of the dynamic relationship between Ur-texts and texts-in-action. Indeed, many of these texts emerge over the course of the negotiations and are folded into them. In terms of the specific negotiation activities, Jayne Docherty has written authoritatively about the FBI negotiators at Waco. Noting that the parties to the conflict negotiate nothing less than reality itself, she writes, "In other words, [the parties] cooperatively name self and other and name the world (or at least their immediate context) in ways that enable them to engage in issue-specific negotiations."[125] This naming process is at the heart of the generation of the texts that propel the standoff forward.

Pace and rhythm

All of the above activities need time to develop and yet we have seen how complicated and unpredictable the temporal parameters of standoffs are. It should not surprise us to find preoccupation precisely about the timing of negotiation. When does/should it start? When does/should it stop? Should it be sustained or intermittent? What does its "breaking off" mean?

A certain perplexity about negotations that kept starting and stopping was evident in the standoffs at Wounded Knee, Waco, and Lima. The FBI negotiators involved with the Branch Davidians were, we recall, particularly thrown by David Koresh's claim that God had told him to wait at the exact point that the negotiators were expecting evacuation of Mt. Carmel. This apparent intervention of the deity into the rhythm of expectations of the negotiations meant that the end of negotiations (and thus of the standoff itself) was subject to an uncomfortable deferral. After about two weeks of talks at Wounded Knee, Bureau of Indian Affairs Superintendent Stanley Lyman wrote: "On March 10 a major concession was made by the federal government *in an effort to put an end to the on-again, off-again agreements* and to effect a real settlement: government roadblocks would be withdrawn."[126] In reading Lyman's first-hand account of this standoff, one has the sense of frustration equally divided between the content of the crisis and the rhythm of its attempted resolution.

Always, the pace of negotiations is interpreted as meaning something about the situation. "The faster the better" may seem the intuitive read, but those charged with gauging the progress of standoffs oscillate between optimism and pessimism in such a way as to sometimes suggest the counterintuitive. Thus, two weeks into the occupation of the Japanese Ambassador's house in Lima, a diplomat monitoring the situation was quoted as saying: "I think when you look at it over the long haul, we've got a series of good signs, without any blood being spilled . . . The lack of movement isn't necessarily a bad sign. The two sides appear to be studying the situation."[127] Movement, or its lack, is the key here and the self-conscious tracking of timing of negotiations acts as a kind of existential pump at the heart of the standoff.

Location

We have seen that negotiators at Wounded Knee sat with representatives of the occupying group first in tipis and then in school buses that had been brought to a spot in the demilitarized zone. Negotiators in Waco spoke by phone to Branch Davidians from several miles away. Over the fifty-one days, negotiators had phone conversations with fifty-four people inside the compound for a total of 215 hours. Negotiations in Lima took place in a house designated as the Red Cross headquarters, across the street from the Japanese Ambassador's house, after initial talks had occurred in the occupied residence itself. Congressional representatives and, later, FBI agents sat at a table and folding chairs set up outside of the Clark ranch during the Freemen standoff.

These different spaces selected for negotiations, as well as the different orientations of the participants to each other in the spaces, all structure the situation of negotiations. Emergent issues have to do with whether the talk is direct or technologically mediated, whether it is in a neutral space or one that is charged with a particular position or stand, what kind of a structure is erected for negotiations, and whether the parties stand or sit. The chosen options for these issues will combine with each other to produce action that will indeed be read as meaningful to the larger questions of safety, trust, and progress. For example, direct, face-to-face contact that takes place in the standoff center creates a kind of wedge, opening up the very binary opposition of center and perimeter itself. As the *New York Times* put it, in regards to the standoff in Lima:

> Marxist rebels released the Ambassadors of the Dominican Republic and Malaysia and 18 other hostages today after a Peruvian Cabinet official entered the residence of the Japanese Ambassador in what appeared to be the first direct contact between the rebels and the Government . . . The very fact that he did not fear being taken hostage himself demonstrated that the Government and the rebels had reached some kind of understanding, at least to talk.[128]

Relations between tactical team and negotiators and negotiators' superiors

Worldviews not only differ between authorities and their antisystem antagonists, they also differ between different units within the same organization. Thus the study of standoffs reveals a certain tension between the negotiating wing of law-enforcement organizations and their tactical colleagues and between the negotiators and their administrative superiors. As former supervisory special FBI agent Frederick Lanceley put it during the Senate hearings on Ruby Ridge, after being asked by Senator Kohl if negotiations were given too low a priority in that standoff:

> Yes, sir. I think part of the problem goes back a little bit further in that the advanced team that went out there consisted of tactical people. If you send an advanced team of tactical people to evaluate a situation you are going to get tactical recommendations. If you send a doctor out to look at a scene you are going to get a medical recommendation. If you send a Senator out there you are going to get a new law. [Laughter][129]

The laughter, transcribed here in the official, bound transcript of the hearings, is important. Everybody who occupies an institutional social role knows the parameters of that institution's possible action repertoire. It is a funny self-consciousness because it co-exists with the consciousness of the incredible complexity of most situations in life. And thus the paradox: narrow repertoires of discourse and action, broad ranges of issues in situations. We all simultaneously rely on, and feel inadequate because of, our chosen social roles.

At a more practical level, the simple fact of communication difficulties and competing agendas and timetables make for some of the tension between negotiators and tacticians. An example from Wounded Knee demonstrates the logistic and political problems of co-ordination between these two wings of law enforcement. After having negotiated an interim agreement to remove the Armed Personnel Carriers from the area around Wounded Knee, government negotiator Kent Frizzell finds out that indeed the APCs have moved into the area: "Well there's no excuse for the APCs [Armed Personnel Carriers] coming down. I've been assured daily for the last three days by all the law enforcement personnel that they would not allow this to happen, to spark off an incident. And I will again bring it to their attention."[130]

Finally, there are the tensions between negotiators and their superiors, superiors who are often some distance from the scene. Kent Frizzell speaks of having to deal with the "hardliners" back in Washington during the Wounded Knee standoff. And the case of Ruby Ridge is particularly important here, precisely because there were really no successful official negotiations. On the parts of the US Marshals who were handling the standoff, this lack of negotiations both was and wasn't Randy Weaver's choice or fault. The complex and contradictory testimony that two of the Marshals, Henry Hudson and Michael Johnson, provide during the Senate Hearings reveals the degree to which any hypothetical negotiator must navigate among a wide range of co-participants even to be able to declare negotiations a possibility:

Mr. Hudson: I will have Marshal Johnson, if you do not mind, go into the seven specific attempts he made to negotiate Randy Weaver's surrender. But the bottom line is that we went through neighbors, we went through friends, we went through intermediaries attempting to establish a line of communications and the response from Randy Weaver was there would be no negotiations. Come on my mountain, and we kill you . . .

Senator Abraham: In that process, was there ever any point where Mr. Weaver conveyed in any way, to anybody, that there might be any circumstance by which he would submit to an arrest, short of the satisfaction of those conditions he was raising?

Mr. Johnson: Senator, we had the one occasion that Mr. Weaver sent down some demands, and those demands, some of them, to us seemed reasonable, that we could put a package together and make an offer back. We answered a lot of those questions, went to the US Attorney's office – I didn't personally, my deputies did – ran it by them. At that time, they told us to stop and not make any negotiations like that, that those would be negotiations that could be made later on, during the trial process, so we stopped at that time.[131]

Intermediaries

US Marshal Hudson laments the inability of the authorities successfully to convince Randy Weaver of the usefulness of intermediaries, and he names

some particular kinds (neighbors, friends) and the generic model "intermediaries." Indeed, intermediaries are among the most semantically and syn-
tactically unstable of the various *dramatis personae* of the standoff. They
must always create and reproduce their identities in the actual doing of
their intermediation. As we have seen, identities attempt to achieve stability through their tethering to institutional roles. We have seen that this is
true of such participants as law-enforcement officials, the antisystem antagonists, and even the hostages/"hostages." Given their overtly metaphorically spatial title (inter-mediary) intermediaries can't even pretend this
preemptive attachment to institutional roles. They must respond contingently to the discovered space in between.

This does not mean, however, that they are without a certain type of
authority. Because of their only indirect and minimal implication in the
specific dispute that set off and snapped into the standoff, they have a recognized freedom and autonomy. As well, they have what Carol Greenhouse
calls a "surplus authority." She writes: "Third parties emerge as a salient
comparative feature in ethnographic studies of conflict because the third
party is, in effect, the figure of surplus authority, the 'extra' authority a
social system can generate beyond the direct influence of disputants over
each other."[132] Like surplus value, the system is actually able to intermittently and temporarily imagine modes of being beyond those that are
inscribed in the organizations and structures of the involved parties.

But it is important to recognize that intermediaries may be with or
without official portfolios. Some intermediaries are specifically selected by
the parties in the standoff and these are close to the role of full-fledged
negotiator. The occupiers of Wounded Knee designated the Council of
Elders of the Teton Sioux as their envoys to present their final negotiating
proposal to the government. Three negotiators from the CAUSE Foundation, a foundation that had represented a former Ku Klux Klan member
and the survivors of the Branch Davidian standoff, were brought to the
Freemen standoff by the FBI to be of assistance. The Tupac Amaru group
designated four released diplomats (Canadian, Greek, German ambassadors and French cultural attaché) as a negotiating team. This group
included Anthony Vincent, the Canadian Ambassador, who seriously
tried to assert his authority as a mediator. And the Peruvian government,
before ultimately storming the occupied house, appointed a Guarantor
Commission, comprised of a Catholic bishop, Juan Luis Cipriani, and a
Red Cross delegate, Michel Minnig, to engage in official talks with the
Tupac Amaru.

Within the group of intermediaries without official imprimatur to
engage in talks, there is a subcategory that have organizational portfolios.

There have been members of religious organizations, professions, and political organizations. At Wounded Knee, a Methodist minister named John Adams led a group from the National Council of Churches to the occupied town and managed to arrange several short-lived ceasefires.[133] Bishop Cipriani was a frequent visitor to the Tupac Amaru-held residence in Lima and a member of the Guarantor Commission. Professors of religion, including most notably Drs. Phillip Arnold and James Tabor, offered their own interpretation of the Seven Seals section of the Book of Revelation on a radio show broadcast in the Branch Davidian listening area (a tape of that show was brought into Mt. Carmel by David Koresh's attorney). Finally, the political offshoot of the "patriot" community, the Independent Grand Jury Formation Committee, offered themselves to the Freemen standoff, proposing that "laws derived from the Magna Charta, the Constitution, and the Continental Congress be brought into play, specifically with regard to the function of the Grand Jury, without whose indictment no one may properly be brought to trial."[134]

Those intermediaries who are without any official portfolio, either designated by the participants in the standoff or designated by membership in a religious, professional, or political organization must work the hardest to gain a voice and a role. Often they may be relatives of those inside the standoff center. Or they may be individuals who have had previous experiences of their own with such standoffs. In most cases, relatives are allowed to make appeals to their kin to exit their redoubts peaceably, often via tape recordings, phone calls, or, as in the case of the mother of a member of MOVE, by way of a bullhorn from the corner of the block. However, when they actually offer themselves as potential negotiators, they are often rejected.

This reluctance to involve the noninstitutionalized as interlocutors in a standoff extends to former standoff antagonists themselves. Unlike former hostages, who are sometimes allowed minimal, interim authority (the case of Anthony Vincent), former antagonists are viewed with suspicion. When Randy Weaver showed up with Bo Gritz at the Freemen ranch, they were turned back by the FBI:

Weaver told reporters Friday he wanted to convey to the Freemen the heartache that can come from losing family members in a violent confrontation . . . "It's better to talk it out than to shoot it out." Asked what he would say to the Freemen, Weaver said: "I'd like to come in and see you guys. I know what you're going through. I'd like to come in and give you a hug or something."[135]

Even though Weaver has moved from Nazi salutes to hugs, he is still not a stable enough narrative character to gain official entry into the story.

In this narrative instability, Weaver is similar to that group of intermediaries I have termed "organic mediators" in my study of the MOVE standoff.[136] These individuals attempted to assert their authority as more than witnesses and as more than simply residents of the community. Their understanding of their own, self-designated mandate and portfolio is generally built up from their participation in previous community and civil rights struggles and conflicts. The Philadelphia police did not embrace these intermediaries; in fact they rejected their services on the day of the confrontation in 1985. One, Charles Burrus, stated that he had:

fallen into a role, more or less, of negotiator . . . Me not being that familiar with the legal system, I don't know if I'm using the proper terminology. Fortunately, in my life style, I was able to stay out of the [legal system] . . . We were acting as mediators instead of negotiators . . . No one asked me to negotiate, I negotiated on my own, as a concerned black man.[137]

For all of their empirical marginalization, organic mediators, those without official portfolios or mandates, are the most analytically, semiotically pure form of intermediaries. What's essential about their (often hypothetical) syntactical role in the standoff is that it is necessarily empty and multiple at the same time. It is empty because they are truly there as supplements and points of intersection. It is multiple because they point to a kind of self-conscious Simmelian hybridity. They are positioned at the intersection of multiple "social circles," resisting the oddly anachronistic monologic nature of the institutional social roles that litter the standoff. Sometimes, rarely, such societal intermediaries are actually also incumbents of recognized roles and are contingently permitted to articulate the hybrid identity in the service of resolving a crisis. This was the case in Italy in the early 1990s during the *Mani Pulite* (Clean Hands) judiciary campaign to root out corruption. At that time, chief Milanese prosecutor Francesco Di Pietro led the attack and did so by indicting and interrogating many members of the entrenched political class. Sociologist Pier Paolo Giglioli has written about Di Pietro's language in the courtroom and the way in which it provided for a powerful doubling and mixing of identities:

In Di Pietro's language, the concrete quality of the bureaucratic-juridical lexicon is clear. So, as well, is the ordinary, man-in-the-street lexicon, characterized by metaphors and the like drawn from daily life, a lexicon that ostentatiously distances itself from the technical jargon of jurists. This mixture is revealing because it shows the double role played by Di Pietro in the trials, the formal one of Public Minister and the substantial one (for our purposes) of the representative of the moral indignation of the citizens.[138]

The problem is that in most cases, intermediaries do not have the kind of even temporary status of a Di Pietro (who was, himself, later to be the subject of judicial investigation). Their attempts at mobilization fall on deaf ears. Some standoff participants recognize their structural indeterminacy and yet also recognize their structural utility. Thus, the Branch Davidians actually requested intermediaries to assist in the negotiations between themselves and the FBI negotiators – negotiators to deal with the negotiators. The issue of the mobilization of multiple identities is a complicated but critical one to thinking through the paralysis of the standoff.[139] In the conclusion, I will try to get at this through the concept of improvisation.

The expert

I asked the Mayor as humbly as I could, I even called him His Excellency, if he would please reconsider the action that was about to take place. I told him that there were children in the house . . . I thought maybe if we could continue talking we might be able to accomplish a peaceful end or at least save their lives, because I told the Mayor that I was convinced that if there was a police assault on that house that the people would be killed. Q: And what did the Mayor say? A: He told me that he had been assured by the experts that no one would be hurt.[140]

While the Ghost Dance was taking place, some warriors reported hearing over the Government's radio that the marshals became worried and called in a "BIA dance expert" to tell them what was going on. He informed them, inaccurately, that it was a war dance that had not been performed since just before Custer's massacre . . .[141]

I want to end this chapter with the character of the expert because it is this character, along with that of the intermediary, who points the way to improvisation as a conscious method of dealing with the contingency of the standoff. And improvisation is a focal point of the next, and last, chapter. Experts show up at the sites of all standoffs. They can be members of other categories of the *dramatis personae* but in the moment of inhabiting the role of expert, their syntactic charge becomes highly specific and focused. They appear in the various guises of scholar, professional, and even negotiator. Mostly we find the obvious ones – experts in equipment, experts in tactical maneuvers, experts in negotiation, experts in psychological profiling, experts in cults. The issue I am most interested in is not whether experts should or shouldn't be incorporated into the *dramatis personae* of the standoff, nor is it the slightly more interesting question of the manner of their involvement. Rather, I am most interested in asking the situationally focused, Pragmatist question: what is it that we want these experts to be expert in?

According to Shupe and Hadden, experts are "individuals and agencies who are neither directly involved nor responsible for dealing with the crisis event . . . [they] can generally be categorized as either corroborators or doubters."[142] Experts are turned to precisely where the relevant event has offered up a moment of uncertainty and we do, in fact, think of them as providing certainty on highly specified topics. There is more though to make of this certainty–uncertainty dialectic and it intersects with the broader role of uncertainty in all narratives. As noted in the first chapter, all narratives are about the relationship between certainty and uncertainty. Because the standoff is a frozen narrative, experts, with their official certainties, are looked to for the impetus they give other participants to take action. But it may be that it is sometimes actually the expert's ability to locate uncertainty (rather than to provide certainty) that makes them valuable to those attempting to find an escape hatch out of a standoff. This is what religious scholars Arnold and Tabor attempted at Waco and, as Tabor later wrote: "It was this uncertainty [in the temporal vectors of the prophecy in Daniel 11:40–12:13] which offered the best hope for a peaceful resolution of the conflict."[143]

Of course Arnold and Tabor were not embraced by the authorities and so their expertise could only play itself out around the margins of the situations. A similar rejection of an expert-in-identifying-uncertainty occurred in the standoff at Ruby Ridge, when FBI negotiator Frederick Lanceley attempted a creative management of Randy Weaver's predilection for mountain tops and social isolation. Lanceley testified that :

I went down the mountain to our command post, and I encountered Assistant US Attorney Ron Howen whom I had met earlier. And I said, "Ron, we're going to have to come up with something really creative here to get Randall Weaver out of that house alive . . . I don't know what. Perhaps a legal solution such as if convicted he will do his time on top of the mountain, something like that, Ron." And he said, "Randall Weaver will never talk to you," and he turned and walked away. I was extremely angry at that, but that was the attitude of everybody, the townsfolks, the marshals I talked to.[144]

Alternatively, in some of the standoffs examined here, the desperation to cut through the paralysis and the uncertainty prompted the agents in charge to gather any and all experts they could find. We hear this perplexed hope in the following statement from Wayne Colburn, Director of the US Marshals at Wounded Knee: "We must defuse this situation. We must bring in the Civil Rights [people], bring in the HEW people. Let's saturate this area and see if we can come up with a viable plan that will satisfy everybody."[145]

Saturating the area with experts, selecting certain experts and rejecting others, expecting certainty from experts, or hoping that they can help identify flexible areas of uncertainty – these are all possible official attitudes towards this character in the narrative. Such choices highlight the way in which interpretation and action move each other across the dance floor of social life, often without it being clear who is leading.

5

Endings and improvisations

> The innovation introduced by the Latin system above all consists in the ordered and regular way in which the theme of temporality, so to speak, is reduplicated through the contrast between the infectum [describing the process on its way towards completion] with the perfectum [describing the completed process].   (Ferdinand Gonseth, *Time and Method*, p. 151)

> At a demonstration that passed close to the Ambassador's residence today, Peruvians, in tacit acknowledgment of how delicate the standoff had become, spoke not for a quick end to the crisis but for a peaceful one. "It would be a shame for this to all end in bloodshed after we've come so far," said Lucia Perez, a nurse. "I don't care when it ends as long as it ends peacefully."   (*New York Times*, January 2, 1997, A1)

It may seem either self-serving or dangerous for a book's concluding chapter to begin with the assertion that conclusions are extremely important. But it is indeed the case that the way a standoff ends will have much to do with whether its management as a situation of conflict and paralysis will be considered a success or a failure. As the times and spaces of the standoffs have taken their various shapes, and as the actions of the standoffs have engaged the participants in the generation of a variety of texts, speeches, and gestures (that have fed back dynamically into the participant identities themselves), the standoffs have all moved through time towards their resolutions.

Endings

I have discerned three ideal-typical modes of ending for standoffs: deals, surrenders, and violence. In reality, the designation of any given standoff's ending as consisting in one or another of these modalities is something of a judgment call, for elements of two or more approaches are often found cohabiting the same standoff. For example, there may be attempts made to work out deals or surrender agreements only to have these attempts fail. As well, the fact that a standoff ends in a deal or a surrender doesn't mean it hasn't experienced violence somewhere along the line. On the other hand, it is important that the main protagonists share a dominant sense of an ending – that both sides facing each other across the perimeter agree that they are participating in a deal, or in a surrender, or in a fiery conflagration, no matter how they got there and no matter how they may even disagree on the details. Endings do, then, at least temporarily, provide for the elusive overlap of meaning that allows a situation to proceed.

This chapter will designate and describe the three ideal types of ending and will match them with specific cases. Once again, it is important to remember that while the examined standoffs in this book are those of religious, ideological, or political groups confronting a state, the fundamental parameters of space, time, and action that have emerged from the analysis are relevant to all social interactions, because all social interactions harbor the standoff within them. Thus it is possible to say that all social interactions end in deals (discoveries of some area of mutuality), surrenders (assertions of hierarchy and asymmetry), or violence.

Finally, the implications of the different types of endings will then be further explored in a discussion of the theoretical and practical meaning of improvisation and of a vision of standoffs as an aesthetic emergency. And the gains of a combined Structuralist and Pragmatist approach to contingency will be assessed.

Deals

Deals imply strategic actors calculating the costs and benefits of making specific concessions to the enemy, whomever the enemy has been determined to be. A provisional, and generally largely symbolic, recognition must occur in order that any deal can be made. However, this recognition adamantly does not necessitate, or even make likely, a legitimation of the anti-authority groups.[1] Arrests still can, and indeed have been, attendant upon standoff-ending deals.

Deal endings were not common among the cases under examination. Of the seven cases, only Wounded Knee and the Republic of Texas ended with the codification of deals for further, post-standoff, action. Official agreements were signed in both of these cases. And in both, the occupiers of the standoff centers were arrested upon exiting.

At Wounded Knee, several disarmament agreements were signed by various combinations of representatives of the occupying force in the final weeks of the standoff. Those signing did so contingent upon their being assured that they would be permitted to meet with White House officials and that a Presidential Treaty Commission would be formed to discuss the status of the panoply of treaties made between Native Americans and the US Government over the centuries. Coming as it did on the cusp of the disintegration of the Nixon White House, mired in the Watergate scandal, this agreement actually shriveled to one or two meetings with White House officials. Nevertheless, disarmament, evacuation, and arrests all occurred without violence.

In the Republic of Texas standoff, all but two members of the group holed up in the Davis Mountain cabin agreed to a "cease-fire agreement," that permitted Richard McLaren to argue his case before a federal judge in Washington, D.C. As noted by a television reporter, "The word 'surrender' was never used in the agreement. State police spokesman Mike Cox described an almost theatrical scene of McLaren and his cohorts putting down their weapons: 'They had a military-style ceremony at which they laid down their arms . . . in a circle,' he said."[2]

While in each of these cases, there was some prevaricating between the contending parties as to the specifics of the meaning and expanse of the cease-fire agreements, the agreements did make it possible for the endings of the standoffs to occur in a predominantly nonviolent manner.[3]

Surrenders

Surrenders can be singularly decorous and honorable or singularly disheveled and humiliating events. It all depends on the forms they take. Of the two surrender endings in our set of standoffs, the Freemen surrender fell in the former category and the Ruby Ridge surrender represented the latter.

Surrenders announce a universally acknowledged asymmetry, usually of strength and power. From one point of view, there is a clear winner and there is a clear loser. As well, surrenders demarcate a clear ending to the standoff and a beginning of the post-standoff situation. On the other hand, depending on the manner in which the surrender takes place, the winner can be made to feel humiliated and the loser can feel that his or her social persona has come through the situation intact. These counter-intuitive reactions reveal the degree to which the rituals and ceremonies of surrenders draw the grammar of a situation into reconfigurations of character.

Barry Schwartz has written about one of these counter-intuitive moments of surrender, that of the surrender ceremony at Yorktown during the War of Independence in the United States. Writing about General

George Washington's response to the delivery of the vanquished enemy's sword, Schwartz notes: "As the victorious commander, he was entitled to receive the sword of surrender directly from Cornwallis, his vanquished counterpart. Cornwallis never showed up; instead, he delivered his sword to Washington through an aide. Refusing to accept the instrument himself, Washington instructed Cornwallis's aide to present it to his own aide, General Lincoln."[4]

On the other side, a vanquished foe may, through the respect tendered him or her during a surrender ceremony, experience some (however temporary and relative) elevation of status during the event. In the surrender of the Freemen of Montana, a deal was folded into the general surrender agreement (just as, in its own way, there was a "surrender" folded into the Republic of Texas deal). That deal, revealing the importance of texts in crises such as standoffs, provided for the files and legal documents that were on the Clark/Bliss/Justus Township ranch to be turned over to Republican Montana State Senator Karl Ohs and that these documents ultimately be used as evidence for the Freemen's alternative legal theory and claims. As well, the FBI allowed the Freemen to surrender to arrest without the indignity of being handcuffed. Such ceremonial gestures give a dignity to the end of the standoff.

Randy Weaver's surrender at Ruby Ridge was noticeably lacking in these ceremonial niceties. His surrender followed the deaths by shooting of his wife and son and the wounding of his friend Kevin Harris. Only Bo Gritz could convince him to end the standoff without further bloodshed.

Along with the actual surrenders, there are several failed surrenders. All groups in standoff situations have an awareness of the possibility of surrender. Some, such as the Tupac Amaru, took an adamant position against it. Thus during the first weekend of their occupation of the Japanese Ambassador's residence, in early March, 1997, the group hung out a banner that read, "Surrender is not the way of the Tupac Amaru." Other groups, such as the Branch Davidians, seemed to be moving in the direction of surrender, but that movement was propulsive, intermittent, and difficult for FBI negotiators to interpret. On the one hand, FBI agents maintained a literalist, quantifiable idea of surrender. As two of the agents recounted later, they wanted to break down the actual surrender into physical movements:

Jeff Jamar: We worked out a surrender plan in minute detail. And that's what you want. See, you want a plan, you want a surrender plan because you put that in their heads.

Byron Sage: If they can visualize – and you actually use those words – "Can you picture this? Can you – can you visualize – okay, you're going to come out the front door. You're going to turn left."[5]

On the other hand, scholars of religion claimed that David Koresh had an altogether different image of surrender, one that was mediated by biblical hermeneutics: "What the authorities never perceived was that Koresh's preaching was precisely such to him, the only matter of substance and means through which to work out a 'surrender.'"[6]

Violence

"If acts of communication – exchanges of gifts, challenges, or words – always bear within them a potential conflict, it is because they always contain the possibility of domination."(Pierre Bourdieu, "Structures, Habitus, Power," p. 196, Note 47)
"In the end, Mr. Fujimori conceded nothing to the Tupac Amaru guerrillas, who had demanded the freedom of hundreds of their jailed comrades, and reclaimed his reputation as a decisive leader ready, even eager, to back up his will with force." (*New York Times*, April 23, 1997, A1)

Three of the standoffs analyzed here ended in violence. Both the MOVE standoff and that of the Branch Davidians involved a fiery conflagration in which the standoff centers burned to ground, killing most of the inhabitants. In both of these cases, the logic of the assaults, from the perspective of law enforcement, was to force the inhabitants to exit their compounds. In both cases only a minority of those inside actually exited alive. Thus, there are the lingering mysteries of the no-exits: did they constitute collective suicides, did they indicate a greater fear of being killed by those involved in the assaults? Various theories of collective mentalities get drawn into these calibrations. Alternatively, the Tupac Amaru standoff ended with an assault by the Peruvian military on the Japanese Ambassador's residence, an assault that was programmed to kill all of the Tupac Amaru occupiers. One hostage was also killed in the assault.

Violent endings are, despite all we know and cherish about the sanctity of human life, the most cathartic ways in which to end a standoff. They provide a kind of social-psychological release (in the manner of the analyses of crowds and power of Elias Canetti) after a period of sustained paralysis. As well, as we have heard in the testimonies of the negotiators, there are all of the institutional pressures on tactical wings of law-enforcement agencies to be true to themselves, that is, to use their tools.[7]

Notwithstanding these three decisively violent endings, episodes of violence litter all of the standoffs. Each episode is calibrated differently by different participants and agencies. There is legitimate violence, illegitimate violence, professional violence, random violence, reasonable violence, unreasonable violence, defensive violence, offensive violence, collective violence, individual violence, and so forth. Various trials and investigations and hearings held after the several standoffs attempt to characterize the violence that occurred within them and attempt to blame or exonerate its perpetrators. The minute cataloguing of specific acts of violence reveals society's preoccupation with separating the legitimate from the illegitimate. After the Ruby Ridge standoff, for example, the US Department of Justice issued a report in which such precision was demonstrated: "With regard to the two shots fired on August 22, we concluded that the first shot met the standard of 'objective reasonableness' the Constitution requires for the legal use of deadly force but that the second shot did not satisfy that standard."[8]

Another way out: improvisation

Perhaps, after all, we are not entirely satisfied with the fact that the standards for "objective reasonableness" for the use of deadly force have been met. Perhaps we have higher, more ambitious goals for the outcomes of the standoffs. Perhaps, regardless of our opinions of the ideologies, methods, and lifestyles of the antistate groups who find themselves in standoffs with the state, we hold the state, to the degree that it's possible, to the very highest standard – that being aiming to get everyone out intact.

It might seem unaccountable for normativeness to enter this essentially agnostic book so late in the game. On the other hand, Pragmatists hold that if situations are truly the focus of attention, the goals will be found within them, *in media rerum*. And thus, we have found a goal in the process of combing through the standoff cases and in tracking their trajectories. Given that standoffs are existentially temporary, and given that they all must end, it is not irrelevant to consider the contingent nature of their endings and the things they leave in their wake. We have seen that some standoffs end in deals and surrenders that leave all participants with their lives and key aspects of their *personae* intact. And we have seen that others end with violence, death, and destruction.

So the question becomes: is it possible to work with the radical contingency of the standoff as a situation, to attend to structures and standard operating procedures but also, when those procedures restrict rather than facilitate movement, to put Pragmatism into practice as a method of proceeding through a frozen and congealed present?

One way to think about putting Pragmatism into practice is to think about improvisation. Improvisation signifies a making-do with the materials at hand. *Improvviso*, in Latin and Italian means "unexpected," but it need not, at least in modern usage, mean completely unprepared. In fact,

I'd go so far as to say that when we use the term improvisation we imply some background knowledge of whatever forms the situation "normally" calls forth. When improvisation is practiced in music or in theater, there is the assumption that the musicians and actors are working without scores or scripts. They have a few stimuli, some chords, some sketchy situations, to start them off. But the performances must have an immediacy and a spontaneity that reflect their improvisatory stance. And yet, these performers must still abide by the extant rules of composition, melody, and drama. Rules and spontaneity that work together at a deep level pull coherence out of an evolving and unpredictable situation. In terms of locating improvisation in sociological theory, I argue that improvisation is a sort of halfway house between the Meadian "I" with its playful and idiosyncratic experience of the self and the Meadian "Me" with its learned taking of the role of the generalized other. This involves the temporal looping of the past through the present, as memory and creativity join forces.

This coordination of memory and creativity is most explicit in theatrical improvisation and in musical genres such as jazz and rap, where knowledge of dramatic genres, traditional plots, musical variations, and so forth clearly provide the epistemological ground for the improvisation. Thus, improvisations both carry out and reconfigure our aesthetic and narrative expectations. But improvisation is found as well outside of the world of theater and music. The *bricoleur* is, in many ways, the archetypical improviser – someone who, as Karl Weick has written, "routinely act[s] in chaotic conditions and pull[s] order out of them. Thus, when situations unravel, this is simply normal natural trouble for bricoleurs and they proceed with whatever materials are at hand . . . knowing these materials intimately . . ."9

Weick thus proposes the existence of situational *bricoleurs* (akin to our organic mediators) alongside the more concrete, handyman, *bricoleurs* made anthropologically famous by Lévi-Strauss. What exactly do situational *bricoleurs* do? What kinds of strategies do they employ? Is it possible to systematically account for their asystematicity?

In fact, I want to claim that there are certain parameters of improvisational action that can be identified. They include: 1) a strategic acknowledgment of categorical insufficiency and a concomitant withholding from naming and claiming the situation; 2) a simultaneous recognition of binary oppositions and continua; 3) a relational approach to alternative frames of space, time, and action with concomitant bridging mechanisms from one frame to another; 4) an ability to intercalibrate chance and necessity; and 5) an aesthetic sensibility.

Given these identified parameters, of what does improvisation consist in a political or social crisis of the standoff variety? SWAT teams, hostage negotiators, dispute-resolution practitioners, anti-institutional groups, all have vocabularies of motivation, argument, persuasion, and the like (even if such vocabularies, in the case of the SWAT team, are gestural rather than linguistic). When the standard operating procedures that derive from these vocabularies of motives fail to elicit the peaceful endings our higher standards require, how can representatives of these organizations or other specially imported participants reconfigure their approaches?

All of the identified parameters of improvisatory action must be fundamentally based on a commitment to situational uncertainty. Recalling (and, further, anticipating) the discussion of the role of experts, uncertainty in situations of crisis poses both constraints and opportunities for action. In such situations, where violence casts its shadow, uncertainty can be frightening and frustrating. On the other hand, uncertainty also provides a space for action and a sense of a future that has not been foreclosed. Moving with such uncertainty constitutes what I have called operating in the subjunctive mood. Thus rather than seeking to negate uncertainty through devising scenarios of strict linear causality, a commitment to uncertainty must stick it out in the elemental uncertainty of forking paths, sideshadowed alternative histories and future trajectories, and so forth. In a related manner, Jeffrey Alexander has developed a critique of what he terms the materialist Structuralism of Bourdieu by counterposing a complexly developed analysis of the creativity of human agents confronting the contingent situations of social life: "To acknowledge and attempt to theoretically incorporate the ad hocing procedures first identified by Garfinkel and the turn-taking procedures detailed by Schegloff and others would demonstrate that there is, indeed, a space of indeterminacy – a space for practice or use in Wittgenstein's sense – between institutionalized expectations of any kind and any particular individual act."[10]

Improvisation works with this accentuated space of indeterminacy, or uncertainty. And it does so in the ways enumerated above. In what follows, I will flesh out these aspects of improvisation.

Withholding the categories

The strategic acknowledgment of categorical insufficiency during an ongoing standoff opens the door to improvisation. The improvisation of situational *bricoleurs* precisely foregrounds the acknowledgment of the insufficiency and the existential openness of given categories of objects, participants, event genres, and issues. It makes these categories subsidiary to the recombinatorial principles of improvised action. One might imagine temporarily adopting a stance of categorical agnosticism. Rather than working as quickly as possible to name the situation and to set its terms (these two processes engaging each other dialectically), this alternative approach withholds these claims. I'd like to suggest imagining an experimental approach to categorical representation and engagement. This implies an ability to both embrace categorical imperatives as participants ply their way through the situation and to slough these imperatives off if they are found not to work. Something as basic as not calling a situation a standoff, or not calling a particular set of actions at the end a surrender, is at the heart of categorical agnosticism.

Another way to think about this is to use the analytic rubric of Kenneth Burke's "God-terms." Complex situations present competing God-terms that describe and situate the situations' primal motivators and ultimate ends. Thus, in one and the same situation, one might find a notion of "the law" setting your highest stakes and goals, next to "rationality," next to "holiness," next to "efficiency." Rather than expending the social energy to attempt the match-up between situation, worldview, and God-term, and then to enforce that particular planetary system over all other competing ones, improvisation would suggest purposely abandoning the particular vocabularies of motive and goal for the sake of getting everybody through the situation intact.

Allowing a serendipity through discursive, or categorical interaction, might appear to be synonymous with adopting an attitude of neutrality. But withholding categorical determinations, resisting and delaying categorical action is very different, I think, from being neutral. For I read neutrality to mean being neutral between two or more opposed and clearly defined parties or positions, and the point here is to deliberately forestall precisely the seemingly inexorable process of the naming and defining of parties and positions.

In terms of what it means to embody "withholding" stylistically, a key distinction is that between linear, causal descriptions and experiential, relational stories. Here, scholars in fields as various as psychology (White and Epston), rhetoric (Schon), and conflict resolution (Docherty) converge in pointing up the difference between a good argument and a good story. In his work on problem setting and social policy, Schon writes about the ongoing process of reconfiguring complex situations as the description–action dialectic plys its way. In doing so, he emphasizes the importance of storytelling:

Although the inquirer has suspended the earlier conflicting descriptions . . . he has not yet achieved the restructuring that will enable him to make a new description. In this intermediate state, he needs a way of representing to himself the particularity of the situation in which he is involved – one which is dominated by neither of the descriptions with which he began. At this point, storytelling can play an important part. The inquirer can tell the story of his experience of the situation . . . and he can do this before he has constructed a new, coordinated description of the situation.[11]

Storytelling has a particular relationship to time and temporal experience. Structurally, a story must extend itself through time (as well, we have seen, it often pivots on issues of spatial displacement). This commitment to time requires a certain patience in and of itself and diverges dramatically from the cross-section-like simultaneity of categorical description. As White and Epston write: "A good argument uses the indicative mood, deals with general causes, and strives for certainty. A good story uses the subjunctive mood, deals not with universal truth conditions but connections across across time, and leads not to certainties but to varying perspectives."[12]

Some policy-oriented organizations have discovered the communicative benefits of storytelling, as the recent strategy of the "Welfare Truth Squad" organized by the Jewish Council on Urban Affairs demonstrates. This "Welfare Truth Squad" consists of seven former welfare recipients who make presentations to various groups about their experience of welfare. The group has actually turned to professional storytellers to advise them on how to tell their stories, indicating, perhaps, a sense of the ability of stories to hold attention and create alternate worlds in ways that graphs and statistics cannot.

Of course, there are more or less effective stories, more or less satisfying stories, and more or less evocative, suggestive stories. As well, any form of narrativization of experience confronts H.P. Grice's dicta of truthfulness, adequacy, parsimoniousness and so forth. At the end of the chapter, I will revisit the vexed question of the political implications of the appeal to a narrativized reading of social life. Here, I would simply enjoin the reader to think about the potential of the genre of storytelling in which, as literary theorist Franco Moretti says of the paratactical structure of Joyce's *Ulysses*, "multiplying developmental directions and making them independent of one another conveys . . . an open present, where the various developments are still all equally possible."[13]

Respecting and transcending the binaries

We have encountered many pairs of binary oppositions over the course of this analysis of standoffs. There are the temporal binaries of past and future, patience and impatience, and times of action and times of stasis, among others. There are the spatial binaries of inside and outside, civilized and wild, and permeable and impermeable. Finally, there are the action binaries of offense and defense, ingress and egress, expanding and narrowing, and so forth. As well, in a semantically derived typology of the participants of the standoff, there are similarly several operational pairs of binaries. We find guilty and innocent, defender and offender, hero and villain.

The Structuralist mode of analysis places binary opposition at the very core of symbolic meaning – where the individual terms of opposition derive their meaning from their oppositional relationship to each other. So we really don't know what an innocent is unless we are able to juxtapose it to one who is guilty, and vice versa. Thus, it has been absolutely crucial to locate and calibrate the relevant binary oppositions as they give literal and figurative shape to the standoff and to the way it is represented by and to participants and audience alike.

By contrast, a Pragmatist approach to ongoing situations sets its perceptual sights on continua and transformations rather than on binary oppositions. Meaning unfolds over time in a manner that is simultaneously developmental and recursive. If semantics is the key to the Structuralist world of paired opposites, syntax is the key to the processual orientation of Pragmatism. Thus, this analysis has also sought to develop a syntactical understanding of participant identities, for example, as their ongoing actions figure and reconfigure their meaning. Improvisation must then, at one and the same time, respect the structures of the binaries and push to overcome them in its quest to find its shape (ends) within the situation at hand. As Lars Engle puts it; "One of [Pragmatism's] central intellectual moves is the conversion of binary oppositions into continua, for instance, the conversion of the opposition 'necessary/contingent' into a continuum with 'more stable' and 'more fluid' as its directions, and no end point imagined either way."[14]

Relational approach to time, space, and action

Each simple substance has relations that express all the others and is in consequence a perpetual living mirror of the universe.

(Gottfried Wilhelm Leibniz, *Monadology*, 1965, p.157)

It is obvious that no matter how complete the theory may be, a middle term is required between theory and practice, providing a link and a transition from one to the other. For a concept of the understanding, which contains the general rule, must be supplemented by an act of judgment whereby the practitioner distinguishes instances where the rule applied from those where it does not.

(Immanuel Kant, *Kant's Political Writings*, p. 61)

In a manner similar to the above dictum to intercalibrate the binary oppositions with the continua of a situation, this third improvisational aspect aims at a contingent overcoming of absolutism. Standoffs, with their highlighted antitheses, indicate and emphasize the uncomfortable coexistence of different frameworks of space, time, and action. Or, what is the same thing, they highlight the difficulty of acknowledging such coexistences without a concomitant sense of threat or intimidation. This latter sense characterizes many interactional moments where coexisting temporal, spatial, and action frameworks slide unknowingly together, or out and out collide with each other. David Harvey refers to just such a moment when Europeans and Native Americans engaged in initial transactions of exchange. He writes: "Incommunicability of the sort that characterized the negotiations over land sales between colonial settlers and Indian groups in the early stages of colonization of New England, then becomes part of the clash of different social definitions of spatio-temporality."[15]

Ultimately, however, if one follows Marshal Sahlins' notion of the "structure of the conjuncture," the shapes that these transactions will come to take will reflect more than mere mutual incomprehensibility. If the situation doesn't devolve into the finitude of destruction or massacre, what looks at first glance to be pure imposition of one time–space frame onto another is actually the transformation of both. Such transformations have many, contingent, implications. But we need to remain focused on their implications for the (existentially) short-term goal of resolving the paralysis of the standoff.

In order for the diverse frameworks to communicate with each other and forge areas of (however temporary) overlap, mediating bridges must be found. In his study of the use of improvisation in conversation, Reyes Ramos identifies the particularly important bridge moments in conversation during which the speakers change topics. He refers to this process as one of modulation, making a case for its analogy to modulation in musical improvisation:

The smooth modulation process is usually accomplished in four stages, and they are as follows: the establishment of the home key, the use of a pivot chord, the entry into the new key, and the establishment of the new key . . . When a pivot chord is played, the listener does not know which key the chord is being played in and whether or not the key has changed or is about to be changed.[16]

The playing of the pivot chord, which can be recognized as belonging to the initial key and can also be recognized as belonging to the upcoming key, creates a moment of uncertainty, frame coincidence, and potentiality. Certainly, its existential status is temporary, but that does not diminish its salience. The musicians, conversants, or situational participants can make what they want of it.

Bridges can take several forms and serve several purposes. There can be bridges oriented primarily toward temporal parameters and bridges oriented toward spatial parameters. There can also be action bridges (modulations in gestures, speech, texts). In the standoffs under examination here, there are a few examples of such pivot chords. Perhaps not surprisingly, most of these examples represent suggestions that emerged over the course of a standoff and were subsequently rejected.

A proposed temporal bridge was suggested by the head of a city agency, the Philadelphia Crisis Intervention Network, approximately one year before the final confrontation between MOVE and the Philadelphia police. Bennie Swans, the agency head, sent a letter to then Mayor Wilson Goode, in which he proposed negotiating with the MOVE group about its use of the loudspeaker system that they had mounted on the side of their house. Recall that MOVE had initiated its campaign of shouting invectives against local and national politicians and against some of its own neighbors on Osage Avenue through this loudspeaker, as well as emitting long diatribes against "the system," based on MOVE's philosophy. Swans writes:

I recommend that some discussion take place around the use and time of the loudspeaker system. While clearly negotiating around the speaker system will not serve as a resolution, it does provide more time. This may minimize chances of a forced reaction by the law enforcement community and may allow for the development of a more creative approach to handling the MOVE organization.[17]

Swans' suggestion was not taken up by Mayor Goode. On the face of it, it might indeed seem a paltry suggestion – the neighbors will still have to put up with the noise and psychological oppression of the loudspeaker diatribes at certain points of the day, and the "MOVE problem" is not solved by this proposed action. However, temporal parameters are forced into prominence here and notions of quiet-time and noisy-time bring the diverse frameworks into communication with each other. Hypothetically restricting the loudspeaker times to, say, daytime, insures that the neighbors can sleep at night. From the perspective of MOVE, hypothetically permitting the loudspeaker to be used during certain moments of the day recognizes MOVE's membership in the community and makes (temporal) room for its actions. It is, of course, impossible to know if such an approach would have led to any amelioration in the situation or, more importantly, if it might have acted as the thin end of the wedge toward a transformation of the structures.

In terms of spatial pivot chords, the actions of the FBI during the

Freemen "standoff" can be understood as constituting a series of experiments with space (among other dimensions). As the *New York Times* reported: "When the resisters, who call themselves the Freemen, refused to surrender, the FBI agents employed a novel technique for an agency steeped in a tradition of aggressive law enforcement: They retreated out of sight."[18] The act of retreating indicates a radically novel approach to the spaces of the standoff. It involves a dissolution of the perimeter and a redomestication of the just previously militarized space. It also puts territorial claims in abeyance. In this case, such strategic and epistemological moves proved to be ultimately successful in staving off the devolution of the situation into violence.

Beyond temporal and spatial bridges, there lie other bridge modalities of action. Two key modalities for this study are that of text hybridity and alternative experts. Text hybridity refers to both the ability of different readers of "the same text" to interpret the text's meaning differently. It also refers to texts that are the product of diverse discourses and that can thus be read from a series of angles. The category of alternative experts raises the question about which kinds of experts ought to be imported into the scenes of standoffs.

Hybridity in texts (both Ur-texts and texts-in-action) can be accidental and disavowed or it can be purposeful and embraced. The degree to which such heterogeneity is acknowledged and worked with as hybridity is, I think, absolutely at the heart of this project. If, as scholars of law and society claim, complex societies such as those under examination here demonstrate conditions of legal and social pluralism,[19] then the kinds of contradictory or just plain different categorical imperatives of different institutions will confront each other over the course of a standoff. As we have seen, these confrontations will inevitably take the form of textual exegesis and formulation. Sociologists need to develop ways of analyzing these various forms of hybridity. An ability to identify and articulate the diverse worldviews (for example, secular or religious), structuring genres (for example, tragedy, melodrama, comedy), and discourses (for example, means-oriented or ends-oriented) that inhere in the texts, and that move a situation on in its existential trajectory, is crucial to the next step, that being an active working with hybridity.

Anthropologist William Hanks analyzes one historical example of an actively hybridized series of texts that were theoretically open to diverse interpretations and could also be viewed as transforming the structures in the process of apparently reproducing them. These sixteenth-century texts from early colonial Mayan society in Mexico, written by native Mayan officials, reveal aspects of both Spanish and native conventions of textual production. Hanks writes:

On the one hand, the texts fit nicely into contemporary Spanish categories such as carta (letter), informacion de derecho (statement of rights), and concierto (agreement) . . . But native conventions also laid claim over official Maya in at least some of its features, and lead to another reading. For instance, the texts are written in Maya, showing indigenous forms of address, along with prose and verse styles common to other kinds of native discourse. It is also typical of official Maya works that they arise as part of an intertextual series of two or more versions of what seems to be a single template.[20]

Such hybridized texts represent moments of improvisation as antagonists confront each other and the new situation that their interactions (however amicable or hostile) create. In the standoffs examined, there were a few attempts at devising and working with hybridized texts. We can recall the officially neglected "organic mediators," religious scholars Arnold and Tabor and their attempts at an alternative biblical exegesis of the Seven Seals on the radio talk-show to which David Koresh listened. There was, as well, an attempt on the part of several US Marshals, Ron Evans, Warren Mays, and Dave Hunt, to develop a letter to be sent to Randall Weaver in the period just prior to the Ruby Ridge standoff, that period during which Weaver was under general surveillance after not appearing for his trial for selling two shotguns to an undercover agent. Two proposed variations on a theme of this letter were reproduced in the set of documents accompanying the Senate Hearings on "The Federal Raid on Ruby Ridge." It is interesting to read them, both for their complex, hybrid form and content, and in the light of the knowledge that they were prevented from being sent by US Attorneys in charge of the case.

The first, and longer, letter states its official purpose at the outset: "I have been asked to write to you and discuss how we might find a reasonable solution to this matter [the pending status of criminal charges filed against Weaver]." It then lays out the nature of Due Process and of the authors' admittedly somewhat limited knowledge of cross-examination in trials. Two US Marshals sign the letter. However, the first person pronoun "I" appears along with the second person plural pronoun "we" throughout for self-referencing the author(s), making somewhat uncertain the nature of the author's agency. They write: "Due Process requires that you also take part in the proceedings. From your letter we received through Allen Jeppesen there is some suggestion that you are willing to discuss your concerns about the judicial system. It is my hope that through discussions I might relieve some of your anxieties about the federal process."

The structure of the letter presents several opening paragraphs in letter form, then a six-point set of responses to issues raised in Weaver's prior letter to the US Marshals Service, then some more paragraphs in letter format and an interesting postscript that I will discuss below. The tone of the letter manages to stay in a middle zone somewhere between official bureaucratic, impersonal distance and a more colloquial, personal, intimacy. The Marshals try to address some of Weaver's more tendentious claims about a conspiracy against him (and other ex-Green Berets) on the part of the United States federal government. They do so in a sustained, respectful manner; "I am unaware of any concerted effort to 'set up' for prison or murder all ex-green berets. In addition I do not understand your bases for believing this, unless you explain it further to me." Finally, the authors seek to simultaneously allay Weaver's fears that his wife, Vicky, has already been charged in any criminal proceedings, but also to warn Weaver that "the longer this matter remains unresolved, the stronger the likelihood that she or others could be charged with obstruction of criminal process."

Tempered, sober, helpful in its tone, the letter seems to end with an expressed hope that the situation can be resolved. However, there is an unexpected and revealing postscript to the letter which reconfigures the letter's generic repertoire. I will reproduce the postscript in its entirety:

On several occasions you have asked Warren and I to refer to various scriptures. We have done this on every occasion you have referenced scriptures to better understand your beliefs and why we may be in conflict. You have caused us to think about many of the issues you raised. It is clear that you have studies [sic] the Bible extensively. For this reason I would ask you why Deuteronomy 16:18–19, does not present some question in your mind that you should face your accuser as stated in this passage?[21]

While roughshod in manner, this attempt at biblical hermeneutics does display a desire to open the letter to heterogeneous voices, to communicate on several channels simultaneously, to, in a word, hybridize. Again, as in the proposal to find the temporal pivot chord for the times of the loudspeaker in the MOVE case, this hybridized letter, a textual approach to the problem with Randy Weaver, was never actually sent. Thus the sideshadowing analytical endeavor enjoins us to imagine what might have happened if it had.

The various relational approaches to time, space, and action draw the project of improvisation into an oblique colloquy with issues of prediction, expectation, and hindsight. There is something of a logical paradox in the linking of standoff improvisation with Pragmatism on the one hand (which finds its goals in the actual concreteness of the situation) and with a pre-articulated goal of getting everybody out intact, on the other. Finding goals and predetermining goals might seem like contradictory imperatives. I will take up this rather thorny theoretical and normative issue at the very end of the chapter. Here, I simply wish to note that a probabilistic mode of linking expectations about certain kinds of conflicts, such as those standoffs examined here, to certain outcomes assumes a variety of things that improvisation holds in abeyance. It assumes that given empirical events can unproblematically be determined to be categorically given "kinds of conflicts," and it assumes that standard operating procedures act as strict causal agents in moving toward the anticipated outcomes (or, perhaps even more frequently, that the specific anticipated outcome of violence could not have been prevented because of the recalcitrance of the antagonist to standard operating procedures).

Hindsight provides a strange vantage point on such issues. According to political scientist, Marc Howard Ross, hindsight must also manage to incorporate a vision of originary expectations in order to be minimally useful. He writes:

> . . . on the technical level it is difficult to evaluate the probabilities associated with outcomes that did not occur and compare them with those that did. Because such judgments are generally made after an outcome is known, hindsight frequently affects evaluations. In this regard, assessing conflict management . . . is much easier from the point of view of apparently self-evident outcomes than from the perspective of the unfolding events. But not all outcomes were most likely ones when viewed from the outset, and it is necessary to construct explanations in order to discern the ways initial expectations as well as proximate actions, nonactions, and other factors shape the outcomes.[22]

The relational approach to time, space, and action engages improvisation as a mode of creating alternative worlds within an extant world held in temporary suspended animation, where self-evident outcomes are purposely deflected.

The final type of pivot chord mechanism to be explored in this section is that of the category of alternative experts. Unlike the experts who are usually imported into such scenes as standoffs – ballistics experts, psychologists, hostage negotiators, tactical experts are a few – the kinds of alternative experts configured here are precisely experts in various kinds of improvisation. These would include the organic mediators whose portfolios include community-based experiences as well as official credentials. Another image of expert conjured here reflects Ron Jacobs' and Philip Smith's idea of the critical social roles of the jester and the bard.[23] The jester has a commitment to irony and contingency. The bard spins epic stories to mobilize the past in the service of the present. Both types of narrative experts point to the sacred, though they do so in different registers. Both, because of their essentially poetic origins, are as much invested in the modality of communication as they are in its content.

Another quality of alternative experts in crisis situations such as standoffs is that they should keep changing. At any given point in a crisis, certain kinds of skills, and not others, might be required. Writing about the Uruguayan soccer team that survived for ten weeks after its aircraft crashed in the Chilean Andes, Karl Weick notes that,

Demands shifted from caring for the wounded . . . finally to finding someone able to explain and rationalize their decisions to the world once they had been rescued . . . What also becomes clear is that any attempt to pinpoint *the* leader or to explain survival by looking at a single set of actions is doomed to failure because it does not reflect how needs change as a crisis unfolds, nor does it reflect how different coherent groupings form to meet the new needs.[24]

Part of the reason for the alternation of experts is thus clearly tied to the matching of situational needs and available skills. However, another reason is tied to the self-preservation of the experts themselves. Some of the very best and most satisfying of theatrical and musical improvisation is that done in tandem by a series of interacting performers, where the initiating theme is tossed back and forth by the members of the group. On the one hand this magnifies both the risk and the expansiveness of the performance. On the other hand, it diffuses the responsibility for sustaining the creative maneuvering. Such diffusion is clearly not news for trained law-enforcement negotiators who do work in teams. But the stakes are even higher for alternative experts of the aesthetic variety because of the residual sense of the dangerousness of "poets." As literary theorist Houston Baker writes: "The exclusion of poets from the republic by Plato is the primary Western site of this contest [between poetry and the state]."[25]

Thus the need for experts to appear in many and diverse forms, both for reasons of contingency and reasons of self-preservation. Walter Benjamin put this most poetically in his discussion of the "righteous man" role in the stories of Johann Hebel, and makes explicit the link between aesthetic improvisation and moral improvisation:

But because no one is actually up to this role, it keeps changing hands. Now it is the tramp, now the haggling Jewish peddler, now the man of limited intelligence who steps in to play the part. In every single case it is a guest performance, a moral improvisation . . . for any principle can at some time become the instrument of the righteous man.[26]

Chance and necessity in a situation of uncertainty

In Chapter 1, I proposed narrative as the connecting bridge between typologies of situations (the Structuralist program) and theories of situations (the Pragmatist program). As well, narratives were put forward as the best way of formulating experience that contained both recognizable archetypes and contingent features, certainty and uncertainty, necessity and chance.

Recalling these frames here in the context of intercalibrating the Structuralist and Pragmatist moments in improvisation, we need to clarify the relations between chance and necessity.[27] One might resuscitate and reconfigure the Structuralist analytical enterprise of charting the situational implications of the narrative movement through time as discursive moves are *selected* along the synchronic axis and *combined* along the diachronic axis. Such attention to the way that the punctuated and lurching tacking along the two axes weaves the discontinuous choices into an unfolding continuous narrative of contiguous choices highlights the phenomenological insights about temporality of Mead and Merleau-Ponty.[28] It also exactingly catalogues the influence of particular choices along each axis on subsequent configurations of the story. Predetermined repertoires of choices of ways of characterizing a situation, its participants, and its anticipated trajectories may be reconfigured as improvisation leads to counter-intuitive choices and combinations. In a sense, this project is analogous to a genome project of mapping a recombinant DNA. Of course here the DNA is social rather than molecular in nature.

An example comes from the political decisions in the MOVE crisis. At any given point in the period leading up to and including the standoff, there was a competition (however tilted in particular directions) among an assortment of discourses of comprehension and control. This competition reflected provisional answers to the question: Should we use a language of religious cults, political movements, neurotic acting-out, or terrorists to describe the MOVE group? Thus at specific time-points, choices were made along the synchronic axis that suggested, though didn't absolutely determine, an action/narrative direction. Supplementing, and carrying this forward through time, were the effects along the diachronic axis of the combinations, or contiguous transformations, as each chosen discourse was supplanted by its successor. In *Discourse and Destruction*, I referred to this action along the diachronic axis as discursive "handings-off": the Mayor's office (Bureaucracy) handing off to the District Attorney's office (Law), the District Attorney's office handing off to the police (War). Discourses change as responsibility is transferred. One thing suggested by this way of looking at the relation between institutions and discourses in on-going situations is that the hybridized discourses I theorized at the end of the study of MOVE short-circuit the weaving selections and propulsions along, respectively, the synchronic and diachronic axes. The narrative is stopped in its tracks and, perhaps, a space of pure invention and improvisation opens up. By refusing the restrictive mechanism of adopting a single discourse (with its attendant institutional worldview) at any given time, the responsibility for action may reside more with the resultant *interactions* than with the institutions that would lay claim to the situation.

However, it is also crucial to keep in mind that any situation, crisis or otherwise, will inevitably involve some structured falling back on unarticulated assumptions, rules, roles, and discourses (necessity) and some pragmatic improvisation, mixing, creativity (chance). The important question is what is the relationship (proportionality, relative weighting, timing and sequence) between the use of structures and the use of creativity?

The aesthetic sensibility

At this point I want to suggest that it might prove analytically and practically revelatory to consider the literal and metaphorical standoffs discussed in the book as "aesthetic emergencies," as well as social emergencies. The aesthetic perspective is one that is self-conscious about reflecting on how we must cope with time, space, and action in situations. The difference between the aesthetic and the instrumental perspectives are nowhere better elaborated than in French poet Paul Valéry's analogizing of poetry and prose to dancing and walking.

First Valéry differentiates between prose and poetry by giving the example of someone asking another person for a light: "It may be observed that in all communication between men, certainty comes only from practical acts and from the verification which practical acts give us. I ask you for a light. You give me a light: you have understood me." This prosodic moment, according to Valéry, tends to lead to the negation of language itself, as the giving of a light abolishes the speech in the successful action. Poetry, on the other hand, draws attention to itself as language, as the very phrase "Have a light?" takes on a new and substantially different kind of meaning through its repetition: "It has acquired a value; and has acquired it at the expense of its finite significance. It has created the need to be heard again . . . Here we are on the threshold of the poetic state." Indeed, it is this threshold that this study would like to foreground. For the standoff can also be understood as a threshold moment. Similarly, Valéry's distinction between walking and dancing succinctly addresses the vexed question of goals in situations.

Walking, like prose, has a definite aim. It is an act directed at something we wish to reach . . . There are no movements in walking that are not special adaptations, but, each time they are abolished and, as it were, absorbed by the accomplishment of the act, by the attainment of the goal. The dance is quite another matter . . . It

goes nowhere. If it pursues an object it is only an ideal object, a state, an enchant-
ment . . ."[29]

Its pleasure is in the discovery of itself as it finds and creates shapes in the
environment.

Perhaps it is going too far to bring pleasure into colloquy with the
standoff, but it is nevertheless an aspect of the aesthetic perspective that
taps something deep within human beings. As well, along with pleasure
there are other aesthetic impulses that track human needs, the impulse
toward coherence, harmony, counterpoint, and the narrativization of
social life. Given that even standard operating procedures engage their own
rhetorical forms, we are all fatalistically implicated in an aesthetic dimension of life, regardless of how practical and instrumental we believe our
goals to be. So rather than reject the aesthetic, the goal might be to locate
those aesthetic genres, principles, and devices that best anticipate the
restructuring of situations in a less deadly direction.

One might begin by asking what genres are being relied on to "make
sense" of the situation? What culturally characteristic plots and narratives
are engaged (here the cultural themes and set-points of normalcy I
described earlier can provide many narrative variations on these themes)?
Archetypal stories about happy families and sad families provide a grid
through which authorities and public alike "recognize" types when they see
them. What then will they recognize as a denouement? In an earlier study
of the kidnapping and assassination of the former Italian Prime Minister
Aldo Moro by the Red Brigades, I considered the existential and political
ramifications of political forces playing the ongoing sequestration of Moro
as either tragedy or melodrama.[30] But genres are only one of the relevant
aesthetic forms by which the aesthetic dimensions of a standoff can be
evaluated. I would submit that other aesthetic elements at this "site of
hybridity of textuality," might be illuminating. For example, recalling my
discussion of temporal expectations for standoffs, the literary and linguistic discussions of the functions and impact of repetition might prove fruit-
ful. How, for example, would the ten-day rule be assayed in the context of
Herrnstein-Smith's revelation about the expectations built into poetic repetition: "When a stimulus continues to be repeated exactly over a considerable period of time, our expectation of further repetition must contend
with our desire for closure or at least for change. Up to a certain point, this
produces a heightening of tension; but after that, it is as if the nerves 'give
up' and simply fail to respond altogether. . . ."[31] Does the ten-day rule indicate a "failure of nerves" in this aesthetic sense as well as the more prosaic
political "failure-of-nerve" sense?

Further, one might look beyond the traditional plot and character structures and actually aim for the short-circuiting of expectations: separate where merger is expected, merge where separation is expected, use repetition in ways that delay the "failure of nerves" that Herrnstein-Smith writes about. Metaphors might prove useful bridging devices between one genre and another, one discourse and another, or one worldview and another. While all language is essentially metaphorical, the overt deployment of metaphors in conversations usually calls attention to itself as an arrow that points beyond the practical world referenced by the conversation to an altogether alternative reality. It can open the space of freedom or indeterminacy for situational recombinations.[32] Of course, not all metaphors are equally engaging or rich. Umberto Eco argues that, "The best metaphors are those that represent things 'in action.' Thus the metaphorical consciousness is consciousness of the dynamism of the real."[33]

Short of a full-scale move across the threshold from the prosodic to the poetic state, an expert sensitivity to the charge and effectiveness of sociolinguistic and narrative features could help in the development of an improvisational orientation to standoffs. These features include such things as repetition, pronominal usage, the appearance of silences and pauses, the meaning of question–answer sequences (and perhaps the disruption of this into question–question sequences), speech overlap, over- and underlexicalization and the like.[34]

Conclusion

Finally, I want to say a few words about goals – a particularly sensitive area for Pragmatism and, as noted above, the area where my own story is tempted to go from analysis to prescription most clearly. Here lies a basic problem for the pragmatic stance and for the project of articulating the *forms* and *substance* of temporal, spatial, and action parameters that are congruent with the pragmatic stance. If it is true that, as Hans Joas writes, Pragmatism "finds its ends within situations . . . we find our ends in the world and . . . prior to any setting of ends we are already, through our praxis, embedded in various situations,"[35] then we must wonder what it means to (even temporarily) abandon our preconceived goals as we enter the situations of social life. The question then is, how are goals "found" and articulated in the middle of things? It is not difficult to move from the claim that Pragmatism finds its goals within situations to the conclusion that Pragmatism is essentially without its own absolute principles and thus lives parasitically off other systems of value and meaning. And from there it is easy to claim that Pragmatism can therefore be used for any purpose or goal. Is there an indigenous, as it were, moral valence to Pragmatism? And, if not, how is it possible to theoretically distinguish between the kind of opportunistic and totalitarian aestheticism of a Hitler or a Mussolini and a complex, humanly expanding aesthetics of improvisation? Clearly, the kind of aesthetic and linguistic sensitivity I have in mind here is not the same thing as Mussolini's choreographing of a successful fascist regime, built on such attention to language that he even wrote in the codebook for his fascist Gran Consiglio the rule that he, and only he, had the power of interruption at his disposal.[36]

As genealogists of Pragmatism, such as Cornel West, have tracked its history, there do seem to be certain constants that flow from Emerson to Dewey, to James, to Trilling and up to the contemporary philosopher Richard Rorty, to West himself with his own form of "prophetic Pragmatism." These constants are a conviction that the moral development of human beings is an ongoing project and that human thought is capable of great creativity in the face of changing situations. Rorty, a premier social constructivist, goes so far as to claim that "J.S. Mill's suggestion that governments devote themselves to optimizing the balance between leaving people's private lives alone and preventing suffering seems to me pretty much the last word."[37] So some kind of existential ground has not been foreign to Pragmatism's proponents. On the other hand, Pragmatism does resist grand theories, and might thus be accused of abandoning the kind of utopian vision offered by Marxism or Christianity. Is it really sufficient to propose that the pragmatic stance acts with a type of hovering "least harm" principle? On the other hand, even if one were not willing to go so far as to claim a moral grounding for Pragmatism (either as theory or as action strategy), is such a grounding necessary for the *situationally specific invocation of Pragmatism*? Here I would respond to Jeffrey Stout's question, in his *Ethics After Babel*, "Can any moral language worthy of use survive more than a moment if defended primarily in pragmatic terms?"[38] with the claim that it precisely does not need to survive for more than a moment, if the moment is an emergency moment, a crisis that is, by definition, momentary.

Finally, if one is willing to make the claim that a pragmatic stance is the most appropriate and useful one to adopt in the kind of crisis situations I've alluded to, is there a certain way to identify when it is that you are in that kind of crisis? Associated with that, might it not be true that some crises call for a reinvestment in structures, disciplines, expert discourses, and institutions? Standard operating procedures provide frameworks in situations of confusion and can be contingently anchoring and reassuring. Might there also not be, ironically, something to be said for the lugubrious delays endemic to bureaucratic institutions, as such delays have the merit of slowing things down, allowing individuals and institutions to catch their breaths?

My strategic and theoretical intervention here is to insist that it is crucial to examine the precise nature and contours of the "effort" actors exert in situations such as standoffs. The contingent is, in the words of Niklas Luhmann, "all that which is neither necessary nor impossible."[39] This study has sought to develop a formal vocabulary for, and a three-dimensional understanding of, the indeterminacy that is the existential stuff of contingent social life. We also need to recall Castoriadis' admonition to keep present the "imaginary moment" in institutions, and, when necessary, to retrieve that momentum in the willful disinvestment in institutional prerogatives and discourses so that we might emerge from crises such as MOVE or Waco, Ruby Ridge, or Lima, at the very least, intact.

Notes

Preface

1. Walter Benjamin, quoted in Richard Wolin, *Walter Benjamin: An Aesthetic of Redemption*, p. 125.

Chapter 1: Theorizing contingency

1. Thus it cannot be the case that this project, in its development of a theory of contingency, will eschew the analysis of empirical cases in favor of a more abstract theorizing. The cases are key, and in this attachment to the empirical, I share the following sentiments of Geoffrey Hawthorn, expressed in his book *Plausible Worlds: Possibility and Understanding in History and the Social Sciences*, p. 26:

   > Explanations, we can say, are dependent, as explanations, on context. If this is so, and if we add the assumption that the world is contingent, or at least, not known to be necessary, and the belief also . . . that the human world is in part constructed by practical reasoning which has to be seen as the practical reasoning of particular agents then in so far as any explanation in history and the social sciences will increase possibilities as it also reduces them, we can only consider the possibilities suggested in explanation, and thereby enhance our understanding, by considering particular instances. We must discuss examples.

2. Engle, *Shakespearean Pragmatism*, p. 19.
3. An interesting footnote, for this project, concerns a scene in which one of the contingent main characters, the party hack, plays the role of mediator in a literal standoff in the film.
4. Bernstein, *Foregone Conclusions*, p. 14.
5. In posing such a question, this project is similar to that undertaken by Philip Smith in his 1996 article, "Executing Executions." In this piece, Smith proposes that we analytically explore and exploit the narrative and aesthetic

238

elements of the public execution in order better to understand the repertoire of displays of personal identity in society.

6. Mead quoted in Rosenthal and Bourgeois, *Mead and Merleau-Ponty*, p. 44. The introduction of George Herbert Mead here points to the Pragmatist pantheon. Mead, Peirce, Emerson, Dewey, and the Symbolic Interactionist school in sociology broadly represent the Pragmatist wing of theorizing relevant to this project. They are often represented in opposing pairs with the proto-Structuralists and Structuralists proper: Descartes, Durkheim, Lévi-Strauss, Saussure, etc. For example, Norbert Wiley writes: "For Durkheim, all knowledge is in categories; for Mead all knowledge is in reflexive symbols. Like that of Descartes, Durkheim's knowledge is linear, intuitive, and direct, fitting neatly into classes. For Mead (and Peirce) knowledge is non-linear, semiotic, and reflexively indirect, fitting not into classes but triads" (*The Semiotic Self*, p. 128).

7. I would argue that we bring modern narrative expectations to standoffs, where chronology charts a series of action over time and space. Thus these narrative conventions are not typically those of some archaic and postmodern narratives which, according to Michael André Bernstein, "show that stories need not have a single beginning and a single end; indeed, they need not even have a single, chronological ordered series of actions," *Foregone Conclusions*, p. 27. The standoff seems to say to its participants and its audience, "I am from somewhere and sometime and I am going somewhere and sometime."

8. William Hanks, "Discourse genres in a theory of practice," p. 670.

9. Robin Wagner-Pacifici and Barry Schwartz, "The Vietnam Veterans Memorial," p. 383.

10. Greimas, *On Meaning*, p. 19.

11. The MOVE standoff of 1985 figures as one of the seven standoffs to be inter-calibrated in this book. The predominantly African-American group calling itself MOVE had been a thorn in the side of official Philadelphia for many years, beginning in the early 1970s, with its adamant and complicated public persona of being antitechnology, back to nature, advocating animal rights (protesting outside of zoos and refusing to use antirodent pesticide), black nationalism, and so forth. It had also made "normal" life in the West Philadelphia row homes near Cobbs Creek Park unbearable for the long-time, African-American, home-owning residents. An attempt to serve four arrest warrants in May of 1985 resulted in a standoff with 500 Philadelphia city police and a horrific confrontation in which eleven MOVE members died (including five children) and two city blocks were consumed by the huge fire that resulted from the igniting of a satchel full of explosives that was dropped on the roof of the MOVE house from a police helicopter.

12. Lévi-Strauss, *Totemism*, p. 89.

13. In reading the manifold documents accumulated to move the crisis forward and to chart its history (police records, memos from the Mayor and the District Attorney, letters written by neighbors to various politicians, broadsides from MOVE) as well as the entire transcript of the MOVE Commission

Watergate-style Hearings), I discerned four dominant discourses (or disciplines in Foucault's terms): the discourses of Domesticity, of Bureaucracy, of Law, and of War. Two of these, Domesticity and Law, were essentially oriented toward the ends of action. Domesticity-talk presented ideal-typical images of family and neighborhood, society's aspirations for emotional and moral succor. The Law also contained a vision of the good society and the good citizen: it distinguished among the guilty and the innocent, the victim and the villain, terrorism and misdemeanors. Two, Bureaucracy and War, were essentially oriented toward the means of action. The discourse of Bureaucracy spoke of rules and regulations, hierarchies and categories. It found its ends elsewhere, external to its worldview. As well, the discourse of War left the ends to politicians and dwelt in the world of means: strategies, tactics, weapons, enemy locations, and so forth.

14. Shupe and Hadden, "Cops, News Copy," p. 196.
15. Rochberg-Halton, "Situation, Structure . . .," p. 458.
16. Harvey, *Justice, Nature and the Geography of Difference*, p. 256.
17. In recognizing the analytical virtue of a processual, relational approach to situations, this book shares an animus similar to that laid out by Emirbayer in his "Manifesto for a Relational Sociology." It represents an advance upon the framework provided there, however, in bringing the interactional into dialogue with the structural to give a total picture of situations that both evolve and emerge over time and through space *and* have stopping-points where boundaries and entities temporarily crystallize. Thus, the combined Structuralist/Pragmatist analysis of the standoff, as one such exemplary situation, responds specifically to the boundary specification problem acknowledged by Emirbayer.
18. Alexander, "Action and its Environments," p. 296.
19. Castoriadis, *The Imaginary Institution of Society*, p. 132.
20. Alexander, "Action and its Environments," p. 300.
21. Granovetter, *Getting a Job*, p. 97.
22. Lévi-Strauss, *Totemism*, p. 98.
23. Ibid.
24. Pragmatist writers do account for structure as well within their understanding of situations. Such accounting approaches my own attempt to intercalibrate Pragmatism and Structuralism. See, for example, Dmitri Shalin, "Pragmatism and Social Interaction," p. 15: "Structure does compel the behavior of individuals in a given situation, but the conduct of individuals structures the situation into a definite pattern. Structure is only a possibility, a 'virtual' reality until it becomes an 'event,' is eventualized, i.e., made to happen in the here and now of the practical situational encounter."
25. Sahlins, *Historical Metaphors and Mythical Realities*, p. 5, my emphasis. Charles Tilly, in his own discussion of the contingency of social relations, and the impact of error-correction on the emergent coherent structure, assesses a similar dynamic:

Incessant error intersects with counterfactual explanation at two different points. First, the order-producing imbrication of error-filled interaction in shared understandings and interpersonal networks constitutes a causal domain requiring explanation of what actually happens with what else might have happened. Second, the implicit computation of possible interactions and their possible outcomes that inheres in every initiation of interaction, erroneous or otherwise, takes place within limits set by the actor's social location and the previous history of the interaction in question. ("Invisible Elbow," pp. 596–597)

26. Blackburn (ed.), *Oxford English Dictionary of Philosophy*, p. 297.
27. Charles Perrow, *Normal Accidents: Living with High-risk Technologies*.
28. Weick, "The Collapse of Sensemaking,"p. 635, emphasis mine.
29. Greenhouse, *A Moment's Notice*, p. 103.
30. *Frontline*, "Waco: The Inside Story," transcript, p. 8.
31. Herrnstein-Smith, *Poetic Closure*, p. 117.
32. Rosenthal and Bourgeois, *Mead and Merleau-Ponty*, p. 61.
33. Greimas, *On Meaning*, pp. 154–155.
34. Symborska, "Reality Demands", from *View With a Grain of Sand*, p. 184.
35. For an in-depth analysis of the MOVE confrontation, cf. my 1994 book, *Discourse and Destruction: The City of Philadelphia versus MOVE*.
36. MOVE, "Twenty Years on the MOVE," p. 6.
37. See Wessinger's forthcoming book, *How the Millennium Comes Violently*, for a complete analysis of the nature of the Branch Davidians under the leadership of David Koresh.
38. Wessinger, *How the Millennium*.
39. See Pate, "Freeh's Men vs. The Freemen," p. 83.
40. Reported in Wessinger, *How the Millennium*.
41. Pate, "Freeh's Men," p. 51.
42. Movimiento Revolucionario Tupac Amaru (MRTA) Communiqué #1, December 17, 1996.
43. Archie Lowe, Secretary of Defense, "An Open Letter to All Texas Sheriffs," p. 1 www.republic-of-texas.com.
44. May 11, 1997, www.republic-of-texas.com.
45. Roberto Unger, *False Necessity*, p. 272.
46. For example, one of the Tupac Amaru communiqués issued during the standoff in Lima identified something called "Andean culture": "whose main laws are: to work, not to steal, and not to lie (*Ama quella, Ama sua, Ama Llulla*)." The claim in this section of Communiqué #9 is that Fujimori did not understand or respect that culture.
47. Alexander, "Action and its Environments," p. 313.
48. Poovey, *Uneven Developments*, 1988.
49. Docherty, *When the Parties Bring their Gods*, p. 24.
50. Phil Linsalata, "Montana townspeople have had enough of the Freemen," *Detroit News*, April 21, 1996.

51. Interestingly, the symmetrical question, "Who is a Peruvian?" is not absent from the Tupac Amaru standoff. A certain self-consciousness about Peru's standing in the world system of nation-states is highlighted when the targets of terrorist action are corporations with centers in the US, or when the very site of the standoff is the residence of an ambassador from another country. The symbolism of the Japanese Ambassador's house, referring as it did to Peru's dependence on Japan, was lost on nobody.
52. Transcript of phone conversations between David Koresh and FBI negotiators, posted on the Internet by Cary R.W. Voss.
53. "Federal Raid on Ruby Ridge," p. 43.
54. Greenhouse, *A Moment's Notice*, p. 230.
55. Bourdieu, "On the Family as a Realized Category," p. 20.
56. *Frontline*, transcript p. 10.
57. "Federal Raid," p. 603.
58. *New York Times*, August 26, 1992, p. 14.
59. *Boston Globe*, August 24, 1992, p. 6, emphasis mine.
60. *Frontline*, p. 13.
61. Sokol, "How do Modern Jewish Thinkers Interpret Religious Texts?" p. 28.
62. As Edward Gaffney, Jr. writes: "Suppose that, although the government has vague general interest in gun control, it does not in fact enforce this policy very vigorously. And suppose the government waits until it gets a case with a group – the Branch Davidians – to hold up to the nation as a bunch of religious crazies who deserve whatever grief they get." ("The Waco Tragedy," p. 344–345). In a similar vein, Shupe and Hadden reproduce the multi-issue ATF agent mandates that led to the raid: "1) a statutory mandate to search for illegal weapons; 2) a humanitarian in loco parentis responsibility to rescue Branch Davidian children and dependents from abuse and neglect; and 3) an obligation to round up illegal aliens." ("Cops," p. 188.)
63. Hall, "Public Narratives," p. 207.
64. "Waco Tragedy," p. 332.
65. Anderson and Hevenor, *Burning Down the House*, p. 284.
66. Testimony of Gregor Sambor, MOVE Commission Hearings, October 17, 1985, p. 199.
67. Editorial Collective *Voices from Wounded Knee*, quotation from Frizzell, p. 230.
68. Docherty, "When the Parties," p. 24.
69. Senator Herbert Kohl, "Federal Raid," p. 3.
70. "Federal Raid," p. 287.

Chapter 2: The times of standoffs

1. Hannah Arendt has a critical discussion of the difference between the Ancient Greek concept of immortality and the Christian concept of eternity in which the latter, unlike the former, opposes itself to the *vita activa* in its contempla-

tive orientation toward the world. Writing about the rise of the Christian gospel, Arendt argues: "And they succeeded so well in making the vita activa and the bios politikos the handmaidens of contemplation that not even the rise of the secular in the modern age and the concomitant reversal of the traditional hierarchy between action and contemplation sufficed to save from oblivion the striving for immortality which originally had been the spring and center of the vita activa." *The Human Condition,* p. 21.

2. Harvey, *Justice, Nature, and the Geography of Difference*, p. 225.
3. See David Landes, *Revolution in Time*, pp. 78–79.
4. *Frontline*, "Waco: The Inside Story," transcript, p. 11.
5. See Jayne Docherty's dissertation, "When the Parties Bring Their Gods to the Table," for a discussion of the impact of divergent world-views on the Branch Davidian standoff.
6. Hanks, "Discourse genres in a theory of practice," p. 678.
7. *Los Angeles Times*, December 19, 1996, A1, emphasis mine.
8. Steven Rea, "Big name hostage snooze off," *Philadelphia Inquirer*, Weekend Section, p. 3, November 7, 1997.
9. Carol Greenhouse writes: "The expansion of Christianity into Europe brought with it two ideas about time which had long roots in Jewish and autocthonous Christian tradition: first, the origin of time in creation and, second, the end of time in a day of judgment. The linearity of time derives from the geometric connection between these two end points" (*A Moment's Notice*, p. 20).
10. See Eviatar Zerubavel, *The Seven Day Circle: The History and Meaning of the Week*.
11. Hall, "The Time of History," pp. 127–128.
12. Hall specifies a case of such alternations apropos of his study of the People's Temple group and the disaster at Jonestown: "In *Gone From the Promised Land*, I saw People's Temple basically drawn back into the strategic time of apocalyptic struggle, when they couldn't reach their 'timeless' heaven on earth. In the end, they chose a different eternity than the one on earth, after a last strategic time strike against their opponents" (personal communication).
13. Cavicchioli, in Giglioli *et. al.*, *Rituali di degradazione*, pp. 80–81, translation mine.
14. For a theoretically sophisticated analysis of a variety of common, contemporary understandings of the law by people in everyday situations, including the way that people understand the temporal and spatial boundaries of the law, see Patricia Ewick and Susan Silbey 1998. *The Common Place of Law*. The following testimony by Former Director of the US Marshals Service, Henry Hudson, during the Senate Hearings on Ruby Ridge, confirms the contingent role of neighbor pressure:

> There was another factor here. Toward the early part of August 1992, we began receiving phone calls from the neighbors, the Raus, who suspected that the Weavers may be stealing some of their property, may be

harassing them. They continually called and said that if the marshals
do not come out there and do something about it, that they were going
to take it into their own hands and do something with Mr. Weaver.
(Hudson, "The Federal Raid on Ruby Ridge," p. 265)

15. Eric Henson and Edward Rendell, MOVE Commission Hearings, October 22,
    1985, pp. 9,19. Cf. also Paul Sutton, "The 4th Amendment in Action," p. 410:
    "Most police officers we spoke with described in varying detail what they often
    regarded as an unnecessarily protracted wait for the magistrate [to determine
    probable cause]."
16. "Department of Justice Report of the Ruby Ridge Task Force," p. 10231.
17. "Federal Raid," testimony of Henry Hudson, p. 263.
18. Gaffney, "The Waco Tragedy," p. 337.
19. *Voices from Wounded Knee*, p. 67.
20. Greenhouse, *A Moment's Notice*, p. 183.
21. See Mark Hansen, "(Cult)ure of the State: The Branch Davidians and the
    ATF," Chapter 2, p. 11.
22. Harvey, *Justice, Nature*, p. 214.
23. "Federal Raid," testimony of Gerry Spence, p. 72.
24. *Frontline*, transcript p. 2.
25. *Voices*, p. 164.
26. Ibid., p. 122.
27. *Frontline*, transcript, p. 4.
28. Associated Press, May 18, 1996.
29. Reuter Information Service, May 20, 1996.
30. Wells, "Narrative Figures and Subtle Persuasions," p. 220.
31. "The Last Words of David Koresh," web-site posted by Cary Voss, downloaded.
32. Leach, "Two Essays Concerning the Symbolic Representation of Time," p.
    227.
33. Eviatar Zerubavel, "The Social Marking of Time: A Study in Structural
    Sociology."
34. Bourdieu, "Structures, Habitus, Power," p. 166.
35. Phil Linsalata, *The Detroit News*, April 21, 1996, emphasis mine.
36. Reuter Information Service, April 26, 1996, Nando.net, emphasis mine.
37. Wagner-Pacifici, *Discourse and Destruction*, p. 42.
38. Sebastian Rotella, *Los Angeles Times*, December 19, 1996, p. 1.
39. Clifford Krauss, "Siege in Peru: The Overview," *New York Times*, December
    21, 1996, p. 6.
40. Reuters News Service, by-line Gene Laverty, May 13, 1996, emphasis mine.
41. Hunter, "The Roots of Environmental Conflict," p. 25.
42. Alvin Josephy, Jr., in Lyman, *Wounded Knee 1973*, p. x, emphasis mine.
43. *Frontline*, transcript, p. 8, emphasis mine.
44. *Ibid.*, p. 10.
45. "Officials Surround Armed Tax Protesters in Montana," *New York Times*,
    March 3, 1996, p. A16.

46. CNN, April 29, 1997.
47. Hal Spencer, Associated Press release, May 31, 1996, emphasis mine.
48. "Last Words," April 18, 1993, phone conversation with FBI negotiator, Cary Voss web page.
49. Hal Spencer, Associated Press, April 8, 1997.
50. "Federal Raid," Frederick Lanceley, p. 586.
51. *Frontline,* transcript, p. 14.
52. "This Time, FBI Avoids Military-Style Tactics," *New York Times*, March 27, 1996, p. A16.
53. *Voices*, p. 224.
54. Program narrator, Peter Boyer, *Frontline* transcript, pp. 17–18.
55. Lewis, "The Absence of Narrative," p. 30.
56. Bernstein, *Foregone Conclusions,* p. 27.
57. Herrnstein-Smith, *Poetic Closure*, p. 2.
58. Hunter, "The Roots," p. 48.
59. *Voices*, p. 229.
60. *Ibid.*, p. 135.
61. From "An Open Letter to All Texas Sheriffs," April 15, 1996, written by Archie Lowe, Secretary of Defense, Republic of Texas.
62. *Ibid.*
63. *Ibid.*
64. Roger Friedland and Richard Hecht develop an in-depth analysis of the political resonance of religious violence at sacred centers in Jerusalem and Ayodhya and find a similar genealogical dimension to both contemporary clashes at these places: "The conflicts in Jerusalem in 1990 and Ayodhya in 1992 have parallel precursors in 1929 and 1949. All these violent conflicts coincide with contests between and within each nation over the territorial extent of the collectivity." ("The Bodies of Nations," p. 144)
65. Quoted in Munn, "The Cultural Anthropology of Time," p. 97.
66. *Ibid.*, p. 98.
67. "Hearings before the Subcommittee on Public Lands, National Parks and Forests," United States Senate, July 29, 1993, p. 13.
68. "Public Narratives," p. 210.
69. *Philadelphia Inquirer*, March 17, 1996, p. 1.
70. CNN Report, April 29, 1997.
71. "Officials Surround Armed Tax Protesters in Montana," *New York Times*, March 27, 1996, p. A16.
72. "Public Narratives," p. 207.

Chapter 3: The spaces of the standoff

1. Vladimir Propp, *Morphology of the Folktale*, p. 26.
2. Greimas, *On Meaning*, p. 22.
3. It is often the case that the authorities will characterize one or another type of person in the standoff center as a hostage, even if the individuals in that

category may not conceive of themselves in that way. This occurred in the case of MOVE, when the MOVE children were ambivalently characterized as "hostages" (the quotation marks giving with one hand and taking away with the other); in the case of the Branch Davidian children and, to some extent, the women, in the standoff at Waco; and the children of Randy Weaver at Ruby Ridge. We will examine the categories "hostage" and hostage in the following chapter.

4. Quoted in Wagner-Pacifici, *Discourse and Destruction*, p. 36.
5. Quoted in Jayne Docherty, "When the Parties Bring Their Gods to the Table," p. 154, emphasis mine.
6. "Federal Raid on Ruby Ridge," p. 625.
7. Reuter Information Service, March 29, 1996.
8. Cohen, *Masquerade Politics*, pp. 60–61.
9. Ian Hacking, *The Taming of Chance*, p. 23.
10. Simmel, "Bridge and Door," p. 6.
11. Treasury Department Report on the Standoff at Waco, pp. 43–44.
12. Reuter Information Service, March 29, 1996.
13. *Frontline*, "Waco: The Inside Story," transcript, p. 6.
14. "DOJ Probes Wreckage at Ruby Ridge," *Legal Times*, March 13, 1995, p. 15.
15. Frederick Lanceley, "Federal Raid on Ruby Ridge," p. 593.
16. Editorial Collective, *Voices from Wounded Knee*, p. 57.
17. *Ibid.*, p. 43.
18. *Voices*, p. 118.
19. "During the Ruby Ridge seige, ATF was assigned to maintain a roadblock approximately 3 miles from the Weaver cabin on this same bridge that Weaver was arrested a number of months before, and also to assist the Idaho State Patrol in patrolling the outer perimeter so that no one could infiltrate into the back . . ." (testimony of John Magaw, Director, BATF, "Federal Raid", p. 198).
20. Testimony of Michael Johnson, "Federal Raid on Ruby Ridge," p. 313.
21. I am grateful to Mark Hansen for this information. See his Senior Thesis, "(Cult)ure of the State," p. 22.
22. Testimony of Mark Tilton, "Federal Raid," p. 328.
23. Foote, *Shadowed Ground*, p. 235.
24. Friedland and Hecht, "The Bodies of Nations," p. 148.
25. Hunter, *Culture and Government*, p. 65.
26. See Philip Smith, "Executing Executions."
27. Charles Taylor, *Sources of the Self*, p. 28.
28. Palestine, Texas was the city to which David Koresh and a few followers moved in 1985.
29. Pate, "Freeh's Men," p. 50.
30. Wessinger, *How the Millennium Comes Violently*.
31. Schama, *Landscape and Memory*, p. 201.
32. Lindecker, *Massacre in Waco*, pp. 2–3.

33. Gwen Florio, "In isolated Montana town, some see omens of disaster," *Philadelphia Inquirer*, March 17, 1996, p. A16.
34. *Los Angeles Times*, August 28, 1992, p. 1.
35. "Federal Raid," p. 12.
36. *Los Angeles Times*, August 28, 1992, p. 1.
37. "Hearings Before a Subcommittee of the Committee on Appropriations," p. 167.
38. See Wessinger, *How the Millenium*.
39. Testimony of Randy Weaver, "Federal Raid," p. 21.
40. MRTA Communiqué #1, December 17, 1996.
41. MRTA. Communiqué #13, March, 1997.
42. Professor Stephen Presser, Testimony Before the Senate Judiciary Committee with Regard to Appropriate Statutory and Constitutional Responses to the Supreme Court's Decision in *Texas* v. *Johnson*: September 14, 1989, pp. 589–590.
43. Here I'll insert my own note to refer to the brilliant work of Michel Butor on "The Book as Object," in his book *Inventory*. Butor takes on the very structure of the book and the page and has the following to say about such things as footnotes and other marginal notes: "Notes are usually placed outside the main body of the page, below, sometimes deferred to the end of the chapter or volume. The reader is manifestly invited to read the text twice: once by continuing straight through the sentence, the second time via the detour of the note" (p. 50). Such readerly paths and gambits indicate how ideas and positions can be influenced by their combined spatial and temporal parameters.
44. McConnell, "Reading the Flag," p. 107.
45. Ibid., p. 110.
46. Daniels, "The Montana Freemen," www.channel1com/mpr/Free.html, Vol. 5, No.2, 1996.
47. Wessinger, *How The Millennium*.
48. Cox, "My Life in MOVE," pp. 171–172.
49. *Voices*, p. 231.
50. Foote, *Shadowed Ground*, p. 278.
51. Schirmer, "The Claiming of Space and the Body Politic," p. 210.
52. Victor Turner, *Dramas, Fields, and Metaphors*, p. 175.
53. *New York Times*, August 26, 1992, p. 14.
54. *Voices*, p. 42.
55. Reuter Information Service, May 29, 1996, Nando.net., emphasis mine.
56. Ross, *The Management of Conflict*, p. 131.
57. *Voices*, p. 40.
58. See "Decibels, Not Bullets, Bombard Texas Sect," *New York Times*, March 25, 1993.
59. Cunningham, "A Linguistic Analysis," p. 554, downloaded text.
60. *Frontline*, transcript, p. 11.
61. Gaffney, "The Waco Tragedy," p. 340.

62. "Federal Raid," p. 146.
63. CNN, "World News," Web posting, January 23, 1997.
64. Simmel, "Bridge and Door," p. 7.
65. "Federal Raid," p. 89.
66. *Ibid.*, pp. 373–374.
67. *Ibid.*, p. 89.

Chapter 4: The action of standoffs

1. Hayden White, *Metahistory*, p. 36.
2. *Ibid*, p. 6.
3. Of course it is important to recall Alexander's epistemological caveat here that even acts of typification are inventive in that the project of matching the empirical event with the predetermined category requires an interpretive leap of faith: "Reality is resistant, however. To make it typical is a creative act and not merely a reproductive, typifying act, for we are usually (unconsciously) finding ways of understanding in a slightly new key. Typification actually camouflages shifts in classification. These shifts are what invention is all about." (Alexander, "Action and its Environments," p. 301).
4. Here it is important to recall that the law-enforcement authorities surrounding the Freemen stronghold made an adamant point that they were not calling the situation a standoff. Such decisions reflect a quite sensitive understanding of the power of labels to shape ongoing situations.
5. *Law and Contemporary Problems*, "Impact of Arrest Records," p. 291.
6. "Federal Raid on Ruby Ridge," p. 287.
7. Gaffney, Jr. "The Waco Tragedy," p. 334. The Treasury Department's Report on the Branch Davidian confrontation provides the following description of the ATF mandate:

    > . . . the Treasury Department on July 1, 1972 created the Bureau of Alcohol, Tobacco, and Firearms under the general oversight of the Assistant Secretary of the Treasury for Enforcement, Tariffs and Trade, and Operations. For the past twenty-one years, ATF has enforced the collection of federal taxes on alcohol and tobacco and the federal regulations on firearms, with particular attention to their use by criminals. Although on its face the bureau seems a discordant collection of separate duties, the techniques for enforcing the taxes and ferreting out the illicit products, whether cases of whiskey, cartons of cigarettes, crates of automatic weapons, or containers of bombs, are strikingly similar.
    > (*Report of the Department of the Treasury on the BATF Investigation of Vernon Wayne Howell,* G-4 5)

8. Wessinger, *How the Millennium.*
9. US Department of Justice Report of the Ruby Ridge Task Force.
10. Jeffrey Alexander, "The Sacred, Mundane, and Profane."

11. Phil Linsalata, "Montana townspeople have had enough of the Freemen," *Detroit News*, April 21, 1996.
12. Henry Hudson, "Federal Raid," p. 265.
13. Charles Goodwin, "Professional Vision," p. 620.
14. "Federal Raid," p. 625.
15. Goodwin, "Professional Vision," p. 609.
16. Friedland and Alford, "Bringing Society Back In," p. 254.
17. Edward Lincoln quoted in *The Los Angeles Times*, December 20, 1996, A p. 6. An important clarification should be made here, and will be reiterated later in the book. The goal of exploring the potential roles of improvisation in standoffs is decisively not the same thing as proposing or exploring a radical ad-hocing through the situation, such as Lincoln seems to be describing here.
18. Meyer and Rowan, "Institutionalized Organizations," p. 46.
19. Hacking, *The Taming of Chance*, p. 89.
20. Editorial Collective, *Voices from Wounded Knee*, p. 67.
21. *New York Times*, February 17th, 1997, p. A3.
22. Shupe and Hadden, "Cops," p. 193.
23. Associated Press, June 1, 1996, Nando.net.
24. Ambulances represent another symbolically key piece of equipment that might appear at the scene of a standoff. Ambulances admit of the possibility of physical injury and death and are thus linked causally (metonymically) to the guns, tanks, and other weapons that are copresent. Significantly, during the initial ATF raid on the Branch Davidians, despite the heavily armed dynamic entry plan of the raid, and despite what officials knew about the arsenal of the Branch Davidians, there were no ambulances in the vicinity. When the raid did turn violent and after several ATF agents had been shot, one agent actually turned to a news reporter on the scene and asked *him* to call 911 for an ambulance. Thus, not only were there no ambulances, the ATF also had no radios or other means of communications with them with which to request one.
25. This same narrative dilemma affected the few police officers involved in the rescue of the two surviving MOVE members who escaped from the burning house. The key rescuer, Officer Berghaier, was lauded by the MOVE Commission as a hero but he was never able to recover from the complicated trauma of his act and, after going through a severe depression, he quit the police force.
26. Wessinger, *How the Millennium*.
27. Quote from *Waco: The Rules of Engagement*.
28. "Federal Raid," p. 778.
29. The exact wording of the Rules has been the subject of contention by those who participated in their codification. The controversy is played out in the Senate Hearings, "The Federal Raid on Ruby Ridge," especially in the testimony of Larry Potts, pp. 621–674.
30. Government Exhibit 41–3, "Federal Raid on Ruby Ridge," p. 296. R, V, and K refer to Randall and Vicky Weaver and Kevin Harris.

31. See *Tennessee v. Garner*, 471 US 1, 3 (1985).
32. While Freeh did discipline bureau officials for issuing rules that were poorly drafted and confusing, he determined that Lon Horiuchi, the sniper who had killed Vicky Weaver, "had done so accidently and had operated according to standard FBI procedure." (Daniel Klaidman, "DOJ Report May Halt FBI Official's Rise,"*Legal Times*, March 6, 1995, p. 4).
33. Larry Potts, "Federal Raid," pp. 632–633.
34. Danny O. Coulson, "Federal Raid," p. 630.
35. Greg Urban, "The Role of Imperatives," p. 21.
36. Parenthetically, no surrender announcement was actually made.
37. Christopher Whitcomb, "Federal Raid," p. 327; italics mine.
38. Dale Monroe, "Federal Raid," p. 314.
39. Lon Horiuchi, the agent who actually shot Kevin Harris and Vicky Weaver, did not testify before the committee as he was at the time under investigation for possible criminal charges.
40. Dale Monroe, "Federal Raid," p. 330.
41. Edward C. Wenger Jr., "Federal Raid," p. 337.
42. Gonseth, *Time and Method*, p. 126.
43. A name that neatly expresses the existential issue of determining whether actions are taken for defensive or offensive purposes.
44. Ken Tilsen, quoted in *Voices*, pp. 128–9.
45. The characterization of a situation as a "standoff" is, interestingly, somewhat agnostic on the question of scope. It is almost as if, in neutralizing instrumental action through reciprocal threat, it also neutralizes the symbolic action of characterizing tropes.
46. Authorities can have their own motives for widening the scope of the scene. Their form of widening may not engage a process of categorical shift in naming the event. Rather, as in the case of the Tupac Amaru standoff, they may want to literally widen the scope of the event. There, the Japanese and Peruvian authorities alternately emphasized and diminished the international nature of the scene. When emphasizing it, they stressed the various nationalities of the hostages and the specific diplomatic portfolios of so many of the hostages. As such, there was a logic to the Japanese Foreign Minister, Yukihiko Ikeda's call for the Group of Seven nations to draw up a united strategy in a letter to the leaders of these countries and to Russia. This group then did collectively issue a statement condemning the hostage taking and reaffirming the no-concession position.
47. *Voices*, p. 250.
48. *Boston Globe*, August 24, 1992, p. 6.
49. "Federal Raid," p. 39.
50. Goodwin, "Professional Vision," p. 624.
51. Greimas, *On Meaning*, p. 23.
52. "gestural praxis: the uses of a person's own body to produce movements organized into programs having as a project an ordinary meaning. Thus, within

this generalized programmed activity, a specifically practical gestuality can be distinguished that can be opposed to mythical gestuality" (Greimas, ibid, p. 31).

53. In the last chapter, on the spaces of standoffs, the discussion of the raising of flags rested on an analysis of flags as markers and makers of territory. Here it is also important to note the role of flags as situational diacritical markers of phases, signifying changes that occur over the course of a standoff. For example, the raising of the Confederate Flag outside of the Freemen compound indicated to those on the outside that the Freemen had agreed to end the standoff and would soon be coming out.

54. Chapter 5 will examine the varieties of standoff endings and propose a paradigm of ending types that includes a category of "deals," of which such prisoner exchanges are clearly examples.

55. *New York Times*, December 21, 1996, p. 16.

56. *New York Times*, December 27, 1996, p. A6.

57. *Waco: The Rules of Engagement.*

58. Wessinger, *How the Millennium.*

59. Lyman, *Wounded Knee 1973*, illustrations following p. 60.

60. Reuter Information Service, May 16, 1996, Nando.net.

61. "Federal Raid," from prepared statement by Bo Gritz, p. 582.

62. "The guerrillas permitted a steady flow of Red Cross workers to bring carts of food, water, clothes, toilet paper, fans and other items to the front steps of the residence,": *Los Angeles Times*, December 20, p. A6.

63. *New York Times*, April 24th, 1997, p. A1.

64. *Voices*, p. 73.

65. Communiqué #10, Tupac Amaru.

66. *Voices*, p. 186.

67. A more Simmelian idea of individual identity as being constituted of multiple and overlapping roles will provide an analytical key to the later discussion of the "organic mediators" who act in standoffs.

68. "[The verb] acts primarily as a factor of integration of the temporal aspect with other aspects of the process, of the action, and of the activities expressed by language," Gonseth, *Time and Method*, p. 90.

69. *Ibid.*, p. 162.

70. Associated Press, April 28, 1996, Nando net.

71. Aho, *This Thing of Darkness*, p. 54.

72. See Gibson's *Warrior Dreams* for a compelling analysis of this legacy.

73. "Federal Raid", p. 303.

74. Writing about the presence of the police in London's Notting Hill Carnival in the tense period of the 1980s, anthropologist Abner Cohen invokes the "hands" of the police and explicitly, if ironically, juxtaposes the actions of the hands to a gesture of attempted comity, the smile:

> The police too, were fully aware of the rage and uneasiness their presence stirred among the young carnival goers and also of the severe

criticism sometimes meted on them by the national press for their "high handedness." They did their best to present a friendly image. They sought to understand the ideology and the traditions of the carnival. They sent police officers to attend the Trinidad Carnival on which the Notting Hill Carnival was modelled, in order to learn more about its organization and problems. In Notting Hill, police officers met regularly with the carnival organisers to seek their advice. In the 1984 carnival offical orders were even given to members of the force to smile.

(*Masquerade Politics*, p. 57)

75. Docherty, "When the Parties," p. 89.
76. *Frontline*, "Waco: The Inside Story," transcript, p. 7.
77. "Federal Raid," pp. 10–11.
78. American Friends Service Committee, *Voices from the Community*, p. 32.
79. Swett, "Cultural Bias in the American Legal System," p. 81.
80. "Federal Raid," p. 269.
81. *The Moro Morality Play*, pp. 173–4.
82. "Federal Raid," p. 308.
83. David Johnston, "This Time, FBI Avoids Military-Style Tactics," *New York Times*, March 27, 1996, p. A16.
84. Wessinger, *How the Millennium.* Pronounced over a loudspeaker by FBI negotiator Byron Sage, April 19th, 1993 at the outset of the final assault.
85. Of course actual threat and symbolic threat are different things, and the Tupac Amaru group, for example, was understood to represent a symbolic threat to the Fujimori government in the sense that that government's legitimacy was thought to hinge on how the occupation of the Japanese Ambassador's residence was resolved.
86. Halliday, "Anti-languages," p. 570.
87. *Voices*, p. 61.
88. *Ibid.*, p. 114.
89. *New York Times*, January 1, 1997, A1.
90. "Federal Raid," p. 24.
91. *New York Times*, Aug. 26, 1992 p. 14.
92. Richard Rogers, prepared statement to Senate Subcommittee on Terrorism, Technology, and Government Information:

> . . . it was clear to me that there was a shooting situation taking place at this location. It appeared to me that it would have been irresponsible for me to send my agents into the situation without at least giving them a set of rules within the greater framework of the standard FBI rules, that would allow them to defend themselves. With that in mind, I proposed that the rules be that if any adult is seen with a weapon in the vicinity of where this fire-fight took place, of the Weaver cabin, that this individual could be the subject of deadly force . . . [Any] child is going to come under standard FBI rules, meaning that if an FBI agent

is threatened with death or some other innocent is threatened with death by a child, then clearly that agent could use a weapon to shoot the child . . . [That's] the way it's stated, but quite frankly, we try to prevent ourselves from being put in positions where children can threaten us and where we would have to use deadly force.

93. "Federal Raid," p. 303.
94. Leo Brooks, MOVE Commission Hearings, October, 10, 1985, pp. 55–56.
95. See my discussion of the transformation in the public representation of former Prime Minister Aldo Moro during his fifty-five day sequestration as a hostage of the Red Brigades in Italy in 1978, for an example of the work of contamination in *The Moro Morality Play*, pp. 220–230.
96. "Federal Raid," p. 171.
97. *Voices*, p. 55.
98. Of the particular books of the Bible on which Koresh focused his interpretive vision, James Faubion writes:

> David Koresh remains sociologically and culturologically ambiguous. At first, even at second sight, he is counter-modern, anti-modern, even pre-modern. So, too, his favorite book. But here as elsewhere, historicism proves to be too simple, too simplistic. Many Biblical scholars have urged a generic distinction between such strictly "prophetic" books as those of Isaiah or Jeremiah and the visionary, properly "apocalyptic" books of Daniel and Revelation. The former date largely from the period preceding the Babylonian exile, the latter from the politically more pessimistic period following it. The former tend toward explicit exhortation and practical application, the latter toward an occult eschatology . . . Part epical, part tragic, part sublime, the book that David Koresh believed himself appointed at last to unlock is at once totalizing and individualizing.   ("Deus Absconditus," pp. 397–398)

99. According to James Aho, the *Protocols* "pretends to detail the tactics used by the High Jewish Council, the Sanhedrin, in its quest for world domination" (*This Thing of Darkness*, p. 30).
100. Sokol, "How do Modern Jewish Thinkers Interpret Religious Texts?" p. 39.
101. *Frontline*, transcript, p. 12.
102. Greenhouse, *A Moment's Notice*, p. 181.
103. Roe, *Narrative Policy Analysis*, pp. 144–145.
104. *Los Angeles Times*, August 27, 1992, p. 1.
105. Moshe Sokol, "How do Modern Jewish Thinkers?" pp. 31–32. The apocalyptic religious exegete has different interpretive challenges than those of the modernist. As James Tabor writes, "Biblical apocalypticism involves the interplay of three basic elements: 1) the sacred text, which is fixed and inviolate; 2) the inspired interpreter, who is involved in both transmitting and effecting the meaning of the text; and 3) the fluid context, in which the interpreter or group finds itself" ("Religious Discourse," p. 270).

106. Stephen Toulmin, *An Introduction to Reasoning*, pp. 44–45. What's interesting for me, in the context of standoff arguments, is how often they are precipitated by practical and not just conceptual warrants; that is, *arrest* warrants.
107. Sometimes, as in the standoff at Waco, this "talking the event into life" is quite literal. In her doctoral dissertation, "When the Parties Bring Their Gods to the Table," Jayne Docherty writes, "Koresh often said he had been sent both to 'explain and to do the Scriptures.' In other words, the Davidians believed that opening these seals involved not only explaining their mysterious meaning but also bringing about the events they prophesied" (p. 113).
108. Writing about the contested sacred center in Ayodhya, India, alternatively configured as the birthplace of Ram for Hindus and as a mosque honoring the sixteenth-century Muslim emperor (Adyondhyais Ramjanmabhumi or Babri Masjid), Roger Friedland and Richard Hecht detail the various interpretations of the texts surrounding the center, and the alternatives among them: ". . . the texts from which Ayodhya's theological significance derives have been subject to conflictual interpretations, used variously as a template for socialism, nationalist unity between Muslims and Hindus, and, of course, particularistic Hindu Nationalism." ("The Bodies of Nations," p. 111).
109. "Federal Raid," p. 380, emphasis mine.
110. *New York Times* News Service, April 11, 1996, Nando. net. Note that women, along with nonwhites, were considered to be second-class citizens. They were called "contract citizens" by the Freemen, meaning people who required acts of Congress to grant them their status.
111. Department of Justice Report of the Ruby Ridge Task Force to the Office of Professional Responsibility, p. 10231.
112. *Voices*, p. 136.
113. Reuter Information Service, April 2, 1996.
114. Phil Linsalata, "Montana Townspeople have had enough of the Freemen," *Detroit News*, April 21, 1996.
115. "Federal Raid," pp. 576–577.
116. Weick, "The Collapse of Sensemaking," p. 644.
117. Charles Goodwin and Allesandro Duranti, "Rethinking Context: An Introduction," pp. 25–26.
118. In the next chapter I will develop the idea of improvisation in standoffs and there the seeming finitude of responses to ultimatums will be problematized.
119. Stanley Lyman, *Wounded Knee 1973*, pp. xxxv-xxxvi, emphasis mine.
120. *New York Times*, January 5th, 1997, p. A8.
121. Mark Hansen, "(Cult)ure of the State," p. 20.
122. Associated Press, April 28, 1996, Nando.net.
123. Maines and Charlton, "The Negotiated Order Approach," p. 280.
124. See the work of Catherine Wessinger and of Jayne Docherty, both of whom have written on the specific nature of negotiation in one or several of the standoffs under examination here.
125. Docherty, "When the Parties," p. 156.

126. Lyman, *Wounded Knee: 1973*, p. xxix, emphasis mine.
127. *New York Times*, December 31, 1996, p. A3.
128. *New York Times*, December 29, 1996, p. 1.
129. Testimony of Frederick Lanceley, "Federal Raid," p. 586.
130. Quote from negotiator Frizzell, *Voices*, p. 145.
131. "Federal Raid," p. 271.
132. Greenhouse, *A Moment's Notice*, p. 106.
133. Ultimately, Adams and his team of mediators were barred from the Pine Ridge Reservation by Tribal Chairman Dick Wilson.
134. Associated Press, June 11, 1996.
135. Reuter Information Service, April 26, 1996, Nando.net.
136. See *Discourse and Destruction*, pp. 118–124, for a discussion of the attempted actions and interpretations of the organic mediators in this case and the way in which they were appraised by the authorities and the MOVE Commission.
137. Charles Burrus, MOVE Commission Hearings, October 22, 1985 pp. 10, 16, 41.
138. Giglioli *et al.*, *Rituali di degradazione*, p. 20, translation mine.
139. As Ron Jacobs and Philip Smith write of the insufficiencies of extant theories of communicative reason and democratic procedures: "The problem is that none of these theories can conceptualize the possibilities or consequences of multiple, contradictory, or hybrid identities, nor the ways in which these identities might be mobilized (or not) by particular types of public discourses." "Romance, Irony, and Solidarity," p. 7.
140. Novella Williams, MOVE Commission Hearings, October 22, 1985, p. 43.
141. *Voices*, p. 90.
142. Shupe and Hadden, "Cops, News Copy," p. 187.
143. Tabor, "Religious Discourse," p. 272.
144. "Federal Raid," p. 592.
145. *Voices*, p. 113.

Chapter 5: Endings and improvisations

1. I have previously developed this thorny recognition/legitimation dialectic issue in my book, *The Moro Morality Play*.
2. Ron Howell, ABC News, May 3, 1997.
3. Two Republic of Texas members did not agree to the cease-fire and fled the cabin on foot, only to be killed or captured at a later date.
4. Barry Schwartz, *George Washington*, pp. 140–141.
5. *Frontline*, "Waco: The Inside Story," transcript, p. 5.
6. Tabor, "Religious Discourse," p. 266.
7. Bo Gritz, one-time commando himself, goes even further in his characterization of these agents when he recounts his conversations with them on Ruby Ridge and speculates on their animus:

    I had gone back up to negotiate more with Randall. I was told by Dick Rogers that tomorrow, being Monday, the 31st of August, if you don't

get them all out, we're taking them out. I really couldn't imagine why
the acceleration. It put a lot of pressure on me . . . And it's just my skin
feeling. But believe me, these are not Efrem Zimbalist, Jr.'s in the HRT.
These are commandos like I have trained and led most of my adult life.
To me, Dick Rogers did not want to be denied his kills in this instance.
I really don't believe he wanted to see them come out in one piece.
                                   "Federal Raid on Ruby Ridge," p. 579.

 8. US Department of Justice Report, pp. 10232–233.
 9. Weick, "The Collapse of Sensemaking," p. 639.
10. Alexander, *Fin de Siècle*, p. 139.
11. Schon, "Notes on Generative Metaphor," p. 278.
12. White and Epston, *Literate Means to Therapeutic Ends*, p. 78.
13. Moretti, *The Modern Epic*, p. 139.
14. Engle, *Shakespearean Pragmatism*, p. 13.
15. Harvey, *Justice, Nature and the Geography of Difference*, p. 254.
16. Ramos, "The Use of Improvisation and Modulation," pp. 327–329.
17. Bennie Swans to Mayor Wilson Goode, June 18, 1985, MOVE Commission
    Files, Urban Archives Collection, Temple University.
18. David Johnston, "This Time, FBI Avoids Military Style Tactics," *New York
    Times*, A16.
19. As Carol Greenhouse writes, ". . . legal pluralism is an empirical state of
    affairs in society . . . Drawing on Sally Falk Moore's view that complex soci-
    eties consist of multiple intersecting social bodies capable of generating and
    enforcing norms, John Griffiths concludes that legal pluralism and 'social plu-
    ralism' are congruent," *A Moment's Notice*, p. 57.
20. Hanks, "discourse genres," p. 688.
21. "Federal Raid," pp. 314–315.
22. Marc Ross, *The Management of Conflict* , p. 126.
23. Jacobs and Smith, "Romance, Irony, and Solidarity," pp. 74–76.
24. Weick, "The Collapse," p. 648.
25. Baker, *Black Studies, Rap*, p. 95.
26. Benjamin, "The Storyteller," in *Illuminations*, p. 106.
27. "[Nietzsche and Peirce] believed that our world, which others find orderly, is
    a product of chance . . . Gilles Deleuze has a succinct summary of one of
    Nietzsche's thoughts here. The dice of creation 'thrown once are the
    affirmation of chance, the combination which they form on falling is the
    affirmation of necessity'. . ." Hacking, *The Taming of Chance*, p. 147.
28. This approach brings to mind John Hall's dictum to "Begin at the hermeneu-
    tic end of interpretive analysis, invoking the Durkheimian model of binary . . .
    distinction only where the play of meanings takes that, rather than some other,
    form," "Public Narratives," p. 233. I would add here that one could similarly
    also begin with the binary model and invoke hermeneutics as the situation
    progresses in it temporal, spatial, and action parameters.
29. Valéry, "Poetry and Abstract Thought," pp. 919–922.

30. In that book, *The Moro Morality Play*, I proposed the greater cognitive and normative adequacy of Tragedy (over Melodrama) as a social genre in complex, large-scale, mass-mediated societies. Similarly, in his theorizing of the idea of "sideshadowing," Michael André Bernstein proposes the inadequacy of allegory and ties it to the counterpoints of necessity and contingency: "There can also never be any real sideshadowing in allegory. Historical events that unfold through time involve the succession of non-necessary events and contain sideshadows at each moment of their unfolding; they are thus inherently in contradiction with the terms of an allegorical understanding/narration," Bernstein, *Foregone Conclusions*, p. 115.
31. Herrnstein-Smith, *Poetic Closure*, p. 75.
32. Richard Rorty writes: "In [Donald Davidson's] view, tossing a metaphor into a conversation is like suddenly breaking off the conversation long enough to make a face, or pulling a photograph out of your pocket and displaying it, or slapping your interlocutor's face, or kissing him. Tossing a metaphor into a text is like using italics, or illustrations, or odd punctuation or formats." Rorty, *Contingency, Irony, and Solidarity*, p. 18.
33. Eco, *Semiotica e filosofia*, p. 164, translation mine.
34. Writing about the antilanguages of the criminal underworld, Halliday notes:

    So we expect to find new words for types of criminal act, and classes of criminal and of victim; for tools of the trade; for police and other representatives of the law enforcement structure of the society; for penalties, penal institutions, and the like . . . It is noticeable, however, that even these purely technical elements seem to be somewhat larger than life. The language is not merely relexicalized in these areas: it is overlexicalized. So in Mallik's account of the Calcutta underworld language we find not just one word for "bomb" but 21; 41 words for "police," and so on."   Halliday, "Anti-languages," p. 571.

35. Joas, *Pragmatism and Social Theory*, p. 130.
36. This dictum is in an interesting radical polar opposite to Seyla Benhabib's Habermasian communicative principle of "egalitarian reciprocity" that stipulates that "within such conversations, each has the same symmetrical rights to various speech acts, to initiate new topics, to ask for reflection about the presuppositions of the conversation, etc." "In the Shadow of Aristotle and Hegel," p. 6.
37. Rorty, *Contingency, Irony, Solidarity*, p. 63.
38. Stout, *Ethics After Babel*, p. 244.
39. Luhmann, *Osservazioni sul Moderno*, p. 61.

Bibliography

Aho, James, *This Thing of Darkness: A Sociology of the Enemy*. Seattle, WA: University of Washington Press, 1994.

Alexander, Jeffrey C., "Action and its Environments," in Jeffrey C. Alexander et al., eds, *The Micro-Macro Link*, Berkeley: University of California Press, 1987.

Fin de Siècle Social Theory: Relativism, Reduction, and the Problem of Reason. London: Verso, 1995.

"The Sacred, Mundane, and Profane: Why Evil is Basic to Culture," paper delivered at the Cultural Turn Conference, University of California at Santa Barbara, February, 1997.

Alexander, Jeffrey C., and Philip Smith, "The Discourse of American Civil Society: A New Proposal for Cultural Studies," *Theory and Society*, 22 (2), April: 151–207, 1993.

American Friends Service Committee, *Voices from the Community*. Philadelphia: AFSC National Community Relations Committee, 1986.

Anderson, John, and Hilary Hevenor, *Burning Down the House: MOVE and the Tragedy of Philadelphia*. New York: W.W. Norton, 1987.

Archer, Dane, "Unspoken Diversity: Cultural Differences in Gestures," *Qualitative Sociology*, 20 (1): 79–105, 1997.

Arendt, Hannah, *The Human Condition*. University of Chicago Press, 1958.

Baker, Houston, *Black Studies, Rap, and the Academy*. University of Chicago Press, 1993.

Bakhtin, Mikhail, *Speech Genres and Other Late Essays*, Caryl Emerson and Michael Holquist, eds. Translated by Vern W. McGee. Austin: University of Texas Press, 1986.

Benhabib, Seyla, "In the Shadow of Aristotle and Hegel: Communicative Ethics and Current Controversies in Practical Philosophy," *The Philosophical Forum*, XXI (1–2): 1–31, 1989–90.

Benjamin, Walter, *Illuminations*. Hannah Arendt, Ed. and Introduction. New York: Schocken Books, 1976.

Berlin, Isaiah, Sir, *Against the Current: Essays in the History of Ideas*. Henry Hardy, ed. and bibliography. Introduction by Roger Hausheer. New York: Viking Press, 1980.

Bernstein, Michael André, *Foregone Conclusions: Against Apocalyptic History*. Berkeley: University of California Press, 1994.

Blackburn, Simon (ed.), *Oxford Dictionary of Philosophy*. Oxford University Press, 1994.

Bourdieu, Pierre, "Structures, Habitus, Power: Basis for a Theory of Symbolic Power," in Nicholas B. Dirks, Geoff Eley, and Sherry B. Ortner, eds., *Culture/Power/History: A Reader in Contemporary Social Theory*, Princeton University Press, 1994.

"On the Family as a Realized Category," *Theory, Culture and Society*, 13 (3): 19–26, 1996.

Brenneis, Donald, "Performing passions: aesthetics and politics in an occasionally egalitarian community," *American Ethnologist*, 14 (2): 236–250, 1987.

Burke, Kenneth, *A Grammar of Motives*. Berkeley: University of California Press, 1969.

"Terms for Order," in *On Symbols and Society*. Joseph Gusfield, ed. and Introduction. University of Chicago Press, pp. 282–293, 1989.

Butor, Michel, *Inventory*. Richard Howard, ed. New York: Simon and Schuster, 1968.

Castoriadis, Cornelius, *The Imaginary Institution of Society*. Translated by Kathleen Blamey, Cambridge, MA: MIT Press, 1987.

Cohen, Abner, *Masquerade Politics: Explorations in the Structure of Urban Cultural Movements*. Berkeley: University of California Press, 1993.

Cooke, Maeve, *Language and Reason, A Study of Habermas' Pragmatics*. Cambridge, MA: MIT Press, 1994.

Corcoran, Paul, E. "Godot is Waiting Too. Endings in Thought and History," *Theory and Society*, 18: 495–529, 1989.

Cornell, Drucilla, *Transformations*. New York: Routledge, 1993.

Cox, Sharon Sims, "My Life in MOVE" (as told to Carol Saline). *Philadelphia Magazine*, September: 170–172, 1985.

Cunningham, Clark D., "A Linguistic Analysis of the Meanings of 'Search' in the Fourth Amendment: A Search for Common Sense." *Iowa Law Review*, March: 541–543, 1988.

Dayan, Daniel, and Elihu Katz, *Media Events: the Live Broadcasting of History*. Cambridge, MA: Harvard University Press, 1992.

Diggins, John Patrick, *The Promise of Pragmatism: Modernism and the Crisis of Knowledge and Authority*. University of Chicago Press, 1994.

Docherty, Jayne S, "When the Parties Bring Their Gods to the Table: Learning Lessons from Waco." Unpublished doctoral dissertation, George Mason University, Fairfax, VA, 1998.

Eco, Umberto, *Semiotica e filosofia del linguaggio*, Turin: Einaudi, 1996.

Editorial Collective, *Voices from Wounded Knee, 1973: In the Words of the Participants*. Rooseveltown, NY: Awkesasne Notes, Mohawk Nation, 1974.

Emerson, Caryl, "American Philosophers, Bakhtinian Perspectives." Paper delivered at Transnational Institute, Moscow 13–19 March, 1993.

Emirbayer, Mustafa, "Manifesto for a Relational Sociology," *American Journal of Sociology*, 103 (2): 281–317, 1997.

Engle, Lars, *Shakespearean Pragmatism*. University of Chicago Press, 1993.

Ewick, Patricia, and Susan S. Silbey, *The Common Place of Law: Stories from Everyday Life*. University of Chicago Press, 1998.

Faubion, James, "Deus Absconditus? Waco, Conspiracy (Theory), Millennialism, and (the End of) the Twentieth Century," in George Marcus, ed., *Paranoia Within Reason: A Casebook on Conspiracy as Explanation, Late Editions*, Volume VI. University of Chicago Press, 1999.

Foote, Kenneth E., *Shadowed Ground: America's Landscapes of Violence and Tragedy*. Austin: University of Texas Press, 1997.

Fox, Elaine, "The Struggle for Legitimacy: A Study of Contingencies and Constraints in Emergency Medicine," *Sociological Spectrum*, 4: 311–333, 1984.

Frake, Charles O., "Struck By Speech: The Yakan Concept of Litigation," in John Gumperz and Delly Hymes, eds., *Directions in Sociolinguistics*. New York: Holt, Rinehardt and Winston, pp. 106–129, 1972.

Friedland, Roger and Richard Hecht, "The Bodies of Nations: A Comparative Study of Religious Violence in Jerusalem and Ayodhya," *History of Religions*, 38 (2): 101–149, 1998.

Friedland, Roger, and Robert R. Alford, "Bringing Society Back In: Symbolic Practices and Institutional Contradictions," in Walter Powell and Paul di Maggio, eds., *The New Institutionalism in Organizational Analysis*. University of Chicago Press, 1991.

Frontline, "Waco: the Inside Story." ABC television documentary broadcast October 17, 1995.

Gaffney, Jr., Edward McGlynn, "The Waco Tragedy: Constitutional Concerns and Policy Perspectives," in Stuart A. Wright, ed., *Armageddon in Waco*, University of Chicago Press, 1995.

Garfinkle, Harold, "Good Reasons for Bad Clinic Records," in *Studies in Ethnomethodology*. New York, Prentice-Hall, pp. 186–207, 1967.

Garfinkle, Harold, and Robert J. Stoller, "Passing and the Managed Achievement of Sex Status in an Intersexed Person," in *Studies in Ethnomethodology*. New York: Prentice Hall, pp. 116–185, 1967.

Gibson, J. William, *Warrior Dreams: Paramilitary Culture in Post-Vietnam America*. New York: Hill and Wang, 1994.

Giddens, Anthony, *The Giddens Reader*. Philip Cassell, ed. Stanford University Press, 1993.

Giglioli, Pier Paolo, Sandra Cavicchioli, and Giolo Fele, *Rituali di degradazione: Anatomia del processo Cusani*. Bologna: Il Mulino Editore, 1997.

Gonseth, Ferdinand, *Time and Method: An Essay on the Methodology of Research*. Translated by Eva Guggenheimer. Springfield, IL.: Charles C. Thomas, 1972.

Goodwin, Charles, "Professional Vision," *American Anthropologist*, 96 (3): 606–633, 1994.

Goodwin, Charles, and Alessandro Duranti, "Rethinking Context: An Introduction," in Alessandro Duranti and Charles Goodwin, eds., *Rethinking Context: Language as an Interactive Phenomenon*. Cambridge University Press, 1994.

Granovetter, Mark, *Getting A Job: A Study of Contacts and Careers*. Cambridge, MA: Harvard University Press, 1974.

Greenhouse, Carol J., *A Moment's Notice: Time Politics Across Cultures*. Ithaca, NY: Cornell University Press, 1996.

Greimas, Algirdas, J., *On Meaning*, Minneapolis: University of Minnesota Press, 1997.

Hacking, Ian, *The Taming of Chance*, Cambridge University Press, 1990.

Hall, John, "The Time of History and the History of Times," *History and Theory*, 19 (2): 113–131, 1980.

"Public Narratives and the Apocalyptic Sect: From Jonestown to Mt. Carmel," in Stuart A. Wright, ed., *Armageddon in Waco*, University of Chicago Press, 1995.

Halliday, M.A.K., "Anti-languages," *American Anthropologist*, 78: 570–584, 1976.

Hanks, William, "discourse genres in a theory of practice," *American Anthropologist*, 14 (4): 668–692, 1987.

Hansen, Mark, "(Cult)ure of the State: The Branch Davidians and the ATF," Senior Thesis, Swarthmore College, 1994.

Harvey, David, *Justice, Nature and the Geography of Difference*. Oxford and London: Blackwell Publishers, 1996.

Hawthorn, Geoffrey, *Plausible Words: Possibility and Understanding in History and the Social Sciences*. Cambridge University Press, 1991.

Herndl, Carl, B. Fennell, and C. Miller, "Understanding Failures in Organizational Discourse: The Accident at Three Mile Island and the Shuttle Challenger Disaster," in Charles Bazerman and James Pardis, eds., *Textual Dynamics of the Professions*. University of Wisconsin Press, pp. 279–305, 1991.

Herrnstein-Smith, Barbara, *Poetic Closure: A Study of How Poems End*. University of Chicago Press, 1968.

Hunter, Ian, *Culture and Government*. New York: Macmillan Press, 1988.

Hunter, Susan, "The Roots of Environmental Conflict in the Tahoe Basin," in Louis Kriesberg, Terrell Northrup, and Stuart Thorsen, eds., *Intractable Conflicts and Their Transformation*. Syracuse University Press, 1989.

Jacobs, Ronald, and Philip Smith, "Romance, Irony, and Solidarity," *Sociological Theory*, 15 (1): 60–80, 1997.

Joas, Hans, *Pragmatism and Social Theory*. University of Chicago Press, 1994.

The Creativity of Action. The University of Chicago Press, 1996.

Kant, Immanuel, *Kant's Political Writings*. Hans Reiss, ed. and Introduction, Translated by H.B. Nisbet. Cambridge University Press, 1970.

Lalli, Pina, and Alessandra Dino, *La babele quotidiana: Forme e modi della comunicazione Sociale*. Palermo: Edizioni la Zisa srl., 1996.

Landes, David S., *Revolution in Time: Clocks and the Making of the Modern World*. Cambridge, MA: Harvard University Press, 1983.

Law and Contemporary Problems, "The Impact of Arrest Records on the Exercise of Police Discretion," *Law and Contemporary Problems*, 47 (4): 287–302, 1984.

Leach, Edmund, "Two Essays Concerning the Symbolic Representation of Time," in William A. Lessa and Evon Z. Vogt, eds., *Reader in Comparative Religion*, 4th edition, New York: Harper and Row, 1979.

Leibniz, Gottfried Wilhelm Von, *Monadology and Other Philosophical Essays*. Translated by Paul and Anne Martin Schrecker. New York: Bobbs-Merrill, 1965.

Lévi-Strauss, Claude, *Totemism*. Boston: Beacon Press, 1963.

Lewis, Justin, "The Absence of Narrative: Boredom and the Residual Power of Television News," *Journal of Narrative and Life History*, 4 (1 & 2): 25–40, 1994.

Limon, José E. "Carne, carnales, and the carnivalesque: Bakhtinian batos, disorder, and narrative discourses," *American Ethnologist*, 16 (3): 471–486, 1989.

Lindecker, Charles, *Massacre in Waco, Texas*. New York: St. Martin's Press, 1993.

Luhmann, Nicklas, *Osservazioni sul Moderno*. Rome: Armando Editore, 1995.

Lyman, Stanley David, *Wounded Knee 1973: A Personal Account*. Lincoln and London: University of Nebraska Press, 1991.

McConnell, Stuart, "Reading the Flag: A Reconsideration of the Patriotic Cults of the 1890's," in John Bodnar, ed. *Bonds of Affection: Americans Define Their Patriotism*, Princeton University Press, 1996.

Maines, David R., and Joy C. Charlton, "The Negotiated Order Approach to the Analysis of Social Organization," in Harvey A. Faberman and Robert S. Perinbanyagam, eds., *Foundations of Interpretive Sociology: Original Essays in Symbolic Interaction*. Studies in Symbolic Interaction, Supplement 1. Greenwich, CT: JAI Press, pp. 271–308, 1985.

Marx, Gary T., *Undercover: Police Surveillance in America*. Berkeley: University of California Press, 1988.

Meyer, John W., and Brian Rowan, "Institutionalized Organizations: Formal Structure as Myth and Ceremony," in Walter Powell and Paul di Maggio, eds., *The New Institutionalism in Organizational Analysis*. University of Chicago Press, 1991.

Moretti, Franco, *The Modern Epic: The World-system from Goethe to Garcia Marquez*. Translated by Quintin Hoare. London, New York: Verso, 1996.

MOVE, "Twenty Years on the Move." Philadelphia: MOVE, 1992.

Munn, Nancy D. "The Cultural Anthropology of Time: A Critical Essay," in *The Annual Review of Anthropology*, 21: 93–123, 1992.

Musil, Robert, *The Man Without Qualities*. Burton Pike, ed., Translated by Sophie Wilkins. New York: Vintage International, 1996.

Pate, James L., "Freeh's Men vs. the Freemen," *Soldier of Fortune*, July: 1996a, 50–84.

"Big Sky Surrender," *Soldier of Fortune*, September: pp. 54–71, 1996b.

Perrow, Charles, *Normal Accidents: Living with High-risk Technologies*. New York: Basic Books, 1984.

Pizzorno, Alessandro, "Decisioni o interazioni? La Micro-descrizione del cambiamento sociale," *Rassegna Italiana di Sociologia*, 37 (1): 107–132, 1996.

Poovey, Mary, *Uneven Developments: The Ideological Work of Gender in Mid-Victorian England*. University of Chicago Press, 1988.

Propp, Vladimir, *Morphology of the Folktale*, Louis A. Wagner, ed. Introduction by Alan Dundes. Austin: University of Texas Press, 1968.

Ramos, Reyes, "The Use of Improvisation and Modulation in Natural Talk: An Alternative Approach to Conversational Analysis," *Studies in Symbolic Interaction*, 1: 319–337, 1978.

Rochberg-Halton, Eugene, "Situation, Structure, and the Context of Meaning," *The Sociological Quarterly*, 23: 455–476, 1982.

Roe, Emery, *Narrative Policy Analysis: Theory and Practice*. Durham, NC: Duke University Press, 1994.

Rorty, Richard, *Contingency, Irony, and Solidarity*. Cambridge University Press, 1989.

Rosenthal, Sandra and Patrick Bourgeois, *Mead and Merleau Ponty: Toward a Common Vision*. Albany, NY: SUNY Press, 1991.

Ross, Marc Howard, *The Management of Conflict: Interpretations and Interests in Comparative Perspective*, New Haven, CT: Yale University Press, 1993.

Sahlins, Marshall, *Historical Metaphors and Mythical Realities: Structure in the Early History of the Sandwich Islands Kingdom*. Ann Arbor: University of Michigan Press, 1981.

Schama, Simon, *Landscape and Memory*. New York: Alfred A. Knopf, 1995.

Schirmer, Jennifer, "The Claiming of Space and the Body Politic within National-Security States: The Plaza de Mayo Madres and the Greenham Common Women," in Jonathan Boyarin, ed., *Remapping Memory: The Politics of TimeSpace*. Minneapolis: University of Minnesota Press, pp. 185–220, 1994.

Schon, Donald A., "Notes on Generative Metaphor: A Perspective on Problem-Setting in Social Policy," in Andrew Ortony, ed., *Metaphor and Thought*, Cambridge University Press, 1979.

Schwartz, Barry, "Waiting, Exchange, and Power: The Distribution of Time in Social Systems," *American Journal of Sociology*, 79 (4), Jan, 841–870, 1974.

  George Washington: The Making of an American Symbol. Ithaca, NY and London: Cornell University Press, 1987.

Shalin, Dmitri, "Pragmatism and Social Interactionism," *American Sociological Review*, 51: 9–29, 1986.

Shupe, Anson, and Jeffrey K. Hadden, "Cops, News Copy, and Public Opinion," in Stuart A. Wright, ed., *Armageddon in Waco*. University of Chicago Press, 1995.

Simmel, Georg, "Bridge and Door," *Theory, Culture and Society*, 11: 5–10, 1994.

Smith, Philip, "Executing Executions: Aesthetics, Identity, and the Problematic Narratives of Capital Punishment Ritual," *Theory and Society*, 25: 235–261, 1996.

Sokol, Moshe, "How do Modern Jewish Thinkers Interpret Religious Texts?" *Modern Judaism*, 13: 25–48, 1993.

Stewart, Ann Harleman, "The Role of Narrative Structure in the Transfer of Ideas," in Charles Bazerman and James Paradis, eds., *Textual Dynamcis of the Professions*. University of Wisconsin Press, 1991.

Stewart, Susan, "Shouts on the Street: Bakhtin's Anti-Linguistics," *Critical Inquiry*, 10: 265–281, 1983.

Stout, Jeffrey, *Ethics After Babel: The Languages of Morals and Their Discontents*, Boston: Beacon Press, 1988.

Sutton, Paul, "The 4th Amendment in Action: An Empirical View of the Search Warrant Process," *Criminal Law Bulletin*, 22: 405–429, 1986.

Swett, Daniel H., "Cultural Bias in the American Legal System," *Law and Society Review*, 1: 79–110, 1969.

Szymborska, Wislawa, *View With a Grain of Sand*. Translated by Stanislaw Barazczak and Clare Cavanaugh. New York: Harcourt Brace and Co, 1995.

Tabor, James, "Religious Discourse and Failed Negotiations," in Stuart H. Wright, ed., *Armageddon at Waco*. University of Chicago Press, 1995.

Taylor, Charles, *Sources of the Self: the Making of the Modern Identity*. Cambridge, MA: Harvard University Press, 1989.

Terdiman, Richard, *Present Past: Modernity and the Memory Crisis*. Ithaca: Cornell University Press, 1993.

Tilly, Charles, "Invisible Elbow," *Sociological Forum*, 11 (4): 589–601, 1996.

Toulmin, Stephen, *et al.*, *An Introduction to Reasoning*. New York: Macmillan, 1979.

Turner, Victor, *Dramas, Fields, and Metaphors: Symbolic Action in Human Society*. Ithaca, NY: Cornell University Press, 1975.

Unger, Roberto Mangabeira, *False Necessity: Anti-Necessitarian Social Theory in the Service of Radical Democracy*. Cambridge University Press, 1987.

Urban, Greg, "The Role of Imperatives in the Rhetorical Unconscious," Paper presented at Swarthmore College, April 16, 1997.

Valéry, Paul, "Poetry and Abstract Thought," in Hazard Adams, ed., *Critical Theory Since Plato*, New York: Harcourt Brace Jovanovich, 1971.

Waco: The Rules of Engagement, Documentary film produced by Dan Gifford, William Gazecki, and Michael McNulty, Fifth Estate Production, 1997.

Waelchli, Heinz, and Dhavan Shah, "Crisis Negotiations Between Unequals: Lessons from a Classic Dialogue," *Negotiation Journal*, April: 129–145, 1994.

Wagner-Pacifici, Robin, *The Moro Morality Play: Terrorism as Social Drama*. University of Chicago Press, 1986.

    Discourse and Destruction: The City of Philadelphia vs MOVE. University of Chicago Press, 1994.

Wagner-Pacifici, Robin, and Barry Schwartz, "The Vietnam Veterans Memorial: Commemorating a Difficult Past," *American Journal of Sociology* 97(2): 376–420, 1991.

Weick, Karl E, "The Collapse of Sensemaking in Organizations: The Mann Gulch Disaster," *Administrative Science Quarterly*, 38: 628–652, 1993.

Wells, Susan, "Narrative Figures and Subtle Persuasions: The Rhetoric of the MOVE Report," in Herbert W. Simons, ed., *The Rhetorical Turn: Invention and Persuasion in the Conduct of Inquiry*, University of Chicago Press, 1990.

Wessinger, Catherine, *How the Millennium Comes Violently*. Dulles VA: Seven Bridges Press, forthcoming.

West, Cornel, *The American Evasion of Philosophy: A Genealogy of Pragmatism*. Madison: University of Wisconsin Press, 1989.

White, Hayden, *Metahistory: The Historical Imagination in Nineteenth Century Europe*. Baltimore, MD: Johns Hopkins University Press, 1973.

White, Michael, and David Epston, *Literate Means to Therapeutic Ends*. Adelaide: Dulwich Centre Publications, 1989.

Wiley, Norbert, *The Semiotic Self*. University of Chicago Press, 1995.

Wolin, Richard, *Walter Benjamin, an Aesthetic of Redemption*, New York: Columbia University Press, 1982.

Zerubavel, Eviater, *The Seven-Day Circle: The History and Meaning of the Week*. New York: Free Press, 1985.

    "Horizons: On the Sociomental Foundations of Relevance," *Social Research*, 60 (2): 396–413, 1993.

    "In the Beginning: Notes on the Social Construction of Historical Discontinuity," *Sociological Inquiry*, 63 (4): 457–459, 1993.

"Lumping and Splitting: Notes on Social Classification," *Sociological Forum*, 11 (3): 421–433, 1996.

"The Social Marking of Time: A Study in Structural Sociology," paper delivered at the Cultural Turn Conference, University of California at Santa Barbara, February, 1997.

Zimmerman, Bill, *Airlift to Wounded Knee*. Chicago: Swallow Press, 1976.

Transcripts

Department of the Treasury, Waco Administrative Review, *Report of the Department of the Treasury on the Bureau of Alcohol, Tobacco, and Firearms Investigation of Vernon Wayne Howell (also known as David Koresh)*. Washington, DC: US Government Printing Office, 1993.

Hearings Before a Subcommittee of the Committee on Appropriations: Bureau of Alcohol, Tobacco and Firearms "Operation Trojan Horse," Raid of the Branch Davidian Compound, Waco, Texas. Washington: Government Printing Office, 1993.

Senate Hearing before the Select Committee on Indian Affairs, 102nd Congress (103–193), First Session "To Establish a National Park and Memorial at Wounded Knee." April 30, 1991. US Government Printing Office.

Senate Hearing before the Subcommittee on Public Lands, National Parks, and Forests of the Committee on Energy and Natural Resources, 103rd Congress, (103–407), First Session, "Truman Farm Home; Wounded Knee National Memorial; Bodie Bowl; Preservation of Taliesin Site; and Alaska Peninsula subsurface Consolidation Act." July 29, 1993. US Government Printing Office.

"The Federal Raid on Ruby Ridge, ID," Hearings before the Select Committee on Terrorism, Technology, and Government Information of the Committee on the Judiciary, United States Senate 104th Congress, First Session on Examining Certain Federal Law Enforcement Actions with Regard to the 1992 Incident at Ruby Ridge, ID, September and October, 1995, Serial No. J-104-41. US Government Printing Office.

Department of Justice Report of the Ruby Ridge Task Force to the Office of Professional Responsibility, Government Printing Office.

Philadelphia Special Investigation MOVE Commission Hearings, Urban Archives Collection, Temple University, Philadelphia, PA.

Index

public address systems, 130
  loudspeaker at MOVE house, 226
Purgatory, 62

racial alignment, 94–5
Ramos, Reyes, 225
Rashomon, 3–4
relational approach, 224–31
religion
  moving away from oppressors, 113–14
  as setpoint for standoff, 48, 53–5
  spiritual messages, 128–9
  Ur-texts of, 192–3, 194–5, 197
  see also spiritual time
Reno, Janet, 37, 40, 100, 104
Republic of Texas members, in prison,
  124
Republic of Texas standoff
  beginning, 83
  end, 216
  historical time-line, 89–90
  participants
    law-enforcement agents, 45
    neighbours and hostages, 44, 45, 146,
      168–9, 188
  setting of, 117
  summary of, 43–5
  symbolism of place names, 112
  texts-in-action, 198
  Ur-texts, 192
reservations, spatial narratives of, 122–3
residence, spatial narratives of, 121–2
retreat, 227
retrospective approach, 3–4
ritual time, 71–4
Rochberg-Halton, Eugene, 14
Roden, George, 35
Roden, Lois, 35
Roe, Emery, 194
Ross, Marc Howard, 131, 230
routine arrest, 166
Rowan, Brian, 150
Rowe, Joe, 44, 45, 168
Rowe, Margaret Ann, 44, 45, 168
Ruby Ridge standoff
  end of, 172–3, 217, 219
  equipment used, 153, 155–6
  gestures, 172–3
  initiation of, 143, 144, 146, 147, 197
    gun ownership setpoint, 56, 57
    religion setpoint, 54
  internal spatial divisions, 71–2, 120–1
  negotiations, 206, 207
  participants
    antagonists, 187, 189; *see also* Weaver
      family; Weaver, Randall; Weaver,
      Sammy; Weaver, Vicky

on both sides of law, 177
go-betweens, 131
hostages, 189
informants, 32, 190–1
law-enforcement agents, 33, 34, 100,
  147, 181, 182
neighbours, 146
perimeter, 104–5, 106–7, 129, 130
property rights, 133–4
Rules of Engagement, 157–9, 161–2
scene clearing, 107
setting of, 114, 115, 116, 164, 165–6
shooting in doorway, 135–6, 167
summary of, 32–4
texts
  hybrid texts, 228–9
  texts-in-action, 197
  Ur-text, 192
and time
  duration, 85
  past subjunctive, 62–3
  routine temporal framework, 71–2
  timing of warrant, 68–9
Rules of Engagement, 34, 157–63

sacred space, 109
Sage, Byron, 37, 85, 180, 193
scene clearing, 107
scenes *see* standoff scenes
Schama, Simon, 114
Scheidt, Bob, 44, 124
Schirmer, Jennifer, 125–6
Schon, Donald A., 222–3
Schwartz, Barry, 9, 216
Schweitzer, LeRoy, 39, 40
search warrants, 67–8, 69, 133
sentimental and bureaucratic discourse,
  12
Seven Seals manuscript, 76, 79–80, 197
sexual relations at Waco, 51, 120
shapes of marches, 125–6
sideshadowing, 3, 5
Simmel, Georg, 102
situations, identity of, 140–1
Skurdal, Rodney, 38, 39, 177, 196
sociology, project of, 1–2
Sokol, Moshe, 54–5, 192
sound transgression at Waco, 132
space
  binary oppositions in, 97–100
  codifications of, 102–3
    literal spaces, 103–8
    symbolic spaces, 108–13
  concept of, 23–6
  divided by Tupac Amaru, 24, 98, 121–2
  location of negotiations, 205–6
  mediation across, 100–2

Continued from front of book

LYNN RAPAPORT, *Jews in Germany after the Holocaust*

0 521 58219 9 HARDBACK 0 521 58809 X PAPERBACK

CHANDRA MUKERJI, *Territorial Ambitions and the Gardens of Versailles*

0 521 49675 6 HARDBACK 0 521 59959 8 PAPERBACK

LEON H. MAYHEW, *The New Public*

0 521 48146 5 HARDBACK 0 521 48493 6 PAPERBACK

VERA L. ZOLBERG AND JONI M. CHERBO (eds.), *Outsider Art*

0 521 58111 7 HARDBACK 0 521 58921 5 PAPERBACK

SCOTT BRAVMANN, *Queer Fictions of the Past*

0 521 59101 5 HARDBACK 0 521 59907 5 PAPERBACK

STEVEN SEIDMAN, *Difference Troubles*

0 521 59043 4 HARDBACK 0 521 59970 9 PAPERBACK

RON EYERMAN AND ANDREW JAMISON, *Music and Social Movements*

0 521 62045 7 HARDBACK 0 521 62966 7 PAPERBACK

MEYDA YEGENOGLU, *Colonial Fantasies*

0 521 48233 X HARDBACK 0 521 62658 7 PAPERBACK

LAURA DESFOR EDLES, *Symbol and Ritual in the New Spain*

0 521 62140 2 HARDBACK 0 521 62885 7 PAPERBACK

NINA ELIASOPH, *Avoiding Politics*

0 521 58293 8 HARDBACK 0 521 58759 X PAPERBACK

BERNHARD GIESEN, *Intellectuals and the German Nation*

0 521 62161 5 HARDBACK 0 521 63996 4 PAPERBACK

PHILIP SMITH (ed.), *The New American Cultural Sociology*

0 521 58415 9 HARDBACK 0 521 58634 8 PAPERBACK

S. N. EISENSTADT, *Fundamentalism, Sectarianism and Revolution*

0 521 64184 5 HARDBACK 0 521 64586 7 PAPERBACK

MARIAM FRASER, *Identity without Selfhood*

0 521 62357 X HARDBACK 0 521 62579 3 PAPERBACK

LUC BOLTANSKI, *Distant suffering*

0 521 57389 0 HARDBACK 0 521 65953 1 PAPERBACK

PYOTR SZTOMPKA, *Trust*

0 521 59144 9 HARDBACK 0 521 59850 8 PAPERBACK

SIMON J. CHARLESWORTH, *A phenomenology of working class culture*

0 521 65066 6 HARDBACK 0 521 65915 9 PAPERBACK

DATE DUE

Demco, Inc. 38-293